The Return of the Cranes

JOHN HEATH-STUBBS was born in 1918 and educated at the Queen's College, Oxford. He has been awarded the Queen's Gold Medal for Poetry and an OBE. Carcanet have published several previous volumes of his poetry, as well as a *Collected Poems*, a *Selected Poems* and *The Literary Essays*. He is also an anthologist and a translator.

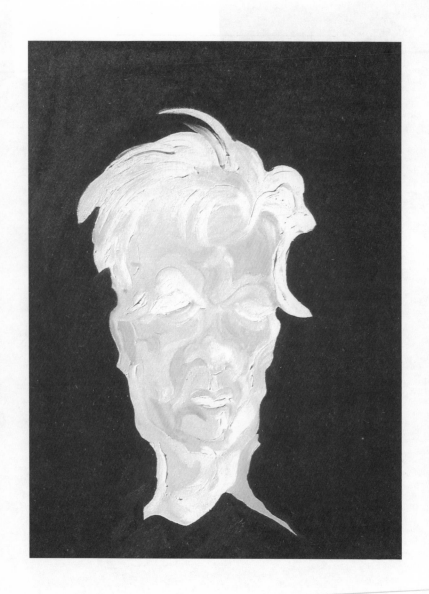

JOHN HEATH-STUBBS

The Return of the Cranes

Portraits by Hammond Journeaux

CARCANET

First published in 2002 by
Carcanet Press Limited
4th Floor, Conavon Court
12–16 Blackfriars Street
Manchester M3 5BQ

A CIP catalogue record for this book
is available from the British Library

ISBN 1 85754 606 7

The publisher acknowledges financial assistance
from the Arts Council of England

Set in 10pt Palatino by Bryan Williamson, Frome
Printed and bound in England by SRP Ltd, Exeter

Contents

Acknowledgements

Some of these poems have appeared in the following publications:
Acumen, The London Magazine, New Welsh Review, Shop.

The Return of the Cranes

So they're back – the great grey birds
With their dark legs, and their foreheads banded
With red, white and black – representing,
Robert Graves thought, the three phases of his lunar goddess –
Back on the Norfolk Broads, their stronghold once –
Before the improved firearms of the eighteenth and nineteenth
    centuries
Settled their due. The place is now top secret.
There was, it seems, a reconnoitring.
Some years past it was reported from Barton-on-Sea,
That dull resort village I spent my boyhood in,
Two great cranes
Appeared and lingered for a while – and then flew on,
Upon the undercliff, the Barton beds' blue-slipper clay, bearing
    its crop
Of Eocene fossils – dentalium the tooth shell,
And sometimes sharks' teeth. There grew
The yellow flowering coltsfoot
Which some collected – a wartime substitute for pipe tobacco.
There coiled the adder
And longer swifter grass-snake darted;
Above were sandy cliffs where martins tunnelled
And twittered.
In boyhood days what would I not have given
To have observed those cranes – obsessed as I was
With bird books, old and new, taught by my father
To recognise the songs and calls around us.
But now, too late – my eyesight gone
And I once more become the Londoner
That I was born. Now they've come back,
But not to Barton,
Once more we'll hear their honking calls
And see them flying high,
As over Russian and Hungarian plains –
Protected now of course – though centuries since
Their slaughtered bodies in abundance graced
Tables at Tudor and Plantagenet banquets.

Ostrich

Avis struthio, the great strutter,
Hence our word *Ostrich*, the shucking great sparrow –
Or so I imagine Greek mercenaries called him,
When they came to Egypt to fight for King Amasis,
Just as the locust was a Roman squaddies' name
For the lobster it looked like.
Kit Smart, I remember, enjoined us to pray
For the ostriches on Salisbury Plain. What, in heaven's name,
Was he on about – maybe the bustards?

Mary Kingsley and the Crocodile

While Mary Kingsley was crossing a lake
In her canoe, a crocodile
Attempted to climb into it. She hit him
With her paddle, and he retired.
Only twelve foot long, it was a young crocodile,
She explained afterwards, that hadn't yet learned manners.

And, navigating now the singing lake,
I can perceive much similar beasticles,
And they all want to get into the boat.

Fanny Trollope and the Alligator

A hard-working, all-American guy,
His labour finished, makes his way homeward,
To embrace once more his wife, his children.
But when he opens the door of his cabin
What does he find? An alligator
Has devoured the lot of them, and is sleeping off his surfeit
Under the great bed. Fanny Trollope was told this story
And passed it on. A widow with two boys back in England,
To feed and educate – one of them
The gifted Anthony. Her visit to America
Had not been a success – her commercial venture failed.
There was nothing much she wouldn't have believed
Against that country. It was the land of liberty,
Her neighbours explained. They enjoyed freedoms
She could not conceive of –
'Your King George wouldn't let you,' they said –
'But not far away
You have slave plantations,' she answered.

It was a long trail to Barchester.

Karawan
to Shafik Megally

The thick-knee or stone curlew –
Half plover, half bustard – in England inhabits
Windswept expanses like Salisbury Plain,
With relics of ancient temples – Stonehenge, or Woodhenge.
In Egypt he is called 'karawan' – a name he shares with the lark,
Is found in villages, and nests
On the flat roofs of Arab houses –
Even in the outskirts of Alexandria.
It was karawan and not the Attic nightingale
That soothed the troubled slumbers of Cavafy.
A gypsy singing girl, top of the charts –
If there were such a thing when I was in Egypt –
(Days of the Suez War)
Carried that bird's name for the sweetness of her voice –
Such sweetness and such wildness too!

Rhodope to Aesop

I don't know whether you'll remember me,
But once we were two in the same batch of slaves,
Hawked about for sale in Asian markets
And in Hellenic countries too, by a proficient merchant
Of such commodities as I, a red-faced Nordic Thracian girl,
With a promise of beauty
(In the Egyptian climate I get burnt
But never tanned) – and you a Blackamoor
(If that word's not offensive).
We were sold off – you in Greek cities,
I, in Nilotic lands. But I
Have done pretty well for myself in that profession
I am best fitted for. I bought my freedom,
And what's more, endowed a smallish pyramid
Out of my savings – in honour of Isis – not Ammon-Ra –
The cruel Egyptian sun –
Isis, the goddess who knew
What suffering and bereavement were and exiled wandering –
I do not think
She'll ever be quite forgotten in this country,
Whatever name she goes by. Now
I'll tell you a more interesting story – one time
When I was paddling in the Nile, a fork-tailed shite-hawk
Swooped down from heaven, and picked up one of my sandals,
And miles and miles away eventually dropped it
Bang into Pharaoh's lap.
He fell in love with it, or more precisely
The foot it had contained – and thereupon
A thoroughgoing search was instituted
To find the owner of this piece of footwear.
And that's the way that I became a star,
And got a place at court for a few years,
And moved in very fashionable circles –
Including Greek mercenaries (King Amasis
Employed a lot of them – they all fell for me –
One in particular whose sister was a poet
Back on Lesbos – she was the music mistress
In a posh girls' school. She named me in a poem, addressed to him
Urging his return. She disapproved

Of his entanglement and called me
'A black unchancy bitch' – I won't go on).
Now he tells me that you're famous too
With your African talent for telling stories
About the animals – Brer Jackal and Brer Hare,
And Brer Hyena with his sickening cry
Who's become Brother Ass.
He says you're now at Delphi, but the priesthood
Resent the political point of some of your tales
And one day they will poke you over a cliff –
I hope they haven't succeeded yet.
I'll ask Sappho's brother
To take this message back with him
Hoping it will catch up with you, before
Those toffee-nosed Apollonian clerics do.
For life is short and life could have been worse – for me
And for you too I think. Not so, old friend?
Neither of us ever had children, but one day, maybe
Children not yet born will hear of us –
Me as Cinderella, my sandal changed for fur
And then to glass, where some say worms can spin
Or delicate fleeces are combed from overhanging trees –
Or far to north and westward, and beyond
The backward flowing and Atlantic stream,
You also will turn up – as Uncle Remus.

The Musician Wren

A small brown bird from South America,
Like all his family, shy and unobtrusive,
A troglodyte, creeper into hollows,
And yet – so rare, so sweet his song – they say
Once in a lifetime only will you hear it.
And to possess one feather from his wing
Is to become yourself, a singer
Welcome on every feast-day, honoured among the tribes.

Epithalamium for Two Big Slugs

Within a moonlit wood, two hermaphrodites, two great black
   slugs –
(*Arion ater* was the name of both of them),
Casually met. With one accord
They climbed to the branch of an overshadowing tree,
From which they both let down a long rope
Of slime, mutually extruded. Then together –
They slowly crept down it, and hung there,
Swaying in the breeze. Each appreciating
The maleness, the femaleness of the other,
They hung there, making love – when they had finished,
They mounted that long thread once more,
(The last to reach the top politely snipped the thread).
They both descended to the ground, then parted.
I don't suppose they ever met again,
Or ever knew the offspring that hatched from their eggs.
Their world was a world of menace. Their enemies?
The hedgehog, spiky as a high church curate
And the insidious blindworm, and above all man,
Who'd batter at them with a stick, or crush them with a boot,
Out of sheer hatred and repulsion,
For after all, they were no good to eat.

George Orwell on Paradise

'The Christian idea of Heaven,' said George Orwell –
'A choir practice in a jeweller's shop.'
All right then, honest Orwell,
Except it's the finished performance and not a practice,
And the pearls and diamonds are going free.

Vision and Television

'Without vision, the people perish.'
The reverse of vision is television,
And that, of course, the people cherish.
'Trust you to maintain that –
For you're as blind as a Natterer's bat.
You might as well say that the earth was flat –
Flat as my hat – for goodness' sake.'
So we're back in the company of William Blake –
In his visionary terms it was just that.

The Burger King

Burger king, in my book, should be
A continental light opera
Of the early years of the twentieth century –
Like *The Vagabond King*, or *The Student Prince*.
The schmaltzy music, the clichéd plot, suggest
An over-plus of cholesterol.
But he is a tyrant too – for his pampered beeves
The great rain forest is felled.
The jacamar, the butterfly-snatcher,
Mourns the destruction of his tree bowers;
The watercourses are fouled
For nutria and potamogale.
Where are the hunting grounds
For human beings, noble and indigenous?

John Edward Stubbs
listening to Radio 4 Artesian Road
London 1991   Adam Tournoux

Bunch

Bunch was an unremarkable dog,
Till, to everybody's surprise,
The mess he had made on the drawing room carpet
Was awarded the Turner Prize.

Going Metric

'The first turning on the right,' I said
To the boy who had asked for directions.
'It's about a hundred yards on.'
'What,' said he, 'is a hundred yards?'
He had not been instructed in yards, feet and inches,
And I had no skill in metres and kilometres –
The metric system – that absurd invention
Of the godless philosophers of the French Revolution.
But there wasn't time to explain that an English yard
Was exactly the distance between
The tip of King Henry the Second's nose
And the end of his forefinger.
'Never mind,' I said, 'You'll come to it anyway.'

The Decent Inn

Oh yes, I am old-fashioned enough
To quote G.K. Chesterton – that charitable fancy
That there is an inn at the end of the world, or somewhere
Where the soul, at the last stage of its pilgrimage
May spend one night of refreshment and rest
Before it goes to final arbitration,
Kept, they say, by Saint Gertrude. But there have been other
Licensees, I think – Scottish Kind Kittock –
They say she died of thirst and made a good end,
And sneaked into heaven when St Peter wasn't looking,
Fixing herself a job as Our Lady's henwife.
But the ale of heaven, she said, was sour – so she left
And opened up premises outside the gates.
I pray you, have a drink with her before you go in.

But centuries and millennia before her time
There was that Lady of the Booth, who offered a drink to Gilgamesh
On his hard slog, as he went on his way
To consult the sole survivor of the flood,
The only man granted immortality –
Sisudra, Ut Naphistim or Noah.
But Gilgamesh sought it only for himself,
And not for the hairy barbarian friend he had loved.
Immortality, he found, was a branch of coral
In the Persian gulf. He dived for it,
But a snake filched it while he dried himself:
This was before the Serpent's power was broken.

A Dream Transcribed
Memory of Philip Larkin

Blind as a bed-post I've been, for thirty years or more –
Yet I still dream in images, though now
They're fainter and less easy to remember
Than once they were. And thus, the other night,
I seemed to be travelling northward in a train
To one of those dull Midland towns, where once
He lived and worked. I got out at a station
Where he met me, in a kindly way.
We went to some place where there was a meal –
Either a restaurant, or his apartment.
Waking, I recalled how he had died –
And that was years ago – and how
We'd once been friends – in Oxford days,
And, when we'd both gone down, exchanged letters
Comparing notes on trying to find a job, which he likened
To one of those bicycle races, in which
The first to fall off is a winner. And then
I knew this dream of mine referred to
That world beyond death which, if such things are,
I must be drawing closer to. And to which, he,
Lying sleepless through a long tedious night,
So passionately refused his credence.

Matilda

'You're on your own now,' said Virgil,
'Crowned and enmitred over yourself.' And then he vanished.
Dante was in terror because of the loneliness
He suddenly found himself in. But it wasn't the void,
Nor that dark wood, where the beasts harboured.
After the horror of hell and the pain of purgatory
A springtime meadow, and wild flowers, and a blessing of
    birdsong.
And then, all at once, a young girl who gathered
Selectively the blossoms. She was Matilda –
Whoever Matilda was – and she
Would lead him once again to Beatrice.

Our Lady's Juggler
to John Minahan

If he had written hymns to the Virgin,
They would probably have been boring ones. So he did
What he was best at – he juggled –
He juggled and he tumbled. He stood on his head, and kicked
Simultaneously in the air (in honour
Of the Trinity – I rather doubt it?)
But then the Queen of Heaven, that housewife of Nazareth,
Descended from her plinth, and did what she could do best –
She wiped the sweat and grime upon his brow
With the fringe of her veil, as serviceable for that
As to protect the bulwarks of Byzantium
From a horde of Saracen invaders.

The Miracle of Saint Nicholas

As they arose out of the pickling tub
Crystals of brine still hung
Upon their eyelashes, and on their beautiful soft hair.
Surprised, as if they'd been
Suddenly jerked out of sleep, they gazed
On the saint's face, saw the expression
Of love and pity for those boys – compassion and condemnation
For those others. The innkeeper and his wife
Stood astounded, stricken with guilt and fear –
Sweeney Todd and Mrs Lovett, or whatever
Galatian, Anatolian or Pontic names
They went by then (for they are always with us –
Those who in times of dearth, misgovernment, and war,
In the desperate scrabble for money will sell anything –
Even the flesh of their fellow human beings).

'You'd better get on with your journey, boys,' St Nicholas said,
'Or else you'll miss the opening of term.'

John Heath-Stubbs
Artesian Road
London 1991

Alan Duncan

The Five Faithful Serving Men

Those serving men begin to slack in their duties.
They've served me well enough for four-score years
According to their capacities, though one of them
Discharged himself some two decades ago. Soon it will be time
They should be pensioned off. They have my thanks.
Only the old nurse, Sleep, remains,
With her last and deepest draught – a dreamless slumber
(What's to be feared in death?) or else the unnumbered petalled
    rose that opens
Beyond reality and non-reality.

The Brass Bottle

The story of the djinn in the bottle –
You'll find it somewhere in *The Arabian Nights*:
And various other versions have migrated
Westwards – from Arab sources. I'd surmise
It was intended to discourage Moslems
From opening bottles indiscriminately –
And that was wholesome counsel, but I wonder
How much it ever was observed. Think of yourself
Endlessly trudging on a sandy beach
Beside a limitless ocean – yes, an image
Of this our earthly pilgrimage. You will notice
Inorganic and organic flotsam –
Cuttlebones, mermaids' purses and dead men's fingers;
And there, amid the rest, a brassy bottle
Turned green with verdigris – and on its neck
A seal suspended, which you recognise.
This was the token whereby Solomon
Controlled non-human beings – djinns and afrits –
They know the hidden secrets of the sea
And the deep minds where treasure sleeps, sardonically gleaming.
What would you do then? – leave it alone, pass on,
Or break that seal, releasing
Whatever lurked within? I'd lay a coffin-load of gold,
A jerry-can of carbonaceous diamonds,
That I can guess the answer.

Anti-Daffodil Poem

Whoever was it who decided
This should be the first if not the only poem
Kids were exposed to? Children nowadays
Are not likely to see daffodils growing
The way Wordsworth, or rather Dorothy, saw them.
Some little townees, I'd hazard a guess,
Have only a vague idea what a daffodil is.
And as for the final stanza
It contains a helping of rather sophisticated
Hartleian psychology smuggled inside it. This plugging of his
   verses
Can do no service to the great poet,
Lofty as Skiddaw or Scafell Pike,
Profound and wind-swept as Grasmere or Ullswater.
For a hundred years or so, I must surmise,
This daffodilolatry has been going on.
I was exposed to these verses
When I first went to school, and next came
Alfred Tennyson's 'Lady of Shalott'.
But at least that poem had music and magic,
And for nowadays, a warning
Against watching too much television.

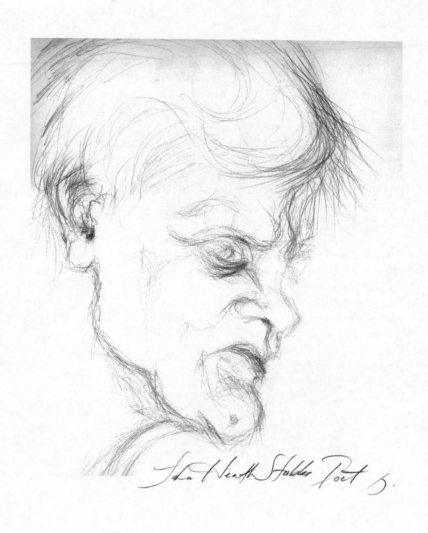

John Heath Stubbs Poet 6.

Reader to the Kaiserin

The Princess Augusta, Queen Victoria's daughter,
And married to an emperor, who was dying
Of cancer of the throat – Bismarck hated her
As a focus of English and liberal ideas –
So did her own son, with his distorted ego
And his withered arm (they skinned a hare alive
To try to cure it) – she needed an English reader
But it could not be one from her native country.
So she engaged that sad deraciné Frenchman
Jules Laforgue, invalide and poet, haunted
By the sound of the pianos in comfortably-off
Quarters of Paris – young girls
With their continual ritornelloes, up and down,
Up and down again, in rigid time:
'He came into my life – he went away.
Life is real, and is a crime.'
And those two strangers, what did they read together?
The sensible church-going Charlotte M. Yonge perhaps,
Or Rhoda Boughton – 'Red as a rose is she.'

An Echo of Schubert
(and Wilhelm Müller)

That young miller's apprentice – he started out
So full of hope, so full of love,
And ended up at the bottom of the mill-pond,
As we all do, more or less. Dusty miller, dusty answer –
Or soggy, under the mill-race.

Dinner in a Dinosaur

Prehistoric creatures, dinosaurs,
Labyrinthodonts, and pterodactyls
And the feathered archaeopteryx, trailing its lizard tail,
Flapping its fingered wings,
Are in the gardens once surrounding
The Crystal Palace – Paxton's greenhouse –
Though that went up in smoke, Father Willis's console
Thundered for the last time.
It was the great Professor Owen who
Designed those creatures, and, when they were finished,
He gave a dinner-party. Bearded and eminent,
In white tie and starched shirts, and tails,
His privileged guests sat down to stuff themselves
Inside the belly of the largest monster.

A visit to South Kensington and the museum,
In boyhood, used to be the high spot,
When I, infrequently, was brought to London.
In the vast entrance hall one first encountered
Enormous models of a flea, a sheep-tick,
A body-louse, a prowling housefly,
Which trod with dirty feet all over
A plate of simulated ham and eggs.
Beyond these auguries of pollution, rose
A wide staircase, which was leading upwards
To spaces of more wonder, more delight;
And at its base there sat two marble statues –
Professor Owen and Professor Huxley,
Awe-full in their academic robes. They glowered
Down on us visitors, and made it clear
They'd stand no fables, nor no fairy tales
Nor shakey hypotheses. On the same stairway
Glass cases stood – 'The Gould Collection',
Where among nectarless and scentless flowers
There hung pathetically the stuffed dried bodies
Of tiny humming-birds, that hummed no longer.

Somewhat Too Sensational
On reading a recent book on the phylogeny and taxonomy of birds.
for Oliver Parfit

It is all as Miss Prism might have said –
Like the chapter on the fall of the rupee –
Somewhat too sensational, the divorce
Of the pigeons and the sand-grouse, the expulsion
Of the pelican from the clan we all thought he was head of; the
   hoatzin
Clambering at last into his untidy communal nest,
Cosying up to Crotophaga, the Anicuckoo, and not
To the plantain-eaters or the curasows, and then the secret alliance
Of the fin-foots with the limpkin. And so it goes on.
Miss Prism, I suppose, knew little of ornithology.
She taught her pupils botany – and as for taxonomy, of plants,
She stuck to Hooker and Frere, with a distant nod to Linnaeus –
A system based on the number and disposition
Of the plants' sexual organs (but she did not call them that) –
Stamens and pistils of course.
But she might have paused for a moment when a chaffinch rattled,
Or a tomtit 'Tea-cher'd' her
Among the trees of that Hertfordshire garden,
And afterwards looked them up in a bird-book –
The Reverend C.A. Johns perhaps, or another clergyman –
The Reverend J.G. Wood. His *Illustrated Natural History*
Followed the system of Gray, who catalogued
The birds in the South Kensington Museum.
I too read these old books in my Hampshire childhood.
I too heard those songs, which my father taught me to recognise,
Taking me for walks when I was six years old.
Later on I wandered in the woods and fields –
Children could do that then – there was no fear of molestation –
Making friends with birds, insects and wild flowers,
Or down on the sea-shore, with stranger creatures.
We were just outside the New Forest
Where the Red King was slain.
People told me how once the wood-spurge was used as a substitute
   for tea,
When that was too heavily taxed; and showed me how to peel a
   rush

To make a rush-light, or cut through a bracken-stalk
To see the picture of good King Charles
Hiding in the oak-tree. Goose-grass
Was called cleavers and clung to one's clothes.
Mushrooms and blackberries were there for the picking
(But the Devil spat on the blackberries in November).
We gathered sloes and pricked them
To steep them in gin. My bird-book was Coward's
(A Cheshire man) and the coloured plates
Were Lord Lilford's. And Coward's taxonomy
Was that of Sharp, pedantic and meticulous.
And so, likewise, were ranged, in suitable poses,
The birds – all stuffed and dead – on London visits to the museum.

The Emperor's Parrot
From the *Geata Romanorum*

He was a Palaeornis, a ring-necked parakeet, and not
A red-tailed African Grey, nor a gaudy screeching Macaw
And certainly not a top-knotted antipodean cockatoo – no ship
    from our world
Had yet made landfall on shores where such were found.
An Indian – swami, or guru, or fakir, or something – at any rate
That's what he claimed to be – had brought the bird
As a present for the emperor – and was handsomely rewarded, I
    may say,
For that same gift. As for the parrot's accomplishments –
He could repeat several Vedic Hymns, Mantras and Sutras
In Sanskrit or other ancient Indian tongues and – in Greek –
Sentences from Plato, passages from Aristotle,
And whole missing chapters of Theophrastus, but what
Delighted the emperor most, was the way that bird
Over and over again, recited
Salutations to his highness – '*Ave Caesar,*
Salve Imperator.' The parrot was housed
In a gilded cage, and sumptuously fed
On hothouse grapes, Lucullan cherries,
Armenian apricots, sweetcorn and popcorn. The emperor
Spent hours listening to the bright-feathered flatterer,
Neglecting the sessions of the Senate and all official duties – till
    one day
The carers found that the cage was empty – its loquacious prisoner
    flown.
A search was instituted. The emperor headed it,
Riding about the adjacent countryside, when all of a sudden –
It seemed a miracle – for there was the bird
Flying at the head of a flock of other wild fowl, who'd been his
    disciples,
And all of them – but all of them – repeated,
Again and again, the same loyal salutation,
Greenfinches, chaffinches, whitethroats, and bluethroats and ruby-
    throats,
Hoopoes and cuckoos, pratincoles and coursers,
And godwits and peewits, redshanks, and greenshanks,
Down by the very margins of the sea, all chorused

'*Ave Caesar! Salve imperator.*' For the Indian bird had instructed
   them.
The emperor was overjoyed, he brought his parrot home
And had it rehoused in an even more expensive
Prison, with more luxurious delicacies to feast on,
And spent still more time just listening, delighted, to what it
   articulated.
'It serves to keep me going,' he said,
'Now that I seem to be turning into a god –
An uncomfortable and rather messy process.
The Senate and the imperial guard can look after the affairs of
   state.' And so it was
Until those Praetorians eventually scrubbed him out,
One day when he was sitting on the lavatory, contemplating
His navel, with its incipient hernia. '*Ave Caesar*'
Still ringing in his ears. After that
The parrot seemed to fall silent. Some thought it was grief
For his eliminated master – but that was not the case – the prudent
   bird
Was secretly practising a fresh repertoire:
Even more flattering formulae of salutation,
Ready to trot them out to a new Caesar,
When the Senate, and the people, and of course the Praetorians
Had settled upon a replacement to the purple.

The Language of Birds
for Carmen Blacker

I seem to be, you said, like one of those
Men one hears about, in old stories,
Who understood the language of birds. Well, maybe,
I have a sort of smattering, though I wouldn't claim
Proficiency in any of their dialects.
Last year I had a spell in hospital –
Nothing much wrong with me, but I was well looked after.
One sunlit day, they let me sit
In a small garden that the place boasted. A crow,
A black carrion crow, had built her nest
Up in a tree there. She was quite clear
That this was her territory, and I
Had absolutely no business there at all.
She cawed and croaked, 'Get out, go off!
You stinking human monstrosity. Don't ever dare
Show your face here again!' Her meaning was quite clear –
I was a threat to her, her nest, and to her new-hatched brood.
That was a rough transcription of what she said –
Though quite unprintable, but actually
The voice of courage and maternal love.

Solomon Eagle

Solomon Eagle, naked except for the sackcloth about his loins,
Beating a drum, a brazier of burning coals on his head,
Strode through the highways and byways of London, crying
'Woe to the bloody city, woe!'
It got on people's nerves, and didn't
Really remedy the situation.
This sort of thing gave harmless Quakers a bad name –
In the year of the plague, 1665,
When the death carts rumbled through the cobbled streets
And the black rats squealed in the stinking gutters.
Solomon Eagle had been a musician,
But after his conversion, had publicly burned
His instruments on Tower Hill. But his son, John Eccles,
Continued the business.
He was friends with William Congreve
And Anne Bracegirdle who created the rôle of Millamant.
Congreve wrote an opera *Semele* on a pagan theme
For Eccles to set, and Bracegirdle to sing in.
Such is the way of the world.
But there was also a cello sonata.
I was awarded a bronze medal, as a boy,
For playing it at the Bournemouth Festival
(The silver medal was withheld – there were no other competitors).
I've had other medals since but I've still got that one –
I found it lately in a box at the back of a drawer.

Bournemouth and Brighton

Bournemouth, with her concert halls,
Her three theatres, and her smart shops,
Her second-hand bookstores, where I picked up
Throw-outs from the library of Hartert the ornithologist –
This was our town in my Hampshire, sub-rural, boyhood.
Bournemouth regarded Brighton not as a rival,
But rather as a Victorian lady might have done
Her slightly scandalous Regency aunt.
Bournemouth's sister Boscombe was less refined –
Marie Lloyd had appeared at her Hippodrome,
But in my day the Charleston was forbidden there. In Brighton
Prinny's stately pleasure dome stood empty and unrefurbished.
Whelks and jellied eels were sold on her seafront,
But not I think on Bournemouth's. Brighton's sister, Hove,
Was reputed to be really a much nicer place. Though it's surprising
How many people with colourful pasts
Were to end up there –
Ethel Le Neve (Crippin's mistress),
Lord Alfred Douglas, and Aleister Crowley –
I might mention my friend John Waller,
But he moved to the Isle of Wight:
Then of course there was Mandy Rice Davies –
But she married and settled in Israel, didn't she?

Sir Percy Shelley Speaks

Me poor old dad – never knew him of course,
Nor Harriet neither, his first wife,
No better than she should be I'm afraid – what's worse,
Both of their heads stuffed with radical ideas –
Drowned herself in the Serpentine. Water
Was the enemy of both my parents. My wife now –
She loves my old dad's poetry. Elderly gentlemen
Get invited up from London, who say they were his friends –
Peacock one of them calls himself, and Hogg, the other,
To give their reminiscences – and latterly
A professor over from Dublin.
My wife – she'll pay good money for a letter my dad signed –
A lot of them fakes I'm told. They'll muddy
The waters of scholarship for at least a century.
And the monument she erected in Christchurch priory,
Showing two ladies – muses I suppose,
Hardly his wives – fishing his body up
Out of the sea. To tell you the truth
It gives me gooseflesh.
Harriet's daughter,
She came to see us too.
We gave her the key to my dad's archive
But one box she wasn't to open –
Then we both went for a long walk
And left her to it. When we came back
She was weeping. Water was the enemy,
But he loved sailing, as I do too,
A freak storm caught him in the Mediterranean – I'm happy to say
We don't have such storms in the Solent.
Allow me to present you with an autographed copy
Of my own little book, *The Romance of Yachting*.

Conversation with an Extra-Terrestrial

'That conflict in your neighbouring island,' asked the Martian,
'What is it all about exactly?'
'That's difficult to explain,' I said to him,
'One of their own poets, centuries past,
Offered this analogy – at which end
Is it correct that you should crack an egg before consuming it?'
'Eggs in my world are all of them perfect spheres,
And none knows or cares where on the shell
One ought to open them – except, one must presume,
The thing inside that's waiting to be born.'
'Next time you visit us,' I told him then,
'You'd better bring a clutch.'

Just Enough Change

The shop sold newspapers, envelopes and things, stamps,
And a certain amount of confectionery.
In front of me, the lady by the counter
Reckoned up her change. 'I've just got
Enough to buy a galaxy,' she said.
And how in heaven's name, in the name
Of all the whirling and twirling stars, was I to know
A galaxy could be a chocolate bar?

Gay?

'You do realise, sir,' said the doorman,
'That this is a gay bar.' He needn't have bothered –
The particular dreariness which pervaded the place,
Could not be described as anything else but 'Gay' –
The camp self-mockery, the parody
Alike of the feminine and of the masculine;
The stranger carefully concealed the bomb
In the fetid lavatory, then left
And crossed to the other side of the road
To survey his handiwork. It was
His own rejected selfhood there
He murdered and mutilated
With gay abandon.

The Frigate Bird in Love

'O frig it!' said the frigate bird,
Using a rather inelegant word,
'I loved a flamingo from San Domingo
But I am no more to her than a turd.

'Just as a Latin mistrusts a Gringo –
I cannot even work out her lingo.
I must take my flight to a very great height,
Or spend the rest of my days playing bingo.'

An English Idyll

'A tedious little place as I recall:
There's really nothing there at all –
Except a fried fish and chip shop,
And also a bus-stop.'
'So what do people find to talk about?'
'They talk of fish no doubt –
Occasionally chips, one would suppose –
What's more, the time the next bus goes.
And others that are good at sums
Work out the time the next bus comes.'

Ancient Wisdom

There was a Chinese sage, so I'm informed,
Deplored the invention of the wheelbarrow –
It led to immorality, he said,
It made it easier for younger folk
From different villages to meet, trundling
Their loads of night-soil to far-off locations.

National Tastes in Murder

English murders usually take place
In respectable seaside resorts, or boring suburbs:
Somebody just happens to open a closet
And a body falls out, or several bodies,
In an advanced state of decomposition.

French murders on the other hand,
Are the product of sheer peasant greed,
So universal a motive that it is difficult
To sort one individual out from among a number of suspects.

American murders are frequently massacres –
Done with a chainsaw or anything else that happens to be lying
    handy,
And presided over by a benevolent Godfather.

The Skeleton in the Cupboard

For what unspeakable scandal they'd stacked him in there,
Discarding then the key, none of the family
Could now remember – but it was centuries past.
There he remained, forgotten, with only the cockroaches
And the mice for company. The mice could sing and dance,
And entertained him, while the cockroaches
Retailed their ancient wisdom, which went back
To carboniferous times. At last
Somehow or other he learned to pick the lock
From the inside. At nights he would slip out,
Pilfering food from the larder, wine from the cellar.
This put flesh on his bones, and a left-over
Carnival mask served him for a face.
But spirit was lacking, till by chance
He turned on the late-night radio and then the strains
Of the *Danse Macabre* filled the air.
He improvised a xylophone obbligato,
Beating his rib-cage with a wooden spoon.
Saint-Saens, that more than competent composer,
With possible skeletons in his own closet,
Infused him with the spirit of his music.
Our skeleton exited by the French window,
And pranced about the moonlit mansion. Subsequently
He was observed in various parts of the county,
And having somehow acquired a suit of clothes
He left for London, and thereafter followed
A series of successful careers – in journalism,
In public relations, and the media.
He held a post as Senior Lecturer
In Cultural Studies at the newly-founded
University of Hogsnorton, wrote a novel –
Its title was *Old Bones* – highly commended
By all the reviewers, and then shortlisted
For the Booker Prize. Finally he entered parliament
And still holds his seat there, but which constituency
He represents, which party has his suffrage,
Even if I knew, I don't think I should tell you.

Tinnunculus in Bayswater

A kestrel, who has lost his usual perch
Upon a convent roof, the sisters having left,
The roof replaced by one of trendy flatness,
Now must take his stance by turns
Upon the dome of the Greek cathedral (Hagia Sophia)
Or on St Matthew's spire (the parish church) or else,
A vaulted gable of the synagogue.
It's seasonable that this should be an omen.

Christmas 1998

El Draque Forbids the Banns
for John Cherrington

This is a story they told down in Devon,
Concerning Francis Drake and his wife – his second wife,
Elizabeth, of a good family,
Of honest West Country folk.
There was an understanding that he would marry her
But not until he had circumnavigated
The whole vast globe. She agreed to wait,
With reservations – 'I don't know how Mary,
His first wife, put up with this sort of thing,
And I wasn't aware that the world was round –
But all the learned say so, so it seems –
But he'll be a good catch, and a good husband
So I might as well wait a few months or so.'
She waited and waited, but no news came.
A second suitor was dangling after her –
I don't know his name, but let us suppose
It was Urchard of Taunton Dean, from the next county,
Already known for an unsuccessful wooer
(There's a ballad about it). But perhaps he'd acquired now
A little more finesse. Eventually she agreed
To this proposal – that the banns be read in church.
She should have thought twice, she should have asked the
    Spaniards
They could have told her El Draque's familiar
Informed him of everything. His crew likewise recounted
How a shag, a boatswain-bird, or a mollymawk
Would fly round his mast, and then, suddenly,
They'd spot a Spanish treasure-ship loaded with gold
Or marketable slaves, or they'd sail to a city
Ripe for the sacking, its great cathedral
Crammed with jewel-encrusted ex votoes.
She should have been wary when a coach-horse beetle
Crossed her path, and erected its tail,
Emitting a stink, or a sharp-nosed shrew
Peeped out from a dunghill, or a yellowhammer
Bread-and-no-cheesed her from on top of a gatepost –
That wicked bird which scribbles on its eggs

Heathen hieroglyphics and cabbalistic symbols,
And drinks a drop of the devil's blood
Every Mayday morning, as the rhyme said –
For any of them could have been Drake's spy,
The vehicle of his familiar spirit.
She took no heed, and got tired of waiting.
At last she submitted to Urchard's suing –
The banns were to be read in front of the altar.
But as they stood there, and the priest had got
As far as that bit which speaks of
'Just cause or impediment' – suddenly
There was a rumbling under the earth,
And through the crypt, and through the church floor,
A cannonball came. And stood there sizzling-hot.
But its momentum continued no further.
For Drake, a little off course
For circumnavigation, was sailing at the Antipodes
And somehow – from demon, or bird, or flying-fish,
Had got to know what was going on.
He gave orders, and fired a cannonball
Down into the depths of the ocean.
It pierced the sea-floor, and infernal strata
Down to the centre, and singed the old Devil's arse
As it flew by. And then it surfaced
Right there in England, and in that church,
Where those two were standing before the altar,
Elizabeth and Urchard. They got the message,
And she dismissed her unsatisfactory suitor –
'I'm plighted to master Francis,' she said,
'And he'll be back in his own good time.'
'Maybe he will,' said Urchard, 'But you
Can marry your sea-dog, your salty sailor –
And "Yo-ho-ho!" I sing to both of you.'
Drake did come back, and he landed at Deptford,
And the queen came aboard and dubbed him 'Sir Francis'
There on the deck of his ship, and greatly appreciated
The gold and the silver which he had brought her.
And after that he went down to Devon,
Claimed his own Bess, and made her his lady.

It was sometime later, as we've all heard.
He had time to finish a game of bowls
Upon Plymouth Hoe, and beat the Armada after.
And as for the marriage, I've no information,
But I'm inclined to surmise
That it worked out.

This story is freely based on one given by Katherine Briggs and Ruth Tongue in their *Folk Tales of England* (Routledge, 1965). A text of the ballad of 'Richard of Taunton Deane' was given in Bell's *Ballads and Songs of the Peasantry of England*. It is one of a group of ballads about a clownish wooer, of which the best known example is probably the 'Scottish Duncan Gray'.

A Genetic Predisposition

'Why, for goodness sake,'
Someone is bound to say,
'Do you write verse about Sir Francis Drake?
He's in his hammock and four hundred years away.'
'All's in the genes – we don't know how they'll act
But can be sure that they will always win.
Sir Henry Newbolt, was, in point of fact,
My fairly distant kin.'

Senecio Recalls Playing Football

'It passes my comprehension,' said Senecio,
'That any sane adult person could possibly be interested
In the fact that eleven healthy young men
(Or is it fifteen?) are better at kicking a ball
From one end of a field to the other
Than eleven (or fifteen) wholly similar young men,
But I realise that the great majority of my countrymen
Find this banality more uplifting,
Awe-inspiring, than the music of Bach, Mozart or Beethoven,
The paintings of Michelangelo, the *Commedia* of Dante,
The tragedies of Shakespeare, and all the wisdom
Of the saints and sages of every epoch.
I know what I'm talking about: as a schoolboy
I was compelled to take part in this dreary game,
And punished if I failed to turn up, which, in the end,
I refused to do – for there was no form of punishment
They would be likely to inflict, that could be worse
Than the game itself.
If I did play, I hoped I would be stationed
At the outside right or left (the wing position).
The ball didn't usually get into that part of the field –
And, if it did, one could generally see it coming
Turn round, and walk away,
In a dignified fashion. But this strategy
Apparently incurred a certain odium.'

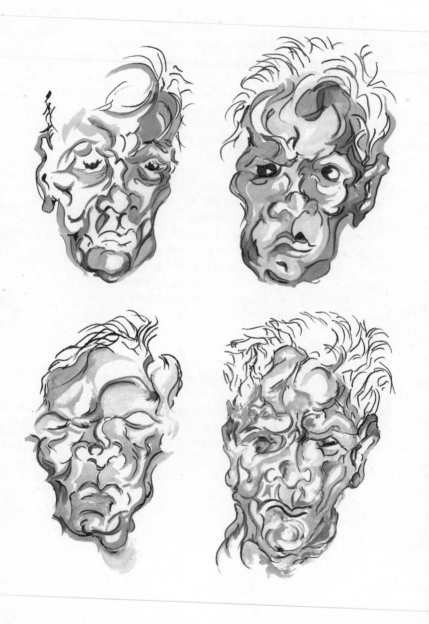

Senecio and Lady Chatterley

'A rather better work, in my opinion
In its expurgated form,' said Senecio.
'But not many bookshops stock that nowadays,
And if it gets around that's how you read it
You'll be a social and a moral outcast.'

Class Distinctions among Lice

The head-lice and the body-lice are not two species
But races simply, though each one clings
To its proper habitat – the body,
Or otherwise, the head.
The head-lice look down on the body-lice. The body-lice
Call the head-lice élitist. The crab-lice
Belong to a different genus, exclusively confined
To the pubic hairs, or sometimes
The coarse ones underneath the armpits –
'A stinking slum,' said the head-lice and the body-lice:
'Aphrodite's Eden,' the crabs rejoined.

The Millennium Bug

Belphegor – he was an ugly bug
Holed up snug in a tatty old rug.
His body was bloated with human blood –
For he hated mankind, and he hated the good.
But what especially evoked his rage
Was the triumph of the computer age.
But in this situation Belphegor knew
There was something a bug could easily do
To stop the computers. Those innocent creatures
Had a fault built in with their other features.
They knew how many make up five beans,
But understood centuries only in teens.
On December the thirty first, ninety nine,
Just before midnight, in cold moonshine,
Belphegor crept forth with evil intent –
It was sabotage on which he was bent.
Through the computers this monster came slinking,
Seeking the weak points in their thinking.
He worked on this, and before very long,
All the calendar dates were wrong.
To rectify which seemed labour in vain –
The world-wide web had been rent in twain.
Nobody now, with Belphegor to thank,
Could get any money out of the bank.
Bewildered satellites strayed through the heavens
And things on earth seemed at sixes and sevens.
But Britons all know – at our direst need
Succour will come to the island breed.
King Arthur and all his knights, who still
Dream in the depths of a sacred hill
Or beneath the waves of a magical lake,
When the hour seems darkest shall awake.
Thus it was now – with a deafening clatter
They issued forth, and 'What is the matter?'
With a single voice those paladins cried.
'The millennium bug!' the people replied.
But not King Arthur nor all his knights
Were able to put those computers to rights.
At derring-do they were most proficient,

But hardly at solving sums sufficient.
Arthur said, 'Merlin might mend those faults,
But he sleeps in Carmarthen's castle vaults.'
So they worked out magical spells – when they'd sung them
Merlin awoke, and was soon among them.
'Why am I summoned?' he asked with surprise,
As he blinked in the daylight his horny eyes.
'Are you plagued by some dragon, or ogreish thug?'
But they shouted out, 'No – the millennium bug!'
'He fills with confusion our days and our nights,
And nobody knows how to put things to rights.'
'Wait a few minutes,' old Merlin said,
And he made calculations inside his head –
'Just tighten those screws, just twiddle that knob –
Be patient until you have finished the job.'
They took his instructions, and – lo and behold –
The computers were working as good as gold.
Their faults were corrected, and now, at ease,
They hummed like a hive of contented bees.
But where was Belphegor the bug to be found?
He was right there, crawling upon the ground,
As bold as brass. You would hardly guess
There was anyone there who might dare to repress
That monster. But the bold Sir Galahad,
On account of the pureness of heart that he had,
And his strength which was as the strength of ten,
In his coat of mail, stepped forth – and then
He did what anyone else would do:
He planted his heavily-armoured shoe
Upon the creature, and squashed it flat –
As flat as my grandfather's opera hat.
Then all the people shouted 'Hurray!'
Millennium springtide was on the way.
Heaven had succoured their utmost need,
And civilisation could proceed.
'New Year's morning, and I awoke –
Nothing had happened, just a joke.'

For a Commonplace Book
To celebrate Carcanet Press's thirtieth anniversary

Volatile and garrulous chaps,
Poets resemble birds perhaps,
Composing sweet melodious strains,
Although they've rather tiny brains.
The figure fits in other terms –
Birds hop about in search of worms,
Berries and seeds and grubs and flies,
Which nature generally supplies;
And poets make (at least a day)
Their living in that sort of way;
With luck, some find a gilded cage
And do quite well in this our age.
A different simile comes to mind –
Creatures of the insect kind,
With delicate wings, and compound eyes –
Ephemerids and butterflies:
Children of the summer sun –
But when he sets, their day is done.
Eternity they only win,
Transfixed by a collector's pin.
Let's take instead the honest toad
Trying to cross a busy road,
In spite of heavy traffic that,
Later or soon, will squash him flat.
Ugly and venomous he may look,
But isn't so – not in my book –
For there's enclosed, as Shakespeare said,
A precious jewel in his head,
And this, if it be duly set,
Shall grace the muse's carcanet.

An Acrostic for the Omar Khayyam Club

Oh how time's passing keeps one on one's toes –
March, and like an early-blossoming rose,
 A poem, which the Omar Khayyam club
Request to grace their dinner. Well, here goes –

Kindly muse lend a judicious ear –
Have you not done so for me many a year?
 A string of words like shining beads, will serve
Your votary, a modest balladeer.

'Your lines,' she said, 'shall picture, on a lawn
A company of drinkers.' One last yawn,
 And then the setting of the youthful moon:
Morning is imminent, here comes the dawn.

Judge some, 'Khayyam was mystical and gnostic –
He'd turn his nose up at your trite acrostic.'
Somehow he mightn't, tipsy old agnostic.

Omar in Autumn
for the Omar Khayyam Society Dinner, November 2001

A great autumnal moon rises in heaven,
The nightingales have left for other climes,
A few late roses bloom. The astronomer
Is poured a drink, and improvises rhymes.

It's no bad thing, perhaps, we should remember
That such a garden was, or might have been;
The eastern skies are dark with threats of violence,
And with fanatic bigotry obscene.

So if, at last, they blow us all to bits,
We will have drunk with Omar and with Fitz.

Porphyry and Plotinus on heaven's payment;
Swedenborg's vision in the darkness of the mine;
Blake in the golden square of Jerusalem,
Terrible as the voice of a lamb,
Innocent as a tiger;
The simplicity of the stone, of the flower that unfurls its petals,
Its stamen and pistils numbered
By Hooker or by Linnaeus;
Ascetics are clustering
About the summits of Mount Meru;
It is a lengthy pilgrimage
That is also the way home.

A Christmas Rose

Roast turkey and plum pudding
Or a suitable vegan dish;
Faith, hope and charity –
What else is there to wish?

Faith and hope in their space-ship
Where a cosmic whirlwind blows;
Love, in her secret garden,
Nurtures a Christmas rose.

Just Once a Year

'Christmas comes but once a year –
And a very good thing too, if you ask me,' said Mrs 'Arris,
The cockney housewife – creation
Of Clifford B. Poultney, a now forgotten comic writer,
Favoured in my boyhood and adolescence.
And if, as some do, you tend to dislike
The over-rich food, the overindulged-in drink,
Commercial ballyhoo, red-nosed reindeer,
And *erythacus rubecula*, with a breast more scarlet
Than bountiful Nature ever assigned him,
Please remember – at the heart of all this
What we are summoned to celebrate is love –
Quotidian and supersubstantial as bread,
And common birth in an unhygienic stable.

Bede's Death Song

He knew he was dying. He summoned his brethren together,
And told them to bring
What he called his box of treasures –
A small package of black peppercorns.
He told them it came over the seas from India,
Over the curve of the round earth.
'And I will share these among you all.'
There can't have been, I suppose,
More than one or two for each of them –
These with gratitude and with tears they took.
Then he began to sing, in his native Northumbrian,
In the alliterative metre – as once
In old pagan stories, heroes had sung
Dying on the field of battle.
But there was peace, as this one passed
Into eternity – as in ages yet undreamt-of
William Blake, David of the White Rock.

Poem for Easter

A stone rolled away, a vacant tomb,
Linen clothes folded, the voice of a gardener
Who was not a gardener – women's tales,
And other rumours – a stranger on the road,
Texts expounded – a recognition
In the breaking of bread. And then
'I go a-fishing' – back
To the quotidian reality, the boring necessity
Of earning a living. A figure on the shore –
The miraculous draught again,
Every species of fish, and then
The acknowledgement, the submission, the commission –
'Feed my sheep' – the renewal
Which every spring contains,
One with the eternal renewal
And the all-embracing, illimitable cosmos of love.

Crichlow, Amandla Crichlow, Barbara Beese, A. Sivanandan, Linton Kwesi Johnson, Max Farrar, Linda Bellos, Margaret Busby, Clare Short, Dotun Adebayo, Sarah White, Farrukh Dhondy, Nirpal Dhaliwal, Trevor Phillips, Narinder Minhas, Marques Toliver, Barry Cox, Caroline Coon, Harry Goulbourne, Lincoln Crawford and especially Darcus Howe, who spent many hours discussing his life with us. Thank you also to Robert Hill, Richard Small, Joe Street, Anne-Marie Angelo, Ana Laura Lopez de la Torre, Anthony Gifford, Dr Vince Hines, Derek Humphry, James Whitfield, Winston Trew, Simon Woolley, Kimberly Springer, David Austin and Krishnendu Majumdar. We also thank the master and fellows of St Edmund's College Cambridge and the president and fellows of Homerton College Cambridge for their support during this project.

We owe a great debt to the expertise of Michael Ryan and Alix Ross at the University of Columbia's Butler Library as well as Jenny Bourne at the Institute of Race Relations Archive and Sarah Garrod at the George Padmore Institute. Thank you to Harry Carr for his editorial work, to Laura Williams, Barry Hart, Grishma Fredric and Farzad Zadeh for their comments on the manuscript and to Mark Richardson and Caroline Wintersgill at Bloomsbury.

We are particularly indebted to Leila Hassan and Priyamvada Gopal. Leila's vivid memory and insights into events over a 40-year period have been invaluable to us, as has her support, friendship and encouragement in writing the book. Priya Gopal took time out of her own teaching, writing and research schedule to generously read and wisely comment on the whole manuscript for which we are extremely grateful. Finally, we would like to thank our respective partners, Lucy and Maggie, and our children, India, Max and Mia. Without their love, support and patience, we could not have written this book.

Introduction –
'Darcus Howe is a West Indian'

C. L. R. James, a man who will appear again and again in these pages, once stated: 'Darcus is a West Indian.' The comment was an attempt to elucidate Howe's character for the benefit of Leila Hassan, deputy editor of *Race Today*, a woman who would later become Howe's wife. So saying, James situated Howe within a specific culture as well as pointing to some fundamental aspects of his personality. James famously argued that West Indians 'have been the most rebellious people in history' (James 1980: 177). This rebelliousness was rooted in a deeply felt love of freedom, a love that sprang from enslavement and the experience of regimented labour on the sugar plantations of the Caribbean.

> But when we made the Middle Passage and came to the Caribbean we went straight into a modern industry – the sugar plantation – and there we saw that to be a slave was the result of being black. A white man was not a slave. The West Indian slave was not accustomed to that kind of slavery in Africa; and there in the history of the West Indies there is one dominant fact and that is the desire, sometimes expressed, sometimes unexpressed, but always there, the desire for liberty; the ridding oneself of the particular burden which is the special inherence of black skin. *If you don't know that about West Indian people you know nothing about them.*
>
> (Ibid.)

Significantly, West Indian slaves experienced conditions akin to those of the modern proletariat. On Caribbean plantations, slaves worked within stratified systems of collective toil, using industrial technology at the cutting edge of the age, disciplined by the clock, producing a single product. The result was riches and industrial development for the West, and for the West Indies, a population characterized by the will to rebel. Howe puts it like this: 'we fought from day one and that fight culminated in Toussaint L'Ouverture in Haiti and Paul Bogle in Jamaica'. In this sense, James was right: Darcus Howe is a West Indian.

Howe would later modify James' aphorism. Today, when he tells the story, he adds a coda: 'Darcus Howe is a West Indian *and he lives in Britain.*'

That, for Howe, is a fuller description, and a description of some political importance. For the past 50 years, he has made Britain his home, fighting all the while for immigrants to enjoy the full rights of citizenship without having to renounce their history or identity: to integrate on their own terms. For Howe, it is a struggle in the best traditions of English radicalism and part of the ongoing struggle of the British working class. Writing in 1998, Howe described his mission thus:

> ...although I spent part of my life in a struggle against England it was, I now know, also a personal and political struggle for England. My life has been largely spent in trying to help force an often reluctant and purblind England to be true to the benign "Motherland" of my parent's vision.
>
> (UC DHP 9/2)

Thirty years earlier, while editing the *Black Eagle*, the newsletter of a small London-based Black Power group, he set out his mission in a similar way. With playful irony he wrote in terms of a civilizing mission; the British had travelled the globe to civilize Africa, India and the Caribbean, now it was time to return the favour (GPI JOU 35/4). Howe and the Black Power Movement would civilize Britain by challenging the state-licensed barbarism of the Metropolitan Police (Met), by teaching Britain to become a harmonious multiracial society, by bringing 'reason to race' (Howe 2011b).

*

There is nothing cryptic about our title. *Darcus Howe: A Political Biography* is just that. The outlines of Howe's story are simple enough: born in Trinidad, he immigrated to Britain where he became the country's best-known campaigner for black[1] rights. Initially, he campaigned on the streets, latterly in the mainstream press, on radio and on television.

The biography is political in two senses. First, it is political in that it concerns Howe's work in the public sphere. Our focus then is on Howe the campaigner, the intellectual, the writer and broadcaster, rather than on Howe's private life. Thus, the biography is neither an intimate portrait nor a psychological one. This may seem to be a denial of the celebrated truth that the personal is also the political. It is not. It is merely a recognition that there is a limit to what can be achieved in a single book. It is political in a second sense too. The book is an intervention, at least obliquely, in a series of debates concerning the extent to which the West has entered a post-racial age, the extent to which racism is and has been an issue in British society and the best ways of advancing racial justice.

Turning to methodological issues, our approach is primarily historical. By this we mean that when dealing with historical actors, we aim 'simply to use the ordinary techniques of historical enquiry to grasp their concepts, to follow their distinctions, to recover their beliefs and, so far as possible, to see things their way' (Skinner 2002: vii). In short, we attempt to understand Howe in his own terms.

*

A number of themes unite this book. The first relates to Howe's consistent focus on the progressive potential of the black underclass. This intuition was clear from an early age. Living in Belmont, Port-of-Spain, in a house looking out on the home of the Casablanca steel band, Howe was part of a community that included the working class and street hustlers. One of his first battles was against his parent's desire to move into a more middle-class area. After winning a scholarship to Queen's Royal College, Howe continued to associate with 'barflies and hustlers', shifting his allegiance from Casablanca to Renegades, the street gang which coalesced around it (Howe 2011c). He admits suffering 'demons of doubt' about the potential of the black underclass of itinerants and unemployed, particularly after a run-in with hustler-turned-faux-radical Michael X. Howe credits James with keeping 'his eye on the ball', by repeatedly demonstrating that the black working class and the black underclass were a progressive historical force (BBC 2002). As a member of the Black Panther Movement, as editor of *Race Today* in the 1970s and 1980s and throughout the summer riots of 2011, Howe continued to believe that radical politics should grow from the ranks of the black working class, black youth and the black unemployed. Howe's faith in the black underclass is based on his view that radicalism is the natural response of immigrants, particularly second-generation immigrants, who refuse to tolerate brutal policing, poor housing, third-rate jobs and social discrimination reserved for them. In this sense, he argues, the economic and social position of the black underclass meant that they had the potential to play an explosive and insurrectionary role in British politics, and to ignite and play a leading role in a wider rebellion of white youth and urban poor.

Secondly, Howe has continually stressed black 'self-organisation' and 'self-activity'. The insistence that black people must shape their own destinies was Howe's rallying cry at the beginning of the Mangrove march and the foundation on which the Race Today Collective was built. His emphasis has changed over the years. In the 1960s and 1970s, Howe was critical of well-intentioned whites who wanted to lead the struggle for black rights. He also rejected the position of anti-racist campaigners who sought to characterize black people as helpless victims, incapable of formulating their own demands. More recently, Howe has questioned attempts to institutionalize the fight for black rights through government agencies. Howe's stance in recent years is evidence of the broader truth that he has eschewed incorporation into the establishment. Rather, Howe continues to identify with the grass roots, striving to articulate the grievances, experiences, goals and concerns of those who have experienced racism most acutely. It is for this reason that Howe often represents a lone voice, and why, at the age of 70, he is still a controversial figure.

Thirdly, Howe has consistently attempted to unite radicalism with reason. Howe describes himself as an instinctive egalitarian. Howe saw the idiocy of racism at school; fielding the best cricket team necessitated Africans and Indians working together on equal terms. Howe rejected colonialism as a young man too, supporting Eric Williams' slogan 'Massa Day Done' (Channel 4 2006). On arrival in Britain, Howe quickly saw that the slogan applied as much to racism in Britain as it did to colonialism in the Caribbean. School, first with his father and later at Queens Royal College (QRC), drew Howe into the 'world of reason'. He recalls the atmosphere of QRC as 'Christian morality, through the lenses of Descartes'; the school's unofficial motto 'I think therefore I am' (Howe 2011a). Howe experienced various kinds of radicalism in Europe. In Britain, in the late 1960s, Howe witnessed the first wave of black militancy. As far as Howe could see, under the leadership of Obi B. Egbuna, Michael X and Roy Sawh, black radicalism was merely a superficial mix of mindless nationalist rhetoric and macho swagger. Howe travelled to Paris in mid-1968 and participated in the revolution. Here, radicalism comprised the esoteric philosophical discussions of students, wholly divorced from the workers' movement. Neither flavour of radicalism appealed. In James, however, Howe found radicalism and reason in their proper proportion. Unlike Britain's black nationalists, James located the black struggle in a universal movement for human emancipation and unlike the French students, James rejected grandiose philosophical abstraction, preferring to face reality (Howe 2011c).

Howe's desire to embrace reason was part of his rejection of black nationalism. Inspired by discussions with James, and E. P. Thompson's *The Making of the English Working Class*, Howe adopted a very English way of conducting politics. Howe's strategy from the Mangrove trial onwards was to appeal to the values of the English dissenting tradition to ground arguments for black rights within a tradition of radicalism that Howe had imbibed at QRC, and which represented the most progressive face of English culture. In this sense, Howe describes himself as 'a natural black heir to the English radical dissenting tradition of Milton, Mill and Tom Paine' (UC DHP 9/2), not so much a black Jacobin as a black Leveller. To some extent, the Englishness of Howe's approach explains his success in the mainstream British media. Indeed, Howe's appeal to an English tradition, in part, explains why programmes like *Devil's Advocate* and the *Bandung Files* entered the mainstream, quickly shaking off the label of 'ethnic programming' and why Howe found success as a columnist for the *Evening Standard*. Crucially, the freshness of Howe's political idiom, which eschewed the moribund rhetoric of the white left while synthesizing English and Caribbean radicalism, is part of the reason that his programmes and his print journalism attracted a loyal white following.

Howe's willingness to collaborate with the mainstream media predates his first appearances on Channel 4. Part of the strategy of *Race Today*, under his editorship, was to produce material that could be easily picked up by the mainstream. In this sense, Howe has played a significant role in recent years by bringing radical ideas into the mainstream. Trevor Phillips, former television executive and current chair of the Equality and Human Rights Commission, argues that Howe has used the media to popularize James' ideas, playing the role of John the Baptist to James' Christ (Phillips 2012). Television producer and Howe's long-term collaborator Narinder Minhas makes a similar point, claiming that Howe was the man who 'brought intelligent discussions about race to primetime' (Minhas 2012).

Howe is also significant as he has continually advocated black and white collaboration, with the proviso that when dealing with racism black people play the leading role. This political principle is rooted in personal experience. He spent his childhood rubbing shoulders with the grandchildren of Indian indentured labourers in rural Trinidad. His school days were enriched by white teachers at QRC, who Howe describes as 'the most enlightened bourgeois' of their generation, whose experiences of war prompted them to leave Europe for the classrooms of the Caribbean (Howe 2011c). In London too, Howe was at home in the late-1960s' scene in clubs like the Flamingo and the Roaring Twenties, where Reggae, Ska and American R&B attracted whitebeats, Mods and the first skinheads as well as black clubbers from Brixton and Notting Hill. Throughout his life, Howe has counted people of all races and classes as his friends, comrades and collaborators. Howe's approach was crucial to securing white involvement in the Black People's Day of Action, against the demands of nationalists who wished to keep the event exclusively black. It is paradoxical, then, that Howe, who has never been a nationalist, has been dubbed 'race chief' and 'race agitator' or 'Britain's first professional black man' as Howe has never embraced separatism or narrow identity politics.

In common with James, Howe saw an important connection between the struggles of the white working class and the fight for racial justice. In his first *Race Today* editorials, Howe set out his view that the treatment of black people in Britain brought the horrors of colonialism and the worst excesses of capitalism to the metropolis. Struggles against racism exposed these injustices and, consequently, had the potential to reawaken the spirit of discontent in the white working class. In this sense, while accepting that the black minority was too small to carry a revolution in Britain to its conclusion, Howe believed that it could play a crucial role in radicalizing the white working class. Howe's faith in the British working class was obvious as early as the Mangrove trial. Accused of inciting riot, faced with the combined forces of Special Branch, the Met, the Home Office and the British justice system, Howe advocated selecting white working-class jurors and making a direct appeal to their experience of police harassment. Significantly, whereas white liberals have tended to see the white working class as a reservoir of unenlightened racism, Howe sees the white working class in a more positive light: as a fluid group who have tended to absorb immigrants from around the world. The inclusive nature of Howe's politics runs through his reports in *The Vanguard*, the newspaper of the Oilfield Workers Trade Union of Trinidad and Tobago, which vividly describe the unity between African and Asian workers engendered by Trinidad's 1970 Black Power Revolution; his editorship of *Race Today*, which focused considerable attention on the position of women; to *Who you calling a nigger?* – Howe's 2004 documentary concerning inter-minority violence.

Howe's campaigning style has synthesized insights from the Caribbean, the United States and the United Kingdom. James' influence has already been noted. *Black Jacobins, Beyond a Boundary, Modern Politics, Facing Reality* and *American Civilisation* are among the works that Howe cites most frequently. This is only part of Howe's radical erudition. With James, he read Franz Fanon, W. E. B. Du Bois, Stokely Carmichael, Walter Rodney, Karl Marx and E. P. Thompson. This list has some notable omissions. Dickens was Howe's first literary love; indeed, at an early age he identified with Philip Pirrip, the protagonist of *Great Expectations*. In *Modern Politics* and *Facing Reality*, Howe saw what he had already intuited from the lives of Caribbean people: that political leaders should play an extremely limited role in organizing and formulating the demands of working people. Specifically, Howe rejected the notion of the vanguard party, the political elite who thought, acted and made the revolution on behalf of the masses.

Rather, Howe embraced James' notion of the 'small organisation' that grounded itself in the lives of ordinary people, educating and learning from the working class, recording their struggle and encouraging them to formulate their own demands (James et al. 1974: 118–19). In the Student Nonviolent Coordinating Committee (SNCC), Howe saw a group that approximated the Jamesian organization. Howe's involvement with SNCC came by a circuitous route. Inspired by James, Howe travelled to Montreal to take part in the 1968 Congress of Black Writers. Black Power had emerged as an ideology and a movement in America in 1966; 2 years later, the Montreal conference served as a Black Power International. The Congress allowed Howe to renew acquaintance with Carmichael, his childhood friend, as well as introducing Howe to Rodney, the movement's rising star. Inspired by the Congress, Howe travelled to New York, where he worked with SNCC during the Ocean Hill-Brownsville education campaign. He played a small role, staying below the radar in order to evade the immigration authorities. Even so, he learnt from the best. The SNCC organizers distinguished themselves by facilitating self-organization, working at a grass-roots level and encouraging black high school students to take centre stage. During his stay in New York, Howe spent time with H. Rap Brown and participated in one of Black Power's defining campaigns which took the struggle for racial justice to the northern states, pitting black radicals against white liberals. Howe first attempted to build a small organization in the run-up to Trinidad's Black Power Revolution. Later in the same year, he applied the lessons that he had learnt in New York and Port-of-Spain to the battle against police racism in Notting Hill. The Mangrove March of August 1970, which took mass protest to the symbolic centres of racism, was in essence a rerun of the strategy used by radicals at the beginning of the February Revolution in Trinidad. Equally, a decade later, Howe used campaigning techniques learnt from SNCC to organize the Black People's Day of Action.

Howe's career has also been distinctive due to his consistent focus on pop culture as a progressive force. The *Black Eagle*, one of the first British Black Power news-sheets, contains images of Malcolm X and Otis Reading united in articulating the same message. The image captured Howe's intuition that political struggle and new forms of popular expression went hand in hand. This was an argument that Howe articulated in Horace Ové's *Reggae* (1971) and later in the 1986 BBC *Arena* series *Caribbean Nights*. Again, Howe found support for his intuitions in James' work, specifically *American Civilisation*, which argued that pop culture often expressed the most progressive aspects of public opinion. Indeed, popular culture and the arts played an important role in *Race Today* and in Howe's later television work.

Finally, Howe has continually shown political courage. This was evident in his decision to defend himself for 55 days at the Old Bailey during the trial of the Mangrove Nine; in his decision to break with the Institute of Race Relations and take *Race Today* on a new course; in his wiliness to confront Chief Buthelezi on *Devil's Advocate* and to tackle taboo topics in documentaries about black parenthood and inter-community violence. He has had the courage to remain outside the political establishment. Indeed, against a consensus that labelled the summer riots as 'criminality pure and simple' (Cameron 2011). Howe was prepared to point the finger at the long-standing issue of stop and search.

*

Howe has been part of Britain's political landscape since the early 1970s. While he has proved hard to ignore, he has often been hastily dismissed. Strategies for dismissing Howe and his arguments have changed. In the late 1960s and early 1970s while Howe was railing against racism in the Met, the authorities adopted a strategy of denial and political slur. Simply put, they argued that there was no racism in the Met and that black radicalism was a front for criminality or even terrorism. By the early 1980s, things had moved on. In discussion with Howe, Michael Mates acknowledged that there was racism in the police and he acknowledged that it was deplorable, but argued it was a reflection of society at large, a relatively small problem that would sort itself out in time. More recently, the narrative has changed again; yes, racism *was* a problem in the 1950s, 1960s and 1970s – in fact, it was a significant problem that blighted the lives of a generation – but racism is now a thing of the past. This was Edwina Currie's response to Howe's radical explanation of the riots of 2011. On this view, while Howe did good work back in the 1970s, his current concerns are a throwback to a bygone age, a sign that Howe is no longer relevant. Around the same time, there has been a resurgence of outright denial, linked to a romantic dumbed-down 'whiggish' view of history that suggests that racism was *always* someone else's problem. On this view it is true that there was terrible racism in Germany under the Nazis, in the American South, in the Belgium Congo, but the British were better than that. As a nation, so the story goes, we had too much common sense to be taken in by fascism, too much decency to introduce segregation, and our Empire, while imperfect, was more humane than those of other European powers. To some extent, this was the message of the 'official' 2007 commemorations of the bicentenary of the abolition of the slave trade. Many of the statements made by senior politicians during and since the bicentennial year reflected the 'abolitionist myth', in which '[t]he history of enslavement has been viewed backwards, through the history of its abolition, and that history in turn has been read not as a complex story involving slave resistance and economic causation . . . but as a story of heroic moral efforts of a mainly white, mainly male and mainly British abolitionist movement . . .' (Smith et al. 2011: 3). David Cameron's recent pronouncements on abolition represent the apotheosis of this view, placing Britain squarely on the side of the angels at every decisive historical moment:

> . . . we have the values – national values that swept slavery from the seas, that stood up to both fascism and communism and that helped to spread democracy and human rights around the planet – that will drive us to do good around the world.
>
> (Cameron 2010)

For Cameron, these national values are ancient:

> Human rights is a cause that runs deep in the British heart and long in British history. In the thirteenth century, Magna Carta set down specific rights for citizens, including the right to freedom from unlawful detention. In the seventeenth century, the Petition of Right gave new authority to Parliament; and the Bill of Rights set limits on the power of the monarchy. By the eighteenth century it was said that: "this spirit of liberty is so deeply implanted in our constitution, and rooted in our very soil, that a slave the moment he lands in England, falls under the protection of the laws, and with regard to all natural rights becomes instantly a free man." It was that same spirit that led to the abolition of slavery . . . that drove the battle against tyranny in two World Wars . . . and that inspired Winston Churchill to promise that the end of the "world struggle" would see the "enthronement of human rights".
>
> (Cameron 2012)

From this perspective, a British black rights movement is wholly redundant, and Howe's criticisms of the British police or of institutional racism are nonsensical; for the nature of the 'British heart', to borrow Cameron's phrase, excludes the possibility of systematic racial prejudice in Britain. Consequently, Howe can be dismissed because his claims run counter to the 'official view' that Britain is a place in which the values of freedom and justice are upheld by all, for all.

Sadly, Britain has not always been the utopia of civilized fair play that the 'abolitionist myth' suggests. Cameron's narrative hides more than it reveals, and it is over-optimistic to think that racism has been pushed now and forever to the fringes of British politics. British culture is Janus-faced, civilized and barbaric, progressive and reactionary. Dismissing Howe ignores crucial aspects of both sides of modern Britain. Therefore, this book contends that we ignore Howe at our peril.

Note

1 Any term with a history escapes definition (Geuss 1999: 13–14). The term 'black' is no exception. 'Black' has been used differently at different moments in the events we discuss. Therefore, rather than attempting to offer an ahistorical definition, we have consciously used the term variously. Our intention is to use the term historically, reflecting the different usages the term has had across the era that we are concerned with.

1

Son of a Preacher Man

We know nothing, nothing at all, of the results of what we do to children. My father had given me a bat and ball, I had learnt to play and at eighteen was a good cricketer. What a fiction! In reality my life up to ten had laid the powder for a war that lasted without respite for eight years, and intermittently for some time afterwards – a war between English Puritanism, English literature and cricket, and the realism of West Indian life. On one side was my father, my mother (no mean pair), my two aunts and my grandmother, my uncle and his wife, all the family friends (which included a number of headmasters from all over the island), some eight or nine Englishmen who taught at the Queen's Royal College, all graduates of Oxford or Cambridge, the Director of Education and the Board of Education, which directed the educational system of the whole island. On the other side was me, just ten years old when it began.

(James 1963: 39)

These words, particular as they are to their author Cyril Lionel Robert James, also carry profound significance for his nephew Darcus Howe. It is no overstatement to say that James' description of his childhood conveys the pattern of Howe's early life. For James, the balance of forces in this formative struggle were overwhelming and his triumph against them extraordinary:

> ... they had on their side parental, scholastic, governmental, and many other kinds of authority and, less tangible but perhaps more powerful, the prevailing sentiment that, in as much as the coloured people on the island, and in fact all over the world, had such limited opportunities, it was my duty, my moral and religious duty, to make the best use of the opportunities which all these good people and the Trinidad Government had provided for me. I had nothing to start with but my pile of clippings about W. G. Grace and Ranjitsinhji, my *Vanity Fair* and my Puritan instincts, though as yet these were undeveloped. I fought and won.

(Ibid.)

The course set out for Howe was almost identical: he was told early on in his childhood 'You will win an Exhibition to Queen's Royal College like CLR James, your uncle,[1] and then you will become somebody.' These were not just the hopes of parents ambitious for their son to use education as a means to ascend the ossified class structure of colonial Trinidad, but also the expectations of a mother and father who were, respectively, Howe's first teacher and headmaster at his primary school in Eckels village, Williamsville. The resources which the young Howe drew upon to resist and ultimately repel this adult onslaught were in some respects just as curious as his uncle's. Instead of James' infatuation with William Makepeace Thackeray's Amelia Sedley in *Vanity Fair*, the first character to become Howe's close friend was Dickens' Philip Pirrup. In the place of James' Puritan instincts, Howe was imbued by his father with the values of Christianity and a love of reason, an incendiary mix which Howe would ultimately employ to ruthlessly question the injustices and myths of race, class and religion itself. Whereas James' youthful rebellion was symbolized by his skipping his duties to illicitly play cricket, Howe rejected the social elitism of Queen's Royal College (QRC) and the middle-class aspirations of his parents by befriending and becoming a Renegade, the street gang of hustlers, street fighters and urban youth who coalesced around the steelband of the same name in East Dry River, Port-of-Spain.

Rhett Radford Leighton Howe was born in 1943 and raised for the first 10 years of his life in Eckels village, a small rural hamlet located 3 kilometres from Williamsville in southern Trinidad. The village folk consisted then, as now, of agricultural labourers, who were the descendants of the indentured Indian sugar cane workers, and a smaller number of black Trinidadians, most of whom worked in the nearby oil refinery at Point-à-Pierre or in the city of San Fernando to its south. Howe's father, Cipriani, had qualified as a teacher at a young age and had gone on to become head teacher of Eckles Village School: English Catholic (EC). It was his second headship, his first Moruga EC. Cipriani transferred to Eckles Village EC when Howe was 3 years old. The family lived in a cottage beside the village school. The house was surrounded by acres of cane plantations owned by Tate & Lyle, and local farmers, and had a clear view of the oil refinery. Howe's father liked to boast that the oil produced in the village kept British warships fighting during World War II. Cipriani's drive to succeed as a teacher owes much to Howe's paternal grandfather who had worked hard as a stevedore and barge driver in Port-of-Spain in order to give his son an education so that he might become a teacher and escape a life of drudgery. He named his son, Cipriani, after Captain Arthur Cipriani, founder of the Trinidad Labour Party,

us, was the victim of random violence on account of being 'brought up by hand' by his older sister, the young Howe seems to have received just one particularly violent beating from his father at the age of 8 when he first sat and failed to win an Exhibition scholarship to the country's top school, Queen's Royal College. The use of corporal punishment was not unusual in Trinidad in the 1950s; Howe's school friend from his Queen's Royal College (QRC) days, David Waddell, describes Trinidad as having 'a teaching culture based around the strap' and remembers the son of a teacher receiving some 'licks' on the hand for being lazy during the Exhibition class he attended at Tranquillity Boys (Waddell 2011).

The beating Howe received at 8 was, however, sustained. He remembers how at that age he could not even write for the 3 hours required to sit the exam. By the time his father had finished beating him with his blacksmith's belt, which he had perversely named 'Betsy', Howe was left with red welts all over his back and buttocks. When Howe's maternal grandmother saw the injuries on her grandson's body, she threatened to report her son-in-law to the police. This traumatic early experience was never forgotten. Howe had a complex relationship with his father. Certainly he loved and admired him on many levels, but he would not excuse this violence, or the injustice it represented visited as it was on someone who was vulnerable and defenceless. Paradoxically, the beating instilled a degree of physical courage that meant Howe never flinched when confronted by violence in later life. When Cipriani was on his deathbed, Howe told him 'so much of what I am is due to you'. His father responded with an apology. 'Is that so? I am sorry I beat you so much when you were a boy.' Howe responded in kind: 'Is that so?'. Looking back he says 'I wasn't going to tell him it was alright, even if that is what he wanted to hear, because it wasn't alright' (Howe 2011a).

Howe's earliest understanding of the world came from the Book of Common Prayer. In the hands of his father, whose services drew a large congregation to the Church of Ascension every Sunday, the message of the scriptures was one of egalitarianism and social justice. Howe recalls that 'in our church Christ was a revolutionary'. He was also the Son of God, the creator of Heaven and Earth. Strangely, Howe's father played a significant role in Howe's rejection of the metaphysical foundations of religion and his 'journey into the world of reason'. Cricket also played a role. One Christmas, Howe was given a bat and ball. He invited Reynold Allahar, an Indian boy from the village, to try them out, but rain stopped play. Howe asked his friend, 'Did you do something bad? Did you steal from your parents or forget to say your prayers, because God is punishing us for something?'. His father overheard the conversation through the bungalow's thin walls and addressed Howe's misunderstanding the next day in school. Drawing a map of South America and arrows from its South East to indicate the trade winds, he said, 'now wind' and blew outwards: 'this wind, blows across South America and hits the Andes. Air rises, condensation and saturation take place and eventually rain.' Howe's conversion to reason and science was completed a fortnight later in a class on English grammar. When a discussion occurred about poetic license and how it allowed exceptions to the usual rules of grammar, Howe asked if the scientific explanation of rainfall was an exception to divine rule. His father replied, 'no it is the rule'. The scientific explanation shattered Howe's faith.

This was a revelation which had both a devastating and liberating effect on Howe's way of looking at the world; it was as if when he pulled at one thread of his religious belief system, the whole thing began to unravel and 'reason became non-negotiable'. In a similar fashion, Howe began to chip away at all the old legends and superstitions which surrounded him in a village permeated with folklore disguised as truth. Here in its embryonic form were the first stirrings of what Linton Kwesi Johnson would, decades later, come to describe as the 'merciless realism' which characterized Howe's analysis of the world. In time, Howe would use the same uncompromising intellectual framework to directly challenge the more poisonous myths on which institutionalized hierarchies of race and class were based in Trinidad, the United States and Britain. Without having read Karl Marx, Howe had instinctively embraced his dictum to engage in 'the ruthless criticism of all that exists, ruthless in the sense of not being afraid at the results it arrives at and in the sense of being just as little afraid of conflict with the powers that be' (Marx 1844).

Howe's thirst for knowledge about the world beyond Eckels village was unquenchable. He would wait for the broadsheet newspaper to be delivered every day on the truck which brought the ice, and when his parents were finished, he would read it avidly. Howe always turned first to a column called 'In the Courts Today' in which a writer called McGee would gently mock the judiciary in his detailed accounts of the trials that went on for weeks in Port-of-Spain's Criminal Court.

He re-sat and won an Exhibition to QRC when he was 10 years old, becoming 1 of only 70 young men in Trinidad to win the prestigious scholarship. By the time the 11-year-old Howe took up his place as an Exhibitioner at QRC in 1954, his family had moved from Eckels village to the suburb of Belmont at the foot of the Laventille Hills in north-east Port-of-Spain. The move represented a new start for the family and a new house which Cipriani Howe had commissioned to be built on Gloucester Lodge Road.

Queen's Royal College

David Waddell remembers his first meeting with Howe vividly. They joined QRC on the same day and both joined the top class 1A, reserved for Exhibition winners. 'Darcus was from Eckels Village and I was from Port of Spain. If a kid from the countryside did come to a city like Port of Spain he would usually get made fun of a bit, what we call "give him a little fatigue". You know the fellow from the country is coming with reservations and is a bit nervous. But Darcus was never nervous. He took it in his stride' (Waddell 2011).

In French class, on their second day, the French master, one Mr Arundel, went around the class asking students their Christian name. When it came to his turn, Waddell replied 'David', whereupon Howe, who was sat at the back of the class, called out 'Splavid' to everyone's amusement. Waddell remembers that within an hour or two of the lesson, the suffix was removed and he was known as 'Splav', a nickname which stuck and by which he is still known by his friends, family, children and grandchildren half a century later.

Howe, Splav and another Royalian Roderick Lewis, who was known by the nickname 'Cheesy', soon established a reputation for being the class rebels. Former West Indies vice-captain and wicketkeeper Deryck Murray also started QRC on the same day as Howe. He had passed an entrance exam but had not won an Exhibition so he took his place in the academic hierarchy below Howe in class 1B. Murray went on to captain Howe in the QRC under-16 cricket team. He remembers Howe as a good friend and talented sportsman but also as someone whose intelligence led him to being rebellious at school. Howe was popular with his classmates because he often got into trouble with teachers, but 'when a particular teacher caught Darcus's imagination and treated him with respect, Darcus excelled' (Murray 2011). One such teacher was their history tutor Mr Rice, a white Cambridge-educated Englishman who was always immaculately attired in white shirt and khaki shorts. Waddell recalls that his friendship with Howe got off to an unlikely start when Rice addressed him in Latin one day as 'piger niger pure' or 'black lazy boy'. In another context, Rice would have become Howe's sworn enemy for such a remark, but the comment concealed the fact that Howe was his favourite student; if he wasn't present on any day, Rice wanted to know where he was and at the end of every lesson, Howe was at his side. Howe recalls striking up a similar bond with his Indian English-language teacher Ralph Laltoo, who, in their first lesson together, told Howe 'your problem is give a dog a bad name and hang him'. Howe took this as a declaration of peace and reciprocated by writing the finest piece of prose he had ever written entitled 'Sunlight in the Morning of Port of Spain', a composition which, Laltoo told the class, was not a school essay but was 'literature' (Howe 2011a).

For every teacher who recognized Howe's potential, there appeared to have been several more who regarded him as a troublemaker. The black schoolmaster Hugo Gunning was one such. Splav had nicknamed him 'pow pow' after the sound of a gun. On one occasion, Gunning overheard the sound of imitation gunfire in the corridor and confronted a group of boys; when no one would own up to having mocked him, Gunning concluded that Howe was the most likely culprit and sent him to the headmaster's study to be thrashed. TV Haynes, or the Sheriff, as he was known by the boys, asked Howe: 'aren't you fed up to keep coming here?'. Howe immediately replied with a Shakespearian flourish, 'Sir, Twas not I.' This clearly amused Haynes who said 'Oh go back to your class and tell them I beat you.' Howe's quick-fire responses were not always so successful. The mathematics teacher Mr Jones was another who singled out Howe, Splav and Cheesy and insisted that whenever he entered the room, they should stand behind their desks. Every time he came into the class and they remained sitting, he would tell them to write 50 lines of 'The way of the transgressor is exceedingly difficult.' If they protested, Jones would double the number of lines. In the end, Howe and his friends refused to do the lines on the grounds that it would leave them no time to do their homework and were promptly sent to the headmaster to be flogged.

Carl Smith joined QRC as Howe moved into its sixth form, and went on to become captain and goalkeeper of its football team before later forging a career associated with professional soccer in the United States. He remembers that Howe had a reputation for knowing all the 'badest fellas' in Port-of-Spain. This alone was enough for some teachers to want to end Howe's school career at the earliest opportunity. QRC is indistinguishable from an elite British public school, and its alumni were a roll call of the country's leading statesmen, lawyers, writers and sportsmen; former student VS Naipaul pays homage to QRC in *A House for Mr Biswas*. Smith believes the only reason why these teachers failed in their vendetta against Howe was because he was very bright and did so well in his exams that they could not deny him his rightful place in the sixth form (Smith 2011).

Outside of QRC Howe was comfortable mixing in the working-class neighbourhoods of Belmont and visiting the slums of Lavantelle to its north. Then, as now, the area was known to be one of the most violent in the country and the scene of many bloody fights between rival gangs, but it is also the spiritual birthplace of the steelpan, calypso and carnival. Whereas most students from elite secondary schools like QRC either shunned the steelbands or formed respectable alternatives with names like Dixieland and Silver Stars, made up of college boys, Howe embraced the authentic grass-roots culture of the panmen. Becoming first a youth member of Casablanca and then later Renegades, Howe easily made friends with the street gang of hustlers, itinerants, gamblers, saga boys and unemployed which coalesced around the Renegades steelband and often did battle with rival gangs of panmen from other neighbourhoods. Trinidadian author Earl Lovelace went on to vividly describe the violent hedonistic world of the pan movement in the late 1950s in his novel *The Dragon Can't Dance*, a time he denotes as 'the war days in which every street corner was a garrison' when young men whispered in awe 'Desperados, Rising Sun, Renegades, Red Army, Hell Yard and Tokyo':

> . . . bands that announced and advertised in their very names the fact and dreams of violence they cultivated all year round, in constant battles fought between themselves, with razors, knives, in hand to hand combat, in night clubs, gambling houses and on street corners . . .
>
> (Lovelace 1979: 69)

Howe became close to the leader of Renegades, a hustler called Stephen Nicholson, who was known by the moniker 'Gold Teeth', and who Waddell describes as 'one of the most prolific fighters in Port of Spain at the time'. Howe would socialize or 'lime' with Gold Teeth and other leading Renegades and would hear their war stories first hand, but whenever a full-scale fight with a rival gang was imminent, it was the policy of all the panmen to send their youth home. Always the rebel, Howe defied one important convention of the pan movement by continuing to visit Wadell, who lived in the neighbourhood of Woodbrock to the West of the Queen's Park Savanagh where QRC is located despite it being enemy territory. Waddell played in his local steelband, Invaders, which was a rival of the Renegades and against whom there had been pitched battles in the past. In time, leading Invaders came to accept and like the young Renegade from Belmont. When Gold Teeth heard Howe was fraternizing with Invaders, he told his young disciple, only half joking, 'change your mind or your address'. Gold Teeth came to tolerate Howe's friendship with Invaders and this, in turn, did a lot to ease tensions and bring old adversaries between the two gangs closer together.

It was around this time that Howe underwent his political awakening as he began attending the regular mass rallies for independence from the British rule held in front of Trinidad's courts and legislature in Woodford Square by the newly formed People's National Movement (PNM) and its leader Eric Williams. Howe began to distribute the PNM paper, *The Nation*, which C. L. R. James returned to Trinidad after 26 years abroad to edit at Williams' invitation. Williams' movement was unstoppable. Tens of thousands of working-class Trinidadians would gather to hear him denounce the injustice of British rule and declare his vision of a new Jerusalem at the mass gatherings which became known as The University of Woodford Square. Williams' former career as an academic and historian in Britain and America had built on the foundations laid by his former teacher and friend C. L. R. James. The 14-year-old Howe was moved by Williams' erudition, and, despite his youth, claims to have understood 90 per cent of what Williams said in his speeches and lectures; speeches which drew on aspects of world history, highlighted the legacy of slavery and the ongoing reality of British colonialism in Trinidad and sought inspiration from the principles of Athenian democracy in founding a new nation. Earl Lovelace describes the movement founded by Williams' as 'something like a religion'; upon visiting a Woodford Square meeting, the character Fisheye, an infamous panman and street fighter from Lavantelle, knows at once 'this was it, something joining people to people and people to dreams and dreams to hope that man would battle for more than to proclaim the strength of his arms, would lift their arms to break down these shanty towns . . .' (Lovelace 1979: 79). By 1962, British colonialism had been routed and Williams had become prime minister of the independent nation of Trinidad and Tobago.

Howe's parents did not know of the double life their adolescent son led as college boy, Renegade and PNM activist. Nonetheless, his mother was horrified when she overheard a conversation between Darcus and his brother and sister, in which Darcus told them that he had heard Ivan, one of the panmen from Casablanca who practised in the neighbouring yard, beating his girlfriend. Howe reported Ivan warning his girlfriend, 'I can beat you all over and on your conscience too.' Howe's mother promptly made this an agenda item at the family's Sunday conference, demanding that they move away from Belmont to a more well-to-do suburb called Glencoe so that her children would no longer be exposed to such brutalities. Howe's father had always encouraged his children to speak their minds at these meetings. Sensing a degree of class prejudice in his mother, the 14-year-old Howe said 'I agree that I heard it and I agree it is unpleasant. But what makes you think I will start hitting women. Why can't we change them? If you have confidence in us and brought us up properly, you should have the confidence not to run away. Our task should be to change people like that.' Moved by his reasoning, Howe's father acknowledged 'you have a point', and his brother and sister concurred. Conscious that she had been beaten, his mother pushed over the milk in a fit of temper.

Howe's comrade and collaborator in later life, John La Rose would say that Howe's distinctive contribution to politics was his ability to engage with movements of the urban poor and unemployed in an unsentimental way. Howe rejected Marxist dogma that regarded the lumpen proletariat as inherently reactionary. Rather, he adopted a more nuanced understanding of their potential; as one of his influences Fanon would later explain, the inhabitants of the shanty towns were capable of both forming the 'urban spearhead' of rebellion as they had in Algeria and being manipulated by forces of counter-revolution as had occurred in Angola and Congo (Fanon 1967: 109). Howe's ability to relate to the urban poor on their own terms came from his early experience as a Renegade; in Waddell's words, he grew up as someone who was equally at home with intellectuals of Trinidad's leading college as he was with 'the rank and file, the people of the street'.

On a personal level, Waddell remembers that his friend was never antagonistic and did not go looking for a fight. Nonetheless, if someone started a fight, Howe would stand his ground. Howe's first experience of racism shortly after joining QRC was such an occasion. The abuse came not from a white teacher, who Howe generally remembers with fondness, but from a lighter-skinned Mulatto boy named Fletcher, whose parents owned an upmarket department store. As they were waiting to buy popsicles outside QRC one afternoon, Fletcher called Howe 'Zork', a reference to the 'primitive' black character who appeared in the Mandrake comic strip. This type of racism towards darker-skinned black people was ubiquitous in the Caribbean; in a 1942 essay, Williams had written that the attitude of the majority of the 'colored' middle class to black workers was one of 'contempt', that these toxic views were the legacy of the role which 'free people of color had performed as a barrier between the slaves and slaveowners' (Williams 1942: 61). He noted that 'no one in the British West Indies talks so glibly of the "lazy" black as his colored brother' (Ibid.). Howe recalls giving Fletcher a good beating and later heard that the decision of his parents to send him to study in Canada was because Howe had told him that he would live to regret his ignorance.

Howe experienced a more insidious form of racism from Trinidad's cricket selectors. Howe's ability at the game was undeniable. As his captain in QRC's under-16 side, Deryck Murray remembers he was an integral part of the team for 2–3 years. He was a medium pace swing bowler, who, in Murray's words, had 'very good control.' Murray says Howe's greatest triumph as a swing bowler was to once take 7 wickets for 26 runs against their toughest opponents, 'Progressive,' from St Mary's College. Howe and Waddell remember his bowling that day was even more spectacular and believe he took 7 wickets for 14 runs (Murray 2011). In any case, it is the sort of performance which should have marked Howe out to the selectors to follow Murray into playing for West Indies. Murray believes that despite Howe's talent, sport was ultimately not his 'bent' and that having succeeded in it he began to lose interest. Howe's view, that his dark skin played a part in his failure to attract the attention of West Indies' scouts and selectors, rings true, given that the game was scarred with discrimination against black players in favour of whites and lighter-skinned players at that time. As Murray acknowledges, until C. L. R. James' campaign in the pages of the *Nation* succeeded in having Frank Worrell selected as the first black captain of the West Indies in 1960, there was 'an unwritten rule that you had to be White and the son of plantation owners to Captain the West Indies', with Worrell himself 'having been captained by a couple of white players who should not have been in the Team far less its captain'. Talented dark-skinned players were routinely overlooked by the West Indies selectors. Learie Constantine, for instance, had ultimately pursued a cricket career in Britain when, as James' later wrote, 'had his skin been white, like George Challenor's, or even light, he would have been able to choose a life at home' (James 1963: 145).

Such disappointment contributed to Howe's sense of alienation. When he left QRC in 1961, he was at a crossroads in his life. He had served his apprenticeship with Renegades at the same time as learning Classics, French, Latin and English Literature from Oxford and Cambridge graduates at QRC. Disillusioned, he appears to have considered taking his place at the side of Gold Teeth as a fully fledged member of Renegades. It was at this time that he picked up a conviction for swearing in public, a record of which would appear on Howe's Special Branch file in London years later. Having turned 18, and worked for a short time in the civil service, Howe decided along with 10 others from QRC, including his close friends Paul Acala and Tony Campbell, to come to England.

Many rivers to cross[2]

From an early age, Howe had believed it inevitable that he would, someday, leave for the motherland. England was simultaneously far away and home. The atmosphere of the Mother Country was imbibed in Trinidad in a multitude of ways, through the Court Circulars that were scrutinized in minute detail, through the radio, through the signs and symbols of Empire, and, for Howe, from the pages of *Great Expectations*. The journey took 2 weeks. On 11 April, Howe's ship docked at Southampton, his mohair suit too flimsy to protect him from the bracing British weather, and he took the train to Waterloo. The England that Howe discovered in 1961 was certainly Dickensian, but Dickensian in a sense that he had not expected. On arrival he found white men doing menial jobs. Evidently, the world of Orlick and the Gargerys lived on in spite of the riches in Britain amassed by the years of Empire.

Howe recalls being told two things by the reception party of fellow Trinidadians who met the group of QRC old boys when they arrived at Waterloo station. First, not to venture out alone at night. It was less than 2 years since Antiguan carpenter Kelso Cochrane had been stabbed to death by a racist gang in Notting Hill as he travelled home alone late one night after an outpatients' appointment at Paddington General Hospital. The murder, coming as it did only a few months after race riots in Notting Hill, had terrorized London's growing immigrant community as had the police failure to protect those under attack during the riots or find and arrest the murderer of Kelso Cochrane. Secondly, Howe was told that if he got a white girlfriend, he mustn't be seen walking alongside her, he should always walk a few feet behind her so that no one would know they were together. Upon hearing this advice, Howe said he was tempted to turn around and go straight back to Trinidad.

For a time, Howe studied law at London's Middle Temple. The path from QRC to Middle Temple was well trodden, and Howe describes the transition from one to the other as 'utterly seamless'. The duality of Howe's life in Trinidad was replicated in England. During the day, he studied law, working 'rather intelligently through the wiles of contract, tort and real property'; in the evenings, he spent his time at The Rio, a small but very chic café in Notting Hill, and the area's shebeens (*New Statesman*, 29 May 1998). At the weekends, when money permitted, he went clubbing at Roaring Twenties, on the lookout for girls and a good time. Howe stuck at the law for 2 years. Trinidadian barrister Desmond Allum took him under his wing. 'He was my protégé really,' Allum recalls: 'He was very, very bright. . . . He had also come from a background of the steel bands, the Renegades and so, and fancied himself as a bit of a bad John' (Channel 4 2006).

Allum, who died in 2010, recalled Howe falling foul of London's Teddy boys. Visiting the Swiss Cottage Odeon, Howe refused to stand when the National

Anthem played at the end of the picture. After the film, a group of Teddy boys who had also been in the cinema followed him as he left, ran him down at the top of Finchley Road and subjected him to a beating. Howe explains his antipathy for the National Anthem thus: "'Born to reign over us" is easily translated with "born to piss all over us". Nobody was born to reign over me.' That much was instinctive to Howe as well as being the culmination of the education he had received as a young PNM activist and graduate of University of Woodford Square, as Eric Williams' mass public lectures and rallies in favour of independence from Britain were known.

There was no disguising the racial motives of the attack. Other instances of racial abuse followed. He was unable to walk arm in arm with his Italian girl-friend, Amanda Bacigalupo, but rather, following advice, had to walk several paces behind so that no one would know they were a couple. Britain was a place where Howe was not even free to love whom he wished. Dismayed at being forced to conceal it, she ended the relationship. Teddy boys were not the only threat. During his time at Middle Temple, Allum and his friend George Hislop were stopped by police, and Allum was falsely accused of stealing a vehicle. The offic-ers planted car keys on him and he was promptly arrested. Allum knew imme-diately what was happening and later went on to win compensation from the police for wrongful arrest with Howe as his witness. This was Howe's first brush with the British police and his first attempt to stand up to police oppression.

After 2 years studying law, Howe dropped out. He was bored and wanted to start a career. With his qualifications, he felt sure it would be easy enough to enter the civil service. Howe sought work in the South London suburb of Catford. During an interview, he produced his certificates and was promptly thrown out for forging documents – clearly no black man could be so well qualified. As a result, Howe lowered his sights, accepting a position as a postman on a weekly wage of £7.15s.6d.

The 19-year-old Howe felt dislocated and isolated. Britain was a hostile place for young black people. The words of Jimmy Cliff's hauntingly beautiful 1969 song 'Many Rivers to Cross' resonate for Howe when he looks back on this period of his life (Howe 2011a). Cliff evokes the sense of rejection, longing and loneliness experienced by Howe's generation of West Indian immigrants as they arrived in post-war Britain to find themselves fast-tracked into low-paid and often unskilled jobs and experience racism on a daily basis. The sense of being 'licked, washed up for years' and 'wandering, I am lost as I travel along the white cliffs of Dover' immediately spoke to Howe's experiences.

The middle of the decade marked something of a political awakening. The Committee of African Organisation hosted visits from Martin Luther King in 1964 and Malcolm X a year later. Howe attended King's St Paul's speech. He remembers being impressed with King's delivery, and being prompted to rethink the position of black people in the West:

> Martin Luther King's attack on the "demolition of self worth" that was at the heart of racism, was the first time I had heard a black person make a challenge about our position. [As a result] I started, like many blacks, to taste the possibility of remodelling our lives.

> (UC DHP Box 9/2)

Malcolm X was a different proposition. Howe shook his hand while Malcolm was touring Notting Hill. For Howe, Malcolm 'embodied the "bad boy" part of me. He was a hustler, he legitimised that part of me which "respectable" Trinidadian and English society feared and despised. The political and the personal fused again when he declared his ruling credo "by any means necessary". That slogan encapsulated everything I felt about escaping "ordinariness". Years later, he recalled, 'I have never seen such a remarkable personality in my life. I've met prime ministers, I've met presidents, I've spoken to Nelson Mandela. He was clear in his bearing and his certainty of language . . . one of the finest political leaders of all time' (Bunce and Gallagher 2006: 73). These two visits made Howe feel that he was part of a global movement. The global nature of Howe's vision was reflected in his first real foray into activism, the campaign against US involvement in Vietnam. Once again, Howe was living a double life, part postman, and later clerical officer dealing with National Insurance, part countercultural agitator. He joined the sporadic anti-war protests that took place in London and in the evenings became something of a fixture at the Troubadour bar, Earls Court, playing the part of raconteur and radical, entertaining and challenging the regulars with sharp wit and uncompromising radicalism.

Notes

1 Howe often referred to James as his 'Uncle'. This was not literally the case. Howe explained the relationship in an interview shortly after James' death. 'I am related to him on his mother's side. She was my Aunt Bessie. CLR was my cousin. Let me tell you a story. We spoke on the same platform at the plenary session of the Black Writers Conference in Montreal in 1968. He referred to me then as his nephew.

At the end of the session, I corrected him. "I am your mother's nephew CLR, I am your cousin." Back came the reply, "what is good enough for my mother is good enough for me." That is the way we lived. I called him Nello generally, but always greeted him as Lionel Robert' (UC DHP Box 1/11).

2 'Many Rivers to Cross' was a song written by Jimmy Cliff. It appeared on his 1969 album *Jimmy Cliff*.

'Dabbling with Revolution':
Black Power Comes to Britain

The Dialectics of Liberation conference of July 1967 brought the 1960s' counterculture to the heart of London. The 2-week conference, convened by R. D. Laing and leading figures in the anti-psychiatry movement, featured contributions from Beat Generation writers William Burroughs and Allen Ginsberg; Emmett Grogan, founder of the San Francisco anarchist movement The Diggers; and the Frankfurt School neo-Marxist, Herbert Marcuse (Cooper 1968: 9). The conference practised the countercultural values that it preached, spontaneously transforming the Roundhouse and Camden's pubs and bars into informal collegiums, the founding event of the anti-university of London (Ibid., 11). Black Power, a movement that had emerged at the cutting edge of the American Civil Rights struggle the year before, had several representatives at the conference. The headline black radical and the most controversial speaker by far was Howe's fellow Trinidadian and childhood friend, Stokely Carmichael, now the harbinger of the Black Power revolution. The British press responded to his visit by branding him 'an evil campaigner of hate' and 'the most effective preacher of racial hatred at large today' (Humphry and Tindall 1977: 63). The British government, conscious of the uprisings in Detroit, Newark and New Jersey, was concerned that his visit might spark similar unrest in the United Kingdom. As a result, Carmichael received a visit from agents of Special Branch who 'advised' him to leave the country. Carmichael clearly took the warning seriously and left earlier than planned, breaking an engagement to speak at a meeting of Michael X's Racial Adjustment Action Society (RAAS). Three days later, he was banned from returning by the Home Secretary Roy Jenkins and shortly after he was denied entry to 30 other territories of the former British Empire, including his country of birth (Ture and Thelwell 2003: 524).

Carmichael's visit did not have the destabilizing effect the government had feared; it did, however, have a radicalizing effect on the British black

movement. Within a week of Carmichael's Roundhouse speech, the United
Coloured People's Association (UCPA) had expelled its white members and
adopted the ideology of Black Power; within a month, Michael X, who quickly
became the media face of Black Power in Britain, was arrested for inciting racial
hatred; and within a year, the British Black Panther Movement was founded. In
essence, Carmichael's visit led to the formation of an indigenous Black Power
movement. For Howe too, the period 1967–68 was of great importance (Bunce
and Field 2010).

Black Power in Britain and the dialectics of liberation

Prior to the Roundhouse conference, there were certainly individuals who
were influenced by Black Power, but there was nothing that could be described
as a British movement. Obi B. Egbuna, founder of the British Black Panthers
and a man who would play an important role in the first wave of the British
movement, goes as far as to say that Black Power arrived in Britain following
Stokely Carmichael's 'historic visit in the summer of 1967' (Egbuna 1971: 16).

Howe attended the Roundhouse conference, keen to see Carmichael speak.
The two men had grown up together in the same part of Trinidad. The young
Carmichael had made quite an impression on Howe. He was older by 2 years
and a stylish dresser. Carmichael's cache among his peers was underlined, Howe
recalls, by the fact that he was the first person in the area to own a pair of roller
skates. The two lost touch just before Carmichael's 11th birthday, as Carmichael
moved to America to join his parents in New York, but became reacquainted at
the Congress, staying in touch until Carmichael's death in 1998.

Carmichael's address created a storm, and like many others, Howe was deeply
impressed. Howe noted that, as a performer, 'he was so brilliant, the change of
tone of voice, commanding the audience' (Howe 2011b). But more than that,
for Howe, the crucial aspect of Carmichael's address was its clarity of thought.
Howe had little time for the thoughtlessness of much of the black nationalism
that was emanating from America at the time. Carmichael, by contrast, was
a serious intellectual, a fact that was all the more remarkable, Howe argues,
given the anti-intellectualism prevalent in black radical circles. His intellectual
credentials were impressive. A Howard University philosophy graduate,
Carmichael had declined the offer of a full postgraduate scholarship at Harvard
to work as a civil rights organizer, before being elected chairman of the Student

Nonviolent Coordinating Committee (SNCC) in 1965. Howe was also struck by Carmichael's ability to communicate directly with the black working class. His oratory mixed references to Camus and Sartre, quotations from J. S. Mill and allusions to Rousseau with street slang (Bunce and Field 2010). Howe found this combination of high culture and the vernacular very attractive. In a way it reflected two aspects of his background. Howe was, after all, as comfortable with the intellectuals at Queen's Royal College (QRC) as he was with the Renegades at East Dry River. It was a verbal style that Howe himself could pull off, and which would come to characterize his own political idiom (Howe 2011b).

Carmichael's message made a lot of sense to Howe, for it reflected a commonality of worldview. Howe explains Carmichael's position in terms of his Caribbean background. Nationalism goes deep in America, and therefore, Howe argues, it was no surprise that a kind of nationalism established itself in the American black movement. Carmichael as a West Indian had never imbibed American nationalism and, therefore, was able to envisage a different kind of radicalism.

In many ways, Carmichael was an inspiration. Yet, Howe did not feel that the time was right to pursue radical politics wholeheartedly. James, one of the first to address the future of Black Power in Britain, put his finger on the issue: Black Power's first great challenge was the police, the front line of the state. Howe saw this clearly. He understood that becoming an activist necessarily entailed persecution by the police. Howe had only recently become a father and therefore had no intention of courting a custodial sentence. He also had other reservations. The Black Power Movement, as it developed in Britain during the latter half of 1967 and early 1968, was yet to become a serious political force. It was a movement of dabblers dominated by nationalist rhetoric.

The first wave of Black Power in Britain was dominated by three rather idiosyncratic figures. All three had flanked Carmichael during his appearance at the Roundhouse. The men in question were Michael X, Obi Egbuna and Roy Sawh. While Howe was never allied with any of these figures, they form the context for the first phase of the development of Black Power. From 1965 to 1967, Michael X was the face of black radicalism in Britain. Christened Michael de Freitas, and later known as Michael Abdul Malik, Michael X described himself as the 'most famous black man' in the Britain. He had risen to prominence following Malcolm X's visit to Britain in 1965. Michael X made his biggest impact on the white counterculture and was regularly interviewed by magazines such as *Oz* and *IT*, where he set out his views on race, poetry, violence and the other burning issues of the day. These utterances never amounted to a coherent political position, and in reality, his organization RAAS failed to make an impact as a grass-roots organization (Wild 2008: 85). Michael X's stature as a black radical was severely damaged by a series of revelations in the tabloid press, which included his association with the notorious landlord Peter Rachman, who was known for renting slum accommodation to black tenants at extortionate rates (Humphry and Tindall 1975: 48). By the late 1960s, most black radicals had rejected him as a serious figure. Nonetheless, his arrest and conviction for inciting racial hatred at the end of 1967 briefly revived his reputation, turning him into a martyr – the first person to be jailed under the Race Relations Act 1965 (Bunce and Field 2010). During the early 1970s, Michael X posed, mendaciously, as the head of various Black Power organizations, but made no real contribution to Black Power as a political movement.

If Michael X was the British movement's would-be-Malcolm, Egbuna was its self-styled Eldridge Cleaver. As Rosie Wild has suggested, Egbuna's book *Destroy This Temple* (1971) is highly derivative of Cleaver's *Soul on Ice* (Wild 2008: 142). A Nigerian-born playwright, author of *The Anthill* (1965) and *Wind Versus Polygamy* (1966), Egbuna had been involved in anti-colonial politics since the early 1960s. He was a member of the Committee of African Organisations (CAO), the group that had organized Malcolm X's visit to Britain in 1965. He had first experienced Black Power during an educational exchange trip to America in 1966, which brought him into contact with the SNCC. Impressed with what he saw, he returned to Britain, determined to establish a Black Power group in London. However, finding little appetite for the new politics in London, he bided his time. Carmichael's visit, which Egbuna described as 'manna from heaven', led to a wave of interest in Black Power, and as a result, Egbuna was elected chairman of the United Coloured People's Association (UCPA) and tasked with producing a new manifesto. *Black Power in Britain*, which set out the UCPA's programme and position, was published on 10 September 1967, only 6 weeks after Carmichael's visit. Egbuna later split with the UCPA, founding the British Panthers. In the summer of 1968, Egbuna was arrested for conspiring to incite the murder of police officers (Bunce and Field 2010). In fact, he wrote a short piece that encouraged black people to collectively resist the police at Speakers' Corner.[1] Egbuna's arrest reflected a new and deliberate strategy on the part of Special Branch and the police to target leading figures within the Black Power Movement. The authorities were not deterred by the fact that the evidence for the charges against Black Power activists was often weak as the primary goal was to disrupt and discredit the movement. This is evident from the surviving documentation. A memorandum from Detective Chief Inspector Kenneth Thompson commended the officers responsible for Egbuna's arrest for having 'put the [Black Panther] party in confusion' (Wild 2008: 184).

Roy Sawh co-founded RAAS with Michael X and was appointed Egbuna's deputy at the UCPA. Divisions between Egbuna and Sawh emerged almost immediately. As a result, the organization split and Sawh established the Universal Coloured People and Arab Association (UCPAA) in September 1967. His flamboyant style, bellicose rhetoric and wish to attract sensational media attention made long-term collaborations difficult. He founded a series of groups, many of which would eventually expel him (Wild 2008: 135).

While Howe was impressed by Carmichael, he had no time for the would-be leaders of the British movement. As a result, Howe did not involve himself in any of the emerging Black Power groups until the summer of 1968.

'L'ennui est contrerévolutionnaire' – Paris, 1968

Speaking at the Dialectics of Liberation conference in 1967, Frankfurt School Marxist Herbert Marcuse had comprehensively written off the working class as an agent of social change. For Marcuse, modern capitalism had made humanity anew. Humanity had been squashed, flattened, and the new 'one-dimensional man' was no longer capable of revolution. Less than a year later, the students and workers of Paris proved him wrong, and Howe was there to witness it.

Howe's path to Paris started in Notting Hill, which became a hot spot for revolutionaries and radicals from across Europe. European radicals, particularly from Germany and France, eager to learn about Black Power, descended on Notting Hill to spend time with black radicals, share ideas and learn from the new movement. This opened up the possibility of a warm welcome on the continent. Howe took the opportunity to travel to France. It was a period, Howe recalls, when all Europe was ablaze, and radicals talked openly about seizing power.

First and foremost, Howe went to France because of the revolutionary situation. The army had intervened, and the French president, Charles De Gaulle, had gone into hiding at the end of May. This was a real revolution, and Howe was unable to resist. Howe was also keen to travel to France as he had learnt about French colonialism through the writings of Franz Fanon and Aimé Césaire and was keen to see the French metropolis for himself. Finally, he wanted to meet the people who were making the revolution and steep himself in the atmosphere of freedom (Howe 2011b).

Howe recalls that while he was there, the students of the Sorbonne were hugely exercised by the question of power. Howe argued vigorously for the overthrow of the government against others who urged caution. But there was a counter-revolutionary edge to the student radicalism. Some of the students, under the influence of New Left and Situationists, had broken so completely with the old left that they had wholly rejected the progressive potential of the French working class (Caute 1988). As a result, they did not wish to collaborate with the 9 million workers engaged in a general strike in defiance of De Gaulle's government.

Howe found the vast majority of the students preoccupied with philosophy, endlessly quoting Camus. The few students who did venture into the factories, such as the Trotskyists, did so didactically, as revolutionary missionaries eager to teach but unwilling to learn. Even so, Howe was moved by what he saw. Nine months later, he wrote about his experience in the pages of *Black Dimension*, situating the events of May '68 within a wider historical context.

> It was the view of Lenin that world revolution had begun with the Russian Revolution of October 1917. A revolution means a total change in all the normal relations of society. We have been watching such changes over the last fifty years and one of them which has appeared in its full and complete manifestation only in the last few years, [is] the entry of students into revolutionary politics. They have already entered twice within the last year in a manner that signifies that a new force has entered into the revolutionary politics of the day. The students, concentrated in Paris, fought and defeated De Gaulle's special police, thereby initiating the most tremendous movement that Europe or any part of the world has known. Ten million workers on strike (whatever their demands) are a political manifestation of the first importance. And this tremendous revolt we owe directly and entirely to the fact that the students fought the police and made the workers aware that the regime was vulnerable.
>
> (GPI JOU 35/2, 5)

The Black Eagles

In August 1968, Howe became involved in the British Black Power Movement. A plethora of Black Power organizations formed in the late 1960s and early 1970s. Significantly, Howe joined none of them. As already noted, he did not feel an affinity with the cultural nationalism that pervaded the bigger groups at the time. Rather, Howe formed his own group, the Black Eagles. The group was short-lived, and Howe's leadership of the group was interrupted by his travels to Canada and America. Initially based in London's Notting Hill, they had a lifespan of around 5 months. Turning racial stereotypes on their head, Howe argued that the Eagles were in Britain on a civilizing mission. This mission took the form of campaigns against institutionalized savagery in the form of police brutality and a commitment to redefining black identity. In spite of the brevity of their existence, the Eagles are not entirely forgotten. Nobel laureate V. S. Naipaul's *The Writer and the World* describes them derisively as a 'Negro fantasy outfit'; America had Malcolm X and the Black Panthers; the British equivalents, Michael X and the Black Eagles were little more than a second-rate copy (Naipaul 2004: 165). But there is good reason to reject Naipaul's assertion, for while there is no denying that black radicals in Britain learnt a great deal from their American counterparts, Howe's version of Black Power went far beyond simple mimesis. Fleeting though they were, the Black Eagles played a significant part in the development of Black Power in Britain. Specifically, the Eagles were the first Black Power group to turn their back on Michael X. Moreover, they set out a legal strategy for dealing with prosecution that would later be employed in the Mangrove trial.

The Eagles were launched during a turbulent period in the history of Black Power in Britain. Egbuna had recently been arrested. Denied bail, he languished for 6 months in Brixton Prison. In response, a benefit evening was organized at the Roundhouse. *IT* carried the following advert for the evening:

> BENEFIT: Third World Benefit for three black playwrights. Obi Egbuna, Leroi Jones, Wole Seyinka. Programme includes plays by Jones & Ed Bullins, Sammy Davis Jr. & Michael X, among others.
>
> (*IT*, 1968: 38, 8)

The evening was covered by *Hustler*, a community newspaper, edited by Courtney Tulloch at Frank Crichlow's restaurant in Notting Hill. The benefit took place at Camden's Roundhouse on 25 August 1968, and according to *Hustler*, it attracted around 1,000 people. The line-up included Sammy Davis Jr, Willie Johnson – better known as Minister Rico of the Chicago Black P. Stones – Michael X, steel bands and readings from the works of the three playwrights. It was Howe's first major speech as a Black Power radical, as well as the launch of the Black Eagles.

The Eagles' first campaign was launched in mid-August. It involved setting up street patrols 'WITH THE AIM OF POLICING THE POLICE' in Notting

Hill (GPI JOU 35/5). According to the *International Times*, the patrols 'work in pairs in 12 hour shifts to observe how the police execute their duty' (*IT* 40, 1968: 19). Although they did not carry weapons, the patrols were inspired by and modelled on the armed patrols organized by the American Black Panther Party. The Black Panther Party's (BPP) aim was to advise those who were the victims of police harassment and persecution, while at the same time, in Eldridge Cleaver's words, creating 'a community structure', where 'the people had control of all local institutions, including law enforcement, instead of being the victims of all local institutions, most visibly the police' (Baldwin 2006: 81).

The campaign led to the arrest of Michael Lee and Robert 'Sammy' Hoyt on Portobello Road on 8 September 1968.[2] Subsequently, the Eagles called a press conference announcing the arrest, which was reported in *Hustler* on 18 September. The *Black Eagle* and *IT* reported that the police had beaten the two activists following their arrest. Lee and Hoyt appeared before Marylebone Magistrates' court on four occasions between 17 September and 14 October (LMA PS MAR/A2/25, PS MAR/A2/26, PS MAR/A3/23). They were found guilty and remanded in custody pending an appearance at the Old Bailey to determine their punishment.[3] According to Special Branch, who took a keen interest in the group's activities, the street patrols soon died out (NA HO 376/00154).

In addition to the patrols, the Eagles published a newsletter, three issues of which appeared from October 1968 through to January 1969.[4] Farrukh Dhondy recalls buying a copy from Howe in the late 1960s:

> I first met Darcus on a tube train when he tried to sell me a newspaper called the *Black Eagle*. It was not much of a paper, more of an agitational rag. My companions and I were on the way back from a demonstration against the Vietnam War . . . when he accosted us. We bought a paper. He tried to sell us another copy.
>
> (Dhondy 2001: xiii)

The magazine was also available through the radical publishing house New Beacon Books. Like many other radicals associated with Black Power, Howe adopted a new name reflecting his African heritage. Howe wrote under the name Darcus Owusu, a homage to Owusu Sadaukai, formally Howard Fuller, who had been closely associated with SNCC and Carmichael in the late 1960s (Woodard 1999: 173). For Howe, Owusu was an attractive figure as he represented a 'thoughtful' brand of black radicalism. Howe used the name from time to time until the early 1973. He claims that he dropped Owusu not for political reasons, but rather due to the protests of his mother (Howe 2011b).

The *Black Eagle* remains a very distinctive publication; it immediately stands out from *Black Power Speaks*, *Grassroots* or other radical magazines of the period due to the artwork, which was produced by Una Howe, Howe's first wife. The first issue, published in late October 1968, comprises a mere eight pages, containing two untitled essays, news about the arrests of Lee and Hoit and quotes from Maulana Karenga (GPI JOU 35/5). The second and third issues are much more substantial. The second issue, which came out in early December, is notable for its coverage of Michael X, including excerpts from his poetry and an account of his arrest on drug charges (IRR 01/04.04/01/04/01/03). Further evidence of his involvement can be found in the two contact addresses that appeared for the first time in the December issue. Both residences were outposts of the counterculture, frequented by friends of Michael X (GPI JOU 35/4). The first was the Ambiance, in Queensway, a small theatre founded by the American radical Ed Berman. Ambiance, which was a lunchtime theatre project, was designed to 'cut across the accepted dichotomy between work and play, by offering entertainment during the working day' (Turner 1997: 221–2). The Eagles could also be reached through the Arts Lab on Drury Lane. The Arts Lab was no less experimental than the Ambiance. It ran for 2 years from 1967 to 1969. The Arts Lab was the centre of many hippy happenings and was regularly featured in magazines such as *Oz*, *IT*, *SUCK* and *Rolling Stone*. The association of these two centres of the white counterculture is an indication of Michael X's influence rather than Howe's. Importantly, Howe was out of the country during its production, and although the reading list and the programme reflect Howe's input, much of the rest of the magazine reflects the work of others.

Howe spent some time with Michael X in late 1968, largely through economic necessity. He was unemployed and Michael X offered him a place to stay (Phillips and Phillips 1999: 241). Michael X set out his reasons for associating himself with the Eagles in an interview published in *Oz* magazine:

> . . . I ran across a group in London, a very small group which was called the Black Eagles and a very young fellow called Dakus Absou [Howe], who is very nice I was very pleased to meet him. He was in Trinidad where he got into trouble constantly, being arrested every so often, so he came to England to do something serious, like study law which he thought would be the right thing to do, in order to understand law somewhat. Studied and qualified as a barrister, then started lecturing at a couple of Universities. In York where I first ran into him, he began to use his energies and his talents towards people inside the ghettoes . . . This was a few months ago when he was getting these brothers together and talking to them and they had the group called the Black Eagles. I started spending a lot of time

with them. Then Dakus offered me a job, he asked me to be Minister without Portfolio and relate with him about my experiences in organising. This I did and I still serve as Minister without Portfolio in the Eagles. My latest job with them was to work out a 5-year economic plan.

(*Oz*, 1969: [18] 19)

Despite a series of exaggerations, the interview contains a kernel of truth. Howe had trained as a barrister, although he had not qualified, and he had indeed gone to the University of York, although as an interviewee rather than as an academic. In essence, Howe's credentials as an intellectual are at the heart of the interview. This is no accident. Michael X knew that in order to be taken seriously as a Black Power leader, he needed to be able to present himself as a thinker. At the same time, he was aware of the limitations of his formal education. With this in mind, he sought out intellectuals in order to learn from them. Robert Lamb, author, playwright and future professor of political science at Columbia University recalled that Michael X 'pumped him for details and quotations of what Black Muslim leaders had said'. He also picked up Lamb's insights and arguments and 'passed them off as his own' (Humphry and Tindall 1977: 94–5). It seems reasonable to assume that Michael X gravitated to Howe for similar reasons. Howe, on the other hand, had little time for Michael X. For Howe, Michael X was essentially a hustler and Black Power was just one more scam.

Howe's return from America at the end of 1968 allowed him to take editorial control of *The Black Eagle* and make changes. Quotes from the nationalist Karenga no longer featured in the magazine. Secondly, and more importantly, all references to Michael X were expunged. James had advised Howe to have nothing more to do with Michael X (Howe 2011b), and therefore, the criticism of Michael X's suffering at the hands of the state was removed from the six demands that prefaced every issue. His autobiography was dropped from the reading list. Expunging references to Michael X from the pages of *The Black Eagle* may seem like a small thing, but the etiquette of the time dictated that black radicals did not criticize each other publically. Dropping the references to Michael X was an important move in the context of the late 1960s. In mid-1968, Michael X still had considerable authority within black radical circles.[5]

The fall of Egbuna

Howe's writings also played a part in Egbuna's eclipse. Early in 1968, Britain's embryonic Black Power Movement began to metamorphosize. The UCPA, which had already suffered one split, split again. Egbuna refused re-election as chair, resigned and, turning his back on the group, set up the Black Panthers. This was quite an innovation, as it was the first Panther group to be set up outside the United States. At last, Egbuna had a vehicle for his vision of Black Power. Under Egbuna, the group was, in theory at least, the epitome of the Leninist vanguard; a secretive and hierarchical brotherhood united by a common ideology. There was talk of paramilitary training, of policing the police and of reaching out to the London ghetto – although how popular outreach could be squared with Egbuna's vanguardism was never made clear. But these activities remained in the realms of theory. From Howe's perspective, Egbuna was a 'Hyde Park revolutionary' (Howe 2010) – his activities largely restricted to giving bellicose lectures at Speakers' Corner. Even this was too much for Special Branch, who, along with zealots in the Metropolitan police, made it their business to nip the British Black Power Movement in the bud. Egbuna, aware of the official displeasure, set out his plans for a fightback in an article entitled 'WHAT TO DO WHEN THE COPS LAY THEIR HANDS ON A BLACK MAN AT THE SPEAKERS CORNER!' (NA CRIM 1 4962), a document that he would later describe, rather sensationally, as the 'Murder Document' (Egbuna 1971: 127). 'WHAT TO DO,' which remains unpublished, advised Panthers to deal with police interference thus:

> The moment the cops lay their hands on a black brother, it is the duty of the black brother nearest to the spot to call the attention of the other brothers to what is happening at once, and the news must spread like wild fire in the park.
>
> The black crowd must surge forward like one big black steam-roller to catch up with the cops . . . The cops must be overcome and beaten till the arrested brother is rescued, freed, and made to flee at once.
>
> (NA CRIM 1 4962/1)

'WHAT TO DO' was due to be published in the fourth issue of *Black Power Speaks*, Egbuna's magazine. However, having read the piece, Egbuna's printer got cold feet and contacted the police. As a result, the Panthers were raided, Egbuna was imprisoned and three of the Panthers were charged, implausibly, with conspiring to murder police officers.

Egbuna's response to his arrest was of great importance for the British Black Power Movement and for Howe himself. The police had acted entirely predictably and yet, faced with a trial, Egbuna had no strategy for dealing with this situation. More precisely, Egbuna's initial strategy of trenchant resistance gave way to a second strategy which contradicted his earlier utterances. Egbuna, the black nationalist, an outspoken critic of white power, the founder of the

Panthers who sanctioned no collaboration with white sympathizers, entrusted his defence to white lawyers and took their advice to play a passive role in court. Egbuna set out his thinking for this astonishing volte-face in an open letter that was circulated at the Seminar on the Realities of Black Power held at the Union of West Indian Students' Centre Earls Court in August 1968. For the sake of his younger co-defendants, Egbuna explained, he would seek a traditional defence:

> You all know that, right from the beginning, my attitude is that, in case of arrest, I will refuse to offer any formal defence in court. Instead, to stand up in court and spit at their white justice, [sic] their white legality, their white judges, the lot – and expose their hypoorisy [sic] to the world. But with young Peter and Gideon right there in the dock, I had to think twice about this line of action. All day in the police cell, I was thinking hard on this question. The police had nothing really on Peter and Gideon. They should not be here. And I know that if my cause is ably defended and whittled down a bit the two boys will get off scot free, or maybe get away with just fines . . . .
>
> (UW MSS 149/2/2/15)

Howe was present at the seminar and followed Egbuna's case. It was in this context that he made his most important contribution to the British Black Power Movement prior to the Mangrove campaign. In response to Egbuna's compromise, Howe formulated an approach that synthesized the experience of black radicals in Britain, the programme of the American Panthers, his legal training and the woeful example of Egbuna. With explicit reference to Egbuna's trial, Howe set out his reasoning in three demands that prefaced the second issue of the *Black Eagle*:

> 3. WE DEMAND AN END TO POLICE BRUTALITY AND THE PERSECUTION OF OUR LEADERS. WE KNOW THAT BROTHERS MICHAEL, OBI, GIDEON AND PETER MARTIN, HAVE BEEN IMPRISONED BECAUSE THEY DARED TO SPEAK OUT FOR FREEDOM.
>
> 4. WE DEMAND FREEDOM OF ALL BLACK PEOPLE IN PRISON. WE KNOW THAT OUR BROTHERS HAVE NOT BEEN GIVEN FAIR TRIALS BECAUSE OF THE VERY NATURE OF THE JURY SYSTEM.
>
> 5. WE DEMAND THAT ALL BLACK PEOPLE BE TRIED BY THEIR OWN PEER GROUP AS IS WRITTEN IN THE MAGNA CARTA. WE KNOW THAT WHITE JURY MEN AND WOMEN ARE IGNORANT OF THE VARIOUS DIALECTS OF THE BLACK PEOPLE IN THIS COUNTRY. HOW COULD A BLACK MAN HAVE A FAIR TRIAL IF MEMBERS OF THE JURY CANNOT UNDERSTAND HIS MEANS OF EXPRESSION?
>
> (IRR 01/04/03/02/031 [1])

Howe's response was double-edged. On the one hand, demands 3 and 4 clearly call for an end to Egbuna's persecution and his immediate release from prison. However, demand 5 sets out a legal strategy more radical than the one chosen by Egbuna. Notably, these demands were published for the first time in early December and, therefore, appeared just days after the beginning of Egbuna's Old Bailey trail on 26 November. As the trial began, it became clear that the three Panthers were defended by a legal team headed by Rt Hon Sir Dingle Foot QC MP, a privy councillor who sat in Parliament on the government benches (NA CRIM 1 4962/1).

Central to Howe's defensive strategy was the demand for an all-black jury. At first sight, this seems to be a simple repetition of the American Panthers. Under closer scrutiny, it is clear that Howe was being far more creative. The American Panthers had formulated their demand in the following way:

> 9. We Want All Black People When Brought To Trial To Be Tried In Court By A Jury Of Their Peer Group Or People From Their Black Communities, As Defined By The Constitution Of The United States.
>
> We believe that the courts should follow the United States Constitution so that Black people will receive fair trials. The Fourteenth Amendment of the U.S. Constitution gives a man a right to be tried by his peer group . . . To do this the court will be forced to select a jury from the Black community from which the Black defendant came. We have been, and are being, tried by all-White juries that have no understanding of the "average reasoning man" of the Black community.
>
> (Newton 2011: 56)

There are several important differences between Howe's formulation of the demand for a black jury and the demand as it was originally set out by the American Panthers. First, the Panthers' claim is rooted in the American Constitution, whereas Howe appeals to Clause 39 of the *Magna Carta* which guarantees the right to 'trial by peers'. In this sense, Howe took the American demand and rooted it in British law. This was an important move, and Ian Macdonald's research 4 years later during the Mangrove case revealed just how much mileage there was in appealing to the British legal tradition. More interesting still is the justification for the demand; Howe argued that it was a question of language. A white jury, however fair-minded, could not be expected to understand the Caribbean vernacular. This argument directly reflected the experience of the British movement. Specifically, it was the argument that Michael X had used when defending himself at his Reading trial when accused of inciting racial hatred. His defence, simply put, was that he was speaking a language that white people could not understand. Thus, a speech that sounded provocative to white people was nothing of the sort to a black audience. In support of his argument, Michael X announced that the novelists William Burroughs and Alexander Trocchi, acquaintances from the Dialectics of Liberation conference, would act as his interpreters during the trial (Williams 2008: 158), although neither were in England by the time of the trial. The October edition of *Oz* contains a partial transcript of Michael X's cross-examination of the *Daily Express* journalist Brian Park during his pre-trial in September 1967:

> *Malik*: Do you understand black people when they talk.
> *Park*: Yes, just as I hope they understand me.
> *Malik*: Are you mamma-guy?
> *Park*: I beg your pardon. I do not understand you.
> After a fruitless quarrel between the Court and the defendant, Malik sighed: "We are not speeking [sic] the same language. We are on a different wave length".
> *Magistrate*: No. We are speaking basic English.
>
> (*Oz*, [7] October 1969: 17)[6]

Whatever were Howe's misgivings about Michael X, he was at the very least persuaded of the language gap that he had identified and saw its implications as far as justice for black people was concerned.

Howe returned to Egbuna's case in the editorial to the third and final issue of *The Black Eagle,* which was published shortly after Egbuna's conviction. Again, he expressed solidarity with Egbuna's cause while criticizing his legal strategy:

> Brother Obi Egbuna, leader of the U.C.P.A. people's movement, was finally released last week, after having spent 5 months in solitary confinement in Britain's official concentration camp – Brixton jail house.... We black people must understand the case history of these Brothers and learn not to repeat it. It must be perpetually stressed that we HAVE THE RIGHT TO DEMAND to be tried by our own PEER group, if ever the need arises for us to do so.
>
> (GPI JOU 35/4)

Egbuna's conviction brought the first phase of the British Black Power Movement to an end. Having been imprisoned for 6 months, Egbuna received a 3-year suspended sentence. He escaped a custodial sentence, but the threat of incarceration and the changes in the Panthers that had occurred during his enforced absence led to Egbuna's exile from the movement.

Notes

1   The unpublished manuscript 'WHAT TO DO WHEN COPS LAY THEIR HANDS
    ON A BLACK MAN AT SPEAKERS CORNER' is preserved among police files in
    the National Archives. See: NA CRIM 1 4962/2.

2   *IT* states that the pair was arrested on 7 September 1968, but the Marylebone
    Magistrate's Court register clearly states that the arrest took place at 5 a.m. on
    8 September. (LMA PS MAR/A2/25) *Hustler*'s account also indicates that the
    arrest happened early in the morning, rather than late at night as suggested by *IT*;
    see *Hustler*, 18 September 3.

3   The committal to the Central Criminal Court was reported in *Hustler*, 14
    November 1968, 4. Sadly the court registers for 1968 and 1969 have been lost so it
    is impossible to determine their sentences.

4   Partial sets of the *Black Eagle* can be found at the George Padmore Institute
    and the Institute for Race Relations, both of which are located in London. The
    sequence of the three issues can be gleaned from the typography. Based on the
    content of the three issues, it seems that they came out in late October, early
    December and early January, respectively. The first issue has eight pages and
    only discusses two events. The first is the arrest of Richard 'Sammy' Hoyt and
    Michael Lee, which took place on 8 September 1968. The second is their court
    hearing, at which two new charges were brought against the pair, and at which
    they were committed to the Central Criminal Court (GPI JOU 35/5 (4)). The
    court appearance in question took place at Marylebone Magistrate's Court on
    14 October 1968, (LMA PS MAR/A2/26) and therefore, it seems that the first
    issue appeared in late October. The second issue refers to several contemporary
    events that took place between 4 November and the first week in December 1968.
    The latest event the petrol bombing of 'George Brown's home, in Colfe Road,
    Lewisham' (IRR 01/04/03/02/031, 13) took place on 25 November (*Lewisham
    Borough News*, 28 November 1968, 1), and the article clearly refers to the incident
    as happening 'On Monday last . . .' which suggests that the second issue of the
    Eagles was published in early December. The final issue discusses current events
    that took place between the release of Egbuna on 11 December 1968 and the
    beating of a group of young black people on 2 and 3 January 1969 at Notting Hill
    Gate police station (GPI JOU 35/4, (2)r and (8)v). Therefore, the final issue of The
    Black Eagles seems to have been issued in early January 1969. The *Black Eagle* was
    superseded by *Black Dimension*, which was first issued in February 1969 (see: GPI
    JOU 35/1).

5   See for example 'Black Power Michael', an article that appeared in a June 1968
    issue of *Hustler*, described him as the man who 'broke the chains here in England
    in the heart of the ghetto' (*Hustler*, 2 June 1968, 3). Equally, Kwame Nkrumah's

pamphlet 'Message to the black people of Britain', which Egbuna edited, presents Michael X and the RAAS in almost identical terms (Nkrumah 1968, [4]).

6 Michael X returned to this argument at the beginning of his autobiography:

> People the world over have always assumed that the English language of the black and the English language of the white is one and the same. This is a false assumption. There is a difference of both thought and expression which makes communication difficult. At one extreme some words used by whites will be found highly insulting by black people and doubtless some words used by blacks are offensive to white ears.
>
> (Malik 1968: 5)

3

Know Yourself

The year 1968, designated by the United Nations as the International Year of Human Rights, is better remembered as a year of revolution. There were barricades in Paris, riots broke out in the American ghettos in response to the murder of Martin Luther King, the Prague Spring rocked Soviet control of Eastern Europe; for a while at least it seemed that anything was possible. The end of 1968 was a turning point for Howe. He had applied to study philosophy at York and, after a successful interview, was set to begin his degree in October. Howe felt deeply that he needed to pursue further study. The decision to apply to study philosophy was not dilettantism on his part, but an aspect of his emerging understanding of revolution. Already Howe had arrived at the view that radical action must be disciplined by reason. Studying philosophy was a step towards a broader social objective. And yet, he was unsure. He had seen the baleful impact of academic philosophy on the student revolutionaries in Paris. On the one hand, discussion of Camus had become a substitute for genuine revolutionary action, and on the other, students who had mastered the Western philosophical canon saw themselves as superior to factory workers by virtue of their education. And yet his experience of British black nationalism, Egbuna's thoughtless rhetoric and Michael X's unprincipled hustling were equally unappealing. Howe was in search of the virtue between two vices: a philosophy rooted in reality that would lead to social change, rather than the academic learning of the French students or the brash, erratic posturing of Britain's black nationalists.

Howe found his *via media* through his friendship with C. L. R. James. Re-establishing his relationship with James was the turning point, for it led to a momentous decision to abandon formal study, sell his house and travel to Canada in pursuit of Black Power (Howe 2011b).

The 'University of Willesden'

I was never heading for Black Nationalism, it [politics] always had to do with thought. . . . I met Nello at a time when I could have gone to University and had all of that shattered, but I met a walking University in Willesden.

(Howe 2011b)

Howe had broken off his legal studies in the early 1960s. However, by 1968, he felt the need to continue with his education. Queen's Royal College (QRC) had provided him with a world-class education, but he felt that he needed to go beyond that. His initial plan was to study philosophy at York. There were two hurdles before he was accepted, an interview with Laurie Taylor and an essay. The first went well. The second was more problematic. He was required to write a piece on Wittgenstein's *Tractatus Logico-Philosophicus*. Howe freely admits that the book made no sense to him whatsoever. His abiding memory of Wittgenstein was the feeling that 'this fucking man needs a psychiatrist!'. Nonetheless, Howe was a proficient writer and was able to turn out an essay good enough to secure a place on the course. In spite of his early involvement in politics, Howe was still toying with the idea of entering a traditional profession, and as a proficient linguist with some legal training, he thought that the degree might lead on to a job in diplomacy (Howe 2011b).

Accepted on the course, Howe was due to start his degree in October 1968, but events late in the summer changed his mind. Ever since arriving in Britain, Howe had been intending to seek out James. The last time he had seen his grandmother prior to leaving for Britain, she had given him one piece of advice, 'Make sure you go and see Uncle Nello, you will never regret it.' The advice obviously made an impact, as Howe read *The Black Jacobins* soon after his arrival in Britain. 'I didn't put it down for days,' he recalls. Meeting James was a different matter. He had no address for his great-uncle so re-establishing contact was all but impossible. Yet, a chance meeting changed things. As luck would have it, Howe and James both boarded the same underground train heading north from Baker Street on the Bakerloo Line. Howe was travelling to Finchley Road, James to his home in Willesden. Once again Howe was struck by the fact that James treated him as an equal and was interested in his ideas and activities. As they parted, James invited Howe to visit him at his house on Staverton Road in Willesden Green.

At the time, Howe knew little of his great-uncle philosophy other than *The Black Jacobins*. He had heard from a friend that James was a 'communist', but that was the extent of his knowledge. That said, once they met, there was an immediate affinity between the two men, a similarity of instinct and concern. They were separated by half a century, yet shared the experience of being brought up in Trinidad, of education at QRC, a love of literature and a love of cricket. The two soon became friends. To Howe, it was more than that. He describes the impression that his great-uncle made on him thus: 'Its remarkable how he sees through you, not in an offensive way, he knows who you are.' QRC had honed Howe's ability to reason, but he only learnt to know himself with James.

Like any friendship, Howe's relationship with James was multifaceted. Soon they were meeting every day. Sometimes, Howe ran errands for James, buying him cigarettes or whatever else he was short of. The two men had a similar sense of humour. 'CLR James' Howe recalls, 'a kind of cynical wit, he would laugh at his own jokes! He was funny! Very, very funny!'. James was always asking questions and was always interested in Howe's life and his experiences. More often than not, conversation turned to politics and sometimes to race. Why race? 'You can't choose your terrain, and you can't choose your issue,' opines Howe, 'but race here returned with a vengeance.' Whether it was remarks made by Enoch Powell in the press, the persecution of black radicals by the police, the legacy of colonialism in Africa and the Caribbean or day-to-day harassment on the streets of Notting Hill, racism was the problem that would not go away. The two would talk about how to deal with the issue. Was black nationalism the right way forward? What about the energies of moderates like David Pitt? What role did the British working class have to play in the struggle for freedom? Where was the battle against racism to be fought, in Britain, America, the Caribbean or Africa? They also talked more generally about Howe's plans and the prospect of studying philosophy at the University of York.

Late 1968 and early 1969 were an extraordinary period in Howe's intellectual development. Looking back, he remarks: 'I did my post-grad with James!'. The metaphor is a good one, because at the post-graduate level, no one has a monopoly on expertise, student and supervisor are forging a new path together into an intellectual *terra incognita*. Indeed, as Howe recalls, James was never didactic in any traditional sense. Rather, he encouraged Howe to read and, through a Socratic method of questioning and discussion to think out loud, to reach his own conclusions. There was also an intellectual rigour to these discussions. Howe recalls that 'his debriefings were the most fantastic thing to witness, and the most terrifying thing to go through; because the questions were so ordinary – they appeared ordinary – and he would get it all out of you in a relaxed way. He was never into, "What do you believe about that?" – No.' James asked apparently prosaic questions. What year did Howe start QRC? Did he play cricket? What books did he enjoy? He took Howe's reading and intellectual life for granted.

Howe also uses the metaphor of a journey to describe the period. The insights that came from this friendship with James should not be understood as a conversion experience or as an intellectual epiphany. Howe was already on a journey and his direction was already set. 'He wasn't recruiting a revolutionary; he wasn't doing that at all. He could see the instinct in the things that I would say, and I knew I needed to educate myself beyond QRC.' James did not alter his trajectory, he 'caught me going somewhere'.

James was always encouraging Howe to read, to know himself through reading. They read together. They read the last three chapters of Marx's *Capital*, examining the way in which work organizes and disciplines the working class. They read Fanon's *A Dying Colonialism* and *The Wretched of the Earth*, considering the brutality of French colonialism and the evolution of revolutionary violence. They also read parts of *Black Reconstruction in America* by W. E. B. Du Bois. One passage they looked at together stood out:

> This the American black man knows: his fight here is a fight to the finish. Either he dies or wins. If he wins it will be by no subterfuge or evasion of amalgamation. He will enter modern civilization here in America as a black man on terms of perfect and unlimited equality with any white man or he will enter not at all. Either extermination root and branch, or absolute equality. There can be no compromise. This is the last great battle of the west.
>
> (Du Bois 1977: 703)

This notion of fighting for the right to participate in society on the basis of absolute equality chimed with Howe's fundamental political commitments.[1]

Perhaps the two most important books that he read during this period were penned by James himself. First was *Modern Politics*, a collection of six lectures given in Trinidad in 1960, which were subsequently suppressed by the Eric Williams' government and only published in 1973. The first two chapters set out the history of a universal struggle from the democracy of ancient Athens and the Paris Commune to the failure of the Second International. The lectures were not written to undercut the black nationalism that emerged in Britain during the 1960s but their universalism underlined Howe's distrust of the nationalist aspects of the black radicalism that he had been exposed to through Egbuna's writings in Britain or Karenga's in America. The second was *Facing Reality*, a book written by James with contributions by Cornelius Castoriadis. The book, which dealt with the Hungarian Revolution of 1956, had a renewed relevance, given the events of the Prague Spring and May '68 which, like events in Hungary before it, pitted democratic socialism against the authoritarian Stalinism of the orthodox left. Section four of *Facing Reality* directly addressed some of the burning issues that the events of 1968 had raised in Howe's mind, specifically, the relationship between philosophy and revolution, and the immediate issue of the value of a philosophy degree.

Section four of *Facing Reality* argues that the dominant tradition of Western philosophy has ceased to be of value as a guide to action. Discussing two contemporary schools of philosophical thought, James argues:

> These learned obscurantists and wasters of paper are of value in that they signify the end of a whole stage in the intellectual history of mankind. Philosophy as such has come to an end.
>
> (James et al. 1974: 65)

James did not write off all philosophy by any means. He argues that the tradition from Plato to Hegel was of considerable value. Classical, medieval and even modern philosophers could not reconcile the competing demands of the classes struggling with one another – no philosophy could do this. But they could expose the 'old and rotten' (Ibid., 66) and in so doing, clear away the dogmas that stood in the way of progress. They could also provide a degree of liberation and foster a worldview conducive to scientific advancement and the emergence of modern democracy. That said, following Marx, he argued that the emergence of capitalism and the growth of the modern proletariat rendered traditional philosophy redundant. First, James argued, the modern intellectual elite was no longer advancing human liberation; rather it sided with the interests of the wealthy. Secondly, the working class now understood reality with greater clarity than any number of philosophers. In sum, philosophy, in the traditional sense, had ceased to be an instrument of social progress; humanity needed to look to the actions of the working class to resolve the contradictions of the modern world. James' words provided an intellectual underpinning to a truth that Howe had already learnt through his experience of the poverty of the philosophical revolutionaries in France.

In *Modern Politics* and *Facing Reality*, James drew together the wellsprings of Howe's intellectual world. *Modern Politics* began with the Bible, a book that Howe had come to know well through his father, the church and Sunday school. *Facing Reality*'s critique of contemporary philosophy explored the significance of Descartes' 'I think therefore I am', the unofficial slogan of Howe's education at

QRC, arguing that Descartes' formulation was the foundation of 'the expansion of individual personality and human powers through the liberation of the intellect', the philosophical foundation, in other words, of the modern democratic impulse (Ibid., 67–8).

While stressing that James never 'propagandized' him, Howe nevertheless quickly grasped a series of foundational approaches to politics. Though Howe had an intuitive sense of them from growing up in Trinidad, James was able to draw out and crystallize their significance. First, James rejected the notion of the vanguard party. Lenin had put forward this notion in 1902, arguing that in the face of the Tsarist police state, a mass party could have no hope of effecting revolutionary change. The idea had been revived after Lenin's death to justify the dominant role of the Communist Party in Russia. In its Stalinist form, it asserted the primacy of the professional intellectual over the passive working class. James had decisively rejected this idea in the 1950s while studying Hegel's dialectic.

Despite his own education in the elite QRC, Howe understood that there was a natural egalitarianism about the working-class culture of Trinidad, for while Trinidad's working class respected education, there was no desire to defer to the learned. Indeed, there was an instinctive suspicion of anyone who sought to raise themselves up above the people and lead. Howe described the process which shaped his view in the following terms: 'in Trinidad and the Caribbean people have a tendency not to genuflect before leaders. So that was spontaneous, I learnt that empirically as I went along with my ordinary life.' Reading James brought out the political significance of these early experiences:

> When I read *Facing Reality* by CLR James, and *Modern Politics*, those two books made it clear that this kind of "I know therefore I lead" . . . the ordinary working person in the Caribbean, descendants of slaves, they weren't putting up with that.
>
> (Howe 2011b)

James' rejection of the vanguard party was, however, only part of the picture. As well as a negative, James provided a positive that had a lasting influence on Howe. Howe encountered one formulation of James' view in Section Six of *Facing Reality*:

> (a) All development takes place as a result of self-movement, not organization or direction by external forces.
> (b) Self-movement springs from and is the overcoming of antagonisms within an organism, not the struggle against external foes.
>
> (James et al. 1974: 105)

These were James' conclusions, based on his readings of Hegel's work on the dialectic. Hegel, for James, constituted the end of Western philosophy. For James, it is the people then, and not the leaders, who make history, the people move when they are ready to move, irrespective of the leader's admonitions. Crucially, for Howe this perspective 'cures that disease of the political leader and the vanguard party'. Howe summarized James' thoughts on the dialectic in the following phrase, which was to become his slogan: 'All movement comes from self movement and not from external forces acting on the organism.'

Note

1   Some of the flavour of Howe's 'debriefings' with James is captured in the reading lists published in *The Black Eagle* and in *Black Dimension*. *The Black Eagle* prefaced the reading list with the Socratic advice, 'HELP YOURSELF – KNOW YOURSELF – BUY AND READ' (GPI JOU 35/3, 5). The final reading list contained much that Howe had read with James, including works by Fanon, Du Bois and James himself.

4

Cause for Concern

In the summer of 1968, a documentary was broadcast by the BBC series *Cause For Concern* that, in Howe's words, turned out to be a 'major watershed in the struggle in which the police and black community were locked' (Howe 1988: 29). The programme would set out in detail a number of shocking cases of police brutality and corruption against members of the black community and then invite senior officers within Metropolitan police (the Met) to respond to the charge that the police were racist.

The BBC's proposal to broach this subject in the mainstream media for the first time unleashed a storm of controversy, and prompted a campaign of threats and recriminations from the Met designed to stop the programme from being screened. The documentary was the brainchild of BBC producer Richard Taylor. In early 1968, he approached Selma James, C. L. R. James' wife and a gifted writer, organizer and activist, to ask her for names of people who could appear in a film exploring the issue of police racism. James was well connected and well regarded at the BBC, where she worked as an audio typist. When James heard what Taylor was proposing, she said that she did not believe he would ever get the documentary aired but agreed to help him try however she could.

Selma James suggested names of black victims of police brutality whose cases she was familiar with from her activist work as a member of the Black Regional Action Movement. As the first organizing secretary of Campaign Against Racial Discrimination (CARD) elected in 1965, James also recommended fellow member and radical barrister Ian Macdonald as someone who could participate in a live studio discussion about how police frequently abused their powers when dealing with members of the black community (James 2011). Finally, James suggested several grass-roots activists involved in campaigns against police racism such as Darcus Howe and Fennis Augustine. Augustine was a Grenadian trade union shop steward and an activist within the West Indian

Standing Conference who would later go on to become the High Commissioner for Grenada under Maurice Bishop's revolutionary government.

Thus, in July 1968, Howe was invited by *Cause for Concern* to participate in a live panel discussion involving black political activists and campaigners alongside senior officers of the Metropolitan Police over allegations that the police were racist. Entitled 'Equal before the Law?', the episode explored issues raised in a documentary to be screened before the live discussion (*Radio Times*, 26 July 1968). The film detailed several cases of the police racism, including instances of brutality, arrests on trumped-up charges and the fabrication of evidence to secure criminal convictions. It showed how in one case, officers from the Met planted car keys on a black schoolteacher and his friend, a barrister, and had charged them with stealing a police car. They were eventually acquitted and the Met was ordered to pay £8,000 in compensation. Black victims of police brutality spoke of how racial abuse preceded beatings while in custody. The documentary ended with an interview with an ex-police officer who spoke of how 'colour prejudice' was 'virtually absolute . . . it extends to probably 99%' (Howe 1988: 28).

In its listing for the programme on 26 July 1968, the *Radio Times* had posed the question: 'Is the black man particularly vulnerable when he comes up against the law?'. After describing the 'hardman cult' which existed among the lower ranks, requiring the young police recruit to prove himself by the number of arrests he made, the former officer was asked this same question by the presenter. His response was damning:

> The old tradition would be that the coloured man is not as fully aware of his rights as a white man would be and on this assumption I suppose he would be more vulnerable.
>
> (Ibid., 29)

Howe realized the significance of the documentary the moment he saw it. Up until that point, 'a conspiracy of silence' encompassed mainstream media, politicians and white liberals. Even multiracial lobby groups had kept the issue of police harassment and racial persecution from public view, 'thereby reinforcing the untrammelled power exercised by the police over the black community' (Ibid., 29). The bold and unambiguous content of the programme was bound to alter the balance of opinion. At the very least it would upset the complacency of white viewers and force them to take a position.

Just as far-reaching was the effect that the programme would have on black organizations. Howe knew that many multiracial and black lobby groups would be profoundly shaken by its revelations. CARD, which in 1967 had prompted disaffiliation by its more militant members by agreeing to partner the new statutory body, National Council for Commonwealth Immigrants (NCCI), together with a host of smaller black support and welfare groups, had a strategy of quietly trying to persuade a liberal section of the British ruling class to ameliorate the worst conditions suffered by the black community (Ibid., 27; Sivanandan 1982: 17). As Howe later explained, this approach had the effect of rendering black people 'as helpless victims whom the liberals, with black middle-class aspirants alongside them, would assist in adjusting to the discipline and control of capitalist institutions' (Howe 1988: 27). These forces reacted with alarm to the Black Power Movement and its calls for direct action and therefore wished to avoid at all costs any high-profile public discussion of police racism, which would inevitably unleash the anger of the black working class.

The programme could not have come at a worse time for the Met. In May 1968, they had fiercely resisted the Home Secretary James Callaghan's proposal to add a clause to the Police Code, making it an offence to discriminate against black immigrants; the Police Federation declared it 'a gross insult even to suggest it', alleging that its purpose was to 'placate the misplaced fears of some immigrant bodies that they may not get fair treatment' (Wild 2008: 199).

When senior officers from the Met were invited to an advance screening of the documentary, they were incandescent with rage. The late Sir Robert Mark, then assistant commissioner for the Met, puts the following gloss on the police reaction to the documentary in his memoirs:

> Representatives of the Met were only allowed to see the film after its completion. They were horrified. The Commissioner objected to its viewing and the BBC got cold feet. Then of course the civil libertarian press began to rage about censorship and to make matters worse the commissioner gave a brief interview to ITV. The BBC therefore decided to go ahead.
>
> (Mark 1978: 100)

As Howe has since pointed out, Mark's account conceals more than it reveals. The Commissioner did not merely object; he authorized his senior officers to deploy a series of increasingly desperate tactics to stop the programme from reaching public view. Senior officers at Scotland Yard threatened to withdraw future co-operation with BBC journalists if the film was shown, and lawyers acting for the Metropolitan Police sent letters the BBC reserving their right to seek a High Court injunction to stop the programme from being aired. Initially, the pressure was effective and BBC management bowed to police pressure, dropping the film from the schedule.

That would have been the end of the affair if Richard Taylor had not telephoned Selma James. As James recalls it, the conversation began with Taylor's acknowledgement, 'you were right, they are not letting it on the air, but don't tell anyone' (James 2011). After receiving the call, James telephoned another producer she knew at the BBC and told him what had happened. He told her to leak the story to the 'Inside Pages' of the *Daily Mirror*. The paper would, he opined, be very interested in the story and would still print it even if she did not provide her name. James followed his advice, and as predicted, the story was front-page news in the *Mirror* and then in every other newspaper thereafter (James 2011).

In addition to the public outcry and scorn of the press and civil liberties groups that followed these revelations of the BBC's acquiescence to police bullying, James, Howe, Fennis Augustine and others organized a daily picket of the BBC Broadcasting House. Howe attended along with his wife Una and daughter Tamara, who in adulthood has followed her father into a career in broadcasting and is now chief operating officer at the children's programmes wing of the BBC. 'I like to remind her that her first experience of the BBC was when she picketed it as a child,' Howe remarks (Howe 2011b).

Entitled *Cause For Alarm,* the daily picket by up to 20 black activists and their supporters became a focal point for the press in their coverage of the campaign against police attempts to censor the BBC's output. As public criticism of the BBC built to a crescendo and threatened to do permanent reputational damage to the BBC, the Corporation bowed to public pressure and rescheduled the programme and the live studio discussion that was to follow it.

The police appear to have made one last bid to have the programme pulled by the BBC. On the day before it was aired, they arrested Blank Panther leader Obi Egbuna on a charge of writing threats to kill police officers at Hyde Park (Bunce and Field 2011). The timing of the arrest and the decision to charge him with such a heinous crime seemed designed to disrupt the fledgling Black Power Movement and put pressure on the BBC to withdraw the programme. Appearing on ITV, the Commissioner contended that the police were now faced with a militant fanaticism and that showing the programme may violate the *sub judice* rule. This last-ditch effort to suppress the programme by reference to an unrelated arrest only served to compound the public impression that the police had something to hide.

With the programme returning to the BBC's schedule, police tactics changed. Assistant Commissioner Robert Mark was given the task of representing the police in the live discussion following the documentary. In his memoirs, Mark describes the documentary as 'one of the most inaccurate and distorted films ever to find its way on to a BBC screen' (Mark 1978: 100). His only evidence of any inaccuracy related to a white building worker who appeared in the first minutes of the film and whose case had been included, no doubt, to show that the white working class were also victims of police malpractice. Mark complained that the BBC had failed to mention his previous convictions for carrying offensive weapons or that a policeman had received £100 in compensation for criminal injuries arising from his last arrest.

Mark managed to track down the officer who had been injured during the white builder's arrest and turned up at the BBC studio determined to present him as a witness for examination and cross-examination during the live discussion. Howe and the other civilian witnesses who were waiting in a hospitality room to go on air were told by a nervous BBC technician that the police were insisting on introducing the new witness. When they protested that this would exhaust the time allotted for the discussion of police racism, they were told by the BBC that Mark and the police had threatened to withdraw from the programme if they were not permitted to call their witness. The police tactics were bold. By ensuring that the live discussion was taken up with the one detail of the programme which did not concern police racism, they would seek to undermine the credibility of the documentary in the public mind without permitting any discussion of the film's substantive allegations levelled at the police.

Howe, Macdonald and the others quickly devised a strategy. They told the technician that they were there to discuss matters concerning black people and that the issue of the white worker was peripheral to this; nonetheless, they were prepared to go on air. Howe describes the strategy that they had agreed upon in the hospitality room:

> Neither the BBC nor the police were told what our trump card would be. We decided to continue the struggle to have the witness removed in full view of the millions who had tuned into the programme. We would expose the history of police attempts to have the film banned and their latest manoeuvre would be explained in that context. Should they persist with their demand, we would walk out of the studio at a prearranged signal.
>
> (Howe 1988: 33)

When the studio discussion went on air and the police persisted in their demand to call their witness, Howe gave the prearranged signal and began to lead the walkout. Conscious of how this was playing out to the watching millions, Reg Gale of the Police Federation relented and the police agreed to engage in a proper discussion of the film's contents.

Selma James watched the programme with Ian Macdonald's family and described the moment when Darcus got up and proposed to leave as 'extraordinary. . . . What was so fantastic is that it was utterly uncompromising and for a good cause.' Howe remembers the moment as 'electric' and says that he was working from instinct and in a way that expressed his political attitude (James 2011).

Having defeated police attempts to railroad the discussion, point after point went in favour of the civilian participants and against the police. Mark's attempts to argue that the cases highlighted within the film were as a result of a few rotten apples, which any institution was bound to contain and against which the black community was protected by the complaints system, were powerfully challenged and refuted by the black participants. Police brutality and harassment, they claimed, was not isolated and fragmented but rampant and pervasive. What was more, the complaints system, with police investigating police, was a sham in which black victims had no hope of redress. One memorable moment occurred when a young black activist from Notting Hill concluded his contribution by stating, 'The police must stop framing and brutalising blacks or the black community will organise to stop them' (Howe 1988: 33). Amid his sweeping attacks on the BBC for making the documentary and 'the mixed bag of the opposition' the police faced, Mark's memoirs say little about the substantive debate other than conceding that he 'didn't think anybody won' and that his reception at Scotland Yard after the programme was 'mixed' (Mark 1978: 102).

The fact that the programme was shown at all was a breakthrough for the black community. Howe describes the tremendous strength and boost in confidence that the documentary gave to activists, in that it showed that the police armour could be penetrated through direct action and a determined campaign. Following the documentary, the popular Left journal *Black Dwarf* reprinted the entire transcript of the programme, thereby enabling those engaged in the struggle against police racism to reach out to wider sections of the Left.

For Howe himself, the lessons were no less profound. His tactical intervention had outflanked the Assistant Commissioner and Metropolitan Police in front of a live audience of millions. A struggle begun on the pavement outside the BBC Studios had been taken on to the live programme and had exposed the police's underhand attempts to first ban the film and then curtail the live discussion of its contents. These were to prove valuable lessons, which Howe would not forget when he was conducting his own defence in the Mangrove trial 3 years later. Howe's dignified challenge to the proceedings during the debate had produced an extraordinary moment of dramatic and compelling television. In this sense, *Cause for Concern* gave him his first experience of the political power of television, an experience that would inform his career with Channel 4 decades later.

5

'Darcus Howe is not a Comedian'

October 1968 was decision time. Howe was faced with a choice; either pursue academic study at York or join James at the Congress of Black Writers. Although the Congress was hosted at McGill University in Montreal, this was no academic affair. Nor, despite the title, was it ostensibly a literary event. The subtitle of the Congress, 'Towards the Second Emancipation. The Dynamics of Black Liberation', is undoubtedly more helpful in understanding the character of the occasion (Walmsley 1992: 227). Howe simply describes it as an 'international Black Power congress' (Howe 2011b). The Congress was organized by the Conference Committee on West Indian Affairs (CCWIA), whose core consisted of Alfie Roberts, Rosie Douglas, Ann Cools, Wally Look Lai and Raymond Watts – a group who were clearly influenced by James (Austin 2001: 61).

It is difficult at this distance to reconstruct how long Howe deliberated, but in the final analysis, he chose to attend the Congress. There was, of course, the issue of financing a trip to Canada. Howe's solution was to sell his house in Crouch Hill, North London. The house had belonged to his first wife's grandmother, and Howe admits that its sale 'disrupted the rhythm of her life for a time' (Howe 2011b).

The Congress of Black Writers

The Congress of Black Writers took place between 11 and 14 October. The Congress was the culmination of a series of events organized by the CCWIA and perhaps the seminal event for the international Black Power movement. Organized in the memory of King and Malcolm X, it attracted around 1,600 delegates as well as many speakers of international stature from the world of Black Power. Speakers who addressed the ballroom of the University Union included James, Walter Rodney, James Foreman and Stokely Carmichael (Austin 2007: 523). Douglas recalls the tenor of the conference thus:

> An attempt was made to analyse our history, our perspective: from the political economy of slavery to the psychology of subjection: from the post 1945 events in the black world and the world in general to the contemporary Black Power Movement, particularly as it related to the third world struggle against imperialism.
>
> (Tulloch 1975: 136)

Howe recollects the Congress thus:

> They had some of the most brilliant speakers at that conference: Walter Rodney, Bobby Hill, Bobby used to bounce on two feet like Fidel Castro! Tim Hector . . . I was terrified, I thought "I'm among the big guns now". CLR mastered it. Carmichael graciously would accept that.
>
> (Howe 2011b)

There were also opportunities for lesser-known figures to speak, and Howe seized the occasion to address the Congress. 'I talked about what I knew, when my mother talked about moving I joined Renegades/Lawbreakers. . . . I was talking about, concerned about, that class in the Caribbean, the unemployed youth and the use of the state against them. And cracking jokes too.' Bukka Rennie, a student at Sir George Williams University in the late 1960s and a delegate at the Congress, recalls Howe's contribution as one of the highlights of the event:

> . . . Darcus spoke about the West Indies Federation or the mash up of the Federation [1958–1962]. He talked about how he was a member of an institution that was born in Trinidad that outlasted the Federation. He was talking about Renegades— Renegades Steel Band. [Laughter]
>
> (*Trinidad and Tobago Review*, 2010)

Howe's humorous take on Caribbean politics provoked a good deal of hilarity. The comedy, Howe recalls, was a testament to his nerves. The Congress was a big arena, and he was surrounded by figures known across the world. Many, like Carmichael, were at the height of their powers. But Howe's speech had a serious idea at its core. Rodney would not give his lecture on 'groundings' until the Congress was over, but this notion of 'groundings' was the essence of what Howe was describing. Quite independently, it seems, Howe had reached the same conclusions: that an intellectual should learn from and spend time in the community from which they are drawn. Fearing that Howe's point would be lost in the mirth, James advised the assembly at the plenary session to carefully consider Howe's words. 'Darcus Howe,' he remarked 'is not a comedian' (Howe 2011b).

The Congress inspired the radicals in attendance to new feats. Almost immediately, black students took on the university authorities on the campuses of McGill University and Sir George Williams University. The final edition of the *Black Eagle*, which contains a brief description of the conference, also noted that once the Congress was over, Rosie Douglas, accompanied by two American Panthers, travelled to Nova Scotia to speak at a meeting of the local black community, only to be arrested for inciting riot (GPI JOU 35/4, 8). Rennie goes further and draws a direct line from the Congress to the Black Power Revolution in Trinidad in 1970.

The Congress wrapped up on 14 October. Howe stayed on. Rodney too remained in Canada after the Congress. In Rodney's case, his presence in Canada was the result of the Jamaican government who, fearing Rodney's influence among local black radicals, banned him from returning to his post at the University of the West Indies (UWI) on the day after the conclusion of the Congress (Small 1969: iv). The ban was counterproductive, precipitating the 'Rodney Riots'. Rodney continued to lecture, and on 18 October, he gave the talk which is now referred to as the 'The Groundings with my Brothers' (Ibid., viii). Howe was present at the lecture. As already noted, the idea of groundings was not new to him, but the lecture did draw out its political significance.

Sojourn with SNCC

Howe's decision to go to Canada rather than York was crucial, for it was the point at which he made radical politics his vocation. The seriousness of his commitment is evident from his decision to immerse himself in political action almost as soon as the Congress was over. The Congress was an excellent opportunity to meet black radicals from across the world. In fact, it was through the Congress that Howe met several members of Student Nonviolent Coordinating Committee (SNCC), who invited him to join them in New York. Eager to work alongside some of Black Power's leading exponents, he accepted the invitation, crossing the Canadian border clandestinely. For two and a half months, he lived in America, and for most of that time, he was based in Harlem, a largely black neighbourhood in Upper Manhattan. Howe's stay in New York coincided with the final phase of the Ocean Hill-Brownsville campaign, a seminal campaign which was on the cutting edge of Black Power politics in America. Working with SNCC exposed Howe to the debates going on within the American Black Power movement, gave him direct experience of SNCC's campaign methods and allowed him to spend time with H. Rap Brown, SNCC's final chairman.

As with all campaigns, the Ocean Hill-Brownsville campaign had a backstory. The issue of race and education in New York had been reawakened in the mid-1950s. The Supreme Court's ruling in the Brown Case effectively tore up the legal foundation of segregation, as well as demanding the integration of all schools across America. The liberals on New York's Board of Education embraced the ruling, but the way forward was unclear. Technically, the Brown Case dealt with formal segregation, that is to say, segregation rooted in 'Jim Crow' laws. In New York, things were different. The segregation in education arose from economic inequalities. Poorer neighbourhoods were predominantly black, more affluent areas almost exclusively white, and this division was reflected in the schools.

By 1966, a hard-fought campaign by Parents and Taxpayers (PAT) had forced the local Education Board to drop its policy of managed integration. The failure of the integration initiative coincided with a new kind of black radicalism. Carmichael was at the forefront of the new thinking. In terms of education, he was concerned to refocus the discussion, taking the emphasis off integration. For too long, he argued, people had conflated integrating education and improving education for black children. This was a problem for two reasons. First, integration did not necessarily lead to improved education for black children. Secondly, integration, as it had traditionally been conceived, was always on white terms, predicated on the notion that there was nothing of value in the black community (Carmichael and Hamilton 1967: 24; Gordon 2001: 16). Consequently, Carmichael argued that future campaigns should focus on community control rather than integration. Carmichael's argument was a game-changer and was soon taken up by other black radicals, including Rap Brown (Peller 1990: 796).

This new perspective made a lot of sense in the context of New York. PAT's campaigns had taken integration off the table, but the issue of improving education remained. Under the circumstances, community control was clearly the best option. Rap Brown, who played an important role in SNCC's campaign to support the experimental schools made the case in the following way:

> White people got hung up on integration. Segregation was the problem and the elimination of segregation was the solution, not integration. It was the unequal nature of segregation the Black people protested against in the South, not segregation itself. Separate but equal is cool with me. What's the big kick about going to school with white folk? Them that want to do that should have the chance. But that ain't no solution.
>
> (Brown 1969, 124)

The campaign for community control started on 12 September 1966, in Harlem. Demonstrators from the Harlem Parents Committee, EQUAL, CORE, SNCC, the Organization of Afro-American Unity and the African-American Teachers Association, picketed Intermediate School 201 in Harlem, demanding community control (Podair 2002: 35). Initially, the notion of community control gained a great deal of support. White radicals, including some academics associated with the New Left, saw community control as an important corrective to the stultifying effects of modern educational bureaucracy. Big business, most notably the Ford Foundation, got on board too. Racial peace was good for business, and in any event, the children of the very rich would never go to schools in the areas affected. Initially, teachers backed the idea as well. In November 1967, the Mayor's Advisory Panel on Decentralization, chaired by McGeorge Bundy of the Ford Foundation, proposed breaking up the New York school district into a series of small districts, controlled in part by elected representatives from the local community. The 'Bundy Plan' designated three pilot districts including Ocean Hill-Brownsville in Brooklyn (Gittell 1968: 65).

The Ocean Hill-Brownsville experiment, however, was dogged by difficulties. Battle lines were drawn over the nature of community participation. The majority of the New York City United Federation of Teachers (UFT), itself riven along racial and social lines, advocated 'administrative decentralisation', that is to say, passing control from the Board of Education to local schools (Gordon 2001: 8–9). However, the community, which was predominantly made up of black and Puerto Rican families, argued that this merely passed power from one group of white bureaucrats to another. In contrast, they advocated community control. Successive school boards, they argued, had failed children of colour, and parental control was the only way to ensure a better deal for their children

(Wilerson 1970: 93–117). The UFT's final response was to brand the leaders of the local community 'illiberal' and 'anti-Semitic', arguing that the educational campaign was an attempt to remove Jewish teachers, who made up the majority of the UFT, from Brooklyn's schools (see, e.g. Berube and Gittell 1969: 120–9, 170–5). Mainstream reporters, who had been characterizing Black Power as a kind of reverse-racism since its emergence in the mid-1960s, took up the claim, distorting the goals of the local community and handing a media victory to the UFT.

The Ocean Hill-Brownsville campaign was significant because it showed a clear break between white liberals and Black Power. The white teachers could claim with considerable legitimacy that they had been committed to integration as it had traditionally been conceived. However, the debate had moved on. The fight was now for 'home rule', a demand that the traditionally progressive UFT bitterly opposed. Howe's involvement, then, exposed him to the debates on the cutting edge of the movement.

Howe had become involved with SNCC in the wake of the Congress. Howe had a great deal of respect for the American black movement. 'Since the end of slavery and Reconstruction period there are no better political organisers than black Americans' (Howe 2011b). His initial thought was to join Carmichael. However, Carmichael had left SNCC in 1967 to join The Black Panther Party for Self-Defense. As far as Howe could see, his old friend was 'drifting' and was no longer in a position to act as a guide. As a result, Howe joined the SNCC team in Harlem. He remembers the invitation to work with SNCC thus: 'they thought "well, this guy can talk" so they invited me down to the SNCC office in New York'. The group comprised the musician and artist Ted Joans, Gwendolyn Patton, who had been fighting for black rights since the days of the Montgomery bus boycott, Fred Meely and H. Rap Brown, SNCC's chair (Ibid.).

Howe arrived in New York towards the end of October. By this time, the dispute over the control of schools in Brooklyn had escalated into a citywide strike. Day-to-day he spent most of his time working voluntarily in the SNCC office. He recalls how the community responded spontaneously to the strike wave, collectively improvising schooling and educational visits for their children. Howe's role was low key, working behind the scenes and answering the phone. Howe kept a low profile for the simple reason that he had entered America unofficially, and he had no intention of bringing himself to the attention of the immigration authorities. There was also the perennial issue of police brutality, all the more serious with armed police. Howe emerged from the Harlem office to speak on a number of occasions. Travelling to Brooklyn, Howe shared a platform with Brown and a group of black school students, who, in the midst of the school strike, made the case for community control. The students impressed Howe greatly. Looking back, Howe remarks: 'I have never heard since people so brilliantly articulate, disciplined by the reason of thought as some of those students' (Ibid.). These were the very students who had been dismissed by educational professionals, psychologists and sociologists as lacking the necessary 'cultural capital' to succeed in education, but for Howe, these were the finest speakers of the campaign. 'That is what the black movement did in the United States,' it led to self-confidence and self-organization among the dispossessed. Howe described his experiences in the final edition of the *Black Eagle*:

> The same situation exists in New York State, where the racist Teacher's Union went on strike because of the Black Community, insisting on the right to control the schools in the community. A patched-up settlement, far short of black people's demands was agreed by the powers that be, and recent events show that the issue is far from being settled. After a rally addressed by Brother H. Rap Brown, only a few days ago, the school kids in the Manhatten [sic] area, took to the streets as a last resort. As per usual, the police attacked arresting and brutalising every black person in sight.
>
> (GPI JOU 35/4)

The SNCC office was a hub of discussion and debate. The crucial lesson Howe learnt was the 'one in ten' method, used to organize small groups who would become the nucleus of mass protest. This was the organizational backbone, Howe learnt, of the March on Washington in 1963 and the Selma March of 1965. 'Martin was the name,' the figurehead of those two great campaigns, but it was SNCC's organization that made them happen. He heard of the conflict within the civil rights movement between King and the Southern Christian Leaders Conference and SNCC over the March on Washington. The story of the march which emerged from the SNCC office was that the idea had come from black farmers in Arkansas, that SNCC's John Lewis had picked up the idea and organized it and that Ralph Bunche and the moderate leadership of the NAACP, which was close to the Democrats, had attempted to co-opt the march and instal King as its figurehead. For Howe, the story confirmed the importance of the small organization and the importance of the initiative coming from the people themselves.

There was also playful criticism of Carmichael, who had earned the nickname 'Starmichael' due to his growing celebrity status. Howe heard stories of campaigns in the south, of black and white students leaving prestigious universities in the north to go and help organize in the south and was moved by their courage in the face of murderous opposition. 'That' says Howe 'is how they built the Student Non-violent Organising Committee, and not one of them was non-violent!' (Howe 2011b). While as some activists were radical pacifists, Howe's comment neatly highlights how, for the majority of those active in SNCC, non-violent direct action was a strategy of mass struggle as opposed to a personal renouncement of all forms of violence.

There was also discussion of 'armed struggle'. For Howe, this meant 'terrorism, basically'. This concerned Howe. 'I was never, ever, ever, going to do that', he comments. For Howe, the discussion of an armed struggle was indicative of SNCC's impending collapse: 'when an organization breaks up . . . one of the things that can easily happen is you get into some kind of terror'. This talk of terror was a sign that SNCC was losing its way. Howe comments, 'if you're morally wrong, you're politically dangerous and you'll pay for it'.

Howe's activities in America were not restricted to New York. He travelled to Chicago to renew his acquaintance with Minister Rico of the Black P. Stones. Chicago was a disappointment; as far as Howe could see, the Black P. Stones was a 'scam'. 'At that time,' Howe recalls, 'gangs were transforming themselves into something resembling Black Power, to rationalise whatever money they were robbing,' and that was the case in Chicago.

The school strikes came to an end in late November 1968. A compromise was hammered out. *TIME Magazine* suggested that in the long run 'the strike seems to have furthered the cause of decentralisation. Thousands of previously uninvolved city parents, white and black, who had been content to let the schools run themselves, became personally involved in their children's schools, and their operation' (*Time*, 29 November 1968).

Howe, as quoted above, struck a more disconsolate note in the *Black Eagle*. Sadly, Howe's premonition proved right; in April 1969, New York passed an educational decentralization law, which gave no ground to community control. The UFT had won, and as Poldar comments, 'In this backhanded way, the Decentralization Law of 1969 announced the demise of the Ocean Hill–Brownsville community control experiment' (Poldar 2002: 146). For Howe and many others in the Black Power Movement, it was a defining moment. It showed that the multiracial coalition of liberal whites and sections of the Left, which had coalesced in support of civil rights and opposition to Jim Crow, would be strained to breaking point when black people began to organize for control of their own communities in northern cities. The struggle underlined the need for black self-organization and leadership in the struggle against institutional racism.

Black Dimension

Early in 1969, back in Britain, Howe started a new initiative. *The Hustler* had closed and Howe had no intention of continuing the *Black Eagle* so there was a need for a newsletter in the black community. Howe set up *Black Dimension*, a 'Community News Service' initially based in Portobello Road (UC DHP Box 5/3).

Black Dimension ran for three issues, February, March and April 1969. It was produced on an old Gestetner machine in Howe's home, a flat in Shepherd's Bush that he shared with Barbara Beese. In some ways, it picked up from where the last issue of the *Black Eagle* left off. The Eagles' programme, now shorn of any reference to Michael X, took up the front inside cover, the graphics, as in the *Black Eagle,* were the work of Una Howe. Nonetheless, there was a crucial difference between publications such as *Black Power Speaks* and the first two issues of the *Black Eagle* on the one hand and *Black Dimension* on the other. The pages of Egbuna's *Black Power Speaks* were devoted almost wholly to doctrinal discussions of the nature of Black Power.[1] Similarly, the first issue of the *Black Eagle*, which was produced largely by Michael X, contained little more than a doctrinal statement, again about the nature of Black Power, and a few quotes from the black nationalist, Maulana Karenga. *Black Dimension*, by contrast, was a determined attempt to reflect the concerns of the community. In this sense, it reflected a Jamesian emphasis on the experience of ordinary people and an equally Jamesian distaste for doctrinal wrangling. James' influence was palpable in the production. Howe recalls that James was continually telling him to 'write it down', to commit his thoughts and experiences to paper.

The first issue of *Black Dimension* was devoted to the police. The leading article 'POLICE STATE IN WEST LONDON' drew together popular reaction to *Cause for Concern,* with personal accounts of police brutality from black people living in the Grove, and Howe's own critique of the Met's community relations counteroffensive in the *Mirror* (GPI JOU 35/1).

Black Dimension's first campaign clearly reflected the dual influence of James and SNCC. The emphasis on people speaking for themselves, both in the amount of reported speech in the newsletter and in its coverage of grass-roots activism, is reminiscent of James' approach to campaigning and to the way in which SNCC put students at the centre of the campaign for community control of schools in Brooklyn.

The police were not the only topic discussed in *Black Dimension*. The first issue included pieces on the experience of black children in schools and an article on Rhodesia. The second focused on Canada and the events at Sir George William University that followed the Congress of Black Writers. The special Canadian issue reflected the contacts that Howe had made during the Congress, and thanks 'Brothers C. L. R. James, Richard Small, and Andrew Salkey, who have brought their experiences and energies to the publication of this issue' (GPI JOU 35/2). The final issue opened with a detailed discussion of the Anguillan Revolution, but rounded off with two further articles dealing with police brutality, the first detailing victimization in Manchester, the second, an interview with a former policeman. The policeman in question was Peter Devereaux, who had left the force in 1967 and had appeared alongside Howe on *Cause for Concern*. Notably, *Black Dimension*'s stories of victimization never presented black people as victims. Rather, it encouraged the black community to come together and act as an agent of change. In the context of police violence, Howe points to a change in the dynamic:

> Only of late, with a series of fine lectures by C.L.R. James – always well attended – have we begun to make any progress towards self realisation and black pride. But now we've started on that road, nothing at all will stop us. We will make quite sure of that.
>
> (GPI JOU 35/3)

Black Dimension's relentless focus on the police did not go unnoticed. History repeated itself: *Hustler* had closed due to its exposés of the police. Howe recalls that '[t]he paper was printed by an old Polish émigré who operated from a basement in Fulham. A visit from the Notting Hill police, who were a target for many of my articles, brought the printing arrangement to an end. We had to fold.' A similar fate befell *Black Dimension*. The police obtained a search warrant and raided the Shepherd's Bush flat. Howe was not charged with anything, but Constable Pulley, who had featured so prominently in *Black Dimension*'s first issue, threatened to bring charges of criminal libel. Howe had no choice. *Black Dimension* had to stop, and Howe was forced to relocate.

Note

1   The first issue, for example, discusses this in the editorial, in 'Lets Face it, Baby', in
    'Black Power or Death!' in T. R. Adam's untitled article, and in Lester Springer's
    'Conversation in Defence of Black Power'. In this sense, it takes up over 10 pages
    of the 19-page magazine. The extent to which the definition of Black Power
    dominated the first issue of *Black Power Speaks* is no surprise, given the factional
    fighting that was reaching its head within the UCPA at the time. In this sense, the
    ongoing attempts to define Black Power were not merely an academic exercise,
    they were a bid for power and influence within the radical Black Movement.

6

Revolution in Trinidad: 'Seize Power and Send for James'

. . . we have been down this road before. On February 26th 1970, when the NJAC stormed the Roman Catholic Church following a protest outside a Canadian bank, they were a small organisation in conflict with the state. It is the sharpness of the conflict centred around support for black students in Canada, which drew thousands into a social movement and hundreds to the membership of NJAC. The then Geddes Granger had to contemplate a new situation. No longer NJAC's particular confrontation with authority but the wider conflict which had beset the social order. Political possibilities soar in times such as these.

(UC DHP Box 9/3)

Having been effectively run out of town by the police, Howe needed to relocate, and quickly, if he was to avoid a criminal libel charge. The move needed to be thought-through. *Black Dimension* had ended prematurely, but Howe had no intention of curtailing his political activism. His thoughts turned to the Caribbean. From the time of the Montreal Congress, if not before, the Caribbean had been a growing part of his political sensibilities. Walter Rodney's *The Groundings With My Brothers* had a particular influence, politicizing his Caribbean identity; for it stressed the need of the black intellectual to talk, spend time, reason and 'ground together' with the dispossessed of their community (Rodney 1990: 78). Following the Congress, Howe had determined to make the Caribbean a conscious part of his intellectual development as well as his political activity. With this in mind, he sought out James. Their discussion settled the matter: for the time being at least he would return to Trinidad.

Bus strike

Howe arrived in Trinidad towards the end of April 1969, returning to his
parents' house. James had provided him with letters of recommendation to
Stephen Maharaj and George Weekes. On arrival, he made contact with Weekes,
the radical leader of the Oilfield Workers Trade Union (OWTU). Weekes, who
had collaborated with James in the days of the Workers and Farmer's Party
(Henry and Buhle 1992: 199), took the recommendation seriously. As a result,
he invited Howe to immerse himself in trade union work. There was a great
affection between the two men. Howe and Weekes did not always see eye to
eye on matters of strategy and organization, but their differences never rankled.
Weekes recognized talent in the younger man and admired his gifts as a public
speaker, writer and organizer. As a result, he asked Howe to join the staff of *The
Vanguard*, the fortnightly newspaper of the OWTU.

   The union was facing a difficult political and economic situation. While
the 1950s witnessed considerable economic growth, the 1960s was a difficult
time for Trinidad. Balance-of-payment problems re-emerged in the middle of
the decade, and industrial modernization led to increasing mechanization and
therefore rising unemployment (MacDonald 1986: 149). For much of the 1960s,
unemployment was hovering between 14 per cent and 20 per cent of the working
population (Palmer 2006: 284). Economic problems coincided with accelerating
industrial unrest. In response, the government passed the Industrial Stabilisation
Act (ISA), which sought to constrain the unions. In the face of the continuing
economic problems and the government's political strategy, a new alliance
emerged, uniting students, who were hard hit by the slump and radicalized by
Black Power, the urban unemployed and some of the radical unions (MacDonald
1986: 162).

   The big news at the time of Howe's arrival was the bus strike, organized by the
Transport and Industrial Workers Union (TIWU). The conflict, which had started
in late April, escalated into a stand-off between the government and the union.
Using the provisions of the ISA, the government declared the strike illegal. The
Act, which had been passed in 1965, gave the government fairly comprehensive
powers over industrial relations. It circumscribed the right of unions to call strikes,
established an industrial court with the power to impose settlements on manag-
ers and workers, as well as allowing for severe penalties for non-compliance. The
People's National Movement (PNM) justified this as an act of modernization,
designed to bring an end to the 'old-fashioned loudmouthed' posturing of the union

leaders. Union leaders, for their part, believed it sacrificed the interests of labour to capital (Ryan 1972: 409–10). Crucially, the TIWU continued its strike in defiance of the ISA. The *Nation* pulled no punches, describing the strikers as a 'lawless breed' (Regis 1999: 247); while the *Trinidad Guardian*, the unofficial organ of official opinion, described the TIWU as 'iconoclasts who would pull down laws, institutions and the very fabric of society in one fell swoop' (*Trinidad Guardian*, 3 May 1969).

Weekes was unperturbed by these reports. There was a long-standing bond between the OWTU and the bus workers, going back to 1961 and the foundation of the TIWU (Alexander and Parker 2004: 309). Moreover, the strike had a broader political significance as it was the most resolute challenge to the ISA since its introduction (Singh 1989: 71; Millette 1994: 344). In this context, Weekes was determined that the OWTU should show its support for the striking bus workers. That said, there were dissenting voices, and there was also the perennial question of tactics. By mid-May, the confrontation had escalated. The problem was now twofold: first, the government had declared the strike illegal and secondly, they had drafted strikebreakers to get the buses moving again.

Conscious that the strike was entering a decisive phase, Weekes called a meeting spanning 11 and 12 May to thrash out a strategy. The composition of the meeting, recorded by Khafra Kambon, attests to the broad range of groups prepared to challenge the government. There were the trade unionists, including Weekes himself and 'a TIWU team'; there were politicians such as 'Vernon Jamadar, official leader of the opposition in Parliament'; academics, like the economist Lloyd Best; lawyers; student radicals 'Geddes Granger, Syl Lowhar, Dave Darbeau, David Murray, Kelshall Bodie'; and Howe, who Kambon described at the time as a 'Trinidadian resident in London closely associated with C. L. R. James' (Kambon 1988: 173). The meeting decided that if the government refused to compromise by 12 May, then the strike-breaking buses would be physically stopped through a campaign of direct action (Abraham 2007: 98). As no compromise was forthcoming, the group agreed to begin their blockade at 5 a.m. the next day.

When Howe arrived at the picket line at 5 a.m. on the morning of 13 May, riot police dressed in khaki, equipped with shields and guns, were positioned outside the depot. At 6 a.m., in time for the first scheduled departures, Clive Nunez of the TIWU addressed the crowd. Weekes, Granger, Darbeau and Howe would play a leading role and risk arrest in order to shield the members of the TIWU. The conflict reached its climax as the first bus rolled out of the depot. Loudspeakers commanded the protestors to get out of the way. They stood firm as the bus advanced, only to be charged by the police. Weekes clung to the front of the bus until he was dragged off and flung into the back of a police van (Kambon 1998: 178–9). Weekes was not alone, as Howe recalls that the police lashed out at the protestors. In total, 17 were arrested and charged with obstructing the free passage of buses out of the Port-of-Spain depot (Singh 1989: 71). Realizing that there was nowhere to run, Howe jumped into the back of one of the police's black Marias, effectively arresting himself.

The cells to which they were taken were squalid. Kambon recalls, '[t]he overused toilet that could not be flushed in one corner, the many signs scratched on the walls, some hand-painted in human excretion . . . cockroaches crawling under the two dirty sleeping bags' (Kambon 1988: 179–80). For most of the detainees, this was their first experience of prison. Howe was one of the few with any experience of 'the rough side of the police' (Ibid., 181).

Thousands flocked to the gaol from all over the island. Rev Cipriani Howe strode through the astonished multitude in flowing ceremonial robes, demanding to see his son. As a general rule, priests stayed out of radical politics, particularly when it involved prison. But he came in the spirit of Mt. 25.36. The first indication of his father's arrival was a huge roar from the crowd outside. On the inside there was talk of a hunger strike. Granger, whom to Howe's mind was capable of being autocratic, was laying down the direction. Ever the pragmatist, Howe favoured a different approach. When his father appeared at the cell door offering help, Howe told him to 'forget the lawyer, George will sort it out. But I want two cheese burgers and a milkshake!'. Turning to Granger, he made his position plain: 'I am for the hunger strike, but only after I've done eating!' (Howe 2011k).

Fortunately, the inmates did not have to wait for long. Around midday, they were taken through the crowd to the court (Kambon 1988: 195). The arrests had handed an important victory to the unions, and perhaps for this reason, the magistrate proceeded with caution. He allowed the students to go, placing them on a bond conditional on their good behaviour. Employing a little subterfuge, Howe identified himself as a student and left the court a free man.

Groundings

The bus strike, which took place a matter of weeks after his arrival, was Howe's first inkling that revolt was a real possibility in Trinidad. His instinct for organization led him to work on a small scale, outside parties, outside unions, outside all established formal structures. Starting in the neighbourhood where he grew up, where he was already known, Howe began speaking and encouraging impromptu discussions. His theme was the country's oil industry. He argued that it could and should be run by local people, his proof text Fanon's *Studies in a Dying Colonialism*. The reception was mixed. For some, it went without saying that only white people had the expertise and technical competence to run the industry; others were won over. But crucially, there was no backchat. His neighbours were prepared to hear him out and engage with his arguments, even when wholehearted assent was unforthcoming.

Howe started small, but his activities created a momentum of their own. Through word of mouth, he publicized a meeting on the bed of St Ann's River, or East Dry River, as it is more commonly known, a large unused artificial waterway where Howe had played cricket as a young man. Around a hundred people showed up, sitting on the dry river bed to hear him speak. Howe spoke and read from Fanon, using a candle to illuminate the pages in the failing light. This was not rabble rousing. As Howe recalls his activity at the time, he was speaking with considerable objectivity, his goal to get people thinking about their own experience. Again, the theme was popular control of Trinidad's resources. The speech became the talk of the town, as people chewed over Howe's argument and discussed who agreed and who disagreed. Struck by what Howe had said, Lenin Woolford, who was in the crowd, remembers avidly discussing the matter with his father, a local PNM councillor and socialist, who said 'Darcus is correct, we could control our own oil industry' (Woolford 2011).

In terms of organization, Howe was on the radical edge of events in Trinidad at the time. Certainly, Weekes had no time for the vanguard party, and in this sense, both he and Howe stood squarely in the revolutionary tradition of James. But he still looked to a party, albeit a mass party drawn from the working class, as the vehicle for change. This was where the two disagreed. Howe was convinced that the people would not wait for the formation of a party and a programme. Working at grass-roots level was fundamental to Howe's strategy. First, working with people at a local level would inspire them to participate in their unions, in marches and in political protest more generally. Moreover, their participation would help to set the direction for existing movements and keep the existing leaders in check. Secondly, Howe was adopting the 'one-in-ten' strategy that he had learnt from Student Nonviolent Coordinating Committee (SNCC). Howe spent time with a small group, inspiring them, encouraging them to think and read for themselves. Then each of them would repeat the process with ten more.

Howe's hope was that within the large demonstrations there would be groups who were ready, not to lead the people, but to publicly reflect their feelings and to encourage them to articulate their own desires. Howe's activities also reflected the influence of Rodney, who argued that the black intellectual 'must attach himself to the activities of the black masses' (Rodney 1990: 77–8). Grounding meant 'getting in touch, working with the people . . . sitting down together to reason' learning from the people themselves (Ibid.). These were the different currents and ideas that Howe and James had discussed in London, working out what form new radical organizations might take. The practice developed in Trinidad, as Howe grounded with the unemployed urban youth around Port-of-Spain.

This new 'organisation' had no hierarchy or formal structure, but there was a small group, which Howe referred to as 'the inner sanctum' who stood out from the rest. This group was partly self-selecting; they were people who would turn up early at demonstrations or meetings, in order to discuss strategy. It was through this informal group that Howe kept in contact with the grass roots during the revolution of 1970, and it was through them that he was able to gauge the pace and direction of events in a way, he claims, Weekes never could (Howe 2011k).

The February revolution

If a revolution can be said to have a beginning, Trinidad's Black Power Revolution began on 26 February 1970, which was, by outrageous coincidence, Howe's birthday. The spark was a demonstration of perhaps 200 people, most of whom were students from the University of the West Indies, in protest at the treatment of their fellow students by Sir George Williams University in Canada. Exactly a year before, over 40 students, many of whom were black and some of whom were from Trinidad, were arrested for the occupation and destruction of a computer lab on the George Williams campus.[1] The occupation was organized in response to the alleged racism of one of the university's staff, and as Rosie Douglas argues, the occupation flowed directly from the Congress of Black Writers (Douglas 1975: 137). Its suppression outraged radicals who identified themselves with Black Power. The response in Trinidad was immediate: Geddies Granger and Dave Darbeau established NJAC (pronounced N-Jack), 'a loose confederation of groups' (Pantin 1990: 51) which started on campus but quickly reached out to the unemployed and radicals in the union movement (MacDonald 1986: 163).

A year later, they took their protest to the sites that symbolized Canadian influence, and more broadly the influence of white power, in Port-of-Spain.

The February protest was part of a broader movement. Black Power had been growing in Trinidad for some time. The government unwisely dismissed the movement as 'noisy and inconsequential' (Ibid., 1986).[2] In so doing, they underestimated its appeal, particularly to the unemployed, who numbered around 45,000 by 1970. Black Power was also attractive to the young, whose high hopes for their newly independent nation had been dashed through the experience of the late 1960s. The mood of the people was evident in the Carnival of February 9. At root, the Carnival was always a celebration of emancipation. The 1970 Carnival mixed masquerade and protest with new symbols: the symbols of Black Power. The *Express* reported: 'The marchers carried huge portraits of Eldridge Cleaver, the Black Panthers leader, the late Malcolm X, Carmichael and others. There was also a caricature of Prime Minister Dr Eric Williams, looking somewhat like a pig' (*Express*, 15 February 1970). Howe recalls that among the J'ouvert there were lots of small groups dressed in fierce costumes. The UWI banner carried a powerful and simple critique of life in Trinidad, 'Black blood, black sweat, black tears – white profit' (Ibid.).

The same mood was also evident on 26 February. The protesters marched from the Canadian High Commission, which occupied the Huggins Building on South Quay, to the Royal Bank of Canada on Independence Square. There was a considerable degree of overlap between the leadership of the February demonstration and leadership of the bus strike a year before, including Granger, Darbeau and Weekes (Palmer 2006: 29). Outside the High Commission, Granger, resplendent in a long dashiki, explained the protest. 'Our students in Canada felt that their dignity was affected. They protested. They were hounded and chained' (*Trinidad Guardian*, 27 February 1970). At the Royal Bank of Canada, it was Granger again who gave voice to the gathering crowd, railing through his megaphone against 'white imperialism'. Howe was there in the front row too, trading insults with one of the police chiefs. In a moment of high political sophistication, Howe pointed at one of the police officers, a man who had grown up with Howe's mother, and shouted 'it's big-moustache Lloyd!'. The policeman responded, 'I'm going to complain to your mother.' 'That would have meant something to me years, and years, and years ago!' retorted Howe (Howe 2011k).

Moving away from the bank, heading down Frederick Street, the protestors began picketing the larger stores. Waving at the displays in the window,

Granger turned to the crowd and remarked: 'They using white mannequins to sell clothes to black people!'. It was at this point that the initiative came from the crowd. Raoul Pantin, a reporter with the *Trinidad Guardian*, describes the moment thus:

> From the depths of the crowd, a man suddenly shouted: "The church! The church! Lets go in church! . . . And among a steadily growing, slowly hand clapping crowd now shuffling along Independence Square, the chant was struck up: "The church! The church! We go in the church!"
>
> (Pantin 1990: 52)

Why the church? Looking back, Carl Blackwood explained, the Roman Catholic Church was the most enduring symbol of the 'white power structure' (Ibid., 54). Williams himself, in his earlier more radical days, had excoriated it as the 'last bastion of colonialism' (Kambon 1988: 197). But as Howe recalls it, the crowd were simply responding to immediate circumstances. The protest had attracted a large contingent of police. In fact, as the *Trinidad Guardian* records, by the time the protestors reached the Bank, a bus had arrived packed with 'a fully armed police riot squad' (27 February 1970). In short, the crowd entered the Cathedral seeking sanctuary from the police.

This turn of events was unexpected. The demonstration was first and foremost a protest about the events at George Williams. Granger and Darbeau had not anticipated or planned for an occupation of the Cathedral. They needed a speaker, someone to address the impromptu sit-in. Howe's cousin, who was part of the student movement, put him forward; as the son of a preacher, he was the obvious candidate. Howe had no time to prepare; 'it was scuffles with police one minute, speaking in the Cathedral the next'. Nonetheless, Howe stepped up and spoke. Next day, the gospel according to Darcus Howe made the front page of the *Trinidad Guardian*:

> Speaker Darcus Owusu told the demonstrators: "The Church which was founded in the name of the greatest agitator who ever lived, is now flaunting the principles of that same agitator."
>
> (Ibid.)

Urging the protestors to respect the sanctity of the church, Howe preached Christ redeemer and revolutionary from the pulpit of the Cathedral of the Immaculate Conception. Blackwood followed, taking up the same theme. 'The Church,' he said, 'had betrayed the message of its founder, Jesus Christ' (Ibid.). The time had come to drive the moneylenders out of the Temple and proclaim the true message of salvation and social justice at the heart of the Gospels. After the speeches, the Black Power congregation engaged in a symbolic cleansing of the temple. The slogan on everyone's lips was 'Power! Power!'; black cloths were draped over the statues of the virgin and the Apostle Paul; a placard proclaiming 'FREEDOM NOW' was hung on St Peter's outstretch hand, the hand which held the keys to the Kingdom of God; St Francis of Assisi, the intercessor for the common people, held a similar banner (Ibid.).

Howe left the Cathedral before the end of the occupation, as clerics debated Black Power and mysteries of the faith with the revolutionary congregation. After about an hour, the demonstrators left the Cathedral and took their protest to business centres on Broadway and South Quay (Meeks 1996: 13). The day ended with speeches in Woodford Square, a place that would later take on a revolutionary significance as the People's Parliament. Before the day ended, Howe could already see the significance of what had happened: a revolution had started.

Acceleration

The events of 26 February showed that the Black Power Movement was much more than the inconsequential nuisance the government had supposed. With hindsight, the government's understanding of the potential of the movement is almost unintelligible, given the ongoing economic problems and the strength of feeling on campus. In a sense, the student movement had picked up from where Williams had left off. Howe recalls the power of Williams' 'Massa day done' speech of 1961. It asserted the independence of the people of Trinidad and Tobago and set Howe's heart beating (Howe 2011k). However, Williams' economic strategy rested on attracting large-scale investment from America and Britain (Palmer 2006: 284) and, in that sense, ceding economic power to white businessmen. As far as black radicals were concerned, Williams had reneged on his promises; the country was independent in name only. For Granger, 'independent' Trinidad was a place where one master had replaced another, where 'BLACK MASSA, DOING WHITE MASSA WUK' (Granger 1969: 65). That said, the economic imperialism was only part of the problem. At a deeper level, there was the issue of 'Cultural Slavery' (Darbeau 1969: 63). Writing in *East Dry River*, a mimeographed news-sheet produced by NJAC, Darbeau argued that the government had detached itself from the people due to a lack of a cultural base:

> Political leaders divorce themselves from their black brothers when they get into Parliament because the black community lacks the cultural bonds which make people love each other, respect each other and understand each other.
>
> (Ibid.)

Fundamentally, Darbeau continued, the new government had crushed the people's spirit of independence:

> We are guilty of the same self-contempt, self-despisement and servility to the whites (all stemming from the white values which dominate the society) which lead the Williams band to hold cocktail parties at the Country Club and trample the interests of the Black Community.
>
> (Ibid., 64)

Williams had inspired a generation and given voice to their desire for freedom (Palmer 2006: 285). A decade on, Williams' neocolonial settlement was not enough for them, but Williams did not fully understand the power of the forces that he had helped to create. Desperately, Williams sought to ban a number of 'subversive' books, including the works of his former teacher and friend C. L. R. James, and his own radical work of history *Capitalism and Slavery* on the basis that 'they might give these half educated Negroes the wrong idea' (Dhondy 2001: 142).

The government could not let the protest of 26 February go unchallenged. The demonstration had focused on the symbols of post-colonial oppression: the institutional Church, the bank, the business district; symbols of three institutions that could be plausibly described as white-dominated (Ibid.). In this sense, protests constituted a direct challenge to Williams' Trinidad. Therefore, 27 February began with a series of dawn raids as the nine leading members of the demonstration, including Granger, Darbeau, Blackwood and Weekes, were arrested. The defendants were charged with 'disorderly behaviour in a place of worship' (Oxaal 1971: 23) and refused bail (Kambon 1988: 199). There was also a government-backed media offensive against the movement. From the government's point of view, the occupation of the Cathedral was a gift. Statements were issued and headlines written appealing to the religious convictions of the populous. Now it was the government's turn to sermonize, condemning the 'desecration' of the holy place by lawless hooligans. 'No demonstration,' the *Trinidad Guardian* opined, 'anywhere has a right to degenerate into the level of desecration and disorder'. 'No self-respecting citizen,' the Editorial continued, 'relishes the thought of an unruly mob wandering around town at random from place to place' (27 February 1970). Yet the government had miscalculated. The arrests turned a protest of hundreds into a movement of thousands. Having spent 24 hours in prison, the nine were granted bail (Kambon 1988: 199). By the time they were released, the campaign for the nine had already begun.

The first wave of protest hit on 4 March. A demonstration of 10,000 people marched from Woodford Square to 'Shanty Town', one of the worst slums in the capital. The destination of the protest was symbolic. Granger explained, 'We are going to Shanty Town . . . because every black man in this country is a Shanty Town!' (*Trinidad Guardian*, 5 March 1970). Granger also imbued the arrests with symbolic significance. The arrests were made under 'slave laws' drawn up by the British in the 1840s (Oxaal 1971: 32). Clearly, he argued, colonialism was alive and well in Trinidad. In that sense, as the *Trinidad Guardian* reported, the protest of 4 March was about much more than the arrest of nine radicals, it was an 'attack upon the "White racist power structure and its black tools"' (Ibid.). The *Express* concurred, the original aims of 26 February has been subsumed by a wider movement demanding fundamental change. The sheer scale of the demonstration was captured in the headlines the next day. The *Express* called it 'Mammoth'. All commentators agreed on the disciplined and peaceful nature of the protests (Kambon 1988: 200).

The strength of the protest intensified over the next 2 days. On 5 March, the demonstrators were charged by mounted police outside the court where Granger, Darbeau, Weekes and their co-defendants were standing trial. Protestors fleeing police violence smashed windows in downtown Port-of-Spain, and a ministerial residence was petrol-bombed (Meeks 1998: 19). The trial was inconclusive. The nine were released and the case postponed. March 6 saw even greater crowds, between 14,000 and 20,000, marching to San Juan, and Granger openly 'declaring "war" on the establishment' (Pantin 1990: 59). Granger declared the demonstration a march of liberation and a march of anger. Nonetheless, the day passed without violence. Property was destroyed in the evening. Eyewitness reports stated that the 'police on duty had stood by and done nothing' (Ibid.), the implication being that the violence was the work of *agents provocateurs*.

Spontaneity, discipline and leadership

Ivar Oxaal, the first writer to produce an extended scholarly treatment of the events of 1970, notes that the emphasis was on spontaneous action during the revolution. In this sense, he argues that the Trinidad's Black Power revolution 'could qualify as an eminently Jamesian revolutionary moment' (Oxaal 1971: 24). This is very much the way Howe sees it. The events of March had made insurrection the order of the day, and as an intellectual, following Fanon, Howe interpreted this as a sure sign that colonialism in Trinidad was finally dying. Howe took his cue from the people. What, then, was the relationship between the intellectuals, the would-be leaders of the movement and the masses? 'This,' Howe comments, 'is where CLR is a genius'; it is not simply that the intellectuals follow where the people lead. More significantly, when the people move, the intellectuals themselves are freed, freed from old ideas, old categories and intellectual constraints. The role of the intellectual in these circumstances is to reflect and give voice to the agenda that emerges spontaneously from the masses (Howe 2011k).

There were several groups and a number of individuals who either led or tried to lead the people during the revolution. NJAC was preeminent. The movement, as noted above, had coalesced in solidarity with the students of Sir George Williams University. It was formed on the St Augustine Campus of the University of the West Indies. The founders included Granger, the president of the Student Guild and Darbeau. The group's focus was broad, comprehending 'the students in Canada, British action in Anguilla and non-action in Zimbabwe, racism, foreign domination of the economy', among other causes (Kambon 1988: 194).

Tapia House was another self-proclaimed centre of the Black Power Movement that emerged from the university. It was founded by George Best, a Cambridge-educated economist. Best was more of an academic than an activist. Kambon describes his rhetorical style as a long-winded mix of 'academic terminology interspersed with popular phrases, folk sayings and sports analogies . . .' (Kambon 1988: 174). Best supported Black Power, but was critical of spontaneous mass action. In essence, Best believed that the protestors understood neither the situation nor the effects of their actions (Meeks 1998: 20). Needless to say, James, who was in Britain during the revolution, was highly critical of Best's approach (Oxall 1971: 85).

Another group associated with the movement, for a time at least, were the Black Panthers. The Panthers were an extremely small group who wore the black berets and the black gloves associated with the American Panther aesthetic. Their leader Aldwyn Primus, a founding member of NJAC, played an ambiguous role in the events of 1970. According to *Tapia*, he was a powerful speaker who was 'able to hold the attention of thousands. . . . His shouts of power were hysterical and orgasmic. They electrified the crowd' (*Tapia*, 21 July 1974). Whatever the gifts of their leader, as a group, the Panthers were too small to bring about any meaningful change (Kambon 1988: 202).

Howe worked primarily within the OIWU as deputy editor of *The Vanguard*. During 1969, Wally Look Lai became editor with Darbeau as his deputy. However, Darbeau's increasing involvement with NJAC lead to his departure from *The Vanguard*. Howe took his place. Look Lai was an Oxford graduate who had formerly written for the *Express*. Howe and Look Lai got on well. There was an ideological affinity as both men were Jamesians, Look Lai having been a member of James' study group in London in 1962 which also involved Walter Rodney, Richard Small, Norman Girvan and others. Look Lai would collect Howe from his parent's home early in the morning in his Volkswagen, and together they would drive to the paper's headquarters in San Fernando. The office was small; Howe and Look Lai effectively ran the paper between them. Howe operated on his own initiative, on occasion referring to Look Lai for retrospective permission when right wingers in the union complained about his radicalism. Day-to-day, Howe's prime task was writing features and editing a mass of contributions from the 'shop floor' (Howe 2011k). Kambon credits *The Vanguard* with being 'a major voice of the revolution' during the heady days of 1970 (Kambon 1988: 236). In addition to *The Vanguard*, numerous news-sheets sprang up during the revolution. These included 'St James Youth Voice; Black Drum; [and] Let The Black Woman Talk' (Pantin 1990: 59).

It was in the pages of *The Vanguard* that Howe revealed his vision for a liberated Trinidad. Central to this was popular control of the nation's oil industry. This was not nationalization in the traditional sense of state control. Rather, Howe envisaged the socialization of the industry, placing the industry under the direct control of the workers. Behind closed doors, Howe was also discussing other aspects of post-revolutionary Trinidad with Look Lai and the radical young army officers Rex Lasalle and Raffique Shah. In this forum, discussions turned to restoring order in the wake of governmental collapse. Howe advocated an alliance between his own organization and the army, the creation of a kind of citizens' militia – a model of socialization that had been advocated by radicals from Rousseau to Marx.

On 12 March, Howe took part in the 'Long March' and also covered it on behalf of *The Vanguard*. The demonstration was a 28-mile march from Port-of-Spain to the sugar belts of Caroni County. The slogan was 'Indians and Africans Unite Now'. Around 6,000 set off again from Woodford Square. Bhadase Maraj, spokesman for the East Indian community, head of the All Trinidad Sugar Estates and Factory Workers Trade Union and the leader of the Democratic Labour Party, had opposed the initiative, threatening marchers with violence if they entered the belts (Bennett 1989: 139). The march was of particular concern to Howe, who had an ongoing desire for Afro-Indian unity. The results were mixed. Maraj kept up his defiance. However, as Pantin records, 'a scattering of mostly young Indian men and women stood at the side of the road to welcome the demonstrators with applause' (Pantin 1990: 65). Others, including Raffique Shah's father, offered the marchers refreshments. The march was disciplined, almost silent, and as Pantin argues, 'it made its point: AFRICANS AND INDIANS could UNITE' (Ibid.). In Meeks' words, at the very least, 'the march served to breach a psychological barrier' between the two communities (Meeks 1998: 22).

Howe's report in *The Vanguard* starts by noting how 'official society' sought to undermine the purpose of the march, Afro-Indian unity. Notwithstanding Bhadese and his 'Al Capone style threats of violence', or the warning of anarchy issued by the Attorney General in his new role as Williams' henchman, the march had succeeded in laying the foundation of unity between the two communities. Howe declared that the triumph of the Long March pointed to 'the unmistakeable and irrefutable fact that a new society is being born, one which is battling on all sides for expression' (*The Vanguard*, 21 March 1970).

Ebb and flow

Williams, who had remained silent about the mass protest following the occupation of the Cathedral, addressed the nation on 23 March. His speech was aired on television and radio. Its conciliatory tone was a surprise to many. He acknowledged the right to march, and in an attempt to regain the initiative, he sacked his industrial minister – a man who had previously accused the Black Power Movement of being directed by communists. He announced new programmes to address unemployment, which were to be financed from a new 5 per cent tax on industry, and demanded an end to racism in the labour market (Bennett 1989: 140). More daring still was the announcement that he intended to extend his nationalization plans, promising that in 10 years, the government's economic control would exceed Castro's control over Cuba's economy (Pantin 1990: 73).

Williams' promises had little effect. According to the *Express*, the speech did nothing to dispel the view that the government was on the side of business and other vested interests (*Express*, 1 April 1970). Howe, too, argues that by this time, Williams had no authority among the people on the streets.

Once again, Williams was out of step with the amazing transformation that was going on in the country. The atmosphere was extraordinary. Howe argues that the protests, the marches, the Peoples' Parliament on Woodford Square, all the grass-roots activism embodied the spirit of Malcolm X's famous adage 'by any means necessary'. Something had finished. Massa day really was done, at least in the minds and hearts of the crowds. Remarkably, the revolution brought healing to the nation. On a personal level, Howe recalls how people who had not spoken for years were reconciled; relationships that had ossified were reinvigorated. Politically too, there was an end of internecine strife: 'all that tension between Indian and African, it swept it away'. There was a unity between the young and the old. There was anger, too, and what Howe described as an explosion of the personality, but machismo was in retreat. Traditional and formal modes of address gave way to 'brother' and 'sister'. Everywhere there was discussion and debate; the revolution changed the very rhythm of people's speech. For Howe, Trinidad was remade. It changed from a place where 'all thought had ceased' to a place where people were plunged into a 'whirlpool of reason'. As a result, people were speaking with greater deliberation, with longer pauses between their words. 'This turned into a style. They wouldn't answer for a second or two, and then answer. There was a social patience. . . . It was *almost*, not quite almost, as if we had turned into angels.' What Howe was witnessing, in nascent state, was what James had been arguing for, for so long: a democracy like that of ancient Athens was emerging on the streets of Trinidad. The discussion was so intense, Howe concludes, that it would have been no surprise to bump into a latter-day Plato or Pericles on the street corner (Howe 2011k).

As might be expected, the British High Commissioner, Richard Hunt, saw things differently. A month or so after the revolution had been put down, he reported back to Britain that the tone of the radicals had been bellicose in the extreme. '[K]illing.' he noted, 'was a commonplace theme in the speeches in Woodford Square.' 'The NJAC leaders', he continued, 'would, I imagine, like to frighten away the white community – if necessary, or for preference, by killing some of them.' This was not what Howe saw, and it should be noted that Hunt was only brought in as High Commissioner after the revolution was over. White capitalists were, as far as Howe could see, 'the least of our worries', they were far away in New York, London or Toronto. Political scientist William R. Lux concurs. 'The paradox here', he argues, speaking of Black Power across the Caribbean, 'is

Figure 2 Howe speaking during the Freedom March in Woodford Square, Port-of-Spain, Trinidad, April 1969.

that these riots, revolts and boycotts are not against white foreign oppressors but against black governments and leaders' (Lux 1972: 214). That is not to say that there was no violence against white people. Howe recalls one incident when a white merchant abused one of his black customers, telling him to 'move your black fucking self out of here'. A crowd gathered outside the business to protest, Granger addressed them, relating the incident, ending his narration, 'and then . . . and then . . . and then . . .' and in seconds the business was burning. Significantly, the violence was against property rather than a person, and this incident was the exception, not the rule. The vast majority of reports, even in the conservative press, stress the discipline and peaceful nature of the protests (Howe 2011k).

The state, by contrast, routinely used violence against people. Early April saw the base of the movement widen. On 1 April, the National Association of Steelbandsmen, traditional supporters of Williams' PNM, joined the revolution. Then, on 4 April, the OWTU officially announced its support for the movement (Meeks 1998: 26). Conservatives in the government urged repression and editorials in the right-wing press demanded the restoration of law and order. It was in this context that Basil Davis, a young man of 22, was shot dead by police in Port-of-Spain during a demonstration. Police violence had accompanied the protests from the beginning, but Davis was the first to be killed and, as a consequence, the first 'martyr' of the revolution (MacDonald 1989: 164).

Davis' funeral on 9 April became the focal point of the revolution. Estimates vary, but somewhere between 30,000 and 100,000 people turned out to mourn his loss (Bennett 1989: 141). Howe, who had been playing a discreet role since 26 February, once again stepped into the limelight. He was asked to read a poem at the funeral. The significance of the event was massive, and Howe chose the moment to bring his organization to the attention of the public.

In the lead up to the funeral, he also laid down a challenge:

I said let's wear a scarlet red dashiki top, and black trousers, black basketball boots. And I wanted to see how many of them would rise to the occasion and get the money and get it made, and quickly . . . when we came into the Basil Davis funeral there were a minimum of 10,000 people at the beginning. And there was this huge gasp, when I walked in with my organisation. "What the fuck is this?" It looked kind of military. . . . It was half men and half young women, they hadn't seen that either . . .

(Howe 2012k)

As Howe looked out, he saw 200 people wearing the red, which symbolized Davis's blood, and black, the traditional colour of mourning. It was a deliberate strategy to recruit women. At the back of Howe's mind was the impact of the feminist movement in America and France, particularly its role in the French revolution of 1968. 'You couldn't get anywhere without women, and they responded immediately.' But Howe's commitment to involving women in the revolution was not based purely on the experience of 1968. Fanon had produced a theoretical account of women in the Algerian revolution which also informed Howe's strategy. *Studies in a Dying Colonialism*, sets out a description and an analysis of the Algerian civil war, which stresses the role of women. In essence, it argued that the moment civil war became revolution was the moment at which the women took an active part in the fight against French colonialism, as the involvement of women itself marked a fundamental transformation in the social order of the colony.

Emergency and rebellion

For a time, the momentum for change seemed unstoppable. Following the funeral, Trinidad's progressive unions began to assert themselves. In mid-April, the strikes started. On 17 April, around 300 workers at the Water and Sewerage Authority downed tools (Kiely 1996: 123). Two days later, a strike started at the

Brechin Castle sugar estate. Both strikes were fundamentally political rather than economic; both were acts of solidarity with the Black Power Movement. The sugar strike was highly significant as it demonstrated the unity between the Indian sugar workers and black-African protestors. Buoyed by this turn of events, Weekes let it be known that he hoped the oil workers would soon join the strike. In the third week of April, almost every business, factory and government agency was hit by at least one strike (Harvey 1974: 46).

It was in this context, with a general strike on the horizon, that Howe proposed a new radical slogan: 'Seize Power and send for James.' The demonstrations and protests had changed Trinidad, but for Howe, protest was not an end in itself. At some point, protest had to turn into a new politics. Howe's connection to the shop floor through *The Vanguard*, his connection to the grass roots through his 'organisation', his participation in the Long March and the funeral of Basil Davis led him to the slogan, not as a call to arms, but as a theoretical point: the Williams government had lost its authority, the time was right for the people to shape the destiny of their nation. Howe was not alone in sensing the imminent fall of the government, the British High Commissioner advised Williams that 'Weekes would be unstoppable unless a State of Emergency was imposed' (NA FCO 63/594).

Following an emergency meeting of the Cabinet, the government declared a State of Emergency on 21 April. Police rounded up the primary leaders of the movement immediately, with the exception of Granger, who evaded capture for a few days. Weekes, Nunez, Darbeau and nine others were then taken under police guard, via Coast Guard patrol boat to Nelson Island. Howe too was targeted. Armed police raided his parents' house on a mission to arrest him. Yet, he stayed out of police hands by making sure he never slept under the same roof more than once. His strategy was simple. He would go to a friend's house, feign illness, sleep over and leave at first light. The story of the confrontation between the police and Howe's parents has entered Howe family lore. The police marched into the house with guns and crowbars. Their initial search yielded nothing, so they started to poke about in the under stair's cupboard. This was too much for Howe's mother. The usually demure Mrs Howe gave the police commissioner a piece of her mind: 'What do think, my son is a fucking cockroach!'. That said, she picked up a crowbar and threw it at the commissioner. Outside, the Commissioner of Police levelled with Howe's father: 'next time you see your son', he said, 'he may be in a box'. The Reverend Howe responded in kind: 'If you make those kind of threats against my son, it will be you who ends up in a box.' Howe was aware of the threats, but he did not take them seriously. There was a body of senior officers who, either due to the fact that they had grown up with Howe, or due to their commitment to the rule of law, would never sanction political assassinations (Howe 2011k).

Small-scale violence in Port-of-Spain was put down fairly quickly, as was an attempt to defy the State of Emergency at the Brechin Castle sugar works (Meeks 1998: 30). The State of Emergency was, however, more precarious than it seemed. It relied on the support of the military, but a significant section of the military refused to turn against their own people. The Trinidad and Tobago Regiment, a force of 750 men based at Teteron Bay in the north west of Trinidad, rebelled. A group of Sandhurst-trained junior officers led by young Lieutenants Raffique Shah, Rex Lasalle and Mike Barzie seized control of the Regiment and Tetron barracks, locking up the senior officers. From the outside, the purpose of the rebellion was initially unclear. In the immediate aftermath, rumours swept Port-of-Spain, that 'the army was coming over the hills' to support the rebels (Kambon 1998: 206). There was also talk that Williams had a helicopter on standby and was preparing to leave the country.

Howe's links to the army connected him to the very officers who had led the rebellion. He had met Shah and Lasalle through Look Lai. What's more, there had been an immediate rapport between Howe and Shah. Howe had grown up with Indians, and he 'had an ease with Raff that some others did not have'. A small group comprising Howe, Shah, Lasalle, Look Lai and UWI lecturer Franklin Harvey coalesced, meeting from time to time to discuss matters of political concern. The rapport was also political. Shah was a self-confessed revolutionary. Many of the junior officers, he recalls, considered themselves '"leftists" and "revolutionaries", although we weren't of the Marxist mould. Our heroes were Argentina-born, Cuban-internationalist Che Guevara, Martiniquan psychiatrist and writer Frantz Fanon, Malcolm X (whose autobiography was considered required reading at Teteron) and Guyanese professor Walter Rodney' (Shah 2011a). Howe was not alone in having connections to the army. As Shah put it: 'Most soldiers, although they came from a PNM family background, also had connections with the young men and women who formed the core of the protesters' (Shah 2011b). Due to his position in the army, Shah, regardless of his political sympathies, had to keep his distance from protests during the revolution. Nonetheless, speculation about the loyalties of the army was published in *The Vanguard* in mid-March.

Inside the base, the objectives of the mutiny were much clearer. For Shah, the purpose of the rebellion was first and foremost to prevent the army being used against the people of Trinidad. There were certainly people in the barracks who argued for an armed overthrow of the government, but this was never the object of those who led the rebellion (Shah 2011). For some time, Howe had anticipated a military rising against the government. Hearing of the rebellion, Howe assembled his organization as best he could and headed for St James, a town *en route* from Teteron to Port-of-Spain. Howe waited on the high street, in hope that the army would march to Port-of-Spain.

In Teteron, the rebels were losing ground. Pantin reported that a convoy of troops was ready to leave the base: '200-odd men who, battle-ready, appeared eager to begin the drive to Port of Spain.' However, Pantin mistook the objective. The regiment were heading to Camp Ogden, located on Long Circular Road in St James. Trinity, a Coast Guard boat which had opened fire on the ammunition bunker earlier in the morning, started firing again. This time, it targeted the troops leaving the base. The first attempt to leave the base was turned back, as was a second attempt later that morning. The rebels had the firepower to destroy the Trinity and the Courland Bay, a second Coast Guard vessel patrolling the bay, but the price would have been too high: it would have involved killing over 100 people. For Shah, there was no question: 'We would die for the revolution, but we would not kill for it' (Channel 4 2006). As a result, the rebels, who had already lost one man, returned to the base.

Howe waited on the St James High Street, backed by his organization, with the commissioner of the police on the other side of the road. He was in a strong position, so an arrest was out of the question. The situation was tense. The police commissioner, no doubt expecting to be swept away by the organized revolutionaries, asked, his voice trembling, what was going on. 'It's too early to say', was Howe's only response. Shah recalls that once the rebellion started, the soldiers had no contact with the movement beyond the barracks for a full 10 days. However, somehow a one-word message reached Howe telling him to 'retreat'. At this point, Howe saw the truth. The balance of power had shifted decisively in favour of the government. There would be no armed rebellion. The revolution was over. Perhaps sensing a change in Howe's mood, the police commissioner, with renewed confidence, came to the point: Was Howe waiting for the army? Howe responded: 'Do I look like an army man to you?'.

Epilogue

On learning of the mutiny, Williams contacted foreign governments for assistance. International white power, that amorphous entity which had been blasted consistently during the revolution, solidified and agreed to aid the government. The British cabinet agonized over the decision, but in spite of their troubled consciences, they dispatched *HMS Jupiter* and *HMS Sirius* to shore up Williams' government, the latter carrying a detachment of Royal Marines who were authorized to defend British citizens and British property in Trinidad. America sent munitions, a helicopter carrier and placed five other vessels on standby. Venezuela too sent warships, one to the waters off Port-of-Spain, the other to the barracks at Teteron Bay (Palmer 2006: 239–40). On the morning of 22 April, the rebels in Teteron Bay started negotiations with the government.

Howe spent the next couple of days evading the police and trying to arrange to leave the country. This was a retreat, not a desertion. Howe remained loyal to his friend, and once he was safely away, he started raising money to provide for the defence of Shah and the other officers who were charged with treason. All would receive lengthy custodial sentences, reduced on appeal, and go on to play important roles in shaping Trinidad's future. In Shah's case, this involved becoming a leader of the Sugar Cane Workers Union, and helping to form and lead, with George Weeks, the United Labour Front which came second in the 1976 Election. In the final analysis, Howe had no need to escape. Old friends from QRC who had risen through the ranks of the customs and immigration service allowed him to leave the country unimpeded. Howe headed for Amsterdam and then returned to London.

Notes

1 For a detailed account of the George Williams Event, see Eber (1969).
2 The government's attitude to Black Power may well have been more nuanced than this statement implies. Indeed, the ban placed by the government on Stokely Carmichael's visit to the Trinidad in 1969 indicates that there were concerns about the movement's potential.

7

A Resting Place in Babylon: Frank Crichlow and the Mangrove

The Mangrove Restaurant was part of no master plan. It was not set up by government fiat, funded by the GLC or founded on the initiative of the Race Relations Board. Black people who wanted to find a place to live or who were having trouble with pig-headed landlords went to the Mangrove. Recent arrivals who wanted to know where to source the ingredients for their favourite dishes went there too, as did black radicals who wanted to discuss the revolution in the Caribbean, or the fortunes of Angela Davis, Stokely Carmichael or Huey P. Newton. 'Whitebeats' dissatisfied with square English culture sought out the Mangrove in search of the best music, good food and radical politics. And so, organically and spontaneously, the Mangrove became the centre of the black community in Notting Hill as well as a hub for London's counterculture.

The emergence of the Mangrove did not go unnoticed. The Restaurant, 'a resting place in Babylon' (Sivanandan 1982: 33), had quite a different significance for the local police. For the 'heavy mob', a group of police who, according to locals, used their authority to intimidate Notting Hill's black community, there was no distinction between black radicalism and criminality. Proceeding on this assumption, the local police raided the Mangrove repeatedly, driving away its customers. For Howe, this was nothing less than a state-sponsored attempt to close the Restaurant and, in so doing, destroy the heart of the community. Howe's solution to the problem was to meet the police on their turf. The police had invaded the Mangrove; now it was time to march on the police stations. The raids led to the march, the march to arrests and the arrests to a trial: the most sensational political trial of the decade, which turned Black Power into a *cause célèbre*, lifted the lid on police racism in Notting Hill and pushed Howe into the media spotlight.

Frank Crichlow, the Mangrove and the Rio

Frank Crichlow owned and ran the Mangrove. Crichlow had emigrated from Trinidad to Britain in 1952 at the age of 21.[1] Initially, he worked for British Rail, maintaining station gas lamps until 1955, when he became a bandleader with The Starlight Four. The band played regularly at a club in Stamford Hill, North London, run by a Guyanese impresario known as Dr Mooksang. The Starlight Four were successful for several years, making appearances on radio, television and in a cinema advert. However, by the late 1950s, a fall in bookings led to the band's dissolution, and Crichlow ploughed his earnings into El Rio, a small coffee bar in Westbourne Park Road, Notting Dale (Phillips and Phillips 1999: 237fn).

The Rio was the favourite meeting place for local West Indians, thrill-seeking nonconformist upper-class 'slummers' and white kids searching for the hedonistic scene created in Colin MacInnes' London Trilogy. The atmosphere in the Rio owed much to Vincent Bute, who sourced the latest Blue Note LPs and EPs to play in the café. According to the filmmaker Horace Ové, '[t]he Rio was the first black restaurant in the Grove', and therefore, it quickly became an informal centre for the local black community (Green 2012: 56). It was to the Rio that black people came to organize in the face of the Notting Hill Riots in 1958. Along with the Calypso club near St Stephen's Gardens and the Notting Hill night club Fiesta One, run by Trinidadian Larry Ford, the Rio was a place where West Indians could socialize until the early hours.

Howe's friendship with Crichlow began at the Rio. Upon his arrival in Britain, Howe made straight for Notting Hill. With no fixed residence, he moved from one place to another around Westbourne Park Road, always one step ahead of the rent collectors. During his abortive period as a law student, Howe was one of many who spent their leisure hours around the Rio. The café was part of London's fashionable nightlife. Indeed, there was a well-trodden path between The Roaring Twenties, a club on Carnaby Street, and the Rio. The Roaring Twenties featured the resident DJ, Wilbert Augustus Campbell, who was better known as Count Suckle. Campbell had moved to Britain from Jamaica in 1952 and by the early 1960s, he had become a permanent fixture at The Roaring Twenties and Paddington's Q Club. Campbell was famous for the 'Count Suckle Sound System' which played an edgy mix of American frat-rock and Jamaican ska and reggae. Apparently, it was common for clubbers to dance into the small hours at The Roaring Twenties and then finish off their night out at the Rio. Money was tight for the student Howe who could only afford to visit Count

Suckle's club perhaps once a month. The Rio was a more regular haunt, indeed he 'spent most of the evenings and weekends at the Rio Coffee Bar in Notting Hill' (*NS*, 29 May 1998).

Spending time at the Rio threw Howe into the path of some of the luminaries who frequented the café. This included the model and showgirl Christine Keeler and her one-time lover, Jamaican-born jazz pianist 'Lucky' Aloysius Gordon. Other patrons included two white radicals, novelist Colin MacInnes and Richard Neville, editor of the countercultural magazine *Oz*. Howe got on well with both and recalls feeling considerable warmth towards MacInnes. Apparently, one of the reasons that MacInnes frequented the Mangrove was to pick up young black men. On one occasion, MacInnes sexually propositioned Howe. Howe told him to 'fuck off' but the event didn't spoil their friendship; indeed, Howe recalls that MacInnes was attractive precisely because he saw no limits or boundaries in his relationship with black men (Ibid.). Howe acknowledges that MacInnes was a friend of Notting Hill's black community. It was MacInnes, after all, who initiated the legal charity Defence as a free legal service, supported by Crichlow and Michael X, for black people who had been arrested or harassed by the police. Prior to its creation, black people often struggled to find lawyers to act for them and when they did, were often pressurized to drop complaints of police abuse.

The Rio was associated with a number of prominent 1960s' love affairs between 'society-girls' and local West Indian men. Christine Keeler met her West Indian boyfriends 'Lucky' Gordon and Johnny Edgecombe at the Rio, sparking a series of events that eventually ended in the Profumo scandal (Williams 2000: 88). In the wake of the Profumo scandal, the press descended on Notting Hill. This media attention affected Howe profoundly:

> Reporters converged on terrain that they knew next to nothing about. They were not averse to filling in missing details from their imaginations: personalities were reviled, a whole Caribbean community abused. I wrote to the editor of one of the nationals, querying the veracity of much of their reports. I eventually received a visit from strange men in grey suits who treated me as someone who was active in undermining British security.
>
> (*NS*, 29 May 1998)

The Profumo affair put the Rio on the map and from that point it was subject to continual police harassment. Charge sheets preserved at the National Archives record that Crichlow was regularly accused of minor offences (NA CRIM 1/5522 3). In the 7 years of the Rio's operation, Crichlow was successfully prosecuted nine times. The majority concerned permitting gambling on his premises; other offences included refusing to admit police to the café, bad language and 'Permitting music and dancing' without a licence (Ibid.).

Police harassment of the Rio was just one example of the aggressive targeting of Notting Hill's West Indian clubs, cafés and organizations during this period. It contained many of the shebeens and gambling houses set up by unemployed working-class West Indians in the early 1950s. Howe frequented the shebeens as they offered cheap entertainment – 'bottles in someone's flat, young men wanting to dance until sunlight was in our eyes at 9 or 10 in the morning. The girls were Australian, Swedish, whatever – it was black men and white girls – mine was Italian. That's how it was' (*NS*, 29 May 1998). The media portrayed the shebeens as criminal haunts, dens of iniquity or brothels. In reality, as Howe has pointed out, this was a myth (*RT*, 1972: 333). The real issue seems to have been the threat they represented to mainstream norms. The shebeens were free from the tyranny of the clock. They served alcohol at all hours and provided the venue for round-the-clock jazz, bluebeat and ska. They were patronized predominantly by West Indian workers keen to escape the racism and strict hours of local pubs. Similarly, the gambling houses where para pinto was played throughout the night compared favourably with the drab state-governed conformity of the English bingo hall.

It was against this backdrop of rising tension, created by the media and politicians' attacks on Notting Hill's West Indian community, that the 1958 Race Riots occurred. It is now known that the rioting, which broke out in August 1958, was manufactured and co-ordinated by white racist groups keen to exploit anti-immigrant feeling and was not a spontaneous reaction of the local community (Bloom 2004: 378). The riots saw crowds of between 400 and 700 attack black homes and businesses around Bramley Road, Notting Dale, amid shouts of 'We will kill the blacks.' The toxic, racist atmosphere pervaded Notting Hill for nearly a year after the riots and finally culminated with the murder of the 32-year-old carpenter Kelso Cochrane in New Road in May 1959. The failure of the police to defend the West Indian community from the lynch mobs, or to find and arrest Cochrane's murderer, resulted in a widespread loss of confidence in the police by West Indian inhabitants of Notting Hill (*RT*, 1972: 38). Howe recalls that at every shebeen and gambling house, the unemployed armed themselves to fight off the marauding racists. Overnight, these institutions became physical bases from which the community defended itself. The riots simultaneously undermined the credibility of the police and cemented the relationship between the unemployed hustlers and the West Indian working class. If these men were outlaws, they were 'social bandits' who, in Hobsbawn's words, were seen as men to be admired, helped and supported by the community, rather than gangs drawn from the professional underworld (Hobsbawn 2009: 20).

The unrest cast a long shadow. On arrival in Notting Hill, Howe was reminded that England was not the genteel and civilized place he had once imagined. Rather, he describes it as a place of great brutality. He had already been told that it was safer to stay off the streets at night for fear of racist attacks which the authorities showed no interest in preventing. Howe soon learnt that the police were part of the problem. He describes the local officers as having a 'colonial mentality', as viewing the local black community as 'savages', people who were not yet fully civilized and more prone to licentiousness and criminality than their white counterparts. This view was summed up in *The Hustler*, a community paper: 'How does the policeman control the ghetto? Like any colonialist trying to control an alien country of which he is secretly afraid, he does it by two means: by a direct show of force, and by corrupting and subverting the people' (*The Hustler*, 24 May 1968).

Police harassment of The Rio prompted Crichlow to move premises, and in March 1968, he opened the Mangrove at 8 All Saints Road, Notting Hill, a much bigger and classier venture. Howe recalls that the Mangrove was a fully fledged restaurant, and that Crichlow served real West-Indian cuisine, learnt from his mother. The new restaurant retained the Rio's reputation for radical chic while losing the association with sleazier patrons such as Profumo and his associate Stephen Ward. The Mangrove features briefly in Horace Ové's *Pressure*, which was filmed around Notting Hill in the mid-1970s. For the most part, the film presents Notting Hill as the epitome of 1970s' decay, but the Mangrove alone stood out. Over the door was a crystalline green neon sign bearing the restaurant's name. A purple awning and glossy paintwork completed the classic 1970s' colour scheme. Against the backdrop of general dilapidation, the Mangrove looked positively space-aged. The interior was also distinctive. Photographs from the early 1970s show that the restaurant was decorated with traditional African art as well as with pictures of hip musicians. The new restaurant attracted Notting Hill's fashionable middle class, including figures such as Mary Tuck, one-time assistant editor of *Vogue*, and Lord Gifford QC, a radical human rights lawyer. It was also the haunt of doyens of London's counterculture like Richard Neville and other writers associated with *Oz* magazine. Its reputation attracted celebrities such as Nina Simone, Sammy Davis Jr, Marvin Gaye, Jimi Hendrix, Diana Ross and the Supremes, the Four Tops, Vanessa Redgrave and the cast of the hit TV show *The Avengers*.

Howe was a regular at the Mangrove. On his return from Trinidad in April 1970, he got a job working on the Mangrove's till. His affinity for the Mangrove is easy to explain. On one level, it was local. Howe lived in Oxford Gardens in Ladbroke Grove – less than two miles away from the restaurant – and he needed the money to provide for his family. On another, the Mangrove was an example of the kind of racial integration that Howe advocated: integration on black terms, integration without the loss of cultural identity and integration without being relegated to the status of second-class citizens. It was also a centre of black self-organization. In this sense, the restaurant was the realization, on a small scale, of much that Howe was committed to promoting.

The Mangrove was also frequented by black intellectuals and radicals such as C. L. R. James and Lionel Morrison. On occasion, James seems to have held court there, using it as a base from which to lecture, attracting crowds large enough to fill half of the restaurant. Following the rise of Black Power in Britain, the Mangrove took on a new significance, serving as a place where the new generation of black radicals could go to discuss ideological matters, the exploits of the American Panthers, or share news of the black struggle in America, Britain and the Caribbean. At the same time, the Mangrove attracted the same unemployed hustlers who had been loyal customers of the Rio. These three groups, the black working class, black intellectuals and the radical whites, would become the coalition that would take on the police campaign against the Mangrove.

The Mangrove, like the Rio before it, quickly became the heart of Notting Hill's black community. The *International Times*, a publication that was associated with the counterculture of the 1960s, described the Mangrove thus:

> The Mangrove Restaurant, All Saints Rd., W11. Is the central eating place for the black community In Notting Hill. It is the one clean, late night social centre which also serves good food, and black families use it as a meeting place as well as a place of entertainment.
>
> (*IT*, 1–11 September 1969)

It is still possible to get a feel for the Mangrove's role in the community from the pages of *The Hustler*, 'a tiny community newspaper' that was published on the premises (Howe 1998). Edited by Courtney Tulloch, *The Hustler* was an eight-page fortnightly magazine launched in May 1968. *The Hustler* provided a window to life in Notting Hill, or 'the Grove' as it was better known to the locals. It dealt with local politics, containing advice on housing and campaigned about the standards in local schools. It had adverts for shops such as Karakata & Son, which stocked 'African and Caribbean Food' (*The Hustler*, 24 May 1968). Regular features included SOULSOUND, which listed the latest and the best singles and LPs, horoscopes and a cartoon, '[t]he adventures of Seraphina', 'a mysterious young Creole with magic powers' who was attempting to bring down an international conspiracy headed by the 'American-Soviet-Republic' (Ibid.). *The Hustler* also kept up a running commentary on international politics which regularly included the American Black Power Movement. The magazine reflected the coalition of black and white radicals who congregated at the Mangrove. Howe recalls that Tulloch's editorial efforts were supported by the several white journalists from 'the *Oz* pack', who brought their publishing experience to bear on the new magazine. For Howe, they were emblematic of a new interest in the black community in the Grove, an interest that was free from condescension.

'Under Siege'

The Mangrove, like the Rio before it, was soon subject to unwarranted police attention. Crichlow's restaurant was raided on numerous occasions. Each raid was predicated on the notion that the restaurant was selling drugs. Yet drugs were never found. For the Mangroves' patrons, the suggestion that Crichlow was a dealer, or that the restaurant was a hive of criminality, was preposterous. Writing to *The Times* in defence of the Mangrove, Colin MacInnes argued:

> I have dined perhaps 100 times in Mr Critchlow's [sic] establishments, and some 20 in the latest of these, the Mangrove. On no occasion have I seen knives flashing, pot puffing, or hip flasks being flourished. On the contrary, such is the command Mr Critchlow exercises over his premises, the atmosphere has been almost decorous: people eat, drink cokes and coffees, and pass the time of day, or more usually night.
>
> (25 September 1970)

Crichlow's propriety was well known, so much so that it became the focus of a joke that celebrated his character by parodying common racial stereotypes: '[h]is education is lacking: he's the only Trinidadian who doesn't know what a great draw of ganja is!' (*Independent*, 13 October 1992). Howe too states that there was no question of Crichlow being involved with drugs, 'no one in their right mind could have described the Mangrove as a drugs den. It was well run and obeyed the rules that governed such institutions' (*NS*, 29 May 1998). This is not to deny that some of the hustlers who were among the Mangrove's loyal customers had convictions for possessing or dealing drugs. Yet, the Mangrove was the last place that any of them would go to deal or take drugs. Crichlow's own anti-drugs stance and projects were well known within the community and would have resulted in the culprit being told to leave. Furthermore, it was common knowledge that the police had the Mangrove under continual surveillance. In fact, some of the clearest evidence of Crichlow's innocence comes from police activity itself: the Mangrove was continually raided, and evidence of drug dealing was never found.

The first raid against the Mangrove took place around 11 p.m. on 24 January 1969.[2] The police arrived with what they claimed was a search warrant. Its authenticity was never established, as the officers refused to allow the manager to examine it. The police also refused to allow the manager to phone Crichlow, who was not on the site at the time. The search yielded nothing. On hearing of the raid, Crichlow contacted the Notting Hill police, who denied any knowledge of the incident and referred him to the Notting Dale station. Officers at Notting Dale also denied any involvement, so Crichlow took up the matter with Scotland Yard. His persistence paid off, and Notting Hill's CID eventually acknowledged that they had instigated the raid.

The second raid took place in the summer of 1969. Again, there were major irregularities. The staff at the Mangrove protested at the police intrusion only to be manhandled by the attending officers. Again, the raid yielded no evidence of wrongdoing at the Mangrove and Crichlow was told that all charges against him would be dropped. This assurance raised concerns as Crichlow had not been informed that any charges had ever been made. What's more, the police subsequently used the raids themselves as evidence of the suspicious nature of the Mangrove in order to rescind Crichlow's licence for late-night trade. In so doing, the police threw their weight behind a local petition started by some white café owners to deny the Mangrove a late-night licence (*IT*, 1–11 August 1969). Paradoxically, the magistrate responsible for the decision dismissed the police 'evidence' while granting their request. From that point on, the Mangrove had to cease serving food at 11 p.m., a ruling seen as clearly discriminatory by the restaurant's patrons. MacInnes' letter to *The Times* complained that the Mangrove had been singled out and forced to close early 'in a city where any white with money can eat and drink legally into the small hours' (*Times*, 25 September 1970).

The ruling paved the way for the police's third raid in May 1970. On this occasion, Crichlow was arrested for '[u]sing premises at night without a licence' and for assaulting a police officer. Matters went from bad to worse, and over the next 6 weeks, the restaurant was raided on nine further occasions. Crichlow's case came to trial in September, about a month after the Mangrove demonstrations, and gained coverage in the national press. The *Times*, for example, indicates that police harassment was evident in the courtroom itself. The trial, which ostensibly concerned a minor breach of local licensing laws, became 'the centre of a large police security operation' with 'more than 20 policemen' patrolling the rooms adjacent to the court and four more at the front entrance (*Times*, 15 October 1970). Crichlow's defence lawyers argued that the Mangrove served no customers on the premises after 11 p.m., but did offer an all-night take-away service, in accord with GLC bylaws. Nonetheless, Crichlow was found guilty and fined a total of £225, including costs.

The final raid took place at 1 a.m. on 14 January 1971 and led to a further trial, again on the basis of licensing laws. The police presented evidence that on entering the Mangrove, they had found three people eating sweet corn and another six drinking tea. Crichlow's defence team, led by Tony Mohipp, demonstrated that there was no evidence of money changing hands, that the door of the café was locked and that the police did not have reasonable grounds for raiding the café in the first place. Clearly, Mohipp argued, there was nothing criminal about a few friends drinking tea together. The magistrate in the case acknowledged that the sentence would affect community relations. Nonetheless, in summing up, he delivered the following verdict: '[w]as the Mangrove used as a night café? I find that it was. I do not feel it is necessary for it to be open when a knock at the door will suffice. It is not necessary to prove that money changed hands.' Consequently, Crichlow was fined £25 and required to pay the legal costs. Crichlow left court with a transcript of the magistrate's decision in order to keep the possibility of an appeal open. However, he acknowledged that he was wary of taking further legal action, as he had been consistently denied legal aid and the legal costs were prohibitive (*TO*, 6 May 1971).

Crichlow's experience at the hands of West London's magistrates would not have come as a surprise to his legal team. A book published the following year by *Sunday Times* journalist Derek Humphry described the quality of some of the justice meted out by London's magistrates at the time as 'harsh and primitive'. He gave the following account of a day spent at Willesden Magistrates Court in North West London:

> The accused – mostly Irish or Black – duck in out of the dock and justice is dispensed in loud tones and with indecent speed. . . . Even the corridors outside are overcrowded, steamy, and the whole atmosphere is redolent of the

Parisian courts at the time of the French Revolution. Willesden Magistrates'
Court dispensing justice for the ghetto of what is Harlesden and Willesden is a
disturbing sight.

(Humphry 1972: 85)

The raids failed to prove that the Mangrove was the drugs den that the police
made it out to be. The two convictions that they secured were based solely on
reports of police officers themselves and were only obtained by ignoring the
eyewitness reports of the Mangrove's staff and patrons. That said, the consistent
harassment had achieved an extra-legal objective. When Crichlow left court
following his conviction in May 1971, he acknowledged that the constant
harassment had led to a decline in trade. The police had driven away many
regular customers. In the late 1960s, the Mangrove had been taking £100 a
night, but by mid-1971, Crichlow reported that he was lucky if he took a tenth
of that. Legal channels had failed, but Crichlow resolved to fight on.

Howe refused to stand idly by. His initial attempts to defend the Mangrove
from the police were journalistic. The first issue of *Black Dimension*, published
in February 1969, opened with an article by Howe. Entitled 'Police State in
West London', it situated the first attack on the Mangrove among similar
stories. The conclusion of the article detailed Howe's efforts to combat police
harassment:

We in BLACK DIMENSION have organised an ACTION COMMITTEE to wage
an unceasing struggle against this organised form of police oppression. We are in
the process of getting together a team of solicitors who would be available to black
people who have been arrested by the police. We have found out that a great deal of
police evidence goes without challenge in the absence of legal representation. The
committee realises that the battle cannot only be confined to the courts, involving
only those who have suffered at the hands of the police. The issue is as large, and
even larger than the community itself, and the mobilization of the masses of black
people behind the demands for an IMMEDIATE PUBLIC INVESTIGATION
into the NOTTING HILL GATE and HARROW ROAD POLICE STATION, and
the SACKINGS of officers concerned in cases of corruption and brutality, are
necessary stages in our struggle.

(GPI JOU 35/1)

On his return to Britain in April 1970, Howe found Crichlow in the midst of
his own campaign to halt the police interference. Crichlow was busy contacting
senior officials, meeting the local MP and talking to lawyers to try and end the
police harassment. Howe was unsympathetic to this approach. His experiences

working with Student Nonviolent Coordinating Committee (SNCC) in Brooklyn and with the oil workers in Trinidad had convinced him of the power of grass-roots campaigning. Howe had no time for Crichlow's approach and told him in no uncertain terms that he was wrong to be looking to white professionals to defend the Mangrove. Howe argued that he should turn to the community for support and take the struggle to the streets, reflecting his view that the black community should organize itself for self-defence.

Howe had no idea how Crichlow would react, as the two men were not close at the time. Crichlow knew Howe by repute as a 'red hot little trouble-making kind of a fellow'. Yet, he liked Howe's suggestion and agreed that a march was his best option though there was no denying this was a high-risk strategy. Howe and Crichlow were both aware that taking to the streets might give the police the pretext to close the Mangrove permanently. Howe recalls that Crichlow acknowledged this, but remained committed to the idea, a decision, which, he admits, showed considerable courage (Phillips and Phillips 1999: 279).

Howe's proposal was rooted in his experience of black radicalism in Trinidad and in America. As he later said:

> You have to organise yourself politically; you have to say my power is not only the power to defend myself in court, but the power of the population to defend itself by taking a collective action against the power structure of this country. And so it boils down to this in my view: that in order to deal with the situation with the police, one would have to unite the experience of brutality not only with the police, but brutality in housing, brutality in education, brutality in all areas of our social lives; unite those experiences in ourselves and that unity must be reflected in our organisation, organise ourselves politically, because this government is not going to take up its responsibility unless it sees people on the street.
>
> (Rosso 1973)

Howe's statement alludes to many ideas in black radical thinking of the time. First, in a tradition that owes much to Malcolm X, Howe stressed the right to self-defence, emphasizing that that right was not simply an individual right, but also that of a community to act collectively against aggression. Secondly, following Stokely Carmichael and the American Panthers, Howe focused his attack on the 'power structure'. His assertion that the impetus for change comes from the people on the streets rather than from the government also reflected a debt to James. In 1967, at the very beginning of the Black Power Movement in Britain, James had highlighted the police as the main target of the movement. In short, Howe saw the battle over the future of the Mangrove as an opportunity

Darcus Howe

to take the radical political strategies that he had seen in New York and Trinidad to the streets in London and, in so doing, put the black community of Notting Hill at the heart of the struggle for black rights.

Notes

1 According to Phillips and Phillips, the date was 1953. The Court records associated with the trial of the Mangrove Nine, however, state that he entered Britain in 1952.
2 The date given for the first raid differs in the agitational material produced at the time. Sometimes it is placed in January, sometimes in February. The earliest published account of the raid was contained in *The Hustler*, which gives the date quoted above.

8

Demonstration

The Mangrove Demonstration sent shockwaves through the British polity. Black Power, which had been such a potent political force in the United States and the Caribbean, was finally flexing its muscles in Britain. The press were horrified, ministers demanded immediate briefings and the Metropolitan Police, determined to stamp out black radicalism, took it as a cue to launch a series of raids on the leaders responsible for the protest. Howe was at the centre of the storm.

August 9

The demonstration took place on the second Sunday in August. Protesters started arriving outside the Mangrove at 2 p.m., and by 3 p.m., there were about 150 demonstrators ready to march. It was a fine day; Howe recalls '[e]ven the unpredictable British weather would come out in support of Black Power' (Howe 1980: 38). The American campaigner Angela Davis has talked of the joy that accompanies political struggle and this was apparent in Howe's speech, which kicked off the march. Talking from a makeshift platform, he addressed the crowd with a mixture of determination and humour:

> It has been for some time now that black people have been caught up in complaining to police about police; complaining to magistrates about magistrates; complaining to judges about judges; and complaining to politicians about politicians. We have become the own shapers of our destiny as from today. The precedent has been set, young kids have committed the most aggressive revolutionary action that has been known in this country for some time. They walked into a police station and took it over, but the objective must be clear.[1] The objective was to free their brothers. What our objective is today, and what it's going to continue to be is a concerted, determined attempt to prevent any infringement of our rights.
>
> (Rosso 1973)

The irony was not lost on his audience, who cheered and laughed as Howe lampooned the authorities and the black leaders who had sought redress through official channels. Photographs show Howe smiling as he talked, clearly in his element. Next to speak was Althea Jones-Lecointe, the driving force behind the British Black Panthers. Speeches over, the marchers, accompanied by 200 police officers, then set off from All Saint's Road, heading west along Lancaster Road to Notting Dale police station, the first of three stations that they were due to visit as part of the protest.

The demonstration was remarkable for several reasons. The casual observer could be forgiven for mistaking it for an American campaign. Some marchers were clearly channelling Black Panther style, wearing black berets, dark glasses and leather jackets. The banners too reflected the rhetoric that had emerged in America, featuring slogans such as 'CALLING ALL PIGS, CALLING ALL PIGS, FREAK OUT OR GET OUT', 'BLACK POWERS GONNA GET YOUR MAMA' and 'POWER TO THE PEOPLE' (NA CRIM 1 5522/1). The police presence was massive. At the beginning of the march, there were more police than demonstrators and the number of officers increased at regular intervals during the march. Under cross-examination, Inspector Aldritt, a senior officer who was present at the march, later admitted that '500 police officers were available that afternoon' (*TO*, 5 November 1971). Files held by the National Archives show that Aldritt significantly underestimated the extent of the police presence. A document dated 6 August and issued by Deputy Assistant Commissioner J. H. Gerrard shows that 588 constables, 84 sergeants, 29 inspectors and four chief inspectors were available during the march. In sum, 705 police officers were present, and this figure does not include the handful of CID and Special Branch officers who were detailed to follow the demonstration (NA MEPO 31/20).

The Action Committee for Defence of the Mangrove and the Black Panthers

The demonstration was organized by the Action Committee for Defence of the Mangrove in conjunction with the Black Panther Movement. According to evidence that emerged at the trial, the details of the march were thrashed out by a small group who met in July at the Willesden home of activist Selma James. The meeting's composition reflected the broad-based community campaign the Action Committee sought to galvanize in defence of Crichlow's restaurant. Along with US-born Jewish radical James, other committee members included Rene

Webb of the community group Advise and barrister Tony Mohipp, secretary
of the North Kensington-based Universal Black Improvement Organisation
(*TO*, 24 January 1971; *KP*, 26 November 1971). As a result of the meeting,
Mohipp wrote an open letter to the Home Office, Prime Minister Edward Heath,
Harold Wilson, the leader of the Opposition, and the High Commissioners for
Jamaica, Trinidad, Guyana and Barbados to announce the march and set out
the community's grievances. Howe would later remark that this approach was
Black Power, but 'tinged with a little British constitutionality' (Howe 1980: 38).
Mohipp's letter, which is preserved in the National Archives, reads thus:

> We, the black people of London have called this demonstration in protest against
> constant police harassment which is being carried out against us, and which is
> condoned by the legal system.
>
> In particular, we are calling for an end to the persecution of the Mangrove
> Restaurant of 8 All Saint's Road, W.11., a restaurant that serves the Black
> Community.
>
> These deliberate raids, harassments and provocations have been reported to the
> Home Office on many occasions. So too has the mounting list of grievances such
> as radis [sic] on West Indian parties, Wedding Receptions, and other places where
> Black People lawfully gather.
>
> We feel this protest is necessary as all other methods have failed to bring about
> any change in the manner police have chosen to deal with Black People.
>
> We shall continue to protest until Black People are treated with justice by the
> Police and the Law Courts.
>
> (NA HO 325/143)

A flyer was also produced advertising the march to Notting Hill locals.

> THE POLICE HAVE DONE IT AGAIN!!!
> THEY ARE SAYING CLOSE THE MANGROVE RESTAURANT,
> A RESTAURANT
> SERVING BLACK PEOPLE IN LADBROKE GROVE.
> WHY?
> WHERE'S NEXT?
> THE METRO YOUTH CLUB?
> EVERYWHERE THAT BLACK PEOPLE GET TOGETHER!!!
> DEMONSTRATE
> IN SUPPORT OF OUR COMMUNITY (THE GROVE)
> on SUNDAY 9th AUGUST 1970
> at 2.30pm
>
> (GPI JLR 3/1/5)

Notting Dale police station

After about an hour, the marchers reached Notting Dale police station on Sirdar Road. Again, Howe addressed the crowd, this time in earshot of the police station, which was surrounded by uniformed officers. The marchers were already outnumbered by their police escort. In spite of this, reinforcements were called. From the statements of an officer given during the trial, it seems that Notting Dale was overcome by a siege mentality. The marchers intended no violence. However, police witnesses argued that they interpreted chanting from the crowd as the prelude to attacks on officers. The marchers spotted an Austin Cambridge on Sirdar Road, the car of PC Frank Pulley and began to chant 'we want Puller, we want Puller'. Pulley was well known in the Grove, and according to some newspaper reports reviled by the local black community. The *Sunday Mirror* reported that his nickname 'Puller' referred to his habit of allegedly 'pulling' local black people into the police station and planting evidence on them or beating them (23 August 1970). Pulley denied these allegations and was never charged with any wrongdoing. At trial, police witnesses claimed that they had interpreted the chant as a threat to Pulley's safety and called in more officers. However, the transcript of radio traffic shows that the re-enforcements were called for when the marchers were still on Lancaster Road, a little more than 10 minutes away from the station, before the chant broke out.

Police anxieties may have been heightened by an incident that took place at Caledonian Road police station on 27 July, less than 2 weeks prior to the march. Howe had referred to the incident in his speech, describing it as 'aggressive revolutionary action', and its proximity to the march ensured both sides were still mindful of the event. Following the arrest of four young black men at Finsbury Park Summer Fair, a group of around 20 of their peers arrived at the police station protesting their innocence and demanding their release. The police viewed the protest as an attack and called for reinforcements who, upon their arrival, arrested everyone on the premises. Activist and *Guardian* journalist Vince Hines had been sent to cover the arrests, and he recalls the events thus:

> The police seemed to have been panicked, by the presence of a large number of Black youth making demands, and more youth were arriving. They packed in the station, including the reception. Urgent police reinforcements were called for. Many police rushed to the station, cars and vans. I heard them arriving and stopping at a screech outside. A large number of police arrived, sirens blaring. Without asking questions, the arriving police arrested all they could. This approach infuriated the

youth. Black youth and police did not mix. A fight broke out between the police and the youth inside and outside the station.

(Hines 2010)

Howe took the event as a sign of a new assertive and radical spirit among the black youth of the Grove. The police, needless to say, saw it differently. Nerves were steadier at the Notting Hill station. The marchers reached the station just after 3:40. Police radio simply described the march as '[w]ell contained by police' (NA MEPO 31/20).

The battle of Portnall Road

The flashpoint came on Portnall Road on the way to Harrow Road station. The demonstrators left the Notting Hill station, turned up Ladbroke Grove and crossed the canal. From this point on, the police reports were becoming increasingly twitchy. At 3.59 p.m. a constable informed his controllers that the demonstration would end imminently. Between 4:02 p.m. and 4:17 p.m., there were six more messages trying to clarify where the march was headed next; 10 minutes later, the number plates of three allegedly suspicious vehicles were radioed in; at 4:33 p.m., the same constable reported that the marchers were heading '[a]long Coomaisie [sic] Road – a predominantly coloured persons dwelling area'. Reading between the lines, it seems that the police feared that the march would grow in number as it went through the largely black area (Ibid.). On Portnall Road, the previously peaceful demonstration became a violent confrontation. Here the police were no thin blue line: rows of officers five deep formed a human barricade at the intersection of Portnall and Marban Road. It was later asserted that this provocative move was an attempt to allow traffic to move. In any case, within minutes of the stoppage, violence erupted, engulfing the march. A police radio signal went out: 'Urgent Assistance required – Shirland Road – all points north – serious fighting – ambulances required' (Ibid.). For a quarter of an hour, chaos reigned:

The demonstration literally exploded. The violence was ferocious, as the combatants continued, for fifteen minutes, to batter, to wound and to maim each other. The police were moved to an orgy of violence and abuse. It was a street fight. Not one single officer entertained that much touted skill of crowd control. It was pure, unadulterated, unlicensed brutality. The niggers were to be beaten into the ground. How dare we, they seemed to be saying, take to the streets in opposition to them? We did not qualify. Anyone but a "bunch of niggers". Crude though the language may be, the words fittingly described the reaction of the British state on that day.

We gave as good as we got. Bricks, stones, bottles, any ammunition at hand we threw at the police. Whole building skips were emptied at them.

(Howe 1980: 38)

In the aftermath, arrests were made and the crowd dispersed. Howe escaped, beating a retreat to the Mangrove to meet his wife and child. According to the police, the violence was premeditated, and the march an elaborate ambush. This account provided the authorities with a narrative that branded black radicalism criminal, as well as giving them a pretext for arresting the radical leadership that had coalesced around the Mangrove.

Howe's arrest came later that evening. The police received word that the leaders of the march were meeting at the Mangrove and arrived there around 6:20 p.m. to make arrests. Sam Morris of the Community Relations Commission described the arrests in a report submitted to the Home Secretary a week after the march. Morris reported that 'several van loads' of police arrived at the Mangrove, cordoned off the area and then stormed the restaurant, laying into the customers, 'who ducked, dived, jumped through windows and took every step possible in self protection' (NA HO 325/143). It was during this attack, which had all the hallmarks of a reprisal, that Howe was arrested, outside the Mangrove. In court later in the year, he described the beating he received, stating that he did not respond in kind. Fearing for the safety of his wife and child inside the restaurant, he did not defend himself, as he had no intention of giving the officers any excuse for hurting his family. The 19 who had been arrested would appear at Marylebone Magistrates Court the next day.

Note

1   Howe's reference to 'aggressive revolutionary action' concerns an incident in the Caledonian Road station in July 1970 and is discussed below.

9

Clampdown

Following the march, police reports and uproar in the press persuaded the Home Office that decisive action was necessary. However, with the help of dissenters within the establishment, Howe and his comrades emerged victorious from the first round of the Mangrove case.

Government reaction

News of the march went straight to the highest levels of government, and the official response was all but immediate. *The Guardian* of 12 August reported that Reginald Maudling, the Conservative Home Secretary, would have 'a complete dossier within 48 hours' due to the fact that 'Special Branch has had the movement under observation for more than a year [and] Police now regard Black Power as, at least, worthy of extremely tight surveillance.' *The Guardian*, however, was wrong on two counts, recently declassified documents reveal. First, Maudling had the report on his desk on 11 August, the day prior to the paper's report. Secondly, as the Branch itself acknowledged, the information it contained was rather outdated.

Over the next week or so, Maudling received a series of reports as well as recommendations on how to proceed against the Black Power Movement. The first, a Special Branch[1] 'dossier' that was extensively discussed in the press, contained three reports. The first, dated 9 August, concluded that the march had been an attempt by Black Power radicals to lure the police into a prearranged trap:

> It would appear most probable that the seemingly aimless march around the back streets of Ladbroke Grove and Harrow Road was designed to lead the accompanying uniformed police as far from reinforcements and aid as possible before a pre-calculated situation led to their being attacked by the demonstrators in a mainly coloured residential area.

> (NA HO 325/143)

The report made no mention of the police decision to stop the march or of the disproportionate police presence. The second report was a more generic Special Branch briefing on the history of Black Power in Britain based on intelligence gathered in the late 1960s. This second report contained an appendix detailing the 19 arrests that followed the march. Notably, Howe was not mentioned in either of these reports or the Appendix (Ibid.). The third report, drawn up by Deputy Assistant Commissioner Gerrard, the officer who was formally responsible for the policing of the march, gave the following account of the Mangrove: '[t]he brief facts are that this restaurant was raided on a drugs warrant over 12 months ago and arrests were made and the offenders subsequently convicted at Court' (Ibid.). This form of words was misleading, implying that the arrests and convictions pertained to drugs, which they did not.

Maudling received the dossier with a covering letter from James Waddell, deputy under-secretary to the Home Secretary (Ibid.). The letter contained advice on how the Home Office might proceed against the protestors. In essence, Waddell considered two possible courses of action. The first was to deport Michael X, Roy Swah and Crichlow, whom Waddell assumed were the organizers of the march, in accordance with the terms of the recent Immigration Act. However, Waddell acknowledged that this might be impossible as it was probable that these men had been resident in Britain for more than 10 years. A second solution, said Waddell, would be to use the provisions of the Race Relations Act. This option was fleshed out in a second letter, apparently from Waddell, which Maudling received on the following day. The Race Relations Act, it suggested, could be used in two ways. First, he suggested referring Michael X to the Race Relations Board on the grounds that he was planning to set up a 'black only' supermarket, a project that Waddell opined 'might be questionable and might have to be considered by the Race Relations Board' (Ibid.). Waddell considered the second option more promising. He suggested using the Act's prohibition of the incitement of racial hatred against Black Power protestors. This view was based on the suggestion that Black Power was an inherently racist ideology. However, Waddell recognized that this was a dangerous approach. Prosecuting Black Power radicals for incitement could be viewed as an attack on free speech and might, therefore, arouse public sympathy for the activists. Equally, such a prosecution could give wider publicity to the activists' 'racialist views' (Ibid.). The letter concluded that Maudling might consider talking to moderates who had proposed greater scrutiny of the police and making a speech decrying the events of 9 August.

Special Branch was not the only organization that reported to Maudling following the march; the Home Office also commissioned a report from the Community Relations Commission (Ibid.). The resulting document, written by Sam Morris, the deputy secretary-general of the Commission, contained a detailed account of police and community relations. In general terms, it argued that the demonstration reflected the strength of feeling in the black community against police harassment. Morris' report contained a detailed description of seven aspects of police misconduct, ranging from the practice of stopping black people who drove cars on the assumption that they are in possession of a stolen vehicle to planting weapons on black people. The report went as far as to say that violence might have been engineered 'by that small section of the force which appears to specialise in either harassing or beating up black people or both, or in preferring bogus charges against them' (Ibid.). The official response to the report was cold in the extreme. The report was sent to Maudling with a covering letter that described it as 'a most disappointing document' due to the fact that it 'merely sets out one view of the recent incidents' (Ibid.). By contrast, the police and Special Branch reports were forwarded to the minister without censure.

Waddell's suggestion of meetings with moderates soon bore fruit and on 18 August, the Home Secretary met with Dr David Pitt. Pitt was the chairman of Campaign Against Racial Discrimination, a civil rights group founded in the wake of Martin Luther King's visit to Britain. Notes of the meeting indicate that Pitt argued that significant reforms were needed to protect black people from the police and to stop the rise of the Black Power groups who capitalized on poor community relations. He suggested reforms ranging from more black police officers and greater use of community relations officers to better record keeping in the police force and the introduction of an independent element to the Police Complaints Commission. Maudling's response to these suggestions was not recorded (Ibid.).

In addition to this flurry of activity at the top of government, Special Branch redoubled their efforts to monitor Black Power groups. From the available evidence, it seems that the Branch had written off Black Power following the release of Egbuna. The Mangrove march changed this, and by the beginning of 1972, they seem to have infiltrated the Panthers and had gathered a great deal of information concerning the internal politics of the group and the nine defendants tried in connection with the Mangrove demonstration.

Press response

The Mangrove march became a media sensation. At first, the tabloids focused on the violence against the police. The *Daily Mirror*'s front page headline read '17 POLICE INJURED IN A MOB ATTACK' (10 September 1970), while the *Daily Mail* led with 'Police hurt by Black Power mob' (10 September 1970). Broadsheets covered the march in more measured tones; *The Times*, for example, carried the headline '19 people held in clash with police' (10 September 1970). The story continued to play out in the press over the next fortnight as papers speculated about the causes of the trouble and what the incident might mean for the future of racial politics in Britain.

Reports in the *Sketch*, the *Mirror* and the *Mail* indicate that reporters had very little grasp of the real nature of the march, and in the absence of a more secure foundation, they fell back on stereotypes and conspiracy theories. Many of the tabloid reports stoked public fear about the threat of Black Power in Britain. The *Daily Sketch*, the perennial rival of the *Daily Mirror*, led the way. Early reports conjured up the spectre of a tightly knit, militant Black Power Movement that was poised to unleash a wave of terror on the country. The paper's article, 'New Threat of Black Violence', claimed that the POQO, a 'terrorist Black Power group', had sent an ultimatum to the commissioner of police (11 September 1970). The report left the exact nature of the ultimatum obscure, but stated in no uncertain terms that the POQO was 'a South African terrorist organisation linked with the Black Panthers' (Ibid.). Some journalists tried to fathom the motives behind the march, often with farcical results. Michael X's comments added to the confusion. In the *Daily Mirror*, on 11 August, he argued that the demonstration had aimed to win the liberation of 'Jamaica, Bahamas, Bermuda, Barbados and St Vincent'. By 14 August, he was advocating the doubling of police pay. Finally, the tabloids were split on the merits of PC Frank Pulley, the first celebrity to emerge from the Mangrove case. On 16 August, *The People* argued that tensions in Notting Hill would be eased by transferring Pulley out of the area. The *Sunday Mirror*, published a week later, gave Pulley a chance to respond. The article, entitled 'My Answer, by Pc Pulley', set out Pulley's view of the campaign to get him transferred: '[a]ll that has happened recently is that villains – and in my manor there are some nasty ones – have decided they would be able to operate better if I wasn't there, and they are out to get rid of me.' In the *Sunday Mirror*'s interview, Pulley dismissed the accusations of police violence, operating a protection racket, planting drugs on black people and harassment. Of his alleged racism, he said:

I LIKE coloured people. . . . They are a sunny race. When I moved house I went to Southall – and there are probably more coloureds there than in the manor. After twelve years in a cosmopolitan place like Notting Hill it's impossible to think in terms of colour. If I see a chap across the street I don't think "There's black Joe." I just think "There's Joe." It's as simple as that.

(*Sunday Mirror*, 23 August 1970)

The broadsheets' misunderstanding of the situation was often as profound as that of any of the red tops. The *Guardian*'s report on 11 August was at a loss when it came to the meaning of Black Power. Apparently, there was no agreed definition among the Mangrove's patrons. *The Telegraph*'s editorial drew broader political lessons from the march. Likening Notting Hill to Ulster, the editor argued that the violence justified W. F. Deedes' proposal, published on the same day, to cut immigration drastically (11 August 1970).

Before the Magistrate

The first hearing, dealing with charges of affray, took place on Monday, 10 August. The police were granted more time in order to gather evidence of incitement to riot, riotous assembly or affray. C. L. R. James was the first to recognize the severity of the situation and called a meeting at the Metro Youth club to discuss matters with Howe, Crichlow and the other leaders of the march (Howe 2010). Six weeks later, the police began a series of dawn raids, initially arresting seven of the marchers (GPI New 38).

Howe's solicitor advised him to plead guilty, assuring him that he would be let off lightly with a 5-year stretch. Appalled at the prospect, Howe rejected the advice out of hand retorting, 'I spend that with your wife, my friend – that five years' (Phillips and Phillips 1999: 280). As a result, he walked out of the solicitor's office with his case notes determined to defend himself.

On 29 December 1970, Howe and his fellow defendants appeared before the Marylebone Magistrates' Court to face the new charges. This would be the first test of the prosecution's case. Fortune, it seemed, smiled on the defendants as the case was heard by David Watcher. Howe recognized the significance immediately. He recalls that in the early 1970s, a few magistrates were beginning to discern the dynamic at work between the police and Notting Hill's black youth. Watcher was such a man: part of the establishment, but a dissenter nonetheless. Howe attributes this to the fact that, as a Jew, Watcher was no stranger to the racial prejudice that dogged the British justice system (Howe 2010). Consequently, he subjected the prosecution's case to serious scrutiny.

The first blow for the police occurred early in the hearings. Nathaniel Stignac and Rudolph Woods, who had been arrested on charges of affray, were acquitted. In a damning closing statement, Watcher told the prosecution that their presentations had failed to achieve the 'necessary stamp of truth' (GPI New 38). The court did not consider the charges of incitement to riot until January 1971. The 5-day hearing that began on 1 January was a major upset for the police case. The prosecution dropped the charge of incitement and Watcher threw out the charge of riot. Fundamentally, the prosecution's case was founded on three elements: first, they argued that the language used by demonstrators showed their intention to riot; secondly, there were reports from police officers concerning the behaviour of the defendants; and finally, the police reports were shot through with innuendo, suggesting that the Mangrove was a den of criminals and that Black Power, as a movement and as an ideology, was inherently criminal. Watcher dismissed all the three lines of argument (NA CRIM 1 5522/2).

On the question of the language used by the demonstrators, *IT* reported that '[s]even officers were asked if they took the slogan "Kill the Pigs" literally and they said that they did.' Watcher dealt with the first line of argument thus:

> Magistrate: Where is the evidence of force?
> Prosecution: They were shouting "Kill the Pigs."
> Magistrate: This is highly provocative but, forgive my language, if they had shouted "Fuck the pigs" or "Bugger the pigs", the police would not have taken that literally would they?
> Prosecution: No, but the word "Kill" embodies some sort of violence.
> Magistrate: So do the other two.
> Prosecution: One man said, "We are going to smash up the Pig House."
> Magistrate: But they passed at least one Pig House and nothing happened.
>
> (GPI New 38)

In a trenchant display of common sense, Watcher refused to allow the prosecution to argue that the shouts of protestors constituted evidence of either intent to riot or incitement.

Records preserved at the National Archives also show that Watcher was sceptical and ruled a large number of comments in the police statements inadmissible. In total, Watcher ruled that statements on 23 pages of police statements were inadmissible (NA CRIM 1 5522/2). Equally, police witnesses did not all speak with one voice. One senior police officer stated that '[t]he melee was spontaneous. As I saw it, it was an occasion when everyone was for himself' (*IT*, 28 January–11 February 1971). But it was a retired postman, Mr Harris, who sounded the death knell for the incitement charge. Taking the stand on the last day of the hearing, Harris told the court that '[t]he demonstrators were peaceful until the police stopped them to allow the traffic to pass. . . . It was then a fight broke out. The demonstrators thought that the police were interfering with them, and they reached for milk bottles, stones, bricks and sticks. The leaders lost control then. I saw several policemen and black demonstrators lying on the ground. The whole thing was a misunderstanding on both sides' (*IT*, 28 January–11 February 1971). The testimony apparently caused panic on the prosecution bench. With their case in disarray, the prosecution quickly dropped the charge of incitement and replaced it with one of riot for six of the seven defendants. Watcher swiftly rejected the new charge. He concluded that the evidence pointed to a spontaneous melee and not to a preplanned riot. Nonetheless, he allowed the charges of affray and possession of offensive weapons to stand and all seven defendants were committed to a trial at the Old Bailey (Ibid.).

In a jubilant mood, the seven defendants finished the day by holding a press conference at the Mangrove Restaurant. The event was James' idea. James was a seasoned activist who, as Howe acknowledges, had more finesse as a campaigner than his nephew in those days. Howe clearly considered Watcher's decision to be a decisive victory for the campaign. Speaking at the conference, he proclaimed:

> . . . the police conspiracy to conceal the truth is over. Black people are going to continue in the spirit of resistance. The question of police maltreatment and persecution of black people may appear to certain classes and social groupings in Britain as a new phenomenon. This does not mean that black people haven't had to live with it for almost a decade. The result of the hearing today demonstrated once again the contempt with which the police hold black people. The police were prepared to go to any lengths to pin incitement and riot charges on us who have exercised our right to demonstrate. The streets are the only platform.
>
> (*IT*, 28 January–11 February 1971)

Sadly, the celebrations were premature. The state had invested too much political capital in the prosecution of the Mangrove demonstrators to allow the central charge of incitement to fall on the decision of a single magistrate. The Director of Public Prosecutions took the highly unusual step of effectively overruling Watcher's decision and reinstated the most serious charges of riot and incitement to riot by way of his own voluntary Bill of Indictment against nine defendants. Howe and his comrades, who were soon known as 'the Mangrove Nine', would have to fight these charges a second time, this time at Court Number 2 of the Old Bailey, with the prospect of up to 10 years in prison if they were found guilty (Macdonald 2010).

Note

1 The Branch's involvement is significant: it was established in 1883 in order to fight 'Fenian' terrorism. The *Metropolitan Police Instruction Book* set out its remit in the following terms: '[t]he duties of the Branch include enquiries concerning the security of the State, and naturalisation of aliens' in addition to border control. Notably, the security of the state and the naturalization of aliens went hand in hand. During the 1950s and 1960s, the Branch kept organizations that campaigned for black rights under continual surveillance in the belief that they were fronts for communists and therefore posed a threat to state security.

10

55 Days at the Old Bailey

There was no denying the seriousness of the situation. From the news stories of Black Power revolutionaries bent on violence, it appeared that the police must have been feeding journalists lurid stories about 'Black Power' agitators. Indeed, police files show that the Met kept a watchful eye on the press reaction to the story (NA MEPO 31/20–21). The sensational coverage was bound to create a hostile public atmosphere towards the defendants and made the prospects of a fair trial seem remote. There was also the behaviour of the Director of Public Prosecutions (DPP), who reinstated the most serious charges. Barbara Beese, one of the defendants, recalls that the DPP's actions 'certainly struck us as outrageous, and certainly struck us as desperate, it was further proof that this was about dealing with a group of black people who had dared to take this action' (Beese 2011). The 'Establishment', as far as Beese could see, was concerned about the impact of Black Power in America and therefore hell bent on stopping the British movement in its tracks. Although they hadn't seen the Special Branch reports, Howe and his co-defendants had read *The Guardian* report on 12 August 1970 stating that Reginald Maudling had ordered urgent intelligence reports on the Black Power Movement. Naturally, they suspected that the DPP was acting on the Home Secretary's political instructions.

Evidently, this was to be a political trial, a fact that was underscored by the manner in which the police had focused their energies and resources on trying to build cases against the most prominent activists from the 27 people originally arrested on 9 August. For 9 weeks before the charges were brought, the energies of sections of the Metropolitan police and Special Branch were devoted to gathering 'evidence' to persuade a jury that leading members and key allies of the Black Power Movement – including Althea Jones-Lecointe, Beese, Frank Crichlow, Rhodan Gordan and Howe himself – were implicated in planning and inciting the riot on 9 August 1970. Ian Macdonald, Beese's defence counsel, acknowledged that the state was more than willing to use tactics that the Nine regarded as 'persecutory' as a means of 'dealing with forces that were revolutionary and were trying to change the system' (Macdonald 2010).

A movement is born

Although the odds appeared stacked against them, Howe knew the Mangrove Nine could draw on the support of the black community. Their trial was the culmination of a year of clashes between the police and London's black community which had seen scores of black youths arrested and charged in Harlsden, Acton Park and Lisson Grove, as well as 16 people arrested following a police raid on the Metro Youth club in May 1971, and more than 50 detained and charged after a week of clashes with police when they failed to take action after a serious racist attack at Peckham Rye Fair in September 1971.

Writing in *Race Today*, the distinguished Black journalist Lionel Morrison described how police attacks on community organizations in Notting Hill, coupled with the prosecution of the Mangrove Nine, had 'produced a tremendous social force of black people who formerly had been apolitical and apathetic but are now anxious to act' (*RT*, 1972: 385).

A number of independent black organizations took up the Nine's cause. The Black People's Information Centre, with its large office above the Backyard Restaurant in Portobello market, provided a base in West London that convened meetings, printed leaflets and posters and even organized a petition taking up the Mangrove Nine's demand for an all-black jury. The Black Panther Movement, which under Jones-Leconite's leadership had transformed itself into a serious community-based organization with hundreds of members and thousands of supporters, now mobilized a sustained struggle in defence of the Panthers' leadership from its political base in South London.

The Panthers' rejection of cultural nationalism and separatism in favour of a class analysis of racism enabled it to reach out beyond the black community to radical white sympathizers, trade unionists and political groups that wished to show solidarity with the Nine. Special Brach monitored these connections closely. A confidential report signed by a Chief Inspector and Chief Superintendent on 31 October 1970 provides a detailed account of a march that day by approximately 260 white supporters of the Mangrove Nine, which traced the same route as 9 August demonstration and at which Jones-Leconite was one of the guest speakers (NA CRIM 1 5522/3).

The protest was called by the newly formed Black Defence Committee, an organization set up by the International Marxist Group's youth section, to raise support for black political activists awaiting trial. This was followed in December 1970 by a national speaking tour by London Black Panthers which led to the creation of a network of Black Defence Committees outside London and a Black Defence and Aid Fund, which aimed to raise funds from white supporters 'who wish to solidarise with the Black Struggle' in this country (BDC leaflet 1970).

Meanwhile, leaflets were distributed, meetings held in black communities across the United Kingdom and briefings, articles and reports sent to sister organizations in the United States and West Indies. Howe later described the initial impact of the campaign thus:

> By the time the trial was scheduled to begin the issues were placed before Caribbean peoples, blacks and whites throughout the United Kingdom. Support poured in from the black movement in the United States. The black community, at a massive rally in Notting Hill, gave the nine defendants a terrific send off on the day before we were to appear at the Old Bailey.
>
> (Howe 1988: 47)

The mass rally of more than 400 people at Faraday Church Hall entitled 'Demand Justice for the Mangrove Nine' appears to have been an important cultural and political event in its own right. *Time Out* reported another big meeting in September. 'Hundreds of blacks and whites filled St Pancras Town Hall . . . to honour the death of George Jackson. . . . But the crowd's greatest response was reserved for an unidentified black woman who spoke on behalf of the Mangrove Nine' (10 September 1971).

Radical legal strategy

With a grass-roots movement behind them, Howe and the Black Panther leadership were anxious that the trial should not be a rerun of previous Black Power trials, which for the most part had been a humiliation for the movement. The majority of cases followed the pattern of Obi Egbuna's trial in 1968, where the accused abandoned militant rhetoric in favour of a traditional legal defence articulated by white lawyers. The handful of activists who had conducted their own defence, such as Michael X, had failed to use the occasion to highlight the discrimination faced by black people or challenge the rough justice many black defendants experienced from the courts.

Howe and his fellow defendants consciously adopted a more radical approach. Rather than abandoning Black Power as they entered the court, Howe and the other leading voices among the Nine were determined to employ a strategy in which the defendants became the protagonists. The first aspect of this Black Power defence was the demand for an all-black jury. Howe had introduced this idea in the days of the Black Eagles, appealing to ancient rights enshrined in *Magna Carta* in the same way that the American Panthers cited the Fourteenth Amendment as the constitutional basis of its call for black defendants to be tried by black juries. Offenbach and Company, solicitors for four of the Nine, informed the court of this demand on 27 September, citing half a page of legal authorities in support of the claim (NA CRIM 1 5522/3). This contentious demand would take up the first 2 days of the trial.

The second aspect of the radical defence was self-representation. Howe and Jones-Lecointe would run their own defence without the aid of professional lawyers. Howe's solicitors informed the court of his decisions at the end of June (NA CRIM1 5522/3). The strategy was, in part, a response to the failure of previous Black Power trials. The Oval House case was a more prescient example of the shortcomings of professional lawyers. On 28 June 1971, Eddie Lecointe and two other Panthers were found guilty of riotous assembly arising from fighting which had broken out during a police raid on a Black Panther dance at the Oval House Youth club in Kennington. All three received suspended sentences. The defendants played no part in their defence, remaining passive as a lawyer put their case before the court. A belated attempt at self-representation by defendant Keith Spencer was cut off by the judge, who refused to sanction 'a political speech in this court' (*The Times* 28 June 1971). Looking back, the radical barrister Ian Macdonald explained:

> The Oval House trial was a disaster for the defendants. The defence's legal team were drawn from the Old Left including John Platts Mills QC. There was no internal leadership from within the defendants themselves and they all got convicted. Then John Platt Mills gave a speech in mitigation in which he referred to the defendants being "excitable."
>
> So when this trial came on, the leadership of the Black Panthers was determined that this would not be a repeat. There were fundamental political issues that they were determined would be dealt with in the trial, including the level of quite blatant individual racism at the time.
>
> (Macdonald 2010)

The Nine decided on a radical strategy that would put these issues squarely before the court. Howe and Althea Jones-Lecointe would defend themselves, thereby releasing them from the strict rigours of legal procedure and allowing them to expose the political nature of the trial and the brutality of policing in Notting Hill. Howe's inspiration for this approach came, in part, from his friend Richard Neville's defence of himself during the *Oz* obscenity trial: 'he defended himself brilliantly. I felt, well, if Richard could do it, I could do it too. More than that, I could do it better than Richard' (KCL 367 Man).

The strategy of black self-representation was not just a legal strategy. It caught the public's attention. Beese recalls: 'the idea of black people actually defending themselves was quite extraordinary, that had not happened before. It was followed avidly. In fact we hadn't realised the extent to which there was this interest across black communities in the country' (Beese 2011).

Self-representation was not a simple matter, for it risked a rift between the radical strategy pursued by Howe and Jones-Lecointe on the one hand and the more traditional strategy of the professional lawyers on the other. The solution came in the person of Ian Macdonald. Barbara Beese, one of the Nine and Howe's partner, approached Macdonald, who agreed to represent her and perform the crucial role of mediating between the defendants who were defending themselves and the barristers acting for the other defendants, in order to stop the court from creating a division between them.

Although now one of the leading human rights lawyers in the country, with just 8 years at the Bar and membership of a Chambers which specialized in planning law rather than crime, Macdonald was, by his own admissions, 'relatively inexperienced at the time' (Macdonald 2010). Yet Howe, who had appeared alongside Macdonald on *Cause for Concern*, trusted Macdonald's political instincts implicitly, as did his co-defendants. In contrast to the others' lawyers, whom they regarded as part of the liberal establishment and therefore prone to speak and make compromises *on behalf of* black defendants, Macdonald's record as an activist lawyer for CARD distinguished him as someone who, in Howe's words, 'had received his education from black proletarians', and on whom they could depend upon for 'unshakable loyalty and support' (Howe 1988: 47).

Macdonald did not disappoint. He fought their corner, challenging his opposite number, prosecutor Michael Hill, and the judge at decisive moments in the trial, an approach which at least one of his fellow defence counsels disagreed with so strongly that he kept pulling Macdonald's gown and saying 'sit down,

Ian, and shut up, you are not doing your client's case any good'. With a smile, Macdonald recalled that this particular civil rights barrister eventually went on to become a Stipendiary Magistrate (Macdonald 2010).

Application for a black jury

The trial began in Court 1 of The Old Bailey on 5 October 1971 and would last 12 weeks. The discovery on the first day that the presiding judge for the case would be Edward Clarke was a blow to the defence. Clarke was well known to Macdonald and his colleagues at the Bar 'as a bully'; his reputation as a judge 'notorious for his heavy sentencing and a right wing law and order approach to justice' extended to Howe and his co-defendants (Macdonald 2010; Howe 1988: 47).

The defendants began the proceedings by applying for the charge of incitement to riot to be removed as it had already been thrown out at the committal hearing for lack of evidence. To strong objections from the defence counsel, Judge Clark stated he had no power to throw out the riot charges. Getting to his feet for the first time in the dock, Howe said:

> My Lord, I have no precedents to state, but I have a sense of justice. I detect a certain vagueness in the way the prosecution has brought back this charge of riot, and as a famous philosopher once said "vagueness in certain matters conceals treachery." Many ordinary people would wonder how I could be tried twice for the same offence having had the charge thrown out once before. As a common man I feel this is a breach of natural justice.
>
> (UC DHP Box VI/5)

Howe's eloquence fell on deaf ears. The charge of riot remained.

Now party to the Nine's strategy, Macdonald presented the application for a black jury, which lasted two full days. He cited old cases from the Pleas of the Rolls that allowed Welsh marchers to have a Welsh jury, Italian merchants to be tried by a jury of 'the half tongue' or half Italian. In addition to the clause in *Magna Carta*, Macdonald pointed out that the established practice for centuries thereafter had been to select the jury from the neighbourhood or '*vicinos*' of the accused. This remained part of the common law and was reinforced by the Juries Act of 1825 which had provided for the continuation of existing practices.

After listening to 2 days of detailed legal argument, Judge Clarke dismissed the application out of hand. Pointedly refusing to engage with Macdonald's argument, he simply stated that he had the prerogative to decide the matter and if Macdonald and the defendants were unhappy they could appeal (*KP*, 6 October 1971). Howe nevertheless regarded the fact that the application was presented at all as a victory. The demand was audacious; it stamped the authority of the defendants on the proceedings and caught the imagination of friends and enemies alike. The public gallery was packed with supporters and the story was picked up widely in the press. For Howe, the 2 days of legal argument was a significant moment which 'served to establish that we were prepared to attack all the worn out and repressive bourgeois legal procedures' (Howe 1988: 48).

Next, Howe and Leconite-Jones began to vet potential jurors politically. The defendants paid a shilling and obtained the array, which was the names, addresses and occupations of all those people who were called for jury service. The defence team pored over the lists and tried to use each of the defendant's seven peremptory challenges to get the best choice of jury. In the absence of black jurors, the defendants wanted jurors from working-class backgrounds who, by virtue of their own experiences, were more likely to accept the defendants' evidence of police harassment and brutality. When he got an opportunity to question prospective jurors, Howe asked each of them what they understood by the term 'Black Power' and which newspapers they read. Again the judge intervened to stop this line of questioning and accused the defence of 'wasting the court's time'. Unperturbed by Clarke's comment, Macdonald replied: 'Your lordship is not above the law.' Clarke responded by saying 'I am well aware of that and I expect courtesy from members of the bar.' Macdonald: 'Yes, your lordship, you will receive the same courtesy I get from you' (*TO*, 15 October 1971).

Nonetheless, the defence dismissed a total of 63 jurors, each defendant using their right to dismiss seven potential jurors. In so doing, the Nine ensured that two of the twelve jurors were black and that a majority of the eight white men and two white women came from working-class backgrounds. Once again they demonstrated that they were determined to take an active part in the proceedings.

Witness evidence

Before Michael Hill made the opening statement for the prosecution, Howe and Leconite-Jones made one further preliminary application to have a friend or assistant with them in the dock to take notes, quietly make suggestions and give advice. Although a relatively new law, the right of unrepresented defendants to be accompanied by a 'McKenzie's' helper, following the Court of Appeal judgement in the 1970 case of McKenzie v McKenzie, was already well established. The same right had been granted to Richard Neville during the *Oz* obscenity trial 3 months earlier and would be extended 6 months later by Mr Justice James to John Barker, Anna Mendelson and Hilary Creek during the trial of the Stoke Newington Eight for conspiracy to cause explosions linked to The Angry Brigade (Carr 2010: 131). In a clear failure to apply the law, Judge Clarke refused the application on the grounds that he had never heard of this being done in a criminal trial.

Michael Hill's opening statement set out clearly how he intended to present the prosecution case. He said that in Britain everyone has the right to peaceful protest but that the march on 9 August 1970 had been an example of people bent on trouble trying to use the discontent of the black community to their advantage. Ruling out any possibility that it was the police who had provoked the violence that day, Hill stated there were only three explanations for what happened:

> ... either a flamboyant demonstration got out of hand or it was led by those who were prepared to take advantage of violence if it occurred, or its leaders deliberately sought to provoke violence.
>
> (*KP*, 15 October 1971)

It was the Crown's case that the defendants deliberately conspired to provoke their supporters into violence.

Contradictions in the prosecution case began to emerge almost immediately. The first major witness to be called, Superintendent Joseph Donnelly, said he was in charge of the police operation that day and had authorized the use of an unidentifiable observation van containing PC Pulley along with other officers. When challenged as to why such a divisive figure had been deployed to police the march, Donnelly said that he had told Pulley not to interfere or get involved in any trouble.

Donnelly said that as the person in charge of the police operation, he was not aware of any plain-clothes officers on the demonstration. Inspector Stockwell of the CID flatly contradicted this in evidence later that day, stating that 12 plain-clothed officers had been there 'to identify trouble-makers', while additional officers skirted the route of the march in private vehicles (*TO*, 22 October 1971).

Howe's cross-examination focused on Donnelly's claim that he had heard Howe begin his speech to the crowd assembled in front of the Mangrove before the march with the words 'Look at the Pigs . . .' Howe stated 'I would suggest to you that I started by saying '"Brothers and Sisters . . ."' After consulting his notebook, Donnelly said he had heard Howe say '"Look at the pigs, we complain to the police about the police, we complain to the council about the council, we complain to parliament about parliament."'

Howe then put it to Donnelly that it was the police which added the words 'Look at the pigs' and that for him to begin with such a statement would have been at odds with what he went on to say and the manner in which he said it. Through cross-examination, Howe established that despite claiming to have listened to the whole 5 minutes of the speech, Donnelly could only recall the first 30 seconds in which the alleged reference to 'pigs' was made. Howe eventually read out the speech, which even Michael Hill had described as 'allegedly eloquent', in full (UC DHP Box VI/6).

Mindful of the fact that several police statements had referred to the defendants' affiliations to 'Black Power', Leconite-Jones then asked the head of the police operation that day what his definition of the term was. He answered: 'I am not in any position to answer. I don't know, maybe it's connected with some left wing movement.' Asked by her if he had given the order to draw truncheons, Donnelly replied: 'I gave no order to draw truncheons but it was every man for himself'(Ibid.).

From such exchanges, Howe and Leconite-Jones were able to speak directly to the jury in a way that no barrister could. Throughout the trial, both provided the jury with an extended opportunity to assess their credibility next to that of the police witnesses in a case where so much evidence was in dispute.

'Criminals, ponces and prostitutes'

Pulley was the first of the three key police witnesses to give evidence on the fourth week of the trial. In his statement, Pulley claimed that the Mangrove was a den of iniquity frequented by 'local criminals, ponces and prostitutes'. Crichlow's counsel, Croft, stated that such a remark showed signs of bias, if not hatred, and asked if 'anyone going there would be likely to be depraved and corrupted?'. Pulley agreed, 'Anyone who ended up there would be depraved and corrupted'(*TO* 29 October 1971). Pulley's words were used in cross-examination of other prosecution witnesses by the defence team, including Howe. Under cross-examination by Howe, PC Lewis agreed with the statement that lots of West Indians who were hard working and law abiding, including students, went to the Mangrove. When asked by Howe if he disagreed with PC Pulley that they would have to be depraved or corrupt to visit such a place, all he was able to answer was that he 'did not know'(*KP*, 29 October 1971).

Pulley's comments were referred to again when Bruce Douglas-Mann, the local MP for North Kensington, appeared later in the trial as a character witness for Crichlow. The MP explained how he had dined at the Mangrove before getting to know Crichlow personally. He said he was initially attracted by the relaxed and pleasant atmosphere and excellent food and had come to know, respect and like Crichlow. Douglas-Mann described Crichlow as 'a very intelligent person' with 'a strong social concern'. Asked in what way he was socially concerned, Douglas-Mann stated: 'I feel he is running the restaurant not so much as a profit venture but as a kind of social centre in the community.' Finally, Croft asked the MP if he had ever seen any prostitutes at the Mangrove. 'I would be very surprised,' was the answer, 'if it was frequented by prostitutes at all.' He added that he had personally heard Crichlow disapprove of violence as a means to an end when others had brought it up in political discussion. Crichlow called a further seven character witnesses, including screenwriter Martin Hall, novelist Colin MacInnes, *Sunday Times* journalist Peter Kellner and BBC Assistant Producer Alan Hayling, who all spoke of the relaxed atmosphere in the Mangrove. None considered themselves 'depraved' or 'corrupted' by having dined there (*TO*, 26 October 1971).

Police witnesses

The riot charges turned on the prosecution's claim that PCs Pulley, Lewis, Rogers and Reid had seen and heard Howe, Crichlow, Kentish and Gordon inciting violence from their vantage point in the police observation van. The credibility of these witnesses was crucial to the prosecution case.

In evidence, Pulley insisted that he had a clear view of the fighting when it broke out from the police observation van and had seen Howe standing on a wall shouting 'kill the white pigs'. But this evidence was problematic, as photographic evidence suggested that a police bus stood between the observation van and the wall at the time. In cross-examination, Howe pointed out that it was physically impossible to stand on a sloping wall unsupported with his arms waving in the manner that Pulley had described. The police case against Howe also contained the claim that he had jumped over a 6-foot fence with railings behind it. When his request that the jury be taken to the fence in Portnall Road to see the impossibility of such a feat was refused, Howe turned the situation into a piece of legal theatre by asking if a replica of the fence could be built in the court room. This too was refused. No doubt aware that the police claim appeared risible, Detective Constable John West pointed out that the fence varied in height from 4 to 6 feet. This prompted Howe to comment to the amusement of the court: 'It would be something of a Billy Smart's circus act and might endanger serious parts of one's body to attempt that jump' (*KP*, 12 November 1971).

In further evidence, PC Pulley said the banners carried by the protestors on the march showed their violent intent in that they read 'Kill the Pigs,' 'Slavery is Still Here' and 'The Pigs will get your mama.' When asked by Bing, counsel for Rothwell Kentish, if he may have been mistaken about this, given that the police photographs of the march only showed banners which read 'Hands off us, pigs,' 'Black Power is gonna get your mama' and 'Slavery is still alive,' Pulley refused to back down (Ibid., 22 October 1971).

Pulley's conduct came under further scrutiny after he had left the dock. He sat at the back of the court while PC Graham Rogers testified to his observations from the police van. As Howe began to cross-examine Rogers, there were cries of outrage from Crichlow, Gordon and Rupert Boyce. The three jumped to their feet when Pulley was spotted nodding to Rogers as he tried to answer Howe's questions. Judge Clarke responded by ordering Pulley to leave the court while the other three officers who had been in the observation van gave their evidence (Ibid.).

'Where was your face?'

Howe's cross-examination of the four officers who had manned the police observation van was a turning point in the trial. It did real damage to the credibility of the prosecution's case by demolishing the evidence on which the riot charge was based. Howe, Jones-Lecointe, Crichlow and Beese met every evening. Beese recalls that they met 'to review how the day's events had gone, and how we planned to move forward and what the strategies were . . .' (Beese 2011). The four formed a core that directed the defence strategy. They considered the juror's responses to the day's testimony, the prosecution's strategy, and tried to anticipate the direction of the case against them. Night after night, Howe pored over witness statements. James was no lawyer, but early in trial he advised Howe 'the devil is in the detail'. Howe took this advice to heart. Copies of witness statements preserved at Columbia University are covered in red pen and marginalia in Howe's hand, a testament to his forensic analysis of the case against him.

For some time, Howe had had a feeling that there was a fundamental flaw in the police evidence, but its exact nature eluded him. The answer came to him in a moment of revelation. Late one night at Beese's house, Howe saw the problem. Four police officers claimed to have witnessed the defendants goading the crowd, simultaneously from the inspection van. But the observation window, which was just a slit in the van, was simply too small for this to be true (Howe 2011e).

Armed with this argument, Howe addressed the court. He demanded, with a theatrical flourish, that the observation van be driven into the courtroom so that the jury could see the problem for themselves. The request was refused. Howe had traced the outline of the window on a sheet of foolscap and the prosecution agreed that it accurately reflected the size of the window. Indeed, the jury were later allowed to inspect the van, allowing them to confirm Howe's claims. Howe confronted the police witnesses with the dimensions of the observation slit. Pulley responded with the farfetched claim that each officer had a single eye pressed to the slit. Howe demonstrated the ridiculousness of this claim with the simple question 'where was your face?'. The effect of Howe's cross-examination was devastating. Beese recalls that 'the more that Althea and particularly Darcus eroded the prosecution's case, the more it became almost a futile effort'. From that point on, the prosecutor Michael Hill had the air of a beaten man. News of Howe's victory quickly reached the streets of Notting Hill where Howe was greeted, for some time, with shouts of 'where's ya face!' (Beese 2011).

Disintegration of the prosecution's case

Serious contradictions began to emerge in the police accounts, further undermining the credibility of the prosecution's case. Beese recalls that by this stage in the case 'the prosecution witnesses were going down like nine-pins, faced with their contradictions'. Lewis, for instance, had claimed in his statement to the magistrate's court that the police van was parked a few feet away from Crichlow, Howe and Gordon when the fighting began. He now said the van was parked 30 feet away, an admission that seemed to cast serious doubt on his claim that he had heard Gordon, amidst the chanting, tell a black youth to 'kill the pigs'.

Challenged about these conflicts in their evidence, police witnesses appeared to have difficulty remembering events and answering questions, which, in turn, prompted Howe to say to Lewis:

> Any consistent lack of memory hinders the process of getting at the truth. Thirteen times you don't remember or you can't say. PC Pulley said 33 times that he did not remember. PC Rogers said so 28 times. . . . About 70 times the three of you can't remember. You were put in the van to observe and record from beginning to end in order to provide information that would give the truth as to what took place. I suggest that you failed distinctly in your responsibility to the court.
>
> (*KP*, 29 October 1971)

At the end of his cross-examination of Lewis, Howe noted that PC Lewis had answered 'I don't know' on 34 occasions to his questions.

If the prosecution team were hoping that their civilian witnesses would advance the prosecution case, they were to be sorely disappointed. The first of these, Corneillus Harris, a resident of 170 Portnall Road for 50 years, told Croft in cross-examination that he saw nothing to suggest that incident was organized or that anything had caused the fighting other than the police decision to stop the march at the junction of Portnall Road and Marban Road. (*TO*, 12 October 1971)

The evidence of another prosecution witness suggested that the police may have actively suppressed exculpatory evidence during their investigation. Stanley Bright, of 176 Portnall Road, had dialled 999 when he saw a policeman knocked to the ground. Howe read a statement that Bright had given to a news agency, which had been published in the *Daily Telegraph* at the time. The statement claimed that the police went into the demonstration with truncheons to disperse it and that black people had retaliated to the attack with bottles and anything else they could find on the street. Howe asked why the same statement had not appeared in his witness statement to either police or Marylebone Magistrates, noting that if it had done, 'none of the defendants would now be on trial'. Bright said 'he was quite sure' that he had given the same statement to the press, to the police and to the Marylebone Magistrates Court and did not know why it had been omitted from the witness statement taken by DC West. When DC West eventually took the stand, he agreed that if Bright had made these observations, they should have been taken down in his statement. Howe put it to him that Bright had made these comments, and West said he could not remember. When Howe said that Bright was clear that he had made these comments, West said Bright's memory may be better than his, but that he had not taken it down (Ibid.).

Judge Clarke's interventions during the course of the trial were regularly challenged by the defendants. Looking back, Beese remarks: 'as far as he could, he tried to assist the prosecution, there was no doubt about that'. That was certainly the view at the time. Howe accused him of 'prejudicing this issue' and of 'railroading the defendants' at a key moment in his cross-examination of a police witness. Rhodan Gordon, who dismissed his lawyers during the trial in order to defend himself, said that Clarke saw his role as running the case for the prosecution. When Frank Crichlow took the stand, he referred to a comment that the judge had made, suggesting that illegal drugs may have been removed from the Mangrove prior to the police raids on the restaurant. Crichlow reminded the judge that when the police made a raid they did not advertise the fact, so to suggest that 'whatever was there' was removed prior to the raid was absurd and unwarranted (*TO*, 26 November 1971). Howe declared: 'the judge says he has 35 years of legal experience. Well, I have 400 years of colonial experience' (Carter, 1986: 108).

Closing speeches

In their closing speeches, Howe and Leconite-Jones referred in detail to the police persecution experienced by the black community in Notting Hill, which had led to their decision to help organize the march on 9 August 1970. It was the police, angry at the demonstrators for openly challenging them, and not the protestors who had provoked and incited violence that day.

Ian Macdonald reminded the jury that 'this is not the Court of Star Chamber. This is not Russia.' Nor, he continued, was it the United States, where a Chicago judge had recently ordered Bobby Seale, co-founder of the Black Panther Party, to be bound and gagged in the dock to stop him speaking out. In spite of this, Macdonald said that Judge Clarke had sought to subject the defendants to a form of 'naked judicial tyranny' and cited several examples of Clarke's conduct, including his threat at one point to cancel the bail of the next defendant who laughed in his court. In a remarkable section of the speech, Macdonald told the jury not to be intimidated by the proceedings or overawed by the atmosphere or architecture of the court; in spite of everything, it was they the jury who held the power in the courtroom and not the judge. Macdonald recently explained the inspiration for this section of the speech:

> Well, I got a lot of inspiration from the American civil liberties lawyers, particularly over issues relating to the architecture and psychology of the court.

I pointed out how the relations of power were mediated by the architecture of the court. The fact that the judge was sat at some height above the defendants, the way in which you stand up when the judge walks in and sit down when the judge sits down. The way in which the defendants in the dock are surrounded by guards so it looks like they have done something wrong even though they are supposed to be innocent until proven guilty. These are all things which psychologically reverse the burden of proof and seem to place it on the defendants to prove their innocence and not the prosecution to prove their guilt.

(Macdonald 2010)

Macdonald stated that the prosecution had not even proved the occurrence of a riot. He asked the jury if the prosecution seriously expected the jury to believe that the police would have allowed the demonstrators to reassemble after the Portnall Road fight and march down Bravington Road if a riot was taking place. In the absence of any riot, the main charges must fail.

In his closing speech, Michael Hill said the issue was whether the jury accepted the evidence of police witnesses alleging a conspiracy by the Nine to incite a riot or whether they believed the defendants. Despite the efforts that had been made to discredit the police witnesses in the case, 'they are officers', Hill claimed, 'in whom you can and should place your trust'. 'There is no grey area about PC Pulley', added Mr Hill. 'He is either honest or totally dishonest' (*KP*, 10 December 1971).

Verdict and sentencing

After eight and quarter hours, the jury reached their verdict. On the most serious charge of riot, the Nine's legal strategy triumphed: the jury believed the defendants, not the police. All nine were acquitted of the principal charge of incitement to riot, while five of the nine, including Howe, Beese and Crichlow, were acquitted of all other charges. Of the 32 charges originally brought, only 9 stood. The jury had spoken: there had been no criminal conspiracy to incite violence by the Mangrove Nine. Acknowledging it was the season of 'peace and goodwill', Clarke suspended the sentences of the four defendants found guilty of assault so that none of the Nine were sent to prison.

But the Nine's strategy had achieved more. The continual pressure on the judge from Howe, Jones-Lecointe and Macdonald and their suggestion that Clarke was essentially on the prosecution's side prompted the judge to close with a public display of even-handedness. Summing up, the judge concluded that the trial had been 'a very unpleasant experience for everyone concerned' and had 'regrettably shown evidence of racial hatred on both sides' (*KP*, 24 December 1971). This was a watershed, an official judicial acknowledgement of racial hatred within the Met. Obviously, he accused the Black Power Movement of the same, but this was nothing new; the government and the press had been accusing Black Power of racism since Carmichael's visit in 1967. This aspect of the judgement reflected the tired rhetoric of the establishment. By contrast, the declaration that there was racism in the Metropolitan Police was wholly new. The importance of the judge's words was not lost on the police or the government. Horrified, the Met's Assistant Commissioner wrote to the DPP seeking a retraction of the judge's statement. Remarkably, given Britain's much vaunted history of judicial independence, the Home Secretary intervened. A meeting was arranged between the judge and senior civil servants. The Assistant Commissioner also wrote to the DPP, asking that Hill should intercede on his behalf with the judge. But Clarke's statement was never withdrawn.

What began as a political trial ended as a political trial. Following the verdict, there was a flurry of internal police correspondence, as senior officers tried to make sense of what had happened. One noted that the 'outcome is disappointing'. Another noted:

> The remarks by Judge Clarke are most unfortunate and appear to have been made to enable him to demonstrate his complete impartiality. . . . Of course they will be used "as a stick" to beat the police with for years.
>
> (NA MEPO 31/20)

On 27 January, questions were asked in the Commons regarding the judge's statements. Interestingly, police files show that they monitored the exchanges in the House (Ibid.).

Lessons of the trial were not lost on the government, who moved to 'modernise' the justice system by restricting the rights of future defendants to remove jurors on the grounds of potential political bias. The Criminal Law Act 1977 formally reduced the number of peremptory challenges that each defendant could make without reason from seven to three. However, in practice, the scope of defendants to remove jurors for political reasons was also greatly restricted long before this by a new Practice Direction issued by the Lord Chief Justice in January 1973, following the use of such challenges by the defence in the Mangrove and Angry Brigade trials. The new Practice Direction advised the courts 'that it is contrary to established practice for jurors to be excused on more general grounds such as race, religion, or political beliefs or occupation' (1973 All ER 240). A few months later, the Lord Chancellor had the occupation of jurors removed from the jury list, because he believed the information was being 'abused by the defence in cases with political overtones' (Gordon 1983: 108).

Shock waves from the trial were also felt among criminal defence lawyers. In a book published a year later, *Sunday Times* journalist Derek Humphry considered the reaction to the verdict within the legal profession, which saw the case as part of a new phenomenon of defendants in political trials successfully defending themselves, and quoted one unnamed lawyer who acknowledged:

> The three of the Mangrove Nine who defended themselves gave the jury their view of police methods, race relations, colonial history, council politics, the prosecution's and judge's conduct of the trial and so forth, something which lawyers could not attempt. The brilliance with which the three defended themselves over a ten-week-long trial showed for the first time that barristers, for a political trial at least, are not indispensable and that much court procedure is dogma, unnecessary good manners or naked blocking device.
>
> (1972: 164)

Perhaps most importantly, the Mangrove Nine had turned the fight against police racism into a *cause célèbre*. As the academic and former Black Power activist, Harry Goulbourne has written: 'In the black communities of London and elsewhere perhaps the single most dramatic event of these years was the trial of the Mangrove Nine in Notting Hill where the police came into direct confrontation with articulate black youths' (1998: 65). Beese considers the trial 'a defining moment for black people in Britain, because it actually gave real meaning to Black Power, in the sense that, here we were taking this stand and taking on the establishment and winning, and not through the artifice of or the words of defence barristers, it was actually black people doing it for themselves'.

For Howe, the significance of the victory also lay in the fact that a majority white jury had rejected the main allegations against them:

> The British State could not convince whites to join them. Racism as a basis for the division of the British working class had taken a beating, particularly since our defence was based on the fact that the police were liars and should not be believed.
>
> (1988: 47)

11

Towards Racial Justice

Breaking up the Panthers

Following the Mangrove trial, Howe joined the Panthers. This was a natural move. He had worked closely with the movement's leadership during the trial, and his performance inside and outside the Old Bailey garnered a great deal of respect from the Panthers' rank and file. Moreover, at Howe's instigation, C. L. R. James had spoken to the Panthers and his words had led to a new direction. James congratulated the Panthers on their campaign in support of the Nine and advised them to go further by bringing out a new type of paper:

> ... "I'll tell you what to write in the Newspaper. Don't write all this Leninist rhetoric, you don't need it." And he pointed to people in the audience and said "What is it you do?", and he said "I'm a bus conductor." "Then write about bus conducting; write about what happens at your garage ... write about what you want, and what you don't want".
>
> (Dhondy 2010)

The resulting publication was the *Freedom News*, edited by the Panthers' Eddie Lecointe, Jones-Lecointe's husband.

The Panther's leadership was not wholly sure of their new recruit. Howe wrote for the *Freedom News*, and his relationship with Lecointe was far from easy. Lecointe derided Howe's education as 'bourgeois', and Howe resented Lecointe's editorial interference. Dhondy, a member of the Central Core, recalls that they recognized Howe's 'star quality' but were concerned that Howe lacked discipline. 'He was treated as an individualistic maverick, I suppose with some justification.' At the time, Dhondy's 'reading was that he was a very valuable rhetorician, a show-off, a dandy and not to be trusted as a political activist, he might go off in any direction he wanted. . . . A loose cannon but extremely valuable in his own way, if he could be tamed and taught some lessons' (Ibid.). As a result, Howe was never elected to the Central Core. Howe recalls:

> ... I was too rebellious to be on the central committee. I had views of my own, so I conserved an independent faction inside of it, but never acquired the discipline that the Stalinist type central committee required. It was built on the same structures as the Bolshevik Party, it was a kind of vanguard party organisation.
>
> (GPI CAM 16/30)

From what Howe remembers, the Panthers never exceeded 300 members, although the Youth League, which met at the Oval House, was much larger.

> The Asians who came into it were young intellectuals. Like Farrukh Dhondy, H.O Nazareth ... and Mala Sen, a Bengali woman, and then there was another man, Suneet Chopra who talked a lot of Maoist garbage, he was in it too, and artist called Vivan Sundaram – there were about four or five Asians in the London organisation. But whereas you had rank-and-file West Indians in it, one did not have rank-and-file Asians in London. In the Midlands and in Bradford it was different. Several Asians, mostly students and young people joined the associated groups of the BPM ...
>
> (Ibid.)

Howe was involved in the ideological education of the Youth League and on one occasion took part in some drama. Cast against type, he played the part of a judge. It was 'the first and I hope the last time that I ever got involved in acting!'. These 'cultural evenings' attracted between '800 or 900 young people with ease' (Ibid.). Linton Kwesi Johnson, who joined the Panther's Youth League in 1969 or 1970, recalls that Howe was 'particularly liked by the members of the Youth section because he was very articulate, a great talker and he had style and charisma. He had a little following amongst members of the Youth League' (Johnson 2011).

Dhondy, who quickly became a close friend, tried to take Howe under his wing and instil some discipline. The two were involved in one of the movement's triumphs. The 1972 Booker Prize went to 'art critic, novelist and Marxist' John Berger for his novel *G* (*Telegraph*, 24 November 1973). At the prize-giving ceremony, Berger, a reader of *Freedom News* and an acquaintance of the Lecointes, announced that he would share his winnings with the Panthers (*Guardian*, 25 November 1972). Berger's largesse presented a problem: the Panthers had no bank account. In fact, Dhondy was one of the only members of the Panthers' Central Core with a steady job and a bank account that could receive Berger's £2,500 cheque. Needless to say, the Panthers were not welcome at the prize giving at the Cafe Royal, so Dhondy, Howe and Berger met in the Albany, a pub on Great Portland Street. Business done, Berger invited the two Panthers to a house in Primrose Hill where a party celebrating his Booker win was in full swing (Dhondy 2011).

The money was put to good use. The Panthers bought a house, a base of operations. With the mortgage arranged in the names of Dhondy and his wife Sen, the Panthers acquired 37 Tollington Park, Finsbury Park. Howe recalls that the house was used, among other things, as a print shop. 'If a pin dropped, within 24 hours we would come out with a leaflet' (GPI CAM 16/30). The Lecointes lived on the ground floor, with other activists above and below (Dhondy 2011).

The house was a mixed blessing. Events at 37 Tollington Park precipitated the break-up of the movement. The Jones-Lecointe leadership was becoming morally prescriptive. The disgrace of Tony Sinclair, a member of the Brixton branch of the Panthers, was the first sign of trouble. Sinclair was sleeping with two women in the movement, and this behaviour offended feminists in the Panthers. 'The feminist branch of the Movement got hold of him and said that he should be punished and exposed' (Dhondy 2011). Sinclair remembers Jones-Lecointe's uncompromising attitude: 'Althea wasn't backward in coming forward in . . . opening a discussion on what she felt was disrespectful behaviour on your part' (Wild 2005: 101).

Communal living in Tollington Park accentuated the control exercised by the leadership. It allowed the Lecointes to police the morality of Tollington Park's residents and, in so doing, set standards for the movement as a whole. The turning point came when the Central Core were assembled to pass judgement on a Panther who had slept with a white woman in the shared house. As far as the Lecointes were concerned, this was a gross breach of revolutionary discipline. Dhondy arrived at the meeting, not realizing what was happening. His first instinct was to defend the unfortunate Panther. He was after all 'a citizen of this country and has a perfect right to screw who he likes' (Dhondy 2011). As the meeting progressed, Dhondy decided to wash his hands of the whole thing. 'I thought, hang on, I'm not participating in this, this is not a Central Core meeting, this is a kangaroo court' (Ibid.). The Core found the Panther guilty and determined to punish him by revealing his misdeeds to the community. Outraged, Dhondy walked out of the meeting and the movement.

Walking away was not enough. In the face of the BPM's degeneration, Howe, Dhondy and Sen decided to break up the movement. They worked 'on the Jamesian principle that organisations become their opposites, which is Darcus' great slogan' (Dhondy 2011). Thinking back to Howe's decision to leave the Panthers, Dhondy opines: 'I'm sure Darcus was inspired at the time by the fact that James moved from one organisation to another, in America for instance . . . so Darcus was not averse to breaking up organisations' (Ibid.). Howe withdrew, refusing to speak at public events, and as a result, audiences and money dried up. Dhondy, who was the legal owner of the communal house, used the mortgage as leverage. The Core retaliated by sending three Panthers armed with machetes to Archbishop Temple's School in Lambeth, where Dhondy was Head of English. Their express purpose was to threaten to kill him, but they had not counted on the Lambeth Sixth Formers who, eager for a fight, offered to take them on. Dhondy and Howe discussed the matter and in the end, Dhondy signed over the house to the movement, but the die was cast and the movement dissipated (Ibid.).

Police and thieves

Having finished with the Mangrove trial, Howe found work with Release. Founded in the summer of 1967 by London-born artist and activist Caroline Coon and 'art school drop-out' Rufus Harris, Release was conceived as a 24-hour emergency service. In founding Release, Coon 'determined to ensure civil and legal rights for all the young people being scooped up by police using drug laws to harass, threaten and intimidate the emerging anti-establishment hippie movement' (Coon 2011). Needless to say, defending young people from police harassment was bound up with the fight against police racism. Early on, Coon helped defend her Jamaican friend Lloyd Ellis, who had been charged with possession of cannabis and possession of a firearm. The case brought Coon into contact with Michael X. Coon, a natural 'ally of the front against racism', tried to work with Michael X during his 1967 trial. However, collaboration was impossible as 'Michael proved elusive' (Ibid.). Nonetheless, Michael X's trial led to Coon's introduction to Raphael 'Dean' Sergeant. Coon recalls that 'Dean worked very closely with us, giving us all the technical legal advice we needed to set up Release. . . . By 1970, when the government clamp down consolidated, Release had an established group of lawyers and barristers (who had to be anti-the death penalty) who were ready to defend all those singled out and arrested on the front line.' By the time Howe joined Release in early 1972, the organization, whose work had been praised by the Rowntree Foundation, had gained charitable status (Ibid.).

Howe worked together with Barbara Beese at Release. Broadly speaking, it was an office job. 'I'd finished the Mangrove,' recalls Howe, 'and I just wanted a job, that would be part of the rhythm of my life, so Release took me on' (Howe 2011e). On a day-to-day basis, Howe handled complaints against police harassment. He also wrote a pamphlet detailing the legal strategy of the 'Old Bailey Three', discussed below.

By now Howe understood the intimate connection between drug pushing and the Metropolitan police. The criminal scam was later exposed in the trial of six drug squad officers in 1973. Barry Cox, a print journalist in the late 1960s and early 1970s, before becoming involved in television and deputy chairman of Channel 4, chronicled the whole affair in *The Fall of Scotland Yard* (1977). Cox describes the system that emerged in the late 1960s and early 1970s thus:

> In the old CID tradition, Pilcher's team of detectives acquired trusted criminal informants, whom they protected as well as they could. But when these informants were drug dealers, a system had to be created whereby certain dealers were in effect licensed by the Drug Squad to deal without much fear of prosecution, in return for providing a number of their customers as "bodies" for the police.
>
> (Cox et al. 1977: 87)

What is more, drug seizures were 'recycled', partially returned to the streets by the drug squad and sold at 'police prices', giving police informants a competitive edge over other dealers (Ibid., 95–6).

Cox met Howe while working for the *Sunday Telegraph* and recalls being introduced to him through Ambalavaner Sivanandan at the Institute of Race Relations. While writing the book, Cox sought out Howe as a man who understood the police's system and the black underclass in Notting Hill, and who had a knowledge of various West Indian informers, including Bartlett, 'one of a small number of West Indian dealers' who was on good terms with the Drugs Squad. Cox remembers the meeting fondly. 'He was an entertaining fellow, so it was hard to believe he'd been badly treated, but I guess he had been' (Cox 2011). Cox recalls that in spite of his own experiences, Howe displayed a critical detachment and a degree of irony about the police during their conversations. Commenting on the structure of the gangs that were working with the police, Howe 'felt that the cell system of pushers created by Bartlett was as good as any revolutionary network' (Ibid., 96). In addition, Cox recalls that Howe confirmed what he had already discovered, that the police were effectively complicit in and profiting from London's drug market. Howe had first learnt of the arrangement while at the Mangrove and opines that one of the reasons that the police targeted the restaurant was Crichlow's unequivocal refusal to be part of the drug 'recycling' racket.

The Institute of Race Relations

Howe joined the Institute of Race Relations as editor of its monthly journal *Race Today* at the end of 1973. Established in 1958, the IRR was initially a wing of the Royal Institute for International Affairs. Its original focus was on race as a dimension of international and colonial politics. When Leila Hassan joined the IRR in 1970, as Secretary to WEL Fletcher, the company secretary, it was still part of Chatham House and retained its establishment feel (Hassan 2011).

While working at the IRR, Hassan joined the Black Unity and Freedom Party, a group that had emerged from the remnants of the UCPA in 1970. George Joseph, the first general secretary of the BUFP, argued that the organization was an explicitly Leninist group (Wild 2005: 94). The BUFP was also influenced by Maoism, which had enjoyed a renaissance in the 1960s due to Beijing's break with Moscow and the radicalism of the Cultural Revolution. Sivanandan, the IRR's librarian, was loosely associated with the group. As Hassan became involved with the BUFP, she became acquainted with Sivanandan, and she was soon transferred to work with him as Information Officer in the IRR's library.

Race Today, like the IRR itself, went through a process of evolution. In its first few years, Hassan recalls, the magazine was dry, academic and patronizing: '*Race Today* would look at the communities that EJB Rose and his team were looking into, and publish stories about them. But very much: here are these nice coloured strangers who've come, these are their habits, this is how they live, it was that sort of journal' (Ibid.). However, by the early 1970s, the magazine began to open its pages to activists. Sivanandan recalls that *Race Today* was at the forefront of efforts to radicalize the IRR.

> *Race Today* was the first stage of our struggle to get black voices heard. Peter Watson was editor of the journal for a few months during which we (the editorial committee of RT was composed of IRR staff) tried to report and represent black

points of view. But this only became policy under the editorship of his successor Alexander Kirby.

(Sivanandan 2011)

What started in *Race Today* soon spread to the rest of the institution. The catalyst which precipitated Sivanandan's 'palace coup' occurred in 1971. IRR researcher Robin Jenkins wrote a piece that was critical of EJB Rose's, *Colour and Citizenship*. Consequently, the board decided to sack him. The staff, by contrast, sided with Jenkins. Controversy over Jenkins was not the only issue. There were also moves to close *Race Today*. Sivanandan recalls:

> The immediate issue was that RT had run an advert for the Anti-Apartheid Movement on its back cover while at the same time having a picture of Lord Goodman (then negotiating with Rhodesia) on the front cover under the headline, "5 million Africans say 'no'". According to our Council this had cost them thousands of pounds in a fundraising campaign that they had going with big business.

(Ibid.)

The issue over the Anti-Apartheid Movement was symptomatic of broader tensions. Sivanandan explains: '*Race Today* had already been transformed by Sandy Kirby and his editorial committee and was now the cutting edge of the IRR. And there was the rub. The management council insisted that *Race Today* had lost its political neutrality and so endangered the charitable status of the IRR' (Ibid.).

Packing the membership was central to the 'coup'. Hassan recalls the process thus: 'anybody who visited, we would ask them to become a member of the Institute . . . so that when it came to the vote, the vote was that we didn't want the council' (Hassan 2011). The strategy was effective, and in April 1972, Sivanandan staged his internal revolution (Mills 2010: 211). The membership voted 94 to 8 against the Board and in favour of *Race Today*'s new direction. Hassan recalls marching into the Board Room chastising the 'capitalists' and their 'blood money', demanding that they leave (Hassan 2011). As a result, Sivanandan took over the direction of *Race*, which became *Race and Class* in 1974, whereas former members continued publishing *New Community* (Harney 1996: 216). In an attempt to be more relevant to the community, Sivanandan relocated the IRR from Jermyn Street to King's Cross.

Howe had first visited the IRR before the coup. He had used the IRR library in preparation for a 2-day National Conference held in mid-May 1971 at Alexandra Palace where he gave a talk entitled 'The exploitation of Black Workers and the Industrial Relations Bill' (GPI JLR 3/2/13). Wilfred Wood, who had become chairman of the IRR following the 'coup', encouraged Howe to apply for the position of *Race Today*'s editor. Sivanandan also backed Howe's appointment for a variety of reasons:

> The reason we had asked him to edit the journal was not specifically because of that [Mangrove] trial. I also knew other people involved in the trial like Althea Lecointe. The kinds of things that made me think Darcus could be a right kind of editor for *Race Today* was that he was well-informed, well-read on political issues and most importantly that he like us saw the concept of "Black" as inclusive of Asians (very important then), he also saw class as well as "race" as an important determinant and he was interested in struggles in the Third World, especially in former colonies. In other words he was not a black nationalist.
>
> (Sivanandan 2011)

Howe agreed to apply on the condition that he got the job. The interview panel comprised Hassan and two others. Howe remembers nothing of the event except for the 'genuine spark' that he felt between himself and Hassan. In any event, Howe was successful and, in spite of competition from Ron Phillips, got the job (Howe 2011d).

Editing *Race Today*

Howe's appointment was made public on 6 November 1973. The *Guardian* announced:

> *Race Today*, former magazine of the Institute of Race Relations, has a new editor, a black activist who promises to steer the magazine yet further from its quasi-academic origins towards the front lines of racial politics.

Speaking to the *Guardian*, Howe set out a new direction thus:

> We have for a long time been told to use the power of the white liberals. But we must now use our own power: we have to show how it can be used.
>
> (Ibid.)

The new direction became clear through a series of early editorials. They stressed a series of themes: the centrality of self-organization, the Jamesian

Towards Racial Justice 145

nature of the paper, the different historical experiences of the black and white working classes and the possibility for greater radicalization presented by the relatively anti-labour policies of the Heath government.

Howe's first editorial, 'From Victim to Protagonist', signalled a radical break with the past. Rather than proceed on 'liberal' assumptions that black people were 'helpless victims', *Race Today* would reflect the 'self-activity' of the 'Caribbean and Asian peoples'. The editorial concluded with a recognizably Jamesian coda:

> Our task is to record and recognise the struggles of the emerging forces as manifestations of the revolutionary potential of the black population. We recognise too the release of intellectual energy from within the black community, which always comes to the fore when the masses of the oppressed by their actions create a new social reality. *Race Today* opens its pages to the tendency which seeks to give theoretical clarification to independent grass roots self-activity with a view to its further development.
>
> (Howe 1974a: 3)

This was radical, even for the new IRR, an implicit criticism of the stance of the Institute under Sivanandan. For Howe, the IRR had become too focused on black people as victims. He wanted to use *Race Today* to present black people as agents of change.

The February editorial addressed the Energy Crisis, the issue dominating contemporary politics. In the context of the miner's strike, Howe argued that anti-government feeling existed in black and Asian communities to a much greater extent than it did in the white working class. The roots of this disparity, he argued, were historical: the British working class had been socialized by capitalism for more than 400 years, whereas the mores of the new arrivals were at greater variance with prevailing values. Nonetheless, the editorial held out the possibility of black and white workers finding a common cause, something that had been impossible, on an ongoing basis, since the explosion of white working-class racism in 1958 (Howe 1974b: 35).

Howe's third editorial was on a similar theme. Discussing the relative positions of the white and black working class, 'Bringing it all back home' argued that there was 'an increasing tendency within the white working class to take on the British State' (Howe 1974c: 67). Howe attributed this to a historical change. Traditionally, British capitalism had exported its most repressive side to the colonies, while at home, the British working class had been bought off by social democracy. However, the policing of recent immigrants had brought the horrors of the colonial system to the streets of Brixton, Handsworth and Notting Hill. Moreover, British capitalism refused to extend the niceties of social democracy to immigrant workers or working women. As a result, some in the white working class were beginning to see through the liberal assumptions about the essential fairness of British society. Consequently, there was a new possibility that black and white workers could draw strength from each other. What was needed, Howe concluded, was an acceleration of black 'self-organisation, indicating that we too are prepared to take on the British state' (Ibid.).

In some ways, Howe's line was a continuation of the radical position that he, Dhondy and Sen had held since the beginning of the decade. Dhondy summarizes his thinking thus:

> We said, you're never going to cause any sort of revolution in this country. But black workers, people who had come here to work – and work on the lowest rung of the ladder – can affect the policies of the unions, policies outside the unions, and we could begin to demand that we have an integrated society which will change things. You can never bring about a socialist revolution unless the white working class moves.
>
>   (Dhondy 2011)

For Dhondy, the position of *Race Today* was a continuation of the best politics of the Panthers. At the same time, the Jamesian influence was accentuated:

> What was *Race Today*? . . . Obviously it came out of the Black Panther Movement's good politics. And then there was the CLR Jamesian influence which told us clearly, write about things that are happening to *you*, not "theory" as in the Socialist Workers Party newspaper. And don't write about great national issues which you can't affect . . . a Leninist party should do that, but we weren't a Leninist Party. We were trying to gather a lot of people to demand the democratic rights of an immigrant population.
>
>   (Dhondy 2010)

The Jamesian influence was self-conscious. Howe was 'driven by the small organisation as opposed to the vanguard party' (Howe 2011d). Specifically, Howe was inspired by the analysis of the journal of the small organization that James had outlined in *Facing Reality*:

> The journal contemplated here . . . exists so that workers and other ordinary people will tell each other and people like themselves what they are thinking, what they are doing, and what they want to do. In the course of so doing, the

intellectuals and advanced workers, both inside and outside the organisation, will have their opportunity to learn. There is no other way.

(James et al. 1974: 126)

This Jamesian approach was evident in Howe's fourth issue. The centrepiece of the April issue was a series of interviews with Asian workers. Evoking the spirit of Marx's *A Worker's Enquiry*, Howe's editorial argued that the interviews were significant because they revealed 'the day-to-day struggles of the Asians on their introduction . . . to factory life, their customs, their values, their ideas, hopes, aspirations and fears as well as their drive toward self organisation' (Howe 1974d: 95).

In the first year under Howe's editorship, *Race Today* covered a multitude of issues. The centrepiece of the first issue was Selma James' 'Sex, Race and Working Class Power' (James 1974). Howe's focus on black people as protagonists was evident in articles on the experience of Asian workers in the April issue, on the community campaign to free Lloyd James, Robin Sterling and Horace Parkinson, the 'Brockwell Park Three'; and in Sen's article concerning the Imperial Typewriters' strike.

Back to Brixton

Relations between the new editorial team and the Institute soon became tense. Technically, *Race Today* had been detached from the IRR in March 1973, when it was 'hived off' and made part of the new charity Towards Racial Justice (*Guardian*, 15 March 1973). As Sivanandan saw it, this was a technical change, which allowed the IRR to continue its work as an educational charity, separate from *Race Today*, which had an overtly political purpose. In spite of this, the first issue bedevilling the relationship between the IRR and *Race Today* was that of control. Howe argues that Sivanandan wanted to retain control of the journal's direction. Hassan concurs: 'Siva basically believed that the institution was his. And he told me, he told us all, "Whatever Darcus says or does, you need to come down stairs and report it to me"' (Hassan 2011). Howe refused to stand for this kind of interference: 'I had just come out of the Old Bailey, for 55 days, fighting for my freedom . . . that was in my head – so I wasn't going to go and be manipulated' (Howe 2011d).

There were also ideological differences. Hassan recalls that Sivanandan 'believed that black people were victims' (Hassan 2011). Howe's first editorial was a broadside against this position, and needless to say, 'Siva didn't agree with a word of it' (Howe 2011d). For Sivanandan, 'it had to be about white racism', Hassan explains, 'racism that had formed us and deformed us, that was our fight. Whereas Darcus said "No, we're forming our own organisation"' (Hassan 2011). Hassan's contention is supported by a *Guardian* interview, from January 1974, in which Sivanandan stated plainly that *Race Today* 'articulates the voices of the victims' (*Guardian*, 20 January 1974). There was also the question of location. The IRR was based in King's Cross, apart from the centres of London's black community. Howe's instinct was to be based in the community.

Finally under Howe's editorship, *Race Today* quickly started to make a name for itself. Dhondy recalls that as Howe took over, several old hands abandoned *Race Today*. As a result, Howe invited him to write a piece on the black experience in the British education system, a continuation of the material that Dhondy had written for the *Freedom News*. The resulting essay 'The Black Explosion in British Schools' became the lead article in Howe's second issue (Dhondy 1974). Dhondy started with Marx's reproduction thesis, arguing that the modern education system was there to skill and grade the workforce of the future. However, young black people refused to participate – they had no intention of being consigned to the lowest strata of the work force and therefore opted out. The article itself was an explosion. It was picked up by the mainstream press and television. The *Guardian*'s education correspondent featured Dhondy's argument in 'Crisis Amongst Young Blacks' (*Guardian*, 16 January 1974). From what Dhondy recalls, Sivanandan was not pleased: 'I don't think Sivanandan liked it at all. Too much attention, too much Farrukh appearing on television. So he started making trouble for Darcus' (Dhondy 2011).

Against this background, a break with the IRR was inevitable. Howe stayed at the IRR's offices until August, when he relocated the *Race Today* office to Brixton. Dhondy recalls: 'One night, literally one night . . . at 11 o'clock when there was nobody there in the *Race Today* offices, we went in and took out all the equipment, the Photostat machine . . . furniture, machinery, the library . . .' (Ibid.). The contents of the office were bundled unceremoniously into Dhondy's dark green post office van and driven to his squat on Railton Road. 'The next day Sivanandan and his staff turned up to find the place cleaned out!' (Ibid.). This was *Race Today*'s home for a few days until Howe, with the help of Olive Morris, found another squat on Shakespeare Road (Howe 2011d).

Sivanandan tells the story quite differently. For him, the relocation was a practical and a tactical decision.

First, there was the question of money. IRR and *Race Today* shared offices in Pentonville Road and money was tight and it became harder and harder to pay the rent and rates . . . *Race Today* realised that they could not pay the rent on their first floor offices and went to squat in Brixton. Second, there was the question of function: a charity could not do the same job as a political body. Nor could the management that served one function serve the other. Besides *Race Today* and IRR saw our priorities differently – and we tacitly eased *Race Today*'s way out of the Institute's governance.

(Sivanandan 2011)

However, the parting of the ways seems to have exacerbated the IRR's financial difficulties rather than remedying them. Some of the IRR's donors decided to back *Race Today*, and as a result, the IRR lost out. In 1974, the World Council of Churches agreed a $10,000 grant to *Race Today*. The WCC increased their support to $15,000 in October 1975 (*Times*, 1 October 1975).[1] Cadburys were also a major donor. 'For them it was much more authentic than what Siva was doing. Siva was very hurt by that, because the money that he should have got, they decided to give to us' (Hassan 2010).

Becoming a Collective

The *Race Today* office was alive with political debate. Hassan comments: 'Our lives, everyday, were spent in political discussion. People would come, and we would talk. The politics of the hour were thoroughly analysed, dissected and discussed and it was through the discussion that the Collective was formed.' The Collective was formed through a process of self-education. Howe invited Selma James to speak to the people around *Race Today*, then Dhondy did the same. The upshot of these discussions was the formation of the Race Today Collective. The organization was built on Jamesian lines.

I was a Jamesian. We weren't trying to mobilise people to follow us – never! That wasn't part of the deal. We would support the insurrection, but we weren't its leaders.

We weren't making any revolution, that's not our business. We had to educate the social group of immigrants that we came from and be sharp in fighting for their rights. But we weren't there to lead anybody. We were there to educate them and to be educated by them.

(Howe 2011d)

Nor was there an attempt to build a mass membership. *Facing Reality* ruled this
out as a course of action for the new kind of small organization:

> For thirty years the small organization knew what it meant by success: success was
> growing membership and influence. . . . But the organization of today will go the
> way of its forerunners if it does not understand that its future does not depend
> on the constant recruiting and training and disciplining of professional or semi-
> professional revolutionaries in the Leninist manner.
>
>   Its task is to recognize and record. It can do this only by plunging into the great
> mass of the people and meeting the new society that is there.
>
> (James et al. 1974: 128–31)

Howe argues that one of the virtues of the Collective was its capacity to include
members with a variety of political views. The Collective was an eclectic mix. It
included Dhondy and Sen, intellectuals and former members of the Panthers;
Hassan and Jean Ambrose, who were part of the BUFP; Patricia Dick, a one-
time member of the IRR; Beese, one of the Mangrove Nine and a former
employee of Release; and Johnson, who initially wanted nothing to do with
the magazine, but after discussions with Howe became *Race Today*'s resident
poet. For Johnson, the politics of the organization was crucial to his decision
to join.

> It was not just the politics of race, it was also the politics of class. The analysis from
> which we were working was that we were part of a working class struggle. So from
> an ideological point of view, the fact that it was a class orientated organisation,
> as opposed to one simply dealing with race meant that I was more likely to join
> than not.
>
> (Johnson 2011)

Visitors to the Race Today squat included Baldwin Sjollema, a leading figure in
the World Council of Churches' Programme to Combat Racism, who, through
ecumenical work, supported initiatives designed to undermine apartheid.
Sjollema moved into the squat for a time with Anthony Wilson, a Quaker
associated with the WCC and Cadburys. Sjollema and Wilson were both keen
that their organizations should support the new Collective, so Howe invited
them to move into the squat and see for themselves what the Collective was
doing. Pauline Webb and Colin Morris from the Methodist Church also came to
find out about the Collective and were keen to be involved and arrange financial
support for the fledgling organization. Politically and financially independent,

the foundation was laid. The Collective was ready to throw its organizational weight behind the fight for racial justice.

Note

1   The decision was extremely controversial. The British Council of Churches initially believed that some of *Race Today*'s material was 'inflammatory' and went as far as to reduce its donation to the WCC by £1,000 in/protest of the WCC's decision (*Times*, 6 October 1975).

12

Race Today: 'Come What May we are Here to Stay'

It may be revolutionary to suggest that we ought now to become a country where immigrants are welcome, but that is really the logical development of our present position in the world. . . . Who is going to pay for the old age pensions and social services we are rightly distributing now, unless we have an addition to our population which only immigrants will provide in the days to come?

James Callaghan 19 June 1946 (Cohen 2003: 74)

The foundation of the Race Today Collective was contemporaneous with a huge conceptual shift in the British Black Power Movement. Members of the Collective made an important transition from seeing themselves as immigrants or children of immigrants to identifying themselves as British. For Howe, this new orientation was summed up in the phrase, which emerged from Asian campaigns in the East End, 'Come what may we are here to stay.' The Collective's overarching objective was to play a part in the fight to secure immigrants the full rights of citizenship. This new orientation reflected the reality of the situation in Britain. Whatever their intention on leaving the Caribbean or the Indian sub-continent, immigrants were having families, buying homes and establishing themselves as a permanent part of British society. What is more, Howe was influenced by James Callaghan's 1946 speech, which acknowledged Britain's dependence on immigrant labour. Howe concluded that economic imperatives and the desires of the black population were pushing Britain in the direction of a multicultural society.

Howe conceived the role of the Collective in a larger context. Speaking in 1981, he argued:

> . . . I do not believe, comrades and friends, that there is anybody in this room who can deny the fact, the historical fact, that black workers in this country,

who are formerly colonial peoples, are in the forefront of contesting trade union bureaucracy, the exploitation of the workers at Grunwick . . .

(James 1981: 6)

In this sense, the Collective would play a role beyond the black community, as the black community itself helped to rejuvenate the British worker's movement. Indeed, the fight for black rights was part of a broader civilizing mission to reclaim British society from state-sponsored savagery.

It is not difficult, comrades, to know that the way the British government is seeking to keep order in Ireland is by means of tanks, guns and torture chambers. It is clear to us that the way the British government, successive governments, seek to keep order among blacks is by way of the Special Patrol Group (SPG), and collaboration of the courts. So we have to be concerned with the creeping barbarism, not only concerned but mustering all our forces to defeat it.

(Ibid., 5)

Undoubtedly, this was a circuitous route to revolution, but a route on which the black population and the fight for black rights would play a crucial role. Thus, with Howe as editor, *Race Today* quickly became a campaigning journal. The Collective helped foster self-organization, while the magazine recorded the struggles.

At first, the Collective was something of an enigma. Howe recalls that local black community mistook them for social workers. The white left were also perplexed. The radical Collective did not fit easily into any of the mainstream leftist schemas. By the late 1970s, however, the Collective had established itself as an essential part of the Brixton community. As a result, the offices at 74 Shakespeare Road, and from mid-1982 at 165 Railton Road, became a hive of activity, a place that was frequented by local people, councillors, community organizers, artists of various descriptions and, on a good day, world-class cricketers. The Collective's influence was felt far outside London. Through contacts with Max Farrar, Ali Hussein and Gus John, through developing a reputation as the authentic voice of the black community, the Collective became, as Hassan puts it, 'the centre, in England, of black liberation' (Hassan 2011).

Backing protests

'Imperial Typewriters' comments Howe, 'that was ours'. The July 1974 issue of *Race Today* covered the strike by Asian workers at Imperial Typewriters in Leicester. Asian workers downed tools at the Copdale Road factory on 1 May 1974 in protest at discriminatory pay and promotions. *Race Today* had a distinctive position on immigrant workers. Immigrant workers, Howe points out, were not born in British hospitals, nor educated in British schools. Therefore, they cost the country nothing. And yet their labour, their skills, their consumption and their tax contributed to the wealth of the nation. Clearly, Howe argued, immigrant workers were a net benefit to the country. Equally, Howe recognized that British employers unwittingly played a progressive role in the creation of a multicultural society. Employers, Howe claims, actively encouraged black and Asian workers to invite their families and friends to Britain and work in their factories and workshops. Certainly, the employers were exploitative, but employing immigrant labour made economic sense. Howe's analysis was distinctive as it undercut the moralizing that characterized the British debate on immigration (Howe 2011d).

The Imperial Typewriter's strike exposed the moral complexity of issues related to immigrant workers. As well as exposing the exploitative nature of the employers, it highlighted the shocking shortcomings of the British labour movement. Rather than backing the workers, the conflict demonstrated the complicity of unions with management. Quickly, the strike metamorphosed into 'a fight against the Transport and General Workers' Union' (Veenhoven 1975: 534). Initially, the TGWU washed its hands of the striking workers. TGWU Chair Bill Batstone summed up the union's attitude thus: '[t]he Asians cannot come here and make their own rules' (Thompson 1988: 73). Howe travelled to Leicester, moved in with one of the striking workers and spoke on the picket line. Along with other members of the Collective, he helped to organize the movement. Without union support, the 3-month strike was sustained by funds provided by local Asian community and businesses. The Imperial Typewriters strike and the Grunwick dispute of 1977 reflected the very political dynamics that the Collective had anticipated. Neither was aiming to overthrow the state or usher in socialism. Rather, immigrant workers won recognition by the union movement, forced the union movement to rethink its essentially conservative position and began to secure immigrant rights. While the Grunwick dispute was the watershed moment, the Imperial Typewriters strike was the first step towards full union recognition for immigrant workers. For this reason, Howe argues that it was 'one of the most powerful strikes of the time. The newly arrived Asians organised themselves skilfully with community support, with women in the vanguard' (*NS*, 25 September 2003). The ensuing victory was a sign that 'black power was coming to industry' (Ibid.).

The Bengali housing campaign, waged in London's East End, was perhaps the most significant campaign that the Collective became involved in during the mid-1970s. From around 1970, Dhondy and Sen had worked with the Anti-Racist Committee of Asians in East London. The group was established in response to a series of skinhead attacks on Tower Hamlet's Mercers Estate. The attacks left several maimed and one dead. ARC-AEL organized small community defence squads, which quickly stamped out the skinhead 'Paki bashing'. Dhondy recalls the campaign thus: 'As soon as you post 10, 12, 15 very, very incensed Bengali youths with staffs and iron rods at the end of a street . . . you put an end to that, they don't come back' (Dhondy 2011). The Collective initiated the organization, the community provided the personnel. In addition to the defence squads, ARC-AEL organized a meeting of around 3,000 Bengalis in a cinema in Brick Lane. After some discussion, it was decided that Howe should address the meeting. Dhondy recalls: 'as Race Today representatives, Mala could have addressed it or I could have addressed it, but we decided Darcus should address it to show that a black guy could address 3,000 Asians, to say "we're here, it's a common struggle"' (Ibid.).

The collaboration with ARC-AEL established a point of contact between the Bengali community in Tower Hamlets and the Collective, which led to Howe's involvement in a bigger, more protracted campaign. The new campaign focused on housing. At first, the Collective fought the GLC's attempts to evict Bengali families from their homes. The evictions had been brought about by a local swindle. Dhondy recalls that a member of the Community Relations Council has conned a Bengali family out of £12,000. The family, parted with their money in the belief they were buying 16 Matlock Street, only to discover that the supposed title deeds were nothing more than a receipt of a donation to the 'Mohamed Social Services'. A month later, the GLC began eviction proceedings against the family, cutting off their gas and electricity (Ibid.).

By chance, Terry Fitzpatrick, a seasoned squatter, lived across the road from the disputed property. Fitzpatrick, a former squaddie, urged the occupants of 16 Matlock Street, and their neighbours who were experiencing similar difficulties, to squat. The decision to squat the Matlock Street houses created a movement. Between 1974 and 1976, hundreds of local Bengalis occupied vacant buildings. The former members of ARC-AEL took the lead, organizing vans, shifting furniture and setting up lookouts at the entrances to each street. The initiative came from the community. The Collective were invited to help organize the movement and began by sending lawyers to advise on the legalities of squatting.

Their primary role was to fend off the local police while local Bengalis moved into vacant houses. After all, there was nothing illegal about living in a vacant house, nor was it a crime to change the locks. Breaking in was an offence, but there was enough latitude in the law for Race Today lawyers to prevent police interference (Howe 2011d).

Fitzpatrick helped with the practicalities of securing the houses, as well as reconnecting gas, electricity and water. Dhondy recalls eager queues of Bengali families ready to move into the vacant houses. Soon all of the empty houses in Varden Street, Walden Street and Old Montague Street were housing Bengali families, who had collectively formed the country's largest squat. In a feature about the families who made up the backbone of the squatters movement, local journalist Mike Jempson described how 'simple mistakes, domestic responsibilities, unfamiliarity with housing procedures and exploitation are among the reasons' why hundreds of Bengalis had ended up squatting Varden Street. 'Their stories are often classic examples of how immigrant families get caught in a trap which leads them nowhere, purely as a result of being homeless, ineligible for council housing, and lacking the right information' (*East London Advertiser*, 8 September 1978). Squatting was the community's solution to these problems.

Dilapidated though the area was, the squatted houses had a value. Indeed, they were the property of the London Hospital who planned to sell two of the squatted roads, Varden Street and Nelson Street, to Tower Hamlets Council. However, the Council would only buy vacant properties. Consequently, the London Hospital and Council used a variety of tactics to remove the squatters. In February 1977, they cut off electricity supplies to many of the houses after London Hospital complained that supplies were being used illegally. Fitzpatrick and Race Today activists made a direct appeal to local unions, some of whose members lived in the squats. They responded with a threat of industrial action if supplies were not reconnected. Not wishing to face a united front of squatters and the local labour movement, the electricity supply was reconnected but not before the squatters were made to foot a £1,200 bill in connection charges (Ibid.).

The squatters movement emerged organically. Sen, Dhondy and Fitzpatrick helped to give it an institutional shape. BHAG, the Bengali Housing Action Group, was set up in February 1976. The first meeting drew together members of dozens of families from the streets which Fitzpatrick and activists from Race Today had helped squat (Forman 1989: 81). Declaring its intention to squat other empty property for families in need of housing, the organization soon took Pelham Buildings in the heart of Spitalfields. BHAG, an acronym chosen in part as it was the Bengali for 'tiger', united the Bengali Squatters under one

banner. In his study of the housing struggle in Spitalfields, Charlie Forman has
estimated that at its peak, BHAG represented several hundred families, with a
core of 150 families in the four main squats (1989: 82). Therefore, it controlled a
large chunk of housing which had been placed under the Council's development
programme and was in a powerful position to demand proper rehousing for its
members. BHAG's programme was simple: it campaigned for the local families
to be rehoused in safe areas, that is to say, areas where there was already a large
Bengali community and therefore less likelihood of racist violence. To this end,
Fitzpatrick and two Bengali activists drew up a list of 13 possible estates in
which no reasonable offer would be refused. The list was agreed at a squatters'
meeting.

The Hospital and Council initially refused to negotiate with BHAG. Rather,
they gained an eviction order to force the Bengali families from their homes.
This was a double blow for the families involved who had collectively spent
more than £10,000 renovating the disputed properties. The folly of the council's
action was highlighted by the *East London Advertiser* which noted how the
once derelict streets had been given a new lease of life by the Bengali squatters
(5 September 1978).

Together with BHAG, the Race Today Collective began to organize a picket
of the Council buildings in protest. Howe proposed the picket as a show of
strength that would take the issue directly to the seat of local government.
However, there were tensions between the Collective and BHAG over the
status of women inside the movement. Women from the Bengali community
played no part in the meetings that directed the movement. This presented a
problem, as the Collective was committed to sexual equality. Key members
of the Collective were prepared to withdraw their support for the campaign
if there was no change. Howe took the lead in defusing the tension. Howe's
strategy was to avoid discussions of principle and appeal to the pragmatism
of the community leaders. Female members of the Collective were playing a
crucial role in the campaign. Sen, for example, was the Joint Secretary of BHAG,
one of the movement's leading forces. Equally, Hassan and Lorine Burt were
crucial to the Collective's contribution to the campaign. Sen, Hassan and Burt
were determined to pull out if the Bengali women continued to be excluded.
Howe's appeal to pragmatism triumphed, and local women were admitted to
the meetings of BHAG and invited to the picket of the Council.

No longer able to ignore the squatters, the chairman of Tower Hamlets
Housing Committee, Reg Beer, acceded to popular pressure and agreed to meet

a delegation from BHAG. A picket was organized to coincide with the meeting. Howe recalls that the Collective had assumed that the squatters would need to be given some guidance in the mechanics of protest. To this end, members of the Collective had produced the placards and were liaising with a group of Bengali youth when a large group of Bengali women arrived. Unprompted, the new arrivals carried out an audacious act of civil disobedience on the steps of the Council. En masse, the women lay down on the steps of the Council Offices blocking Beer's entry, forcing him to face the picket. The police were astonished and had no idea how to respond. One officer, assuming it was a preplanned tactic, approached Howe exclaiming, 'Oh fuck, what the fuck's going on?'. Howe had no explanation, he was just as shocked, but also elated that the women of the community had taken the lead in the protest (Howe 2011d).

As a result of the meeting, the legal action against the squatters was called off. The Tories who had won a majority on GLC in 1977 eventually declared a London-wide amnesty for all squatters and guaranteed those who registered with it would be rehoused (Forman 1989: 84). Forman argues that the GLC were in an impossible position due to the scale of BHAG's support and BHAG's tactical ability to wrong-foot the Council at every turn (Ibid., 83).

The BHAG campaign is emblematic of much that Race Today stood for. It was a campaign that emerged from the needs of the local community; the local community played the decisive role, with the Collective supporting their initiatives. Additionally, local, predominantly white, trades unions supported the action, without trying to dominate the campaign or co-opt the protest to their own ends. The result was victory. Dhondy recalls the end of the campaign in the following terms: 'The GLC moved in and said "Why are you listening to BHAG? We'll give you the tenancy of these places as Housing Associations for £6 a week." At this point we had a meeting and I said "We've won!" But Mala and Fitzpatrick said "No they're trying to undermine the revolution, the GLC is trying to buy these people out." I said, "These people don't want the end of the British state, *we* want the end of the British state, they want a house!"' (Dhondy 2011).

In 1978, the Collective formally set out the kernel of its ideological position:

Race Today is an organisation which has had as its guiding principle, that its content and practice be guided by the activity of the black working class – what it is saying and doing. That the working class will always be in the leadership of any struggle or movement.

(UC DHP Box VIII/1)

The statement reflected 4 years of practical activity and the lessons learnt from a series of successful campaigns.

Relationship with James

From 1982, the Collective began looking after the 81-year-old James. For 6 months in 1981, James moved into Dhondy's spare room at Stormont Road (Dhondy 2001: 174). Later, the pair moved to Hillsworth Road in Lewisham. Dhondy recalls: 'he came to stay because Darcus Howe asked me to put him up' (BBC 2002). Apparently James' marriage was over, and he was engaged in 'an affair of great culture and intellectual cunning!' (Ibid.). From Dhondy's spare room, he moved into a flat above the *Race Today* offices. While there, 'he was mostly content to stay in his room, almost always content to stay in bed' (Ibid.). More often than not, James had no need to travel as people made a point of seeking him out. His visitors included Viv Richards and Ian Botham. Howe was struck by the experience of witnessing 'first class cricketers looking at him with such awe' (Howe 2011).

The Collective supported him in numerous ways. In 1981, in collaboration with Allison and Busby, they organized his Eightieth Birthday Lectures. On a more prosaic level, Hassan remembers shopping and cooking for him. Apparently, he had a particular penchant for saltfish. Dhondy polished his shoes. Others would fetch wine, brandy and flowers when James was entertaining, and on these occasions Howe recalls, 'if anybody called, you were entitled to say "CLR James is dead" rather than interrupt him!' (BBC 2002).

After James moved into the flat on Railton Road, the relationship was more immediate. Speaking in 1992, Howe described the relationship between the Collective and James in the following terms:

> ... he lived with us, the small organisation, for the last ten years of he life. He actually physically lived with us. He lived upstairs above the offices. By and large, people use the word "consultant" these days – I don't think it means anything, but we had this relationship with him, he was a grand old man, suitably respected, who intervened and worked with us over ten years.
>
> (ICA 1992)

Dhondy characterizes Howe's relationship with James as that of the 'respectful nephew ... with C. L. R. it was respect, it was respect and reading, it was always waiting to see what James would say'. Harry Goulbourne, who had known

Figure 3 C. L. R. James and Darcus Howe share a platform during James' Eightieth Birthday Lectures, Kingsway Princeton College, Camden, London, 1981.

Howe since the early 1970s, recalls spending a number of evenings at the *Race Today* offices, sometimes talking to Howe, sometimes talking with James. 'It was wonderful spending evenings there, just sitting around and chatting. It was a part of a great Trinidadian tradition – liming' (Goulbourne 2012). Goulbourne recalls Howe's relationship with James as one of 'nephew and protector. Darcus provided CLR with care, he made sure that visitors didn't exhaust the old man, and one got the impression that he felt very privileged to be in that position, to take care of him in the last leg of his life. There is a caring side to Darcus, in spite of his bravado, he's a caring person' (Ibid.).

As far as Dhondy was concerned, 'CLR was the ideological guide for Race Today' (Dhondy 2011). James' influence was evident in the Collective's attitude to Western culture. Rather than rejecting it, as the nationalists had done, 'the Collective picked up from C. L. R. James that the western intellectual tradition has to be respected and built upon – that is absolutely the basis of *Race Today*, there is no way that that can be gainsaid' (Ibid.). For Linton Kwesi Johnson too, the Collective was a distinctively Jamesian group, 'we followed Jamesian ideas, based on the principle that every cook can and *should* govern. We were a small organisation that was having a big impact – that small meant big' (Johnson 2011).

James' relationship with *Race Today* dated back to the earliest days of Howe's involvement with the magazine. James travelled widely during the 1970s, keeping in touch with Howe through a series of letters that are preserved at Columbia University. James' correspondence clearly indicates that he thought highly of the journal. Writing from Washington in 1976, James commented:

> I continue to receive with great satisfaction, your wholly admirable paper *Race Today*. I am particularly anxious to hear what you have to say about the events which took place between our people celebrating carnival and the police.... I badly want to hear what happened and what is happening from a dependable source.

(UC DHP Box I/3)

On another occasion, on 16 March 1988, James praised Howe's prose:

> I have two letters to write to you but this must be the first. It is about your book, "The Struggle of Asian Workers in Britain." I have talked to you about it but I want to put what I think in writing. It is a masterpiece in the use of the English language."

(Ibid.)

The correspondence is indicative of the scope of James' interest in *Race Today*. Sometimes, Howe's letters chased James' contributions, commissioned articles or reported on his progress setting up James' lecture tours. The two men discussed events in the Caribbean in Britain and in Poland. In one exchange, they considered the definition of fascism, agreeing that the term is too often used loosely as a synonym for dictatorship; on another, James sent a donation to the George Lindo Campaign (Ibid.).

Race Today covered James' writings and lectures extensively. The November 1980 edition, for example, reviewed James' *Spheres of Existence* and *Notes on Dialectics*, the next issue advertised his Eightieth Birthday Lectures; the magazine reproduced many of James' lectures, and from 1983, James had his own column 'Cricket Notes'.

There were disagreements too, most notably over the issue of black police officers. The row started with Howe's December 1975 editorial. Entitled 'Blacks in the Police Force', the piece critiqued a police recruitment drive aimed at the black working class. In essence, Howe argued that the police were following the pattern of all major British employers, seeking black workers for positions that white workers were increasingly reluctant to fill. He also claimed that the initiative was a bid to reassert control of black neighbourhoods. In the light of this analysis, Howe argued that black people should stay out of the force and 'make common cause' with the 'growing movement against police harassment and corruption in the white community' (*RT*, 1975: 266).

James took issue with this analysis. Dhondy remembers that Howe and James were at loggerheads over the editorial. Dhondy recalls it thus: 'James said, "You are being bloody minded. You fellows man, I tell you, you have to be in every institution of the British state. How can you tell blacks not to join where they ought to be?" And Darcus would get angry.' Howe went ahead and published. James responded with a letter that opened the next issue of *Race Today*. Whatever went on behind the scenes, within the pages of *Race Today*, dispute was handled with great tact. James' letter began by complimenting Howe's 'excellent editorial', while Howe ensured that James' letter got the whole of the magazine's first page (*RT*, 1976: 2). In essence, James' letter argued that the police must become a more representative institution. Consequently, he did not want the recruitment drive 'dismissed or attacked'. At the same time, he argued that black people should not rush into the force unless the police committed itself to recruiting and promoting black people on equal terms with white people; and unless the judiciary too became more representative of the community at large. Throughout the piece, James suggested that black officers should be prepared to play a progressive role in the force; they should, he argued, receive special training commensurate with their role as representative of a minority community. Moreover, he argued that black officers could well win back respect of the community as a whole for the force. In the end, Dhondy recalls, 'Darcus acknowledged that James was right!' (Dhondy 2011). Howe's change of mind was evident, in 1986, in the article 'Blacks in Blue: Black Police Officers Speak', which presented extended interviews with three black officers reminiscent of the journal's early pieces with Asian workers. Later in his journalistic career, writing for the *New Statesman*, Howe took on James' role, urging the Black Police Association to drop their opposition to a plan to recruit police officers directly from the Caribbean (*NS*, 17 July 2002).

Putting out the magazine

Howe was no stranger to radical publishing. He had set up and run the short-lived *Black Dimension*, worked on the editorial team of the *Vanguard* and contributed to *Freedom News*. But for Howe, *Race Today* was something different. He was determined to leave behind the rhetorical tropes that had been integral to the first phase of Black Power. Howe's emphasis was on clarity of expression, in the belief that the facts would speak for themselves. Therefore, under Howe's editorship, there would be 'no denigration of the police as "pigs"', which had been part of the style of magazines such as the *Hustler* (Howe 2011d). In this sense, Howe's editorial approach was a continuation of his approach in the Mangrove trial, an approach that had been consciously 'disciplined by figures and facts' (Ibid.). Howe's experience was supported by discussions with James focusing on E. P. Thompson's *The Making of the English Working Class*. Reading Thompson with James persuaded Howe that English racism 'had to be fought in the style and manner of the English dissenting tradition' (UC DHP Box 9/2). This tradition stood in stark contrast to the mainstream radicalism of the day which Howe characterizes as 'leftist ideological anti-racism' (Howe 2011d). Howe was heading in the direction that James had mapped out in his 'Black Power' address of 1968, seeing Black Power as the latest phase of a universal radical tradition. Howe had never intended the magazine to have a mass circulation; rather, he wanted to keep the spotlight on racism. For Trevor Phillips, this was *Race Today*'s greatest achievement; it kept the issue of racism on the map and made sure that the government and media were never able to ignore it (Phillips 2010).

Hassan, who took over as deputy editor after the break with the IRR, recalls: 'usually the stories presented themselves to us, because of what was going on. We never had to scrabble around for stories' (Hassan 2011). Members of the Collective worked as 'in house writers'. Following a £250,000 grant from the GLC, the typesetting, lay-out and design of the magazine were also done in-house. Julian Stapleton, Lorine Burt's boyfriend, helped with the production of the magazine on a voluntary basis (Ibid.). Johnson, who acted as poetry editor and latterly arts editor, describes his role as 'sifting through submissions that came in, finding the appropriate reviewer for the appropriate book' (Ibid.). During 1977, campaigning took precedence over magazine production and therefore some of the issues had to be shelved (UC DHP Box VIII/1).

In addition to the magazine, Race Today Publications put out a series of pamphlets including Selma James' *Race, Sex and Class* (1975), C. L. R. James' *Walter Rodney and the Question of Power* (1981), Dhondy's *Black Explosion in British Schools* (1982) as well as Johnson's poetry such as *Voices of the Living and the Dead* (1974) and *Inglan is a Bitch* (1981); latter publications included a photographic history of black people in Britain from Windrush to the New Cross Massacre, compiled by Hassan and Hilliman, edited by Trevor Esward entitled *The Arrivants*. There were *Race Today* Bulletins too, such as the 1976 *Teacher's Action* which dealt with the Black Parents Movement; the 1977 special

Figure 4 Howe and Leila Hassan, editor and deputy editor at the *Race Today* Offices, Shakespeare Road, during the 1980s.

edition, *The Road make to walk in Carnival* Day; and the 1979 special issues on the Grenada Revolution and the Terror in Guyana.

As the magazine developed, regular features included 'Asian Diary' and 'Caribbean Diary', which were dedicated to reporting the ongoing struggle in the former colonies. John La Rose wrote an occasional column. Howe and the Collective kept in regular contact with radicals in the Caribbean, particularly Tim Hector, and from time to time, they invited activists from the Caribbean to deliver keynote addresses, such as those given to the March 1983 conference on 'The Social Crisis in Trinidad and Tobago'. The meeting was organized jointly by the Black Parents Movement, the Black Youth Movement and the Race Today Collective.

Basement Sessions

In addition to putting out the paper and aiding campaigns, the Collective was involved in self-education through meetings that became known as 'Basement Sessions'. These events were designed, in Howe's words, 'not to build anything, but to discuss the issues of the day'. Sometimes, they were reading groups. Indeed, an early set of sessions was devoted to James' *Nkrumah and the Ghana revolution* (1977). The book is interesting, not least, because James linked the struggle for independence in Africa with the attitudes of the British working class. The book opens with the argument that while Nkrumah and his supporters played the primary role in dismantling colonialism in Ghana, he was helped by the collapse in support for imperialism among the British working class (James 1977: 1). James' discussion of the relationship between the anti-colonial movement and the working-class movement was a crucial part of the ideological education that Howe spearheaded at the Race Today Collective. On other occasions, the Basement Sessions built bridges with other communities involved in their own acts of resistance. In 1983, to take one example, at Hassan's instigation, the Collective paid for the wives of striking coal miners to come to London and tell their stories (Hassan 2011). During the 1983 and 1984 volumes of Race Today, some of the themes discussed at the sessions were written up for *Race Today*. The July/August edition brought these threads together by opening its pages to NUM activist Ron Browne who articulated the miner's case against the Thatcher government.

Annual weekends away continued the work that went on at the Basement Sessions. The weekends took place in a country house, owned by the World Council of Churches, usually used for spiritual retreats. Johnson recalls them as 'fun, they were for bonding, but they were also for ideological discussion' (Johnson 2011). Monopoly and card games were a feature of the Collective's conferences, with Howe always determined to come out on top. It was at one of these occasions that Howe summed up the general feeling, arguing that police action in Brixton was pushing the local black community to the brink of a social explosion. This was no act of clairvoyance. Hassan points out that every edition of the journal had stories about fights with the police and arrests precipitated by the stop and search campaigns (Hassan 2011). Nonetheless, it was an important moment as Howe situated the growing tension within the tradition of Caribbean rebellion and, in so doing, helped prepare the Collective for the coming insurrection.

Beyond London

James advised Howe to get to know Britain, to avoid the mistake of thinking that the whole country was merely an extension of London. Taking James at his word, Howe made this part of his approach to *Race Today* when possible, travelling across the country to participate in campaigns outside of the capital.

One of Howe's ongoing contacts was Leeds-based radical Max Farrar. By the mid-1970s, Howe argues, there was a growing 'educated white radicalism' independent of the major Trotskyite groups and willing to work with Howe and the Collective. Farrar's first encounter with Howe was through *Race Today*. Together with Vi Hendrickson and Annette Francis, Farrar was involved in the production of the *Chapletown News*, a campaigning news-sheet that had been radicalized in the wake of the trial of a number of young black people who were accused of riot during the 1976 Bonfire Night celebrations. On occasion, Farrar promoted stories from the *Chapletown News* to *Race Today*. In April 1977, while fighting racist police in the West Yorkshire force, Howe put Farrar and the Collective around *Chapletown News* in touch with the Bradford Black Collective (UC DHP Box VIII/1). Ali Hussein's 1978 history of the Bradford Black Collective argues that the group emerged in 1976 after conflict between the police and a group of young black people determined to frustrate a National Front rally. This experience, Hussein argues, 'crystallized the fundamental conflicts between Bradford blacks, the state and other hostile forces, and posed the question of independent black organisation' (Ibid.). The nascent Bradford Black Collective soon established links with the Race Today Collective. Hussein argues that this link was crucial to the Collective's political development as it led to the emergence of a coherent group with a clear focus on 'the struggle against the state. . . . This link was personified in Darcus Howe. During his many visits to Bradford we met to review the progress of the Campaign. He made suggestions regarding issues of the Campaign and related his experience in the BPM [Black Parent's Movement] struggles' (Ibid.).

Hussein's narrative accords Howe a crucial role in countering attempts by the white left to co-opt black radicals into existing organizations. Farrar explains the 'fraught relationship' between black radicalism and the traditional white left thus: 'We weren't happy with the slogan "Black and white unite and fight"', he explains:

There was an incipient racism in the white left. It was never verbalised. There was a sort of assumption that black people would join the white left and basically toe the party line. There was no recognition at all that black and Asian people might have something very specific to contribute, coming out of their experience, that might change the nature of these white left-wing organisations.

(Ibid.)

Big Flame was one predominantly white radical group which bucked the trend. Farrar, and some of the other members, had been exposed to the work of James and recognized the importance of black autonomy. Consequently, there was the scope for some kind of collaboration between Big Flame and the Race Today Collective. Farrar acted as the liaison between the two groups. Farrar worked with Howe on several campaigns. The first was in support of the Imperial Typewriters strike: 'Darcus asked me to organise a picket in Leeds against a business who were supplying Imperial Typewriters in Leeds. We had a demo and a picket and made a lot of noise, and then it turned out we were at the wrong place! They were supplying Olivetti or something' (Farrar 2011). Collaborations over the Bradford Twelve and George Lindo campaign were much more successful. Howe describes his role in the Bradford Twelve campaign thus:

> . . . a group of young Asians, hearing that Bradford would be invaded by the National Front, stashed a few petrol bombs in readiness for the attack.
>
> Twelve of them were arrested and charged with conspiracy to cause explosions, I was designated by Race Today to assist in their defence. . . . The Asian youths convinced a white jury to find them not guilty on the grounds of self-defence.
>
> (*NS*, 6 June 2001)

Farrar remembers Howe as 'a great speaker and a great thinker . . . one of the few significant leading figures in British radical and revolutionary politics in the seventies and the eighties' (Farrar 2011).

Howe and the Collective attempted to create a forum in which these disparate groups could co-operate, organizing the Race Today Bradford Black Conference which took place on the weekend of 22 April 1978. Resolutions put forward ahead of the Conference by Hassan state the purpose of the meeting was to ensure that Race Today could 'assist the independent working class activity and organisations against the attempt to re-colonise us' (UC DHP Box VIII/1). The links forged with the Bradford Black Collective, the Collective around *Chapletown News* and smaller groups in Sheffield and the Manchester Black Parents Movement, founded by Gus John in 1978, would prove crucial to Howe's organization of the Black People's Day of Action following the New Cross Fire.

Race Today also kept a constant eye on the politics of Northern Ireland. The magazine reported the Republican struggle as part of its wider coverage of anti-colonial movements. Indeed, in 1980, Howe argued that 'the Irish struggle will in time be the source through which all social relations in Britain are transformed' (*RTR*, 1980: 51). For this reason, it came to the attention of leaders of Sinn Fein and the IRA. As a result, Bobby Sands submitted a short story 'Black Beard in Profile' which Howe published as part of the 1981 *Race Today Review*. 'It had very little literary merit', Howe recalls, but the submission came in the midst of Sands' hunger strike. Moved by compassion for the starving inmate, Howe published the piece. It was one article among many, but its publication clearly meant something for the Republican Movement, for when Ken Livingstone invited Gerry Adams to London in July 1983, Adams requested a meeting with Howe.

Howe recalls that the *Race Today* offices were circled by a police helicopter for the duration of Adam's visit. The two men spoke at length. Adam's physical presence made a deep impact on Howe. 'He did not smile once. To appropriate a Dickensian phrase, he was "so cold and hard". Icy even. He spoke literally without a blink. His stare was razor sharp.' Howe's abiding impression was of a man who had been forced to inhabit a 'dark grim dungeon' (*Evening Standard*, 9 September 1994).

From 1974 to 1988, *Race Today* combined active support for grass-roots protest with powerful journalism. The magazine remained true to its initial commitment to focus on black people as protagonists rather than victims. In accordance with James' vision of a radical publication, it gave space for people to express themselves in their own terms while also acting as a collective memory – situating diverse struggles within a history of the black community in Britain.[1]

Note

1   *Race Today*'s commitment to the arts is considered in Chapter 16.

13

Ten Years on Bail: 'Darcus Outta Jail'

For 10 years, Howe tumbled from one case to another. The arrests came thick and fast, as did the charges. Actual Bodily Harm, Threatening Behaviour, Wilful Obstruction and Obstructing the Police; as far as the authorities were concerned, there was no end to his crimes. By and large, juries saw things differently, and Howe was acquitted at the end of five of his six cases. Police interest in Howe is easy to explain. Howe picked up the theme of police corruption and racism in *Black Dimension* and never let it drop. What is more, he had bruised a few egos by besting officers in the Mangrove trial. Many of Howe's arrests indicate that elements in the Met, and later in the Manchester Constabulary, would seize on any excuse and go so far as fabricating evidence to even the score. Special Branch certainly kept tabs on Howe. Even after his acquittal in the Mangrove case, they continued to keep him under surveillance. According to a Special Branch report from 1972:

> HOWE, is regarded as one of the leading black militants in London. He is a writer of black extremist literature and has taken part in many Black Power activities. He is prominent in the affairs of the Black Panther Movement, although recently he has been critical of the present leadership.
>
> (NA HO 325/143)

With this reputation it is no surprise that he would have trouble with the law for some time to come.

'The Old Bailey Three'

The Mangrove trial was one Black Power trial among many. The pages of the *National and International News Bulletin* and the *Black People's News Service* were full of court reports of 'frame-ups' that ended up at the Old Bailey. As a result, Howe and other black radicals were often at the court, reporting, protesting or giving evidence in one case or another. The case of the Oval House Four was no exception, and on 20 June 1971, Howe was arrested after a scuffle between demonstrators and police outside the Old Bailey (*TO*, 2–9 October 1972). Three protesters were arrested, facing, between them, six charges of Assault and Actual Bodily Harm.

The 'Old Bailey Three' comprised Howe, Olive Morris and Abdul Macintosh. Morris later became something of a Brixton folk hero. She was an active member of the Panthers and 'a genuine rabble rouser' in Howe's words, a founding member of the Brixton Black Women's Group (ROC 2009: 5) and a woman who turned squatting into an art form (Ibid., 40).

The committal hearing took place at the Guildhall in January 1972 with the full trial at the Old Bailey starting at the end of October (*TO*, 2–9 October 1972). In terms of defence strategy, the trial of the 'Old Bailey Three' was a partial rerun of the Mangrove trial. Howe put in a series of pre-trial applications to strengthen his position. He requested a tape recorder, so that he could scrutinize the proceedings; to have a 'McKenzie' and 'a fair representation of black people on the Jury' (UC DHP Box VII/4). Finally, he requested the names, addresses and occupations of the potential jurors. These requests were granted, and Louise London, a law student, acted as Howe's McKenzie.

As in the Mangrove case, the defendants used their right of challenge to influence the make-up of the jury. Consequently, all four of the black citizens in the jury pool made it onto the jury. The defendants selected the remaining jurors '*on a class basis*' (Ibid.), favouring candidates who, according to the information obtained from the court, lived in working-class areas or had working-class jobs. Howe set out his reasoning for selecting jurors from the white working class in a letter to friends in Trinidad dated January 1973:

> Our decision to have white working class jurors needs to be explained. As a class they are presently involved in a continuous struggle against capital and the political regime. At such moments in history sections of the class acquire instincts and attitudes which they are without in times of social peace. Consequently there exists a willingness to explore areas hitherto considered taboo. Such as the bringing on of verdicts which in essence condemn police malpractice and corruption.
>
> (Ibid.)

Finally, the three also looked into the background of the presiding judge. Through conversations with friendly barristers, Howe learnt that John Fitzgerald Marnan Q.C. had been Crown counsel within the Minister of Legal Affairs in Kenya between 1958 and 1959, where he had prosecuted members of the Mau

Mau (*Kenya Gazette*, 2 September 1958). He subsequently transferred to the Federal Supreme Court in the West Indies (*West Indies Gazette*, 1 January 1959). Howe's initial impression was that the Marnan, in contrast to Clarke, was 'mild, courteous and accommodating'. In spite of this, Howe was not prepared to let down his guard. Outright confrontation had failed the state in the Mangrove case, perhaps they hoped to achieve more with a new strategy. After the jury was empanelled, Howe made one last request, that each juror should be given a notebook and a pen so that they could make notes as the trial progressed. The judge's response indicated that he too had been doing some pre-trial homework. He denied the request, appealing to Howe's experience as a public speaker: 'Mr Howe, you are a man who is accustomed to speak to large numbers of people. This experience, you will appreciate, teaches you that if your audience is taking notes while you are speaking, they tend to miss some of what you are saying' (UC DHP Box VII/4).

The trial began on 30 October 1972, in Court number 3, with Howe defending himself. The prosecution's case comprised the testimony of nine police officers. Bizarrely, their case was riddled with inconsistencies. In Morris's case, there were divergent accounts of her footwear, no trivial matter as she was accused of kicking and injuring an officer. In Howe's case, the inconsistencies were even starker. He was accused of assaulting Inspector Murrell, but when Murrell took the stand, he flatly denied that the assault had ever taken place. PC Lomas accused Howe of biting his finger. However, under cross-examination, Howe demonstrated from Lomas' own notebook that the bite was inflicted by a woman. Howe summed up his approach to cross-examination shortly after the trial thus:

> My attitude in cross examination was informed by the fact that their entire story was a pack of lies, and I made no bones about it. I accused them of having no respect for the truth, of being liars and cheats, etc.
>
> (UC DHP Box VII/4)

Lawyers representing Morris and Macintosh took a more circumspect approach. Even so, as the prosecution rested, it was clear that their case had disintegrated. As a result, the judge instructed the jury to retire and reach a verdict on the charges facing Morris and Macintosh relating to the assault of PC Reid. Although he provided no formal direction, it was clear that he was asking the jury to find Morris and Macintosh innocent prior to their defence. Conspicuously absent was any direction regarding Howe. The jury found in favour of the defendants, Macintosh was discharged, Morris faced two further charges.

When Howe took the stand, he argued that he had acted lawfully in trying to prevent an illegal arrest. He concluded with the broader political point that 'if we as black people turned our backs in the face of such persecution, we would be paying much dearer in the future' (Ibid.). The prosecution made no headway during their cross-examination. Finally, Howe called four witnesses, two lawyers, an Indian flight attendant and a doctor, whose names had been taken after the incident by Panthers on the demonstration. Each one stated that the fight had been precipitated by the police and that Howe had done nothing wrong.

Howe's speech on the final day of the trial, 6 November, addressed the politics of the trial. 'I asked the jurors to make a clear social commitment against police corruption by finding me not guilty. I added that if they failed to do this, "then the words of the West Indian poet ring true"':

Sooner or later but must
The dam going to bust
And everyman will break out
And who can stop them
What force can stop this river of man
Who already knows its course.

(Ibid.)

The words were those of Rastafarian poet Bongo Jerry, brother of Richard Small, one of James' collaborators.[1] The poem was a statement of Howe's philosophical position; a political statement but one which Howe had constructed to sidestep the tired phrases that cropped up again and again in the moribund rhetoric of the British white left.

The case indicates that the state's strategy had evolved between the trial of the Nine and the trial of the Three. Marnan and the prosecution made great play of Howe's intelligence and verbal dexterity. It is possible to speculate that their purpose was to appeal to a distrust of intellectuals that is often attributed to the British working class. Another change from the Mangrove case was the behaviour of the judge. Marnan, by contrast to Clarke, stressed impartiality from the first. For Howe, Marnan 'was attempting to pull one on the jury, that he was sympathetic to our case. If he has established that, then he could tilt the case in favour of the prosecution.' That said, Howe's hope rested with the jury rather than the judge, and whatever Marnan's motives, the jury acquitted him and Morris of all charges.

Howe's strategy had also changed between the two trials. His cross-examination was more finessed: 'it wasn't as forthright as the Mangrove . . . you can't go through a huge experience like that and come and do it again in another court, so there was a little more *politesse*, a little more skill, but the punch was always there.' The verdict was reported in *Time Out* under the heading 'Darcus acquitted again' (*TO*, 16–23 November 1972).[2]

'Self defence is no offense'

The year 1976 was another good year for West Indian Cricket. The 25th of May witnessed the end of a 3-day test between the West Indies and the Marylebone Cricket Club. The visiting team won by a staggering 219 runs. An elated Howe watched the '35-over rout' with Basil Jarvis, the Mangrove cricket team's opening fast bowler and his eldest daughter (*Daily Mail*, 26 May 1976). Nonetheless, the news was not all good, for it was also the day on which Enoch Powell's latest speech on immigration made the front page. Speaking in the House of Commons in typically apocalyptic terms, he prophesied: 'I do not know whether it will be tomorrow, next year or in five years . . . but in these divided [immigrant] communities nothing can prevent the injection of explosives and firearms. The thing goes forward, acting and reacting until the position is reached, I dare say it, where Belfast today might seem an enviable place' (*Times*, 25 May 1976). For a man languishing in the political wilderness, Powell still had remarkable clout. His words reverberated around the press, and the next day, Roy Jenkins announced a raft of measures to tighten up on illegal entry to Britain.

It was against this background that Howe journeyed home by tube from Lords. Automated ticket barriers had only recently been installed at Notting Hill Gate station. Preferring not to get nipped, Howe showed his ticket to the attendant. Mr Conlon, the ticket inspector, barred his way. Grabbing at Howe's arm, he bawled 'where the fuck do you think you are going you black bastard . . . black cunt' (Howe 2011e). There was no way that Howe would stand for this, so he whipped off the attendant's cap and slapped him in the face with it, as well as sweeping the change in his ticket box to the floor. As the two men argued, a black ticket inspector intervened, advising Howe 'don't bother, he is not worth it'. The altercation came to nothing, and Howe was preparing to leave when Paul Camp rushed up shouting 'stop I am a barrister'. Howe replied that he didn't care who he was even if he was 'the Prime Minister of England', adding that Camp should go fuck himself. The two men exchanged blows, Camp armed with an umbrella dislocating Howe's thumb. The lawyer's wife called the police and the two men were then taken to Notting Hill police station, Howe in a van, Camp, who had sustained no serious injuries, in a car (Ibid.).

The charge was Actual Bodily Harm. Howe stood trial at Knightsbridge Crown Court on 5 September 1977. The prosecution called Camp and Conlon. Howe once again defended himself. The jury pool, reflecting the denizens of Knightsbridge, was wholly white. During the 3-day trial, Howe argued that he was merely defending himself, and if anyone was guilty of bodily harm, it was the umbrella wielding Camp. In his closing speech, Howe pointed to the inconsistencies in the statements of the prosecution's witnesses; he argued that the arrest should be seen in the light of the local police's long-standing enmity towards him and in the context of Powell's statement. On this last matter, Howe argued that with hatred of immigrants in the air, 'a lot of us are not going to allow anyone to abuse us without a response'. Flyers produced by the Race Today Collective record that Judge Clover's summing up ascribed Howe the role of '*black* aggressor against *white "little Mr Conlon"*'. After 15 minutes of deliberation, the jury found Howe guilty as charged. Clover sentenced him to 3 months in jail and fined him £100, concluding that he was 'an arrogant man who lost his temper' (DH PC 1).

The verdict came as a shock to Howe's supporters. Howe admits that due to illness, he was not as well prepared as he might have been and that he was rude to the judge. 'I was getting fed up with him really. He said to me, "Why don't you shut up." I said, "You shut up!"' (Howe 2011e). As for the accusation of arrogance on Howe's part, the judge saw arrogance because he demanded servility.

Howe appealed immediately, requesting bail pending the hearing. Bail was denied, but Howe did get a preliminary hearing on 9 September at the Royal Courts of Justice. Here, Judge Gibson granted legal aid for the appeal hearing and set a date of 14 September for a full appeal. For Howe, who was sentenced on 7 September, this meant at least a week held at Her Majesty's pleasure (UC DHP Box V/12).

On his first afternoon in jail, some of the Prison Officers identified themselves as members of the National Front and started pushing him around. Howe had no intention of giving them an excuse to persecute him and therefore became 'a perfect prisoner' (Howe 2011e). Howe had never sought martyrdom or seen a prison stretch as a political tool. Therefore, he spent the week unobtrusively playing by the rules. On the Saturday, the first full day, he quit smoking to avoid developing an increased dependence. On the Sunday, it was a choice between joining the IRA contingent in Church and seeing a film. Howe chose the latter.

He soon picked up Pentonville's golden rule: 'you don't do nothing for nothing' so when his cell mate asked him to write to his girlfriend, Howe agreed in exchange for a piece of fruit. As Howe remembers it, 'half of Brixton was in the exercise yard' and they greeted him with shouts of 'Darcus!'. By and large, Howe kept himself to himself – he had no desire to participate in the culture of the prison more than he had to (Howe 2011e).

Outside Pentonville, the Race Today Collective immediately formed the Darcus Howe Action Committee to campaign for Howe's release. The Action Committee quickly came up with a concrete programme, asking supporters to send letters and telegrams to the Home Secretary and the Lord Chancellor 'protesting the savage sentence and conviction', to picket the court during the appeal hearing and to picket Pentonville. Hassan recalls that the Action Committee made use of Race Today's connections in Trinidad, Jamaica and America to create an international campaign. George Weekes, now a Senator in Trinidad, was one of many who sent a telegram to the Home Secretary protesting the sentence (GPI BPM 5/1/6/1).

The Action Committee picketed Pentonville every evening, chanting, singing and wearing army greens. Hassan estimates that there was a core of 20 demonstrating every evening, Dhondy recalls that on some occasions there were as many as 100. During visiting hours, Howe saw Hassan, Ian Macdonald and other members of the Action Committee. As well as legal advice, one or two managed to smuggle in a fortifying drop of brandy. The committee met every evening to discuss the way forward. It was at one of these meetings that criminal barrister Len Woodley came up with the legal strategy that would get Howe out of jail. In essence, Woodley argued that Howe's 16-month period on bail was punishment enough and that the appeal court should order Howe's immediate release.

The campaign seems to have worked. Howe's appeal came to court in a week. The outcome seemed to be a foregone conclusion. Even the Prison Officer who discharged Howe told him that he would not be coming back. On his arrival at the Royal Courts of Justice in the Strand, Howe was greeted by around 50 supporters carrying placards reading 'SELF DEFENCE IS NO OFFENSE' and 'YOU CAN'T KEEP A GOOD MAN DOWN'. Lord Justice Lawton, Mr Justice Park and Mr Justice Michael Davies reduced the custodial sentence to the time served, allowing for Howe's immediate release. In giving the judgement, Lawton recognized that the incident 'might well have been sparked off by an offensive remark'. He justified the court's immediate intervention in terms of

Figure 5 Protest outside the Central Criminal Court during Howe's appeal hearing, September 1977. Leila Hassan and Howe's daughter Taipha hold placards.

the 'staleness' of the case, which had taken more than a year to come to court, and the protracted and no doubt stressful period of bail. Lawton also pointed to Howe's 'valuable service to the community' (*Times*, 15 September 1977). Howe's release was greeted by applause from the gallery. On hearing the news, a chant 'We freed Darcus Howe' broke out outside the court (*Jamaican Weekly Gleaner*, 23 September 1977). Howe left the court a free man carrying his daughter Taiphe (*Telegraph*, 15 September 1977).

Meanwhile, *Race Today*'s poet, Linton Kwesi Johnson, had immortalized the campaign to free Howe in his song 'Man Free (for Darcus Howe)'. The track appeared on Johnson's 1978 debut album *Dread Beat an' Blood* recorded by 'The Poet' (Johnson) and The Roots, a group of nine musicians including dub master and record producer Dennis Bovell. Lenin Woolford, Howe's comrade and friend since the late 1960s, remembers people listening to the song at parties and clubs all over Port-of-Spain throughout 1978 and 1979, even though most did not know who Darcus was or why 'The Poet' was so keen to get him 'outta jail'.

Citizen Howe

The Silver Jubilee of 1977 is perhaps the closest the British people have come to nationwide carnival in recent years. On 7 June 1977, Britains took to the streets in celebratory mood. When people take to the streets for Carnival in Port-of-Spain, the accent is on parade and dancing. During the Silver Jubilee, by contrast, the British were content simply to sit. In ordered rows at trestle tables, millions turned out under red, white and blue bunting to enjoy sandwiches, sausage rolls, tea and jam tarts in plastic Union Jack hats.

In Notting Hill, Frank Crichlow threw the Mangrove Restaurant behind the local street party. This was a party with a difference; instead of the ubiquitous Union Jacks, All Saints Road was to be decorated with the flags of the African nations, flags of the Organisation of African Unity and the red, green and gold of the Rastafari. The road had to be closed and therefore, permissions had to be sought. Crichlow enlisted Howe, and the two men went dutifully to the local police station to inform the Community Relations Officer that they would be celebrating African Liberation Day on the same day that the rest of the country was celebrating the Jubilee. They laid out the timetable for the day and left assured that everything was set for the party.

Crichlow pulled out all the stops. Howe recalls his efforts to get the finest ice cream for the party. On the day, he opened a little kiosk on the corner of All Saints Road and Westbourne Park Road, a couple of doors down from the Mangrove, serving Marine Ices that he had bought in from Camden Town. It was mid-afternoon and the party was winding down, when a car containing four police officers pulled up. The officers were on duty, but in the spirit of the Jubilee they were drunk. Inspector Hunt, who was in the front passenger seat, leaned out of the window and shouted 'Frank Crichlow's a cunt!'. A moment later, he called out again: 'Darcus Howe's a fucking arsehole!' (Howe 2011e). Howe pulled open the car door and performed a citizen's arrest on the inebriated officer. Howe read him his rights London-style: 'You're fucking nicked you cunt!'. The other officers were too intoxicated to put up anything more than token resistance (Ibid.).

Howe incarcerated Hunt in the basement of the Mangrove, making Wappy King, a local hustler who was well acquainted with the penal system, his *ad hoc* warder. Howe asked King to get the officer a sandwich and a cup of tea. King protested – this was better treatment than he had ever received at the hands of the police. But that was part of Howe's point: King, the working-class hustler, would teach Inspector Hunt how to treat his charges. Next, Howe phoned Scotland Yard to put them in the picture: 'I have got Inspector Hunt here under arrest for disorderly behaviour and incitement to riot' (Howe 2011e). The response was swift; 'seven van-loads of police' arrived in riot gear (UC DHP Box V/5). King escaped arrest by jumping out of a window. Evading police capture had never featured large on the QRC curriculum, and Howe's attempts to follow King's example were an abject failure. The police arrested him for kidnapping a police officer (Howe 2011e).

With the benefit of hindsight, it is possible to argue that the citizen's arrest was the apotheosis of the 'policing the police' initiatives which characterized Black Power in the late 1960s. But this is not how Howe saw it. 'I was just rocking 'n rolling', he explains. The arrest was spontaneous; he was making it up as he went along. But at the back of his mind was the adage taken from James: 'all movement comes from self movement'. The citizen's arrest was Howe on the move.

By the time of the trial, the charge had been reduced to 'Threatening Behaviour and Wilfull Obstruction' (UC DHP Box V/5). On this occasion, Howe enlisted the services of the solicitors Clinton Davis and Co., the firm had represented members of the Black Unity and Freedom Party, and were therefore known to Hassan (Hassan 2011). A letter from the Solicitors to the Chief Clerk at Marylebone Magistrates Court, dated 16 September 1977, requested a postponement of the trial due to the fact that Howe was suffering from nervous exhaustion (UC DHP Box V/5). The request was granted and the trial date was put back from September to December. The magistrate seems to have seen the situation for what it was. He dismissed the case after the prosecution rested. He did, however, offer Howe one piece of advice: 'Mr Howe', he said, 'next time you have a party, don't go and talk to the police' (Howe 2011e).

The London case

Howe's next brush with the law occurred in June 1978. The trial, which yielded the clearest evidence of police malpractice thus far, was precipitated by the burglary of Howe's home at 112 Mayall Road in the early hours of Saturday 17 June, the fourth time the house had been burgled. Thieves took jewellery, money and a stereo belonging to Hassan. Hassan quickly found the culprits, who had made no attempt to cover their tracks, and informed the police. The robbery took place on Saturday night, but by Monday, in spite of repeated calls, the police had done nothing (Howe 2011e).

The robbery was a symptom of a bigger issue, a lack of connection between Brixton's black working class and the black intellectuals of the Race Today Collective who had set up shop in one of the poorest areas of London. The decision to move The Collective into the heart of the community was not without its problems. Howe puts the issue in the following terms: 'if you decide to go back into the community, as opposed to where Siva was, then they saw you as social workers...'. Hassan concurs, 'the young ones just thought we were social workers and what you did with social workers was intimidate them' (Hassan 2011). At first, the community had no idea that the offices were bringing out a magazine or engaged in a broader fight for racial justice.

The following Monday in the early evening, Howe, Hassan and Lorine Burt were en route to St Mathew's Church to discuss using their hall to prepare costumes for the Notting Hill Carnival. Passing 60 Mayall Road, Hassan saw the top of her stolen stereo lying in the garden. Leading the way to the basement of 60 Mayall Road, Hassan found a group of small-time thieves and local badmen. Hassan demanded her things back. According to a written statement given at the time, Hassan received the following response, 'res' you blood claatself gal. Which stuff you-a talk 'bout?' (UC DHP Box V/5). It was at this point that Howe was attacked from behind by Michael Dixon who was carrying a large dagger. Howe overpowered him and, holding the knife to his throat, told Hassan and Burt to 'wreck the joint'. Looking back, Howe has the following words of advice: 'never tell women to wreck a joint! I saw the television sailing through the window! And they're trying to pull a stove off its hinges. They wrecked the place!'.

News of what was going on travelled fast, and a crowd started assembling on Mayall Road. Fearing violence, Hassan and Burt hurried to the police station. Howe, having retrieved the stolen property, returned home to find that his place had been ransacked. Howe called up as many members of the Collective as he could to help him defend the house. This was class war: Cambridge graduates and former private school students defending a house against a growing posse of Brixton's lumpen proletarians. Howe, assuming the role of Commander-In-Chief, gave Dhondy and Akua Rugg, *Race Today*'s arts editor, a pep talk to help the miscast intellectuals get into character: 'Farrukh, you killed 15 people in Mumbai. Akua, you killed ten people in Nigeria.' 'I beg your pardon?' responded the nonplussed Rugg (Howe 2011e).

As the posse continued up Mayall Road, it was clear that the Collective was outnumbered. Dhondy recalls that there was a group of around 25 armed with machetes advancing on the house ready to 'teach Darcus a lesson', while the eight or ten members of the Collective armed with cricket bats defended the house.

Confrontation could not be delayed indefinitely, so with no alternative, Howe went out to meet the leader of the crowd, 'a bad fellow', Ivan Dixon, the brother of the owner of 60 Mayall Road. There was a tense stand-off, but before the situation could escalate, the police arrived and escorted Howe back to Brixton police station. Ivan and Elorine Dixon were arrested after a scuffle, Michael Dixon was arrested later. On Mayall Road, the police assured Howe that he was not under arrest. The story changed back at the police station where Howe was informed that not only was he under arrest, but also that he was refused bail, for his own safety's sake. Hassan, who was waiting at the station, remembers the disbelief on the faces of the officers who compared the scene on Mayall Road to a carnival (Howe 2011e).

More than 2 years elapsed between the Howe's arrest and the trial, but this period was anything but uneventful. The next day, Howe arrived at Camberwell Magistrates' Court. By this time, the Darcus Howe Action Committee was already up and running and a picket demanding his release greeted him as he arrived at the court. Bail was granted, albeit against the express wishes of the police. The conditions were punitive. Howe was required to provide two sureties of £500, he was required to present himself three times a week at Tooting Police Station, he was not allowed to go within half a mile of Brixton and he was required to live at his sister's house. Following a second hearing in July, these conditions were moderated; Howe was allowed to visit the *Race Today* offices, but only during office hours. A further 2-hour extension of this 'curfew' was granted by Judge Thomas in December, again against the wishes of the police who claimed that Howe would use any relaxation of the conditions of bail to intimidate prosecution witnesses (UC DHP Box V/5).

The direct action against one of Brixton's hard men proved to be the turning point in the Collective's acceptance by the local community. After all, what kind of social workers would dare to take back their property from the Dixon family and then stand their ground against an armed posse? While it had landed Howe in court again, the confrontation meant that the Collective and its supporters could now go about their business unmolested. Over time, they established close ties with the community and would be trusted enough to be the only organization which was told the story of April 1981 insurrection by those who helped organize it (Howe 2011e).

The trial, initially set for July 1979, was postponed repeatedly (UC DHP Box V/5). The final round of postponements was brought about by Judge David West-Russell who reserved the case for himself. At first, he justified this due to his familiarity with the case notes; later he claimed to have received threatening telegrams and therefore wanted to reschedule the case in order to hear it in a secure court room (UC DHP Box V/5). The judge's behaviour precipitated letters of protest. Patricia Hewitt, General Secretary of the National Council of Civil Liberties, latterly Labour Secretary of State for Health, condemned the judge's intervention in the following terms:

> The Committee, of which I am chairman, feels that the improper intervention of Judge West-Russell interferes with the civil rights of Darcus Howe to a proper trial, and amounts to case-vetting . . .
>
> (GPI BPM 5/1/6/1)

The letter-writing campaign forced a response from Lord Hailsham, the Lord Chancellor. In answer to a protest from Robert Hughes MP, Hailsham acknowledged that the wheels of justice were turning slowly, adding that the delays were, 'for the most part . . . outside the court's control' (GPI BPM 5/1/6/1).

The telegrams were part of a campaign initiated by the Action Committee which encouraged support from the Caribbean. Telegrams from the Oilfield Workers Trade Union, from Pan Trinbago, Trinidad's national steel-band organization, Jewel 22, Third World and the Renegades steelbands arrived at the court; Jamaicans Against Black Repression in Britain handed in a protest petition to the British High Commission in Kingston; and following an interview in the American journal *Black Scholar*, a campaign was launched 'on his behalf in the United States' (*RT*, 1978: 124). The case opened on 20 May 1980. In spite of Judge West Russell's efforts, the case was heard before Judge Oliver Cox. Howe, facing charges of Grievous Bodily Harm and Burglary, was represented by Ian Macdonald. In the event, the trial was a straightforward affair. On cross-examination, Macdonald was able to draw the jury's attention to the criminal records of the prosecution's witnesses. The three main witnesses, Michael Dixon, Glenroy Bailey and Coleman Clarke, had 39 previous convictions between them (GPI BPM 5/1/6/1). They also admitted being heavily armed. More damning still, they testified that in order to escape being charged following the Mayall Road incident, they had agreed to testify against Howe. Macdonald's cross-examinations effectively demolished the prosecution's case. Sensing the jury's mood, Judge Cox advised the defence to make an application for an immediate verdict. Having deliberated for a total of 3 minutes, the jury acquitted Howe of all charges (UC DHP Box V/5).

The Bradford case

The Bradford case was bound up with the campaign to free George Lindo, a young black man wrongly accused, and wrongly convicted, of robbing a betting shop. Bradford Black Collective, publishers of *Bradford Black*, invited Howe and the Collective to organize the campaign to free Lindo. On meeting Lindo, Howe was convinced that 'he was the epitome of a West Indian Christian' and no criminal (Howe 2011e). Howe's intuition proved correct, and Lindo was freed in March 1979. Not only was Lindo innocent, but also the case was a clear instance of police malpractice. Remarkably, the Manchester Constabulary were aware that officers had forged Lindo's statements and therefore that the conviction was unjust 6 months prior to Lindo's release (*Times*, 12 April 1980).

Part of the campaign was a fundraising event, an evening at The Factory, a club in Manchester, featuring The Heptones, a local Jamaican band (UC DHP Box V/5). Howe was on the door in the early hours of 11 February 1979 when two officers demanded admittance. The officers, who appeared to have been drinking, jumped to the front of the queue, called Howe a 'black bastard' and pushed their way in. It was an unpleasant part of an otherwise successful evening, but Howe thought no more of it, until 5 months later, on 27 July, when he received a summons to appear in court on charges of obstructing the police (GPI BPM 5/1/6/11).

The news was shocking. There had been no arrest, no charge and no indication of anything wrong. A press statement issued by the Darcus Howe Action Committee described the charge in the following terms:

> We believe that the charge represents an attempted frame-up by the Manchester police force, and that Darcus Howe has been singled out because of his political activities in the North.
>
> (GPI BPM 5/1/6/1)

From Howe's perspective, the prosecution reflected a police vendetta. He had been leading a campaign exposing corruption in the Manchester Police, and now the police were attempting to get even.

Once again Howe was defended by Macdonald. Pointing to discrepancies in the prosecution's case, Macdonald argued that the police statements were 'a complete concoction, a set of lies, in effect trying to frame my client on concocted evidence' (*Argus, Bradford and Yorkshire Telegraph*, 19 March 1980). Macdonald also invited evidence from two members of the Bradford Black Collective, Courtney Hay and Andrew Clarke, and from Gus John who testified that the police had arrived 'flushed with drink' and had been admitted to the party where they immediately started drinking.

The prosecution's case was untenable. Howe was acquitted and the presiding magistrates awarded him £200 in costs in recognition that he had done nothing to bring the charges on himself. Speaking to the *Argus, Bradford and Yorkshire Telegraph*, John La Rose, chairman of the Darcus Howe Action Committee, argued that Howe's acquittal showed that the prosecution was nothing but 'political persecution of Mr Howe, especially in connection with the George Lindo case . . .' (*Argus, Bradford and Yorkshire Telegraph*, 20 March 1980).

Conclusion: 'Six times framed, six times freed'

'Its strange,' Howe comments, 'where these things begin.' As a teenager, Howe noticed a certain attitude among the police towards the young people who lived in Belmont. It was a working-class area, and on Friday nights, the police would turn up 'and nick you on an obscene language charge'. Howe refused to be intimidated. His father told him 'if you didn't do anything, do not run'. This early experience with officious police and a sense of justice imbibed from his father have stayed with him from his youth to the present day (Howe 2011e).

The Mangrove case was clearly a political trial, involving the combined might of the Home Office, the Met, Special Branch and the British judiciary. Later trials were about more parochial issues; specifically, a long-running vendetta against Howe from certain officers at his local police station. Howe explains the attitude of the police in Darwinian terms.

> You had this detritus of officers who were thrown at the black community, they didn't have to investigate, they just had to lock them up and charge them. And I discovered that later in Brixton. When you come out of training you want to be an Inspector, and there were those that couldn't make it. So they sent them to Brixton or Notting Hill. So we got the detritus, of that I am absolutely sure. As you mature in these cases, you realise they weren't disciplined by any kind of legality at all.
>
> (Ibid.)

Howe never wanted to be a martyr and never courted a prison sentence. But he and the Race Today Collective were determined to expose racism in the police and fight a concerted campaign for justice in the face of corruption in the forces of law and order come what may.

Notes

1 Bongo Jerry's 'Sooner or later' was first published in Savacou (1970), eds. Edward [Kamau] Brathwaite, Kenneth Ramchand and Andrew Salkey.

2 Having been acquitted, Howe wrote to the Home Secretary demanding that the evidence of the police officers given during the trial should be investigated. The Home Office acknowledged the letter in January 1973, contacting Howe again on 26 February 1973, stating that the Director of Public Prosecutions had concluded that there was insufficient evidence to proceed against the officers in charges of perjury (UC DHP Box 6/3).

14

'Thirteen Dead and Nothing Said'

The early 1980s were a turning point in British politics. The post-war consensus, which had been under strain for some time, finally gave way to political polarization and the politics of confrontation. Anti-immigrant sentiment gained new legitimacy with the election of Margaret Thatcher's government in 1979. The Tories had overtaken Callaghan's government in the polls soon after Thatcher's 1978 interview for Granada TV's World in Action. The interview tackled the subject of immigration head on. Speaking to Gordon Burns, Thatcher made a point of seeking to address the purported grievances of those driven to voting National Front. Thatcher said she understood 'that people are really rather afraid that this country might be swamped with a different culture' and declared that she would not allow 'false accusations of racial prejudice' to stop her from tackling the 'problem' of immigration (*World in Action*, 1978). True to her word, a white paper was produced within a year of her election and a new British Nationality Act hit the statute book in 1981, further restricting the right of Commonwealth citizens to settle in the United Kingdom. Clearly, the politics of race played a significant role in Thatcher's victory.

Those on the Tory Right with a track record of opposition to immigration were emboldened by this climate. On 2 January 1981, right-wing Conservative MP Jill Knight was reported as calling for 'noisy' West Indian parties to be banned, following a New Year's Eve party in her constituency which had allegedly gone on for days. A veteran member of the far right Monday Club, which advocated voluntary repatriation of immigrants and defence of white minority rule in South Africa and Rhodesia, Knight appeared to suggest that local whites would be entitled to take direct action to stop such parties (*The Guardian*, 17 January 2011; Manzo 1998: 151).

Two weeks later, in the early hours of Sunday, 18 January, a terrible fire started at a birthday party held at 439 New Cross Road in Deptford, South London. Thirteen young people aged between 14 and 22 lost their lives and many more were injured; all were from the African-Caribbean community. The 14th victim, Anthony Berkbeck, who had survived the fire by dropping from a first floor window, was tormented by the memory of what he had seen. His body was found at the foot of a block of flats 2 years later where he had taken his own life (Steele 1993: 218).

Howe quickly became involved in the movement determined to force the political establishment to acknowledge the horrors of the New Cross Massacre, to conduct a full and fair inquiry into the causes of the blaze and to bring the perpetrators to justice. He was elected by an impromptu grass-roots assembly to give the emerging movement shape. In the tense period following the fire where official misinformation abounded, he played a central role in dealing with the press and the authorities. In the run-up to the Black People's Day of Action, Howe embarked on a whistle-stop cross-country tour, ensuring that New Cross's tragedy became a national campaign. The worst catastrophe ever experienced by the black community was destined to prompt the largest demonstration of black political power Britain has ever seen, when 20,000 black people marched through London on 2 March 1981 to protest at police, media and government response to the fire.

New Cross Massacre Action Committee

Howe received word of the fire on the day that it happened. He was at a meeting with John La Rose, founder of New Beacon Books, and Jessica and Erica Huntley, who ran the Walter Rodney Bookshop and the radical literary publishers Bogle L'Ouverture. The meeting had been called at La Rose's home in Finsbury Park to discuss the proposal to hold a Book Fair of Radical and Third World Books. The planning would later come to fruition in the week-long literary festival which took place in April 1982 at Islington Town Hall and whose success led to it becoming an annual event thereafter (Alleyne 2002: 58).

On hearing of the fire, the meeting ended. Howe, La Rose and Roxy Harris, of the Black Parents Movement, made their way to the Moonshot Youth Club in Pagnell Street, New Cross, where the survivors had gathered in the early hours of Sunday morning. Sybil Phoenix, who ran the Moonshot, had arrived at the scene of the fire while bodies were still being carried from the building. Phoenix had been asked by the police to try to find people who had been at the party to help identify the badly burned bodies. She was to play a crucial role supporting the bereaved through the devastation of the days and weeks that followed.

Howe and La Rose met Mrs Gee Ruddock, who had organized the party to celebrate her daughter, Yvonne's, 16th birthday. Yvonne perished in the fire. Paul, her 22-year-old son, received fatal burns, dying in hospital 3 weeks later. La Rose later recalled the meeting and the Radio interview with Ruddock in the Moonshot. The interview was broadcast live on Alex Pascall's daily 'Black Londoners' Radio Programme:

> In spite of her agony and suffering she spoke to us because she had already heard Radio reports that weren't true. She said that it had been a peaceful party. There were no fights. It was the first party she had given in the house. She'd made a special concession to her daughter, Yvonne for her 16th birthday and she was glad she had because she had never seen her so happy before. (1984: 7)

Howe also remembers that Ruddock was 'lucid, obviously drowned in grief, but in full control of her faculties' (NS, 12 April 1999). Mrs Ruddock and the other survivors all spoke of the party's relaxed atmosphere, at which the 17-year-old Gerry Francis, another of the fire's victims, played the latest reggae tracks on his sound system while Mrs Ruddock superintended the house.

Ruddock told Howe without hesitation that the blaze was caused by a fire bomb attack. Police officers had told her twice, within the first couple of hours of the fire, that it had been caused by a petrol bomb. The first officer to point to arson was on the scene outside the house, the second at King's College Hospital. Other witnesses reported the suspicious behaviour of a man who pulled up and drove off in White Austin Princess. Four days later, the *South East London Mercury* reported that the police were trying to trace the driver of the vehicle which was parked outside the house (22 January 1981).

The horrific events of that night took place in an area known to many as the race hate capital of Britain. Indeed, New Cross had been the scene of pitched battles between the National Front marchers and anti-fascists just 4 years earlier. Invoking the memory of an earlier fire bomb attack on a black party which had left 22 people injured, Joan Anim-Addo recalled 'every black family's nightmare, anticipated by a history of racist threats and actual attacks such as the Sunderland Road fire-bombing a decade earlier, materialised in the news of the dead and injured' (1995: 136).

Howe and La Rose were not the first activists on the scene. Already the West Indian Standing Conference had called a public meeting for the following Sunday. Howe and La Rose proposed that a planning meeting be called on Tuesday 20 January at Pagnell Street. Expecting a couple of dozen seasoned activists to turn up for the Tuesday meeting, Howe was astonished when 300 people came from as far away as the Midlands. The meeting established the Black People's Assembly, or General Assembly as it was known, a body open to everyone who supported the general aims of the campaign. The Assembly met every week. It heard from the survivors of the fire, discussed the troubled history of the black community in Deptford and addressed the question, as Howe puts it, of 'what has to be done?'. In concrete terms, the Assembly's role would be to make recommendations to the New Cross Massacre Action Committee (NCMAC), a body open to Asians, Africans and West Indian activists, who would decide how to carry them through. The Assembly also set up a trust (administered by Alex Pascall and John La Rose) to receive money to organize the funerals for those killed in the fire. In this way, community participation was maximized, the more politically minded could join the NCMAC, while those who were less willing to take a political stand could still demonstrate their solidarity with the grieving families by making a donation to the Parents' Committee.

The immediate aims of the campaign were to establish a Fact Finding Committee which would take statements, gather evidence and oversee the police investigation, and to call a press conference in response to the misleading reports which were beginning to appear in the press. The minutes of the first NCMAC meeting, which took place immediately after General Assembly, record that members of nationalist Pan African Congress Movement (PACM) tried to have Asians and whites excluded from the public and general assembly meetings. Leila Hassan spoke against this, pointing out that Mrs Ruddock was of Indian heritage herself. Another activist objected on the grounds that some white and mixed race youths had been at the party and had been injured in the fire. Howe said the public meeting should be open to everyone. An undercover researcher for the Policy Studies Institute who was carrying out 'participant observation' for a study of relations between the Metropolitan Police and black community, funded by the Met, later reported:

> when feelings were at high pitch and many (especially younger) people sought revenge and confrontation, Darcus Howe, speaking from the public platform, said that while it may be the desire of many people to vent their anger indiscriminately on sections of the white population, a better course of action would be "to turn our emotional rage into better channels".

(1983: 141)

Howe called for the black community to organize itself against racist and fascist groups and 'for the widespread involvement of the black community in the political processes which affect the quality of our lives'. Linton Kwesi Johnson and Frank Crichlow supported Howe's position and his call for public and General Assembly meetings to be open to all races. As a result, the PACM motion was defeated (La Rose 1984: 7).

Passions had run high at the beginning of the meeting when Lewisham Police Commander John Smith arrived uninvited to address those present. His words were drowned out by shouts of 'Go away murderer!'. Smith, who was described by the *Mercury* as visibly shaken by the experience, later called his reception 'rather sad' (22 January 1981). Flanked by Scotland Yard Press Officer, Bob Cox, he left the building without speaking. The fact that Smith and his Force prompted so much anger is hardly surprising considering the widely held perception that the Met had failed to investigate a string of suspected racist attacks in the area properly. The Met's failures, particularly when dealing with suspected arson, were legion. The Moonshot club itself had burnt down in December 1977 a few weeks after reports of it being identified as a target for attack during a local meeting of the National Front. Nonetheless, the police excluded arson as a possible cause (*SELM*, 16 December 1977). Similarly, South London Press openly criticized Greenwich Police's decision to rule out foul play when The Albany Theatre in Creek Road, Deptford, burnt down in August 1978. The suspicion that it was an act of arson aimed at a theatre which hosted a number of anti-racist events against the National Front in the run-up to May local elections of that year had increased when a note was received by those who ran the theatre saying 'Got You! 88'. This was interpreted as being from the neo-fascist paramilitary group, Column 88. When the police ruled out arson without being able to offer any alternative explanation for the fire, local anti-racist activists conducted their own investigation during which they were told by the local Fire Officer that he was 90 per cent sure that the fire had been started deliberately as the theatre's newly installed lighting had been switched off at the mains when it had begun (*SELM*, 28 December 1978).

A week after the New Cross fire, 2,000 people arrived for the public meeting from as far afield as Bradford, Manchester and Leeds. At this point, Howe knew he was witnessing something unprecedented. John La Rose chaired the mass meeting, and Howe spoke on behalf of the Race Today Collective along with other representatives of black organizations such as BUFP and Black Panther Movement, as did Lesley Morris and others. After the speeches, Sybil Phoenix led a march from the mass rally to 439 New Cross Road along a route she had agreed with the police. In the week after the disaster, Phoenix and her co-worker

Ros Howells had performed a vital role in supporting the families who had lost children in the fire and of liaising with outside agencies on their behalf. According to John La Rose, after the march arrived at 439 New Cross Road, Phoenix began a chorus of 'We Shall Overcome' and then tried to lead those assembled away from the house along the agreed route. Only 50 or so followed her. The remaining 2,000 continued to occupy New Cross Road for 3 or 4 hours (1984: 8).

Those, including the police, who were hoping that the influence of militant black organizations would diminish and the movement brought under the control of the more 'respectable' publicly funded Community Relations Council and Commission for Racial Equality, had misjudged the public mood. The black working-class youth who assembled in their hundreds did not so much draw their inspiration from the songs and example of the civil rights movement of the early 1960s as from Black Power and Bob Marley's injunction to them to 'Get up, stand up, don't give up the fight'.

'A general strike of blacks'

At the next meeting of the Assembly and NCMAC on Tuesday 27 January, the decision was taken to call the Black People's Day of Action to be held on a working day and school week, Monday 2 March 1981. Howe advocated a deliberate break with the Left's convention of calling national demonstrations on Saturdays in order to maximize attendance. Howe later explained the reasoning behind the date of Black People's Day of Action:

> I said "Well if they are going to kill so many kids in a fire, we have to show them we got some power in this place, and the only way to do that is to call a general strike of blacks."
>
> (Phillips and Phillips 1999: 328)

The General Assembly and NCMAC voted for Howe, along with fellow members of Race Today Collective, to organize the Day of Action, and it was agreed that Howe would go on a speaking tour of the country to build support for the 2 March protest. The new movement acknowledged that with the Mangrove campaign behind him, Howe was best placed to play this central organizing role. Furthermore, the Collective had consciously reached out beyond London and worked with black groups in places such as Bradford, Leeds and Bristol. Having been elected, Howe packed a bag and headed for Liverpool. At the same time, the

NCMAC printed and distributed 36,000 leaflets across London alone publicizing the Day of Action. From that point, Howe was to play the central role in the Day of Action. For Johnson, 'Darcus's' role was crucial: he was the main organizer. We all played our part, but Darcus was in charge of the mobilization. In terms of the actual committee, that was John La Rose. Darcus was 'the General', John La Rose was 'the Field Marshall' (Johnson 2011).

The new movement was a coalition of different forces, including some more moderate figures and groups from Deptford itself. Leading figures included Grenada-born Ros Howells, who had set up the Mothers Project out of the Moonshot club to help support underage mothers and respond to what she called 'the problem of children having children'. As the project grew, Sybil Phoenix had persuaded her to become a full-time community organizer. On the night of the fire, Howells went to the hospital to support the victims and their families. Now Baroness Howells of St David's, having been made a Life Peer in 1999 for a lifetime of service to the community including the family of Stephen Lawrence, she had this to say of the march and Howe's role in organizing it:

> I did not share Darcus or the other activists' revolutionary politics and being in a mixed relationship did not lend itself easily to being an activist in militant black politics. So I wasn't fronting the march. But I was very much in favour of it and of the criticism levelled at the police. I became very politically involved. I was in the background working with the families, explaining why it was politically important for the black community to make a statement with the march. . . . People like John la Rose and Darcus clearly had a political motive for getting involved, but I would say to you it was the best political motive.
>
> (Howells 2011)

The sense of urgency within NCMAC became more intense as the Fact Finding Committee began to confirm their worst fears about the police investigation (GB 2904 NCM 2/1/1/4). The initial emphasis on tracing the driver of the White Austin Princess was dropped. This coincided with the discovery that Inspector Graham Stockwell, who had been instrumental in reinstating the incitement to riot charges against the Mangrove Nine, was now heading up the investigation. Stockwell's 'form' was not lost on the campaigners. Sybil Phoenix expressed her rage at the appointment during a press conference. Looking back, Howe is convinced that the decision to put Stockwell in charge of the investigation was essentially 'a political decision, because he knew some of the characters in the game'.

Press reports began to appear, sourced to the police, which suggested that the fire had begun within 439 New Cross Road. Equally, the national press started to misrepresent the movement that had emerged following the fire. For example, the *Daily Mirror* of 26 January 1981 purported to give an account of the demonstration following the mass meeting the night before under the headline 'One cool cop calms a mob'. The article omitted to mention anything about the meeting itself. Rather, it provided a sensational account of the march to 439 New Cross Road and ended on the note that the fire may have been started by someone at the party (*Daily Mirror*, 26 January 1981).

The Fact Finding Committee also began to receive reports that the police were detaining the young survivors of the fire, in some cases without their parents' permission; worse still, the detainees stated that they had been pressurized into signing statements saying the fire was the result of a fight at the party. Typical of such reports was the account of 11-year-old Denise Gooding, whose 14-year-old brother Andrew had died in the fire. She was questioned in a police station for many hours before finally being released at 1 a.m. During the interrogation, she was repeatedly told by officers not to lie, just to tell them there was fighting in the house (Phillips and Phillips 1999: 334). NCMAC would eventually expose how child witnesses were made to sign false statements under police duress at the Inquest into the fire, by which point the Met had abandoned the theory of a fight as the cause of the fire altogether. However, as La Rose later pointed out, the movement had been forced to 'exercise every ounce of alertness and vigilance to stop the police framing a group of young blacks who were at the party' (1984: 5).

Spurred on by these events, Howe began his speaking tour. Once again he deployed the organizational strategy that he had learnt during his time with Student Nonviolent Coordinating Committee (SNCC). In each locality, Howe would 'pick people out' and form a small committed group who would, in turn, inspire others. This was the method he had learnt from Fred Meely, Gwen Patton and Rap Brown during his stint in New York. By doing so, he sought to translate the widespread anger which he knew to exist in the black community into mass action on 2 March. In this sense, there was a direct continuity between the Black People's Day of Action and SNCC's initiatives such as Freedom Summer of 1964 or march to Greenwood Mississippi in 1966 which were organized in this way (Ture and Thelwell 2003: 302). Indeed, the Race Today Collective functioned in much the same way that the SNCC had. Both groups were in essence a collection of mobile organizers, who aimed to bring local activists together in each town they visited, and in so doing, generate effective local campaigns.

Howe recalls the dozens of meetings he attended across the country in February 1981, sometimes three or four in one day:

> I would go to a town, say Liverpool and visit Toxteth and I went to the CRE's office and they told tell me where other small organisations were, some political some social. I had been known in the country because of Race Today and the Mangrove and all of that. Then I went to Preston, I didn't know Preston had any black people, but a Liverpool guy said "Lets got to Preston." So I went there, and did the same.
>
> (Howe 2011f)

In Moss Side, Howe linked up with Gus John, chair of Manchester branch of Black Parents Movement at the time, who accompanied him to other meetings across the North, including Sheffield, Huddersfield and Leeds. On the Day of Action, John would bring six coach loads of protestors and a large number of cars from Moss Side alone to the demonstration.

Howe continued:

> I then held meetings across the midlands in Nottingham and in Birmingham where I had invitations to speak to a Pakistani groups I had contacts with. I remember thinking after the first meeting, this is a waste of time, they are not ready for the cross over yet. I wasn't interested in speaking to seasoned left wing groups, I wanted to excavate and channel the real movement I knew was happening all over the country.
>
> (Ibid.)

From there, Howe visited Luton and Bristol and was planning to visit Southampton, when Hassan asked him to come back to London because they were overflowing with requests for speakers. Howe returned and found himself addressing meetings of 200 or 300 black students at campuses all over the Capital every day. This, Howe notes, was the first time in British history when large numbers of black students had entered further and higher education. The mood that he encountered was extraordinary. The black students he met were determined to make a difference, they knew, he recalls, that 'this was their moment'. Johnson was also involved with the mobilization, speaking with La Rose at universities and FE colleges. Students, as Howe recalled, played a crucial role holding parties to raise money for the Day of Action.

The sense of anger among a new generation of black Britons in the schools, colleges and in the streets was palpable. No letter of condolence had been sent to the families of the New Cross victims by the Queen or Prime Minister. The lack of official concern was thrown into stark relief by the government's reaction to the death of 45 people at the Stardust discotheque in Dublin on Valentine's Day 1981. In response to the Irish tragedy, Parliament was adjourned and letters of sympathy were sent immediately by both the prime minister and Queen. It was not until 2 weeks later, a full 5 weeks after the New Cross fire, that a letter was sent by the prime minister. Even then, the message was not addressed to the parents of the deceased but to Sybil Phoenix. Thatcher's letter acknowledged the tragedy, but asserted the police were doing everything they could to investigate it. John La Rose articulated the outrage of the black community when he wrote as chairman of NCMAC to the prime minister to say they considered her letter a 'serious and calculated insult' (Declaration of New Cross 1981).

By late February 1981, 70,000 leaflets and 10,000 posters had been distributed nationally (Policy Studies Institute 1983: 142). Howe recalls that by this point he was thinking that if 5,000 people could be mobilized on a week day, it would be the largest and most significant march of its kind ever held; if anywhere in the region of 10,000 were to demonstrate on 2 March, it would be a serious challenge to the state on this issue.

The police and the media

plenty paypah print pure lie,
fi bline joe public eye
Linton Kwesi Johnson, The New Crass Massakah, 1981

As the Day of Action drew closer, Howe became locked into tense negotiations with the authorities over the route and date of the march. Howe and La Rose headed a small delegation which met with Inspector Pollinghorne, who had been placed in charge of policing the march, at Brixton Police Station in late February. The proposed route of the march went from New Cross over Blackfriars Bridge, through the City and Fleet Street, past Scotland Yard and the Houses of Parliament before finishing in Hyde Park some 17 miles later. The route was symbolic. It had been picked so the protestors could express their disapproval at the distorted press coverage of the fire, protest at the police's handling of the investigation and so that the parents of the dead and members of NCMAC could hand in a statement to Parliament voicing concern at the lack of a government response. Pollinghorne objected to the length and route of the march and said it should go through the Old Kent Road, a route which the campaign had already rejected. Howe defended the NCMAC's preferred route, which had been designed to maximize the support and participation of the black community by going via Camberwell and Peckham. Pollinghorne demanded to know how long it would take the protestors to walk the 17 miles. Howe replied: 'you're a military man, Inspector, we plan to advance a mile a day'. At this, Pollinghorne walked out. The meeting lasted barely 5 minutes.

Russell Profitt, the Labour Councillor whose ward included 439 New Cross Road, was drawn into trying to mediate between the council and police on one side and Howe and the NcMAC on the other:

> It was a very tense and difficult time with little by way of common ground on which to work. Darcus at that time – in my view – saw himself as a conduit of the concerns of young black people in particular and the wider black community in general so had no wish to go against their demands. Council leaders were not in favour of a week day march and wanted to see a de-escalation of the tensions all round. The police who were being criticised for lack of action and causing a cover up to be perpetrated were also not in compromising mood.
>
> (Profitt 2011)

At Town Hall meetings, Profitt argued that with feeling running so high it was essential that the march went ahead. Profitt's status as a local councillor for many of the fire's victims, together with his links with the wider community through his role as the first secretary of Lewisham Community Relations Council and Deputy Head of the local Primary School, meant he was uniquely placed to speak to the concerns of the wider community. His view that it was essential that the march proceed, so local 'concerns were expressed as urgently and in as public a way as possible', eventually prevailed.

Profitt was right, the situation was volatile. But appealing to raw emotion was not part of Howe's strategy. An audio recording of Howe speaking in the run-up to the Inquest shows him speaking slowly, deliberately, choosing his words. He opened by stating his desire to be 'cautious and diplomatic' in his approach. He even went as far as to appeal to the police, 'the feeling of blacks in this country is that this is a God-almighty-mess, and we warn the police not to compound it by the manner in which they behave. . . . It is not too late for them to review their strategy in regards to the calling of witnesses.' Throughout the press conference, Howe was determined to let the facts speak for themselves, deferred to the wishes of the grieving parents and formulated his criticisms of the police precisely. (IRNAA 16 April 1981 Transcript).

Despite having the formal go-ahead for the protest, NCMAC members briefed local organizers to expect the police to try to frustrate participation on the day. Citing examples from earlier demonstrations and carnivals, speakers advised local activists to be prepared for police to delay coaches coming into London or close down local transport on 2 March 1981 as they had unexpectedly done to New Cross station on 25 January 1981.

With only 5 days to go before the protest, an article was published in *Daily Mail* on Wednesday 25 February 1981 headlined 'Killer Blaze Charge Soon', which suggested that a number of black young people had been arrested and would soon be charged in connection with the fire. The story was picked up by ITN and appeared in its news broadcasts later that day. The NCMAC responded immediately by contacting the police who confirmed that the story was 'completely untrue' and that the only black people to have visited Lewisham Police Station about the fire had gone there voluntarily to give witness statements. The NCMAC issued a press statement to the Press Association that evening which condemned the confusion which the article had 'deliberately sought to create', before going on to observe:

> The New Cross Massacre Action Committee has warned the entire public that the police are likely to arrest some blacks on the eve of Black People's Day of Action on Monday 2 March to divert attention from the Demonstration and weaken the Day of Action. The Daily Mail story and ITN news today have served that purpose.
>
> (Declaration of New Cross 1981)

Formal complaints failed to reveal the police source of the bogus story. For Howe, the publication and timing of the story was not a surprise; it was Fleet Street's tradition to act as 'public mouthpiece' for the police in their dealings with the black community. The press performed that role with gusto in its reporting of the Mangrove demonstration as it had done in earlier police investigations of racial crime dating back to the murder of Kelso Cochrane in May 1959.[1]

NMAC and Howe spent the following days anxiously waiting to see if the *Mail* article and ITN report would seriously affect attendance on the day.

The Black People's Day of Action

Howe recalls that the weather on the morning of Monday 2 March was beautiful; not cold but temperate and bright. He arrived at Fordham Park next to the Moonshot in good time and watched the marchers assemble in awe as wave upon wave came down the hill into the valley to join him in the park. Buses, organized by the NCMAC, kept arriving carrying black people from across the country. Among those who gathered for the march that day was the young lawyer and political activist Paul Boateng. In the same year, he was elected as a councillor for Greater London Council, before going on to become an MP for Brent South in 1987 and the United Kingdom's first black government minister in 1997:

> I was struck, first of all, by the numbers, the vast numbers, who were assembling in south London, in Lewisham, on that day. . . . In the main, if you look at street demonstrations, even street demonstrations around issues that affect black people, you get a sense that white people were in command of events. They'd organised it. This was black organised, black led and you felt that. So it was very much a black community event.
>
> (Phillips and Phillips 1998: 242)

The march had been planned carefully. The stewards, who wore identification berets, were briefed by Howe to show discipline and restraint in the face of police provocation, 'otherwise the march would collapse into mass violence and the point would not be made'. With the Collective acting as chief stewards, he knew that if anything went wrong 'we would be held responsible'. Johnson recalls, his job was looking after 'all the rude boys, making sure they didn't rob places' (Johnson 2011). Howe took up position on a lorry containing public address and sound system at the front of the march. Next to him were his 8- and 7-year-old sons, Darcus Beese and Rap Ture Howe, together with other speakers, drummers and the families of the deceased. Howe would later learn that his daughters Tamara and Tenifa were among the hundreds of school children who walked out of their schools to join the demonstration.

The police had said they wanted the march to start at 11.30 a.m. At 11 a.m., Howe called over to one of the officers and said 'Let's go' in the hope it would upset any plans they might have to disrupt the march along the route. It was tactical flourishes like this which led Linton Kwesi Johnson to christen Howe with the nickname 'General'. Tactics aside, Howe opines that the police were unprepared in a second sense. From studying James, from his experiences in the Caribbean and America, from travelling the country during the Lindo Campaign, from the Basement Sessions, and his run-ins with the police, Howe was prepared for the Day of Action. The event was unprecedented, but Howe's years of experience organizing campaigns and his theoretical understanding of the dynamics involved in mass protest meant that he was as prepared as anyone for the march. The police, by contrast, had no idea what they were dealing with. 'They underestimated us. . . . They thought we were a load of little, stupid, black people.' The police were caught off guard by the scale of the march and the sophistication of the organization. 'They had never seen that size demonstration of black people before. So the police didn't know culturally what to do' (Howe 2011f).

As the march set off along New Cross Road, Howe could see that many thousands had missed school or work to protest. By the time that the front of the march arrived at the remains of 439 New Cross Road half a mile away and stopped to pay its respects to the 13 young lives lost in the inferno, the tail end of the march had not yet left the Fordham Park. Of the chants that rang out, three in particular stood out: '13 Dead Nothing Said'; 'Stockwell is a Liar, a Bomb caused the Fire' and 'Come what May, We Are Here to Stay', the slogan which had adorned all the leaflets, badges and posters publicizing the march.

Ros Howells's abiding memory is of her daughter and niece, both university students at the time, at the front of the march. 'The anger and hurt was visible among the young people, for many of them it was the first time they could get their parents to understand what they were going through. Young black people couldn't breathe without being criticised and attacked in the media.' As the march snaked through the South London streets in which the victims had lived and gone to school, its numbers swelled as children climbed over school fences and onlookers left their jobs to join the demonstration. Howells recalls:

> . . . people who were working on buses and school children who were at school came to join the march. I mean conductors literally got off the bus and joined us. As we marched through Peckham children left their schools to join the march and teachers had no control over that.
>
> (2011)

As the mass of people passed through Southwark towards Blackfriar's Bridge, Howe and the organizers estimated that somewhere in the region of 25,000 people may have been on the march. When the chief stewards tallied their numbers together at the end, the final figure they arrived at was a little over 20,000. Howells sensed that the police were frightened, that they had never seen anger from the black community on this scale before and that the movement which had mobilized that day 'shook them to their roots'.

When the march got to Blackfriars Bridge, it started to shower lightly. A small delegation consisting of John la Rose and the victims' families left the head of march to take their protest to Parliament. A group of about 50 young people at the front of the march pressed ahead and overtook the lorry only to find they were confronted by rows of police blocking the entrance to Blackfriars Bridge. The police were determined to stop the demonstration from crossing the bridge. The bridge was symbolic. This was the first protest march since the Chartist Procession of 10 April 1848 to attempt to cross Blackfriars Bridge and the police were determined to block it. As a result, fighting broke out as the youth struggled to break through the police lines and fought to free comrades arrested by the police. One eyewitness account archived at the George Padmore Institute describes what happened next:

> ... Runners amongst the stewards were despatched to bring forward the truck trapped way back from the pitched battle. Chaos was increased as contradictory directives were issued by the police commanders. As Lewisham police tried to ease a way for the truck to move forward, the City police continued with blocking manoeuvres. The impasse was broken as the truck nosed its way through the seething mass, Rasta flag flying aloft. Strengthened now by the presence of the lorry, the crowd with one last heave laid siege to the police line, and with a resounding cheer, broke through the cordon.

Johnson recalls that the impasse was broken by a surge from the 'lumpen elements' of the crowd scattering the police (2011). Among those arrested during the melee by police officers who called him a 'cunt' and 'bastard' was the Policy Studies Institute undercover researcher who was writing a police-funded study of young black attitudes towards the police (1984: 149). Marchers interviewed by Dave Evans for LBC radio clearly viewed police action on the march as unnecessary and provocative.

Russell Profitt, the Labour councillor whose had done so much to overcome opposition within Lewisham Council to the march, was among the thousands of protestors who crossed the bridge. He considers the confrontation at Blackfriars Bridge as predictable, given the strength of opposition within the police to the route. By the same token, he knew it was only a matter of time before the marchers would get across the Bridge; 'we had literally come too far to simply turn around and make our way back' (2011).

Once they had crossed the Thames, the protestors regrouped and continued their demonstration through the City and into Fleet Street. Marching in tight formation past the Red Tops and broadsheets, the protestors offered up the cries of 'Thirteen Dead and Nothing Said' and 'Fleet Street Liars'. All the participant accounts concur in reporting abuse that the marchers received from the offices in Fleet Street. Paul Boateng later recalled 'the taunting and abuse that rained down on us from the *Express* building in particular, I will never forget that'

(Phillips and Phillips 1998: 342). Johnson remembers that as they passed by *The Sun* newspaper 'there was a torrent of racial abuse from people working in the building . . . "Go Back Home you Black Bastards", the usual banal kind of things that these people say' (Ibid). Howe recalls seeing people leaning out of windows making 'monkey noises' and throwing banana skins at the crowd (Howe 2011f).

Against the chants of 'Justice, Justice' and the jeers of journalists, Fleet Street also saw renewed confrontation between the protestors and the police. The eyewitness account held at the GPI claims 'in Fleet Street the whole mood of policing changed. The police imposed themselves on marchers, pushing, shoving, and kicking people off pavements. Scuffles broke out up and down Fleet Street, and, unlike Peckham, it was the police and not the stewards who stood guard in front of shops.'

In an isolated incident, which the vast majority of protesters were oblivious to, one small group broke off from the demonstration to smash and loot a jeweller's shop. As police tried to stop them, an officer was injured. This was the incident that dominated the newspapers the next day. In fact, despite the aggressive police tactics, of the thousands who marched that day, only 25 were charged with minor offences by the police.

There continued to be clashes and altercations with the police for the remainder of the march. Eyewitness accounts criticized the police tactic of riding police horses into families with young children at Cumberland Gate in an apparent attempt to break up the march and stop it reaching Hyde Park. Notwithstanding the provocative methods used to police the march, it did finally reach its destination at Hyde Park 7 hours after it had set out from Fordham Park. Thousands of protestors gathered around the lorry to listen to speeches by Howe and others. Against great opposition, the marchers had triumphed. But Howe was not given long to savour the triumph before the backlash began.

Note

1   Olden details how police officers sold information about Cochrane's murder to the *Sunday Express* before his next of kin had been informed of his death and then furnished *The People* with misleading and inaccurate information which was used in an unsympathetic profile of the victim entitled 'Gang Victim Led Double Life' (2011: 83, 152).

15

Insurrection

From its conception, Howe had intended the Day of Action as a challenge to not only the insouciant racism of police and government as illustrated by their response to the Deptford Fire but also to the way the press had misled and misinformed the public about the Fire. With that background and given the taunts and abuse which had rained down on the marchers from the office blocks in Fleet Street, a less than warm response in the next day's press might have been anticipated by Howe and the organizers. Nothing could have prepared them for the massive hostility which was to follow, as the press attempted to unite the majority white population against the justice of their claim.

Yet try as they might, the press and police could not diminish the newfound confidence which the march had instilled in the black community. As Paul Gilroy has noted, detailed research into police attitudes to People's Day of Action reveals that they saw the success of the march as 'a symbolic defeat' and complained that black people had a new swagger in their step after that demonstration (Phillips and Phillips 1998: 347).

Police efforts to assert their power in the wake of the march through tactics such as the saturation policing of immigrant communities and habitual stop and search of black people would now be met with widespread resistance. 'Operation Swamp 81', whose sobriquet appeared to deliberately echo the term used by Thatcher to describe immigration in her notorious 1978 World in Action interview, was ostensibly called 6 weeks after the march to combat street crime in Brixton. It involved the indiscriminate, and therefore illegal, stop and search of 943 mostly black people by 120 plain clothed officers over the space of 5 days beginning on Monday 6 April. Only 2 per cent of the 'stops' resulted in the detection of street crime (Simpson 1982: 13). By Friday 10 April 1981, this assault on the people of Brixton, unprecedented in its scale, aggression and intensity, had succeeded in igniting a mass youth insurrection against the police. In its initial phase, the uprising in Brixton lasted just 3 days,

Figure 6 Howe leading the demonstration on the Black People's Day of Action, 2 March 1981. Howe is accompanied on the truck by two of his sons, Darcus Jr. and Rap.

but it spread in weeks and months that followed to Southall, Liverpool, Bristol and Birmingham and approximately 60 other cities by the summer of that year (La Rose 1984: 18). In the area known as Liverpool 8, for example, a history of police harassment and racism exploded in a mass uprising which did not die down completely for a period of 6 weeks during which hundreds of buildings were burnt down, 781 police officers injured and 214 police vehicles damaged (Frost and Phillips 2011: 2).

As the most effective black political organization, the Race Today Collective under the direction of Howe, John La Rose and Leila Hassan, had been instrumental in organizing the People's Day of Action. Now it was from their offices in Shakespeare Road, at the corner of Railton Road, Brixton, that Howe and his comrades would witness and experience the police repression which sparked the uprising on 10 April 1981 and would be entrusted with the task of telling the real story of the uprising by those who had led it.

Backlash

As Howe left Hyde Park after the 2 March demonstration, he was asked by a reporter for his response to the People's Day of Action. Avoiding triumphalism, but pleased that so many people had left work and school to join the march and that it had passed off without any major incident which could detract from the dignity of their purpose, Howe simply said 'It was a good day'. In an article which was to set the tone of the press coverage the following day, the *London Evening Standard* published a picture of Howe alongside another photograph of a policeman with blood streaming down his face and the headline 'Race Chief's Verdict on Protest March: It was a Good Day'. Howe later remarked that on seeing the article he thought 'we can only draw this fight, can't win it' (Phillips and Phillips 1998: 343).

The *Daily Mail*'s headline that morning read 'When the Black Tide met the Thin Blue Line'. Likewise, the *Daily Express* described what it called 'the rampage of a mob'. Not to be outdone, the *Sun* ran the headline 'Black Day at Blackfriars'. Inside the paper featured a two-page spread entitled 'The Day the Blacks Ran Riot in London'. It went on to claim that

> ...a cordon was thrown across the bridge in an attempt to halt the march. But militants angrily chanting "Murder, murder, murder" bulldozed their way through with a five-ton truck. As it was driven relentlessly through the police ranks the mob charged across the bridge. Then the rampage began as thousands of blacks stormed up Fleet Street. Urged on by militants on the truck they hurled brick and smashed shop windows.
>
> (*The Sun*, 3 March 1981)

This crude appeal to fear and prejudice prompted a formal complaint to the Press Council and a finding 6 months later that the *Sun* article was inflammatory and 'damaging to good race relations', the first such ruling against a Fleet Street newspaper (Anim-Addo 1995: 138). National press coverage of the event appears to have relied exclusively on the police accounts and briefings, thus following the same pattern of 'reporting' which the yellow press adopted during the Mangrove demonstration a decade earlier. There was no mention that the police made only a couple of dozen arrests, the vast majority on minor charges such as obstruction; or that many of those arrested had been random victims of police snatch squads, among them an undercover researcher writing a police-funded report on police-community relations who was sworn at and bundled into the police van as he tried to cross Blackfriars Bridge.

Only New Cross' local weekly newspaper, the *South East London Mercury*, carried balanced reports of the demonstration. Its articles, entitled 'A Plea for Justice' and 'A Day to Remember: "Stand Firm. We are marching in dignity"' by Marhita Wearing are vivid first-hand accounts of the demonstration. An opinion piece entitled 'Day of Dignity' pointed out the significance of the march as 'the biggest gathering of black people this country has ever seen':

> They came to tell the rest of the country how they felt – not just about the terrible loss of life they had suffered. But about the discrimination they suffer, the fruitless search jobless youngster's face, the problems so many children face in schools. Judging from national newspaper coverage of the march, they haven't managed to bring their protest home, with the Press concentrating on the tiny minority of hotheads who broke away to fight police and rob shops and passersby. But the vast majority of people demonstrated their anger with dignity, their frustration noisily but peacefully, their sense of tragedy with emotion.
>
> (5 March 1981)

The march appears to have prompted a brutal, atavistic response within the police. Research funded by the Metropolitan Police into police behaviour at the time reveals how the Deptford Fire and its aftermath 'had the effect of focusing racialist attitudes within the Met' (Smith and Gray 1983: 116). Unlike the report on black youth which formed the second part of the same study and was written using undercover researchers, the police officers with whom David Smith and Jeremy Gray spent 2 years in the company of knew their purpose but were still prepared to express the most violent racist views to them. Gray and Smith cite five separate conversations in work and social settings (an office party, lunchtime drinks in a pub) involving different groups of up to eight police and CID officers to the rank of chief inspector in which extreme racist views were expressed in response to the Deptford Fire. A typical example of the comments was when Gray was asked by one officer 'how many niggers actually fried in this barbecue at Deptford, then?'. At a CID office party, Smith heard a number of anti-IRA jokes, before being told that they have renamed Deptford as Blackfriars. During the discussion in a pub with eight officers, one constable who had policed the march the day before expressed the view that it had been a defeat for the police before boasting that he 'managed to hit a nigger in the mouth' (holding out his hand to show a mark). That discussion ended with the officers all agreeing that black people 'were animals' and 'that they should be shot' (Ibid.). In a discussion with another group of officers at the same police station later that day, a chief inspector is reported as saying 'If a nigger's coming straight at you, you can put a .38 straight through him and he'll keep coming' (Ibid., 123).

Gray refers to one of the PCs and the same chief inspector talking about 'the return match' or 'second leg' at which they hoped the police would 'get a better score' in reference to a second march scheduled for following Saturday – but which in fact never took place (Ibid., 117).

Howe before the riots

Even for a veteran activist and organizer such as Howe, being at the epicentre of these events and experiencing the juxtaposition of emotions associated with the success of the People's Day of Action and the bitterness of the backlash that followed had a profound effect. As at other crucial moments, Howe looked to C. L. R. James to provide him with perspective:

> I think everybody after that demonstration had to assess who they were; what side they were on. . . . In fact when I was getting a bit over-hyped with it, my uncle CLR James was my political mentor, said to me "I think you ought to retreat. Just calm down, take two steps back, because this is big stuff." I said that we needed some overview to moderate extreme and violent instincts, because there was violence that was obviously beneath the surface. It manifested itself weeks after the demonstration.

> (Phillips and Phillips, 1998: 240)

Approaching middle age by this point, Howe had a stable and happy personal and political life. He was in a loving relationship with his close friend and comrade Leila Hassan which remains to this day. Between editing *Race Today* and his political and family commitments, Howe even found time to fulfil an ambition to teach when he was asked to lecture part-time at South London Tec. No doubt conscious that Howe would be a good role model to many of his young black students, the College's Head of General Studies, one Mr Burke, wrote to Howe asking if he would teach a class of mainly first-generation Caribbean youth who were struggling with grammar. He recalls that one of his students, a young Rasta called Berris, who couldn't read, gave the impression to his classmates of being very tough but clearly liked Howe's no-nonsense approach. As the better weather approached, Howe told Burke that he wanted to organize a day trip for the class to Margate, which prompted Burke to ask Howe if he was crazy, but to which he eventually agreed against his misgivings. Howe recalls it was a fine day and was going well, until he saw his students 'thieving from some shops on the front'. Howe called all his class together and said 'all of you to the bus now if you don't want to be left behind':

> . . . they all came, because no one wants to get left behind in Margate. I told them to turn out their pockets and then made them go from shop to shop returning what they had taken. Anyhow Berris started crying, he said his father had never taught him that.

> (Howe 2011g)

Despite the happy domesticity of his personal life and fulfilling professional life, Howe could tell there were seismic shifts taking place within the black community. In their Basement Sessions, the Race Today Collective set out to analyse the contours of these shifts and changes within the community so they might be better placed to respond to the social explosion they considered imminent. In so doing, their aim was not to try to lead or move the community into mass revolt. Consciously breaking with Leninist notions of revolutionary leadership, Howe and the Collective lived the Jamesian maxim that 'All movement flows from self movement and not from external forces acting on an organism.' As an external force, the Collective saw its role in Brixton as knowing who the community were, helping to connect its struggles and reflecting this back to them so that the community might better understand itself. They were, in Howe's words, 'careful to avoid trying to lead people outside of their reality' (Ibid.).

At its 1980 national conference, members of the Collective instructed Howe to write a series of articles for *Race Today* which would prepare its readership for the impending revolt. The first of these was published in May 1980, just a month after the uprising in St Paul's district of Bristol, and the second article appeared in the November 1980 edition. Together they fluidly analysed the early struggles of the black community against police and state racism, of the police's transformation from 'Bobby to Babylon'[1] during the course of October 1958 Notting Hill race riots and of the incipient forms of resistance associated with Black Power. Howe noted that the first generation of West Indian immigrants were constrained in these early battles by the fact that they were a minority and could not guarantee what whites would do in any major struggles against the police.

What had changed since the Notting Hill race riots of the late 1950s or in the decade since the trial of the Mangrove Nine to lead the Collective to predict a major uprising of black youth with such confidence? For one, young black people no longer feared white reaction. In Bristol, significant numbers of white youth had joined black protesters in attacking the police, and a third of those arrested had been white. By the end of the 1970s, the music and style of a new generation of black British youth spoke directly to the alienation felt by breakaway sections of white working class youth, students and urban poor. In the schools and on the estates of Britain's major cities, there were young disaffected whites who identified directly with the countercultural values of ska, reggae and punk, saw themselves as part of the same rebellious youth culture as black young people and shared their hatred of police and state.[2]

Army of Occupation

'No good general ever declares his forces in a prelude to any attack', Commander Adams, "L District".

(Bays et al. 1981: 6)

Thus answered Brixton's most senior policeman on national television when he was asked why he had not informed the local Police-Community Liaison Committee prior to an 'attack' by the Special Patrol Group (SPG) in Brixton in 1978. The comment was cited at the start of the report of the Working Party on Community-Police Relations which was published by Lambeth Council in January 1981 following an 18-month inquiry into the troubled relations between police and local community, particularly the black community. In a section entitled 'Army of Occupation', the report referred to six such attacks by the SPG on Brixton from 1975 and 1979, involving up to 150 officers at a time, in which the same general pattern was followed each time – road blocks, early morning raids and random street checks. Describing the situation as 'extremely grave', the report anticipated the possibility of unrest.

The Working Party's report made a number of urgent recommendations to defuse tensions, including the immediate repeal of Section 4 of the Vagrancy Act or 'sus', which gave the police the right to stop anyone they suspected, and for there to be no future deployment of the SPG in Lambeth. Submissions referring to police abuses during the interrogation of juveniles said the Working Party 'present a picture of violence, intimidation and induced confessions', thus necessitating basic reforms such as the need for a parent or guardian to be present for any statement given by a juvenile in custody to be admissible as evidence.

It has taken 30 years since the Working Party's report for those directly involved in such abuses to begin speaking out. In a Radio 4 programme to mark the 30th anniversary of the riot in which Howe, Alex Wheatlly, Brian Paddick and others participated, BBC script writer, Peter Bleksley, described his experiences as a young constable in Peckham at the time (BBC, 25 March 2011). Among one of the first to arrive at the scene of the riots, Bleksley recounted how young black men in Brixton and Peckham 'were routinely fitted up, beaten up, tortured and worse' by police. Describing how the culture of the police had turned him from 'a decent 18 year old boy' from Bexleyheath into 'a violent racist, very unpleasant thug', Bleksley recalled how young Rastafarians would have their dreadlocks ripped out by police and how these would then be pinned to police notice boards as trophies. Asked by the programme's host

Sue MacGregor to elaborate on his claim of having witnessed torture, Bleksley described how young black people would be made to kneel with their toes on the skirting boards of police interrogation rooms at which point pressure would be applied and their heels forced downwards causing excruciating pain until they agreed to sign confessions. The Working Report's devastating conclusions were ignored by the police and the political class. Commander Adams had withdrawn police cooperation with the Working Party's inquiry at the outset citing alleged bias against the police even though the inquiry's chairman was a senior QC, David Turner-Samuels, and the Working Party contained Labour and Conservative councillors (BBC, 25 March 2011).

Swamp 81

It was in this tense atmosphere, just 3 months after the Working Party's dire warning to the police and 6 weeks after the mass mobilization of 2 March 1981, that the police launched Operation Swamp 81. Howe recalls the sudden influx of 120 plain-clothed police officers, dressed in jeans, T-shirts and sneakers, onto the streets of Brixton and the harassment and intimidation experienced by the community as they randomly and aggressively stopped and searched hundreds of black people:

> I know what a swamp is. It is water up to your knees, an attempt to overwhelm and corner you. It was happening in front of my eyes. This was an attempt to reassert police authority. That is what empirically was taking place. I don't like writing politics in term of conspiracies but this happened.
>
> (Howe 2011g)

Hassan recalls being stopped with Howe on Railton Road as they made their way towards Brixton market to buy some yam and sweet potatoes to make soup:

> The police approached us and said "where are you going?" Darcus went mad, he said "why are you stopping us?" . . . Everyone was talking about it in Brixton, you couldn't go anywhere without being stopped. It was overwhelming, the sheer numbers of police involved. You'd be stopped and searched at the end of your street and then stopped and searched by a different set of police dressed in jeans and T shirts as you got to the next bloc. It was unbelievable, they stopped young, middle aged, elderly, families, men and women – anybody.
>
> (Hassan 2011)

Howe remembers the incident on Railton Road:

> They shouted "come here, where are you going?" I replied "Go to hell. Law says I
> have be doing something suspicious. What is suspicious about going to buy sweet
> potatoes?" Across the road, I saw a couple local hustlers, Tarzan and Boy Blue.
> They shout "Darco what?" I shouted back "Dunno". They came across to see what
> was happening and the police got back in their car and pulled off. Swamp '81 was
> an assertion of power without reason. I wasn't going to stand for that. I wasn't a
> boy to be ordered around and my wife treated as a pip-squeak. I would have rather
> died than be treated in that way.
>
> (Howe 2011g)

By the end of the first week of Swamp 81, local organizations were overwhelmed
by complaints from black youths at their treatment by the police. As the Scarman
Inquiry would later hear, police claims that Swamp 81 was not an attack on the
black community were undermined by the fact that while whites outnumbered
black people 3 to 1 in Lambeth, the majority of stops were of local black people
and the overwhelming complaints of police abuse and intimidation were made
by Lambeth's black citizens (Narayan 1985: 140).

On Monday night, Howe and the rest of the Race Today Collective met in
their Shakespeare Road office to discuss the situation. Howe argued that the
place was going to explode and that there was no way people would tolerate
police harassment on this scale. In the following days, Howe witnessed a series
'of pushings and shovings' and scuffles break out between black youth and the
'sneaker squad', as Howe referred to the casually dressed, trainer-clad officers. As
tension inexorably rose,

> You would see and hear it time and time again . . . a young black would get
> grabbed and would shout "What you pick on me? Me never doing nothing you
> blood clot!" The "sneaker squad" was drawn from Brixton, Clapham, Stockwell
> police stations, which were dumping grounds that contained the detritus of the
> Met. They reminded me of the police I encountered when I first arrived in the UK.
> They were racist thugs. Those stations got the chance to host this operation and
> seized it.
>
> (Howe 2011g)

Howe remembers one local youth, Ben, seeking him out and asking what he
was going to do about what was happening on the streets. Howe replied, 'What
can I do?'. On the night of Friday 10 April, a local youth, Michael Bailey, was
stabbed. In a practice no longer allowed, he was placed in the back of a police

van and taken away to be treated. Onlookers saw a black man who was bleeding heavily being driven off in a police van. Such was the fear and loathing of the police that onlookers assumed that police were responsible for Bailey's injuries. The incident immediately sparked violence – bricks and bottles were thrown, several cars were overturned, several officers received minor injuries and a small number of arrests were made. That night police held talks with church and 'community leaders' urging them to calm the situation but refused pleas to call a halt to the Swamp 81. In so doing, they refused to take the only action that could have averted serious disorder.

Brixton had experienced unrest of this order before. Significantly, however, word of the confrontation and of what sparked it spread like wild fire. The writer Alex Wheatle, whose novel *East of Acre Lane* is set against the backdrop of the riots, was living in a hostel in Peckham at the time. In the Radio Four Programme to mark the 30th anniversary of the riots, he recalled that he was at a Blues party not far from Railton Road that night, where everyone was saying that 'Babylon whet up a sufferer'; in other words, the police had stabbed someone. Wheatle stayed up all night talking about it with others in the hostel and they decided to go *en masse* on Saturday morning to Brixton and later joined the revolt (BBC 2011).

The fire this time

When a group of black youths gathered to protest at the search of a black mini cab driver by officers on Atlantic Road on Saturday afternoon and police retaliated by arresting one of their number, it ignited a volatile situation. Howe later heard that it was Ben, the youth who had approached him a few nights earlier, who had begun remonstrating with the two policemen at their unlawful use of stop and search and whose spontaneous protest grew into mass revolt when police tried to quell it. Over the course of the next day, Brixton saw the most widespread rioting in Britain that century and the first ever use of the petrol bomb on mainland Britain. Howe would later describe 'the serious insurrectionary proportions of the revolt', 179 vehicles were damaged and 34 vehicles destroyed, 415 police and 172 members of the public injured, 28 premises damaged or destroyed by fire; 7,472 police used to police the area. Leeson Road, Mayall Road, the northern part of Railton Road and the streets to the west of there were in the hands of local youth for hours as they resisted police attempts to advance and counter-attacked in dramatic style. In one incident which Lord Scarman described as 'illustrative of the aggressive spirit of the crowd and the defensive posture imposed on the police', a group of youths commandeered a bus and drove it up Railton Road towards the police line as others charged on foot shouting and throwing bricks: when a policeman threw a brick and smashed the bus windscreen, the youth who was driving it jumped out and the bus veered into the right of the police line before coming to a rest on a wall at the top of Railton Road (Scarman 1981: 56).

As in Bristol, a significant minority of the insurgents were white; Scarman later reported that white men were seen making, distributing and throwing petrol bombs in Railton Road and Leeson Road on Saturday night (Ibid., 75). Despite the scale of the street fighting and arson, its violence was consistently targeted at the police and commercial property; local homes were left unscathed. Bill Bowring, the local Labour councillor whose Herne Hill ward included Railton Road, remembers moving freely from house to house visiting his constituents during the riots to ensure they were safe, including in those streets that the insurrection controlled. Now a professor at University of London, then a young white lawyer and part-time labour activist, Bowring 'never felt under threat' as he moved among the black youth (Bowring 2011).

Similarly, Scarman heard evidence from a local priest, the Vicar of St Jude's of how he tried to intervene to stop a group of black men attacking The George, a pub on Railton Road, and a newsagent opposite. He was told by the men 'that the police have been harassing the black and homosexual communities and they could stand it no longer'. The George had a reputation for refusing to serve black people, earning it the nickname 'Rhodesia', and the newsagents for discriminating against a group of gay men who lived on Railton Road (Scarman 1981: 75). Although initially spontaneous in nature, Scarman concluded from such evidence an 'element of leadership and direction quickly emerged' (Ibid., 74).

Anticipating a revolt after the Friday night clashes, the entire membership of Race Today, with the exception of Linton Kwesi Johnson who was attending a conference in Amsterdam, met throughout the weekend at their Shakespeare Road headquarters. Located in the heart of the insurrection, less than a minute's walk from Railton Road, they monitored events closely while Johnson remained in frequent contact by telephone. For Howe, having a slew of police camped in the road outside his office had its benefit in that it could not be credibly claimed that he was on the streets coordinating the unrest.

This did not stop the *Daily Telegraph* and *Daily Mail* from publishing reports in the aftermath of the uprising which referred to Howe and *Race Today* as local agitators whose role in the unrest should be investigated. In a recently declassified briefing prepared for the Prime Minister and Cabinet in July 1981 after the riots had spread to at least 20 other cities, the contribution of 'extremists' in sparking the initial Brixton uprising was openly discussed. Referring to Howe as someone who, as editor of *Race Today*, was associated with campaigning for H-Block Hunger Strikers and the New Cross Massacre Action Committee, the report ultimately concluded that 'it seemed unlikely that in any major case the extremists have actually instigated the violence or been able to plan it' (NA PREM 19/484, 57).

Race Today's response to the insurrection was twofold. First, it was instrumental in helping to set up the Brixton Defence Committee (BDC) which campaigned for an amnesty for all those arrested during the uprising. As the radical barrister and fellow BDC member Rudi Narayan would make clear in his cross-examination of witnesses during the Scarman Inquiry, such a demand came not as a plea for clemency but rather from the conviction that a revolt was inevitable given such widespread police abuse, that sooner or later people were going to rise up in self-defence against an illegal police operation involving the unlawful stop and search of thousands of innocent people (Narayan 1985: 143). Secondly, and uniquely, Race Today members utilized their close ties within the community to assemble the leaders of the uprising and debriefed them in extensive detail on their activities. Howe later revealed that 'the information was taped and transcribed, and after the contents were digested, both the tapes and the transcripts were destroyed'. Among the plethora of left-wing groups active in Brixton at the time, only Race Today was sufficiently rooted in the area to have been trusted in this role: Howe played cricket alongside and against local youth for Railton Road Cricket Club; Johnson had grown up and gone to school in Brixton and had many friends in the area; Ben's mum cooked and cleaned for C. L. R. James, who was by that point living in the flat above the *Race Today* offices and would debrief all he met about their lives and families. Through James, Howe had got to know Viv Richards, who regularly made a point of visiting Howe and James in Brixton when he was playing cricket in England; such visits by the world's leading batsman drew adulation from a community who correctly saw it as Richards showing his commitment to them. So over time, and in a multitude of ways, Race Today had, in Howe's words, 'become woven into the life of the community' (Howe 2011g).

In November 1981, *The Times* rang the *Race Today* offices to commission a 1,500-word article from Howe on his response to the Scarman Report. His feature article, the first he had written for mainstream British press, was published on 26 November 1981. Drawing on the material acquired from the leaders of the Brixton revolt to help inform his perspective, Howe rejected the plaudits Scarman had received from the liberal press for his report. While Scarman had resisted right-wing demands to recommend the granting of even greater police powers, he failed to 'grasp the nettle' by addressing the systemic abuses which had led to the revolt. Next to Scarman's continued support for 'stop and search', his failure to recommend safeguards against physical abuse and forced confessions of detainees or greater scrutiny of the police evidence used by magistrates to convict black people, his call for a more independent police complaint's system was 'mere tinkering'. Ignoring a wealth of personal testimony of widespread police racism towards black people, Scarman preferred police accounts which explained such racism in terms of a few inexperienced junior officers. He considered the image of a hostile police force held by black people, young and old alike, to be 'a myth' (1981: 106).

Entitled 'My Fears after this Failure', Howe's article highlighted the three central features to emerge from the revolts upon which any report should have rested. First was the fact that within 10 minutes of the uprising, a body of about 30 young men had gathered and had begun to transform a spontaneous reaction into an organized revolt. They had supervised the mounting of barricades and the manufacture of petrol bombs. They had organized scouts who moved around on skates and bicycles to gather information on enemy positions. They had set in train diversionary tactics to confuse the enemy. They had selected which buildings were to be destroyed by fire and saw to it they were. They had organized points at which the injured could be attended to and finally, it was they who gave the order to retreat which the mass of black people promptly obeyed. Such a body of men and women existed within every black community and had been evident in the dozens of other revolts in towns and cities across the county. The second crucial feature to have emerged was a profound transformation in the attitudes of older traditionally more conservative West Indian parents, who had offered sympathy and support to young black people when they had risen up. Thirdly, the much-touted 'white backlash' which had stopped the black community from taking drastic action in the past against their condition had not come and there appeared little possibility that it ever would. Rather, Howe noted, something else has happened. 'Young whites had joined the revolt' (Howe 1988: 67).

It was against this transformed social landscape that Howe predicted that the government's failure to tackle the root cause of the revolt in any fundamental way had ensured that they would necessarily reoccur on an even greater sale in the future.

Looking back 30 years later, Howe is clear about the significance of the People's Day of Action and the 1981 insurrection:

> The Day of Action was the first organised mass intervention with a semblance of the March on Washington and the huge mobilisations in the Caribbean that I had been involved in. The thinking in Race Today was we could replicate it and we did. It represented an end to the easy going way and resignation to our lot, to the belief that things were bad but that we couldn't do anything about it. When the insurrection occurred it fundamentally broke with the past which had consisted of complaining quietly about our lot and whispering in the ear of white power. People acted in a massive spontaneous way and said "if you continue to treat us as you have been doing we will burn down every city".
>
> (Howe 2011g)

Notes

1 Howe's articles were later published as an anthology in 1989 entitled *Bobby to Babylon*.
2 Gilroy notes that Rock Against Racism put on 200 events in just over a year after its formation in 1976; (1987); see also Duncambe and Tramblay (2011).

16

Carnival: Revolutionaries Don't Wear Glitter

For Howe, politics and culture are intimately bound together; his essential insight was that political movements and cultural movements emerge hand in hand. Howe tackled the subject in the pages of *Race Today*. Indeed, the magazine reflected Howe's conception and therefore, as the 1980s progressed, *Race Today* became increasingly oriented towards black cultural movements. Under the direction of Akua Rugg, *Race Today*'s in-house literary critic, the magazine gained sections such as 'Poet's Corner', and 'Creation for liberation', a regular section which covered music, theatre, films and books. The cultural orientation of the magazine was given further prominence from 1980 with publication of an annual *Race Today Review*. The first *Review* contained 'a short story and poems' as well as reviews of 'political tracts, novels, the work of poets, musicians, playwrights and film makers' (*RTR*, 1980: 51). Howe introduced the work that the *Review* contained as a small taste of the 'creative activities which flow from the terrain on which we do political battle', work that was 'forged in the heat of confrontation between the new society in the making and its suffocating and increasingly murderous opposite' (Ibid.). Howe's intuitions about the relationship between politics and culture chimed with those of James. The second *Race Today Review* contained James' essay 'I am a poet', which championed the work of Ntozake Shange. Drawing inspiration from the 1981 Polish Spring, James argued that artistic expression in the modern world would either reflect the desire for freedom embodied in Solidarity or imperatives of the 'regimes that are described by Solzhenitsyn in his book, *The Gulag Archipelago*' (*RTR*, 1981: 2). James praised Shange's work precisely because she wrote about her own experience, 'her own world' rather than serving the ideological vision of the state.

Howe returned to the topic of culture and politics in his 1981 'Introduction' to the *Race Today Review*. The essay addresses the conditions necessary to a flourishing cultural scene. Howe argued that artistic expression must be 'nurtured'.

> . . . artistic creativity is fed and stimulated in an ambience which generates work
> of the highest quality. It requires vibrant, social institutions in which the works are
> concentrated and made available to those who strive to create it.
>
> (*RTR*, 1981: 3)

However, Britain in 1981 was characterized by cultural bankruptcy and therefore black artists should look to 'durable institutions' within the black community such as 'New Beacon Books, Bogle-L'Ouverture Publications and Race Today Publications' which 'continue to foster the ambience' in which artistry could flourish (Ibid.). Rugg's 'Introduction' to the 1984 *Race Today Review* indicates that Howe's notion of cultural 'nurture' was central to her editorial view of literature. 'Artists', she argued, 'need to be nurtured by a receptive and critical audience' in order for their work to mature. Therefore, the 'publishing houses, bookshops, art galleries, theatres and public festivals' that had emerged as part of the 'struggles waged consistently over the years by blacks' were crucial to the black cultural scene (*RTR*, 1984: 3).

Creation for Liberation

Creation for Liberation was one of a number of cultural institutions that thrived during the 1980s to nurture black artists. Established in 1975, the small group of artists and organizers set out the organization's origins and purpose thus:

> Creation for Liberation was born out of the struggles the black community is
> engaged in for freedom. There is a cultural dimension to these struggles reflected
> in many areas of the arts, be it music, literature, the fine arts, the performing arts,
> film or sport. The cultural expression not only draws from the rich and powerful
> Asian, African and Caribbean heritage but also from the British and European
> tradition.
>
> (*RTR*, 1988: 3)

To this end, the organization set up cultural events, organized discussions and published leaflets and books recording and promoting black talent. In practice, Creation for Liberation was responsible for a series of annual Open Exhibitions, starting in 1982, which showcased the work of black visual artists. The Greater London Arts Council and Lambeth Borough Council provided some assistance, but the greater part of the support came from the community itself who gave their time and skills as curators, electricians, carpenters and joiners, painters and decorators to build the show from scratch.

Chila Burnam, who was involved in the 1987 Open Exhibition, described the Open Exhibition as 'dead important because it's the only exhibition by black artists, for black artists' (*BF*, 24 October 1987). Aubrey Williams, the elder statesman of black British art world at the time, argued that the importance of the Exhibitions lay in the fact that it gave young black artists the freedom to 'do their own thing. We're having a do in our own back yard, we're producing our own thing, for our own people . . . it gives an avenue for pure unfettered black expression' (Ibid.). Howe saw things very much the same way. Howe participated in the fourth Open Exhibition of 1987 by hosting a seminar on black aesthetics, a conversation with Williams about black film and painting as well as the experience of up-and-coming black artists in the College system (UC DHP Box VIII/9). In addition to the visual arts, Creation for Liberation did much to nurture black poets, including Maya Angelou, Michael Smith, Grace Nichols, Lorna Goodison and Marc Matthews (*RTR*, 1988: 12). Indeed, the group were responsible for Ntozake Shange and Jean 'Binta' Breeze's 1988 national tour (Ibid.). By 1990, with ticket receipts and various forms of sponsorship, Creation for Liberation was generating revenues in excess of £39,000 (UC DHP Box VIII/3).

Carnival

> Carnival is a festival born out of the socially committed from the Caribbean working class – a festival of the people, by the people, for the people.
>
> Darcus Howe, 11 August 2003 (*NS*, 11 August 2003)

Howe's most significant cultural contribution came through carnival, an art form in which he had been immersed since his youth as a member of Renegades Steelband in Port-of-Spain. Steelband music is in Howe's blood, so from the moment the Notting Hill Carnival was first mooted in 1965, he became a keen participant who 'played the iron' and shared his knowledge of the Trinidadian pan movement with other West Indians and whites attracted by the event (Howe 2011i). The sheer energy and vivacity of the annual celebration attracted thousands of new revellers each year so that by the early 1970s it had already developed into Britain's biggest annual open air festival.

It was in the wake of the violent confrontation between police and black youth which occurred at the 1976 Carnival, when police calls for the Carnival to be banned or relocated reached their height, that Howe emerged as a national spokesman for the Carnival and its organizing committee's first elected chair. At the same time, Howe and the Race Today Collective formed their own masquerade band or 'mas' with the support of hundreds of local youth in Brixton. Via the mas, known as Race Today Mangrove Renegade Band, they brought their radical politics to the streets of Notting Hill with themed floats and costumes. With 'Forces of Victory' in 1977, a tribute to insurgent southern African national liberation movements; 'Viva Zapata' in 1978, an appreciation of the Mexican revolutionary's life, and 'Feast of the Barbarian' in 1979, celebrating Britain's own ancient tradition of native resistance against foreign conquest, the mas won Best Costume for three consecutive years. At the same time, Howe was helping to reconstitute the Carnival's organizing committee on a democratic basis while also articulating a clear and radical vision of what Carnival was and should be. In his study, *Masquerade Politics*, Abner Cohen notes of Howe's impact, that Carnival 'became politically and culturally radical under his influence and he left an enduring mark on its structure' (1993: 110).

The appearance of large numbers of black youth at the 1975 Carnival, the tenth anniversary of the festival, represented a turning point in its history. Attracted

Figure 7 Howe leading the masqueraders during the Notting Hill Carnival, August 1978.

by large stationary discos under A40 flyover and Capital Radio's decision to promote the event, thousands of young black people participated in a way they had not done before, swelling the number of revellers to around 250,000. Inevitably, in such a crowded gathering, some petty crimes occurred such as pick pocketing and camera snatching. Nonetheless, as Howe later pointed out, no more pockets were picked in Notting Hill over Carnival than in Oxford Street during any day in the festive period (Howe 1978: 7). In the aftermath of the Carnival, Police Commander Patterson, who was charged with policing of the 1976 Carnival, openly identified with and promoted the aims of a petition being organized by a small section of the local white community to have the Notting Hill Carnival relocated to White City Stadium or Battersea Park. Patterson claimed that the Carnival 'had outgrown itself' and that if it wasn't relocated police numbers would increase from 60 in 1975 to several hundred at the coming 1976 Carnival. Through the pages of *Race Today*, Howe campaigned to protect the very nature of Carnival as a Notting Hill street festival, winning the support of the organizing committee and its chairman Selwyn Baptiste. Howe insisted there could be no compromise on location, which had been chosen in 1965, as it 'was closest to liberated territory', that is to say, where local West Indians had fought off the racists in 1958 and had put up major resistance to police brutality ever since. Howe's 1976 campaign succeeded in keeping Carnival in Notting Hill but the police continued to threaten a massive increase in their presence.

In a hardening of police tactics from the previous years, Patterson also blocked the organizers' application to obtain a liquor licence for the sale of beer by street vendors. This move gave his officers, quickly branded the 'Pale Ale Brigade', the power to pull down and disrupt numerous stalls which lined the Carnival's route. Two weeks before the 1976 August Bank Holiday, BBC interviewed members of Race Today. Describing the mounting tension between police and West Indian community as 'pretty explosive', they warned the police that 'if anything happened after all we have said, written, publicised, talked officially, if anything happened that's their fault' (*RT*, July 1977: 9).

With the scene set for a confrontation, Patterson deployed 20 times more officers, in total more than 1,200, to police the 1976 Carnival than had been deployed the year previously. Newspaper and eyewitness reports would later describe the appalling violence used by police as they tried to arrest a small group they suspected of pickpocketing at the corner of Acklam Road and Blagrove Road, thereby prompting a full-scale riot (*Daily Mirror*, 1 September 1976). Hassan remembers that when the fighting broke out, hundreds of police reinforcements which had been stationed in green and blue buses in adjoining streets joined the street battle. Not wanting the young children who were with them, including Howe's 10-year-old daughter Tamara, to witness the violence, Frank Crichlow opened the Mangrove Restaurant so they could take refuge from the fighting raging outside. The impromptu plan was thrown into disarray when dozens of riot police stormed the Mangrove without reason, causing its occupants to flee to the basement. After 4 solid hours of fighting, 325 police were reported injured and 60 people were arrested and charged in what was one of the worst riots in London for 25 years (*RT*, July 1977: 11).

In the face of renewed calls from police and politicians for the Carnival to be banned, the Collective issued an open letter to the Carnival Development Committee (CDC) in September 1976, demanding that its next general meeting be opened to all mas men and women, steelbands' men and women, sounds' men and women and interested individuals with a record of positive contribution to the Carnival. It called for the general meeting to elect the Development Committee as their public face, because 'the leadership of Carnival is not a monarchy to be passed on from one elite to the next' (*RT*, July 1977: 18). The Collective's programme for reform was presented to the CDC in stark terms. For the Carnival to survive the threat to its future, it must develop and weld the organizational resources which already shaped the large mas bands, the steelbands, the preparation of stallholders, the local West Indian businesses and individuals with an immediate interest in the Carnival. The case for reform was compelling. In April 1977, Howe became the first democratically elected chairman of the CDC. During his period in office, Howe introduced transparent accounting practices for funds raised and donated for the Carnival, won Arts Council recognition and funding for the Carnival after picketing its meetings and succeeded in opening a constructive dialogue over policing with senior officers in the Met who rejected Patterson's aggressive tactics (Howe 2011i).

Not everyone approved of Howe's new role in the CDC. A rival Carnival and Arts Committee, whose support came from four local community associations without any backing from the steel and mas bands, argued after the 1976 riot that the Carnival should become an explicitly political event. It also called on the Carnival to fully exploit its commercial potential to raise money and create jobs for the local community. Cecil Gutzmore, of Black People's Information Centre, has since criticized the CDC and Howe for establishing a power base among the Steelbands and Massbands on the grounds that such people tended to be 'culturalists' and 'apolitical' (Gutzmore 1993: 227). Howe saw things differently.

He considered any overt, instrumental use of the event for political purposes misconceived. The fact that hundreds of thousands of people came to Notting Hill in the face of opposition from police and authorities was itself a major political event. Howe also resisted attempts to commercialize the Carnival and insisted that grants like that offered by the Arts Council should have no strings attached to them in order to avoid the Carnival from becoming a pecuniary spectacle tied to the interests of the state or big business and thereby nullifying it as a form of cultural rebellion. As Cohen has observed, Howe appreciated the political potential of the Carnival, though he insisted that the celebration was essentially a cultural, artistic event and should be cultivated as such, not only to deny the authorities the excuse to ban it, but also, paradoxically, to make it more politically efficacious (1993: 111).

The Collective's own revolutionary politics were expressed through their own masquerade band with Howe playing the part of Emiliano Zapata one year and Cossack Barbarian Taras Bulba, in 'Feast of the Barbarians', the next. The first time they entered the Carnival and won Best Costume was in 1977 for Forces of Victory celebrating anti-colonial revolutions in Mozambique and Angola. Hassan recalls that the centre piece of their float was a tank which Loretta had built out of polystyrene around the shell of a car. Its realism was such that when a local resident saw the tank with a Renegade from East Driver, Dr Rat, standing on top, she exclaimed 'fucking hell they've got a tank' (Howe 2011i).

Hassan recalls that their mas refused to wear glitter, 'as revolutionaries we wore flat colours, we wanted to show that you could do mas with a revolutionary theme without all the glitter and pomp of the Trinidadian Carnival' (Hassan 2011). Lyn Richards, a white member of IRR staff and mas camp organizer, acted as seamstress, and Una Howe was, by all accounts, a brilliant costume designer. Howe sums up the experience of the Carnival thus:

> The police thought it was a conspiracy and wanted to constrain us within the rigour of some notion of "Englishness". What they found out was that English people liked to dance as much as West Indians. They came to realise that you could not stop hundreds of thousands of people enjoying themselves. To this day it was all spontaneous. Whites began to be attracted in large numbers. There was a beautiful synchronisation of race. Carnival transcended race.

> (Howe 2011i)

17

Playing Devil's Advocate

*Channel 4 . . . has been an integral part of my life . . . Just before its launch,
Jeremy Isaacs, its chief executive, visited a Home Office minister to outline
his plans. The minister congratulated Isaacs, then issued his parting shot,
"As long as you do not have that Darcus Howe on the station."*

*Isaacs returned to his office, called me in Brixton and invited me to
participate.*

(*NS*, 18 November 2002)

When Dhondy was offered the job of commissioning editor for Multi-Cultural
Programming at Channel 4, he sought advice from James. His first instinct
was that commissioning would be a distraction from his vocation as a writer.[1]
He put the dilemma to James. At first, James didn't say a word. He simply
pointed at the bookcase and wagged his finger in the negative, then pointed at
the television and nodded in the affirmative (Dhondy 2010). In his new role,
Dhondy commissioned 'more popular and contentious programmes' than
his predecessor did (Hobson 2007: 70). Some of the most famous were *The
Bandung File* and *Devil's Advocate*, two programmes which allowed Howe to
bring his own brand of radical journalism to a much wider public and become
a household name in the process.

Before Channel 4

Howe had appeared on television and radio on numerous occasions prior to
the advent of *The Bandung File*. These appearances tended to be brief, but in
general terms, Howe's approach to television was a continuation of his approach
to journalism in *Race Today*. Howe's appearance on *Skin*, directed by Trevor
Phillips for the LWT Minorities Unit, in the wake of the New Cross massacre,

is a case in point. Rather than offering a political programme, Howe used the interview to reflect what was going on in the community. His brief interview set contemporary events in the context of black struggle since the mid-1960s and stressed the scale and potency of the self-organization that had followed the fire (*Skin*, 7 June 1981). Howe took a similar tack during his appearance on an episode of the *London Programme* dealing with the Scarman Report in November 1981 (*London Programme*, 20 November 1981). A final example, an ITN News debate chaired by Peter Sissons, featuring Howe, Gerald Kaufman, Michael Mates and Leslie Curtis – the Chairman of the Police Federation – saw Howe setting out a forensic case against the police. Howe's critique of police racism was devoid of florid rhetoric and appealed to the most progressive aspects of British political culture. Indeed, Howe situated the fight against stop and search in a 'remarkable tradition of keeping the police in check . . . what keeps them in check is the alertness, the vigilance of the British democratic tradition' (*ITN News*, 17 November 1983).

In 1984, Howe did a screen test for LWT's *Black on Black*. Inspired by James, Howe viewed television as a progressive force. Radicals had long seen the potential of the media as a propaganda weapon, but for James, the media's progressive role was rooted in the sociological dynamics of modern society. *American Civilization* argued: '[t]he modern popular film, the modern newspaper . . . the comic strip, the evolution of jazz, a popular periodical like *Life*, these mirror from year to year the deep social responses and evolution of the American people . . .' (James 1993: 119). The bureaucratization of modern life, James contended, stripped people of their freedom and threatened their individuality. As life became increasingly restricted, people sought liberty in the field of entertainment, demanding 'aesthetic compensation in the contemplation of free individuals who go out into the world and settle their problems by free activity and individualistic methods' (Ibid., 127). In this sense, the modern media tended to reflect the desire for liberty and self-organization. With this in mind, although he had little time for *Black on Black*, Howe was willing to collaborate with programme makers. *Black on Black* was a false start, the screen test did not go well (Howe 2011j). Howe would soon get a break, with much more scope for creativity, in the form of *The Bandung File*.

The Bandung File

Dhondy was critical of much of the existing multicultural programming. For Dhondy, programmes like *Black on Black* and *Eastern Eye* were essentially exercises in marketing, their sole purpose to present positive images of black people. Dhondy's approach was to try and reflect real life: 'lives have comedy, lives have tragedy, lives have fallacies. I was not going to be an advertising agency for positive images' (Dhondy 2011). As a result, he cancelled *Black on Black* and *Eastern Eye*, programmes which, in any case, were already losing audience share. Dhondy envisioned a flagship show that would take the politics of developing nations and the politics of black and Asian Britain to the centre of the schedule. Dhondy settled on a format revolving around two central journalists, one West Indian and one Asian. 'And who were the best anti-establishment journalists I could find? Darcus Howe and Tariq Ali. I called Tariq and told him "I want to pair you with Darcus." He said, "Oh God!"' (Ibid.).

Having been approached by Dhondy, Ali came up with the title of the show. At the time Dhondy approached him, Ali was working on the manuscript of *The Nehrus and the Gandhis: An Indian Dynasty*, published in 1985.

> I had just reached the point where Nehru arrives at Bandung for the Conference when Greg Lanning, an experienced Producer setting up the company rang and asked for a name for the company and the show. I said: "Bandung" and explained why. Darcus and Greg thought it was a good idea. The show reflected the Bandung experience in the sense of treating the post-colonial world as an entity and not via specific identities.
>
> (Ali 2011)

Ali recalls that the Channel 4 bosses backed the project. 'Jeremy Isaacs, the legendary boss of Channel Four approved strongly. He and Dhondy wanted a hard-hitting show. His only advice: "Let us know first if you're planning something naughty so our lawyers can help in advance."' The show was produced by Bandung Productions, a company jointly owned by Howe, Ali and Lanning (Ibid.).

The Bandung File realized Dhondy's ambition of bringing multicultural programming to primetime. According to Ali, Michael Grade was so impressed by the preview tapes that he granted the show an early evening slot (Ibid.). In its first incarnation, the *Bandung File* had a significant studio-based element. The 45-minute show was split in half by an advert break. The first half was essentially a round-up of national and international news. Sitting at news desks, Howe, Gita Sahgal, Jan Bain and John Buckley introduced short films dealing with specific items.

The show's second section was devoted to longer documentary films made by Howe, Ali and, sometimes, Sahgal. Howe's documentaries included 'The Comediennes', a piece about black comics on London's alternative circuit; 'Black

Police – Behind the Image', which considered why so many black officers left the force; 'Grunwick – Ten Years After', looking back at the significance of the landmark dispute; and 'From Bandung to Harare', an interview with President Robert Mugabe filmed at the 1986 Non-Aligned Movement Summit in Zimbabwe.

By all accounts, Howe and Ali worked together well. Joint editorial meetings at the beginning of the week determined the main focus of each programme as well as assigning researchers and directors to each segment of the programme. For Ali, 'it was a very creative process. I trusted Darcus' judgements on the Caribbean and he mine on other parts of the world so we got on fine' (Ali 2011). Howe agreed: 'Tariq and I never had a row. We were mature enough to know that this wasn't the International Marxist Group, or Race Today' (Howe 2011j). For the most part, Howe and Ali worked quite separately. However, they collaborated on their interview of Julius Nyerere, and when Howe was ill, Ali stepped in to present a programme dedicated to James (Ali 2011).

Howe's television journalism reflected his long-standing concerns. Phillips argues that Howe essentially used his journalism to popularize the work and thought of James (Phillips 2011). There was a continuing focus on the problems of postcolonial government, on police harassment, on James' ideas and on James himself, on the black art scene, black self-activity in Britain, not to mention cricket. During the second series Howe took a steer from James which resulted in the documentary 'Unfinished Revolution'. Dhondy recalls James consistently held that 'if you want to know what the islands in the Caribbean will end up as, go and look at Haiti. That is the degradation into which these ex-slave cultures will descend, without a complete federation of the Caribbean including Cuba' (Dhondy 2011). Talking to James about the programme was natural for Howe. 'Anything big I'm doing I'm going to talk to James about it. I said "Nello, I think part of this has to be the countries we come from." He said "Go to Haiti first, that's where all those little Islands are headed"' (Howe 2011j).

The Jamesian origins were reflected in the finished film which considered the causes and consequences of the revolution that overthrew Jean-Claude Duvalier in February 1986. Broadcast in May 1986, Howe's film read Baby Doc's downfall as part of the Caribbean tradition of revolt stretching back to the Saint Domingo slave revolt. Jamesian too was the emphasis on interviews with the Haitian poor. The documentary presented an extended interview with Father Jean-Bertrand Aristide, who would later become Haiti's first elected President (*BF*, 9 May 1986).

Making the film was a harrowing experience. Howe saw evidence of torture on the bodies of his interviewees. In the slums of Port-au-Prince, he came across a child dying of hunger. Unaware of what he was witnessing until it was too late, the child's final moments were caught on camera. Appalled by what he had witnessed, Howe refused to let the footage be used in the final film (Howe 2011j). In Cite Soleil, a slum that Howe described as 'the dark dungeon of the Caribbean' (*BF*, 9 May 1986), he saw a woman, the very image of his aunt, living in abject squalor. This, more than anything else, brought home the horror of the situation. That evening he cried himself to sleep. Howe brought home a fragment of bullet-proof glass several inches thick, part of Baby Doc's holiday home that had been destroyed in the revolution. For Howe, it symbolized the fragility of dictatorship, however impregnable it may seem (Howe 2011j).

Howe returned to the Caribbean in his February 1987 documentary 'The Gathering Storm' (*BF*, 14 February 1987). The film was made shortly after the National Alliance for Reconstruction won power in Trinidad. 'The Gathering Storm' examined the impact that the fall in oil prices and poor economic stewardship by the previous government had had on Trinidad's economy and society. Howe argued that the mass unemployment, the spiralling inflation and the failure of the government were fuelling nationwide revolt. According to David Abdullah, now general secretary of the Oilfield Workers Trade Union (OWTU), Howe's film 'became infamous in elite circles in Trinidad and Tabago'. Abdullah maintains that 'it was a very important programme which accurately

Figure 8 Howe on Observatory Street Port-of-Spain, the home of the Renegades, in the late 1980s. From *Left* to *Right*, Howe, Victor McQueen, 'Slugger', Tony 'Castro' McQueen and Dr Rat.

foretold the general strike of 1989. . . . Darcus was spot on in his assessment of a seething undercurrent of social conflict and opposition' (Abdullah 2011).

Closer to home, Howe's documentaries dealt with the gentrification of Brixton, conflict between London's pirate radio stations and the authorities and Brixton's art scene. Howe also made several documentaries on cricket. On one occasion, he recalls: 'we were in Barbados filming the West Indies playing New Zealand. I called Viv [Richards] and said "Could you make a hundred?" He just said "Yeah man." I knew he could do it. He did it in ones and twos, he didn't take any chances at all. I thought to myself this is a man who knows what he's doing!' (Howe 2011j).

The show won plaudits from all quarters. 'In general', Ali comments, 'the responses were very positive, although the professional race-relationwallahs hated us because *The Bandung File* did not provide them with a platform' (Ali 2011). *The Listener* credited it with 'some remarkable firsts in both political and cultural coverage'. The *New Statesman* opined that the show guaranteed the Channel 4 boss a spot on the short list for the next Director General of the BBC (Bandung 1988: 2). After 6 years and 91 episodes, the show came to an end. Ali saw the cancellation as indicative of the dumbing-down that was going on in the British media. Dhondy argues that the end of the show was due to changes in the media. The advent of cable television meant that programming from the sub-continent and the Caribbean was available independent of the terrestrial networks; therefore, there was less need for *Bandung* (Dhondy 2011).

The dissolution of the Race Today Collective

In the first few years, Race Today worked closely with Bandung Productions, printing transcripts of segments of the show and publishing pamphlets based on the show's content. Howe's attention was increasingly focused on his television work. In 1985, Howe stepped down as editor and Hassan took over the running of the magazine. Hassan remembers this as a difficult time. 'When Darcus left *Race Today* we were very upset. We used to joke "are you selling out and becoming a TV personality?"' (Hassan 2011). The final issue was published in 1988. The Collective formally dissolved itself on 7 April 1991. The Collective had been extensively reorganized in late 1988, with the establishment of Race Today Enterprises. The move had, in part, been an attempt to solve the magazine's financial problems. Following the closure of the magazines, there were ongoing discussions on the future of the Collective. Howe was keen, at least between 1988 and 1990, to keep an organization going. In a letter to the members of the Collective written in 1989, he argues that the organization should continue as a basis for future interventions in British national life (UC DHP Box VIII/4). The eventual agreement was to dissolve the Collective and found a new organization. Therefore, the formal dissolution, proposed by Patricia Dick and seconded by Michael Cadette, passed all the Collective's assets to a new association, The C. L. R. James Institute (Preparatory) (Ibid.). From Johnson's point of view, Howe had lost interest in *Race Today*:

> Darcus decided that he wanted to be in the media, and I got the impression that he figured that we had more-or-less won the battle that we had been fighting. I wasn't around for any decision making, I just stopped attending meetings, I didn't think the leadership's heart was in the organisation any more.
>
> Also the death of CLR James created a pall over everything. Some members were affected by it. I certainly was.
>
> (Johnson 2011)

For Howe, Race Today had done its job. 'We had exhausted the moment' (Howe 2011d).

The death of James

James' death in May 1989 was a major blow to Howe. Howe was prepared for the end when it came. 'I asked him what do you want, where do you want to be buried? And he says "Please keep me out of a church!"' (BBC 2002). When the time came, Howe took James' body back to Trinidad. James had a long-standing arrangement with George Weekes, and latterly Errol McLeod, that the OWTU should be responsible for his funeral. Together with OWTU officers McLeod, Abdullah, Pat Bishop and the OWTU's representative in Britain John la Rose, Howe played a major role in organizing James' last rites (Abdullah 2011). Howe dealt with all of the legalities of taking James to Trinidad and ensuring that the OWTU had the legal right to oversee the burial. He arranged to have James' remains embalmed. In the meantime, Abdullah and McLeod fended off attempts to turn James' burial into a State Funeral (Ibid.). The rejection of officialdom was evident as James' body arrived in Trinidad. John La Rose read an excerpt from Aime Cesaire's 'Return to My Native Land' in homage to James. In a sense this was an allusion to the Black Power Revolution, as an excerpt from the poem had been published in the *Vanguard* during 1970. Speaking at the airport as James' coffin touched down,

Howe paid tribute to his great-uncle and friend: 'I have brought my friend home, on the last leg of his final journey, into the night' (*BF*, 27 June 1989).

Abdullah recalls that 'Darcus worked closely with myself, Errol, John and Pat on the final programme' (Abdullah 2011). Howe ensured that 'he was buried with his Rite of Spring, his Stravinsky, I was very smart in organising, I knew what I was doing. He was buried as he should have been with all the paraphernalia of advanced European music' (BBC 2002). Music was a major part of the day. The Rite of Spring was played by a steelband and Mighty Sparrow sang his classic calypso 'Memories'. 'Sparrow had written an additional verse about CLR,' and David Rudder sang 'Haiti', a song inspired by *The Black Jacobins*. Howe was one of many who paid tribute to James. Abdulla recalls: 'He spoke on behalf of the family. There is one other relative, Cyril Austin who lives in Belmont, but Darcus was the closest to him personally and politically.' Speaking of James' relationship with the generation that had emerged following the 1981 uprisings, he said, 'they needed him and he needed them. . . . I know no one over forty in the United Kingdom who had such an intimate window upon a completely new generation of people . . . that was James in the last ten years of his life' (*BF*, 27 June 1989).

Devil's Advocate

'In Brixton, my name changed from "Darcus" to "the Dev"!'. In 1992, Howe embarked on a new project. The origins of the show are disputed. Howe claims that the idea emerged from a morning at a West-Indian barbers. 'I left a barber's shop in Balham, and they were all arguing about this-and-that, politics and everything, and I just took it over. I said, if you want to get somewhere with this discussion, talk here, I in charge' (Howe 2011j). Howe approached Dhondy, wanting to recreate the vigour of the barber's shop discussion on screen. Howe was also inspired by *Desmond's*, a Channel 4 sitcom broadcast between 1989 and 1994. Set in a Peckham barbers shop, the comedy emerged from the discussions between a cast of black characters with different aspirations. Howe's vision was simultaneously grandiose and democratic. 'I said, I'll only do it if we can book the largest studio in the country!' (Howe 2010). The studio audience were the democratic element. Not only were they representing the wider viewing public, but also they joined in the debate heightening the scrutiny to which Howe's guests were subjected.

Phillips, the show's Producer, tells a different story. He argues that the show emerged from contemporary media dynamics. *The Walden Interview*, he recalls, ended in the mid-1980s. Its demise, he argues, marked the end of the in-depth 45-minute interview. The dominant model from the late 1980s was the short adversarial confrontation, a style that Jeremy Paxman made his own. Phillip's vision was to revive the 45-minute format. He believed that the longer format was more conducive to forcing public figures to engage with the interviewer. He planned to bring back the 45-minute format but with an added adversarial element (Phillips 2011). Dhondy, too, claims credit for devising the format, as well as coming up with the show's title. In any case, Dhondy, Phillips and Howe all agree that the *Devil's Advocate* format was the perfect vehicle for Howe. LWT picked up the show with Phillips acting as executive producer.

From 1992 to 1996, the *Devil's Advocate* was a regular feature of Channel 4's output. The show ran for six seasons, a total of 36 episodes. Much more than his previous media appearances, *Devil's Advocate* conferred a degree of celebrity on Howe, making him as much a part of 1990s' TV culture as Jeremy Paxman, Richard and Judy, Denise van Outen, Alan Partridge, Chris Evans or Mr Blobby. The first episode of Howe's new series aired at 11:30 on 10 August 1992. According to the *TV Times*, the show would 'challenge conventional wisdom about a major talking point of the day' (7 September 1993). The format of the show changed over the course of production, but in essence, Howe used each episode to subject a person, or a small group – the occupants of the 'Hot Seat' – to intense scrutiny. Usually, Howe would lead the questioning in the first 20-minute segment and then moderate an audience discussion following an advert break. The opening titles added an edge of melodrama, beginning in the first four seasons with a flash of lightning and in the final two with a blaze of hell fire. The theatricality was heightened with two catch phrases. Howe introduced himself with the phrase 'I am the Devil's Advocate' and invited comments from the audience or his guests with the words 'What say you?'. The second phrase had a Shakespearian edge, as well as juridical overtones, recalling the inquiry of the Clerk of Court to the Foreman of a jury at the end of a trial in some American States.

'They say "Get Back" we say "Fight Back!"'

The high point of the third season was Howe's confrontation with Bernie Grant. The show created a stir in the press and serious repercussions for Grant. Howe's relationship with Grant went back many years. Broadly, Howe had supported Grant, believing him to be 'the authentic voice of black people' (*DA*, 13 October 1993). *Devil's Advocate* examined Grant's speech at a fringe meeting of the 1993 Labour Party Conference. Speaking on the 25th anniversary of Powell's infamous 'Rivers of Blood' speech, Grant discussed calls for state-funded 'voluntary repatriation'. Prior to the broadcast, Grant's comments had made the front page of *The Voice*. On 5 October, under the headline 'Take the money and run', Ainsley Okoro reported Grant's statement thus: 'I can tell you that people are coming to me saying that we want voluntary repatriation, that we have had enough of this lousy country. . . . We won't have to wait until the British National Party gets elected and sends us back, we will go back voluntarily. The government should pay for those who want to go.' Smelling blood, the mainstream press jumped on the story. Grant, who was abandoned by his black parliamentary colleagues, responded with a 'clarification' stating that he was not talking about voluntary repatriation (*Guardian*, 6 October 1993).

Howe opened by offering Grant the chance to back down. Grant, however, asserted that he had nothing to apologize for, *The Voice* has misquoted him. At this point, Howe played his trump card, a recording of Grant's fringe speech in which he clearly advocated 'voluntary repatriation'. Faced with the recording Grant apologized, clarifying his position again: he was opposed to 'repatriation', in the sense that he was not advocating a 'return'. That said, he did want a debate; he wanted to ensure that people who wanted to leave Britain were helped to do so; and he wanted Britain to pay reparations to her former colonies. As the show progressed, Grant justified his position in two ways. First, he argued that he was reflecting the concerns of his constituents. Secondly, he argued that black people had no future in Europe:

> Grant: Our future is not in Europe, I think that our future is in Africa in the Caribbean in countries . . .
> Howe: But you're MP for Tottenham!
> [Laughter and applause.]
> Grant: Hang on a minute, I know I'm MP for Tottenham! . . . They have no future because what is happening in Europe is a movement towards ethnically cleansing Europe similarly as has happened in Bosnia, in Europe, that's what I'm saying. And I'm saying that there are two ways you fight against it, you can fight it here in Europe . . . and I'm saying that you also have to join up, because black people in Britain aren't going to be able to sort their own problems out. We have to link up with people in Africa and other countries in order to make sure that that future exists.

> (*DA*, 13 October 1993)

Needless to say, Howe argued that this was a retrograde position. For Howe, it amounted to 'surrender'. Moreover, it shifted the debate away from the fight against racism to repatriation. In so doing, it undermined the gains made by the black community since the late 1960s by questioning the place of black people in British society. Howe argued: '[j]ust when we thought we had established our rights here as British citizens, Bernie has offered us the defeatist position of abandoning ship with our pockets filled with silver'. For Howe, voluntary repatriation was the beginning of a slippery slope that would inevitably lead to forced repatriation. Howe offered an alternative slogan, borrowed from an Asian anti-racist demonstration of the time, 'They say "Get Back" we say "Fight Back!"' (Ibid.).

Grant enjoyed some support from the studio audience. Lady Jane Birdwood, who had stood as a BNP candidate in the 1992 General Election, and had been convicted of distributing anti-Semitic material, stated that she agreed with Grant.

Linda Bellos, former leader of Lambeth Council, offered qualified support:

> I do support the fact that Bernie is reflecting a point of view, which I must say in my several years in working in Social Services, I have had put to me. I have to say, I don't advocate a political strategy of voluntary return home. But I do, on an individual level – on a personal level, feel very sympathetic to people, like my father who's 77, who came here, yes, 50 years ago, he came during the war, expecting not to stay for very long. He is now old, because he was badly paid, as a manual worker, he doesn't have the resources that he thought he would have had, and should have had. So someone like him does frequently say he wants to go home. I don't think he will, I think he's going to die here, like most of us will. But in reflecting that and in saying that, I think Bernie is right.[2]
>
> (Ibid.)

Howe and Bellos were known to each other before the show. During the 1980s, Bellos had lived in Brixton, near the Collective's base; she had been interviewed by *Race Today*; and clashed with Howe over the issue of Black Sections in the Labour Party. Bellos' interest in reparations had led her to work with Grant as part of the African Reparations Movement (United Kingdom) (Sudbury 1998: 186). 'To say that I was less than impressed with Darcus is an understatement,' comments Bellos: 'I just found him so damn negative, sneering and elitist. I could see what he was against, I couldn't see what he was for.' For Bellos, the programme glossed over the subtleties of the reparations issue.

> Ours was a much more sophisticated argument than "take the money and go" . . .
> We had demanded that Britain recognise its role in the enslavement of African

people, I mean the African Diaspora, and pay for some of the repair. What we argued was that the historical legacy of enslavement and colonisation, the relationships that were built before independence, and treatment of people of African descent in Britain; we saw them all connected.

(Bellos 2012)

As treasurer of ARM (United Kingdom), Bellos helped shape the group's demands. Ultimately, Bellos felt that the show had trivialized the issues, missing the opportunity to put a case about the history of Britain to the viewing public.

After the show, Howe claims, Grant left in tears convinced his political career was over (Howe 2011j). Bellos and Grant left together: she recalls that the drive back to London consolidated their mutual 'loathing of Darcus' (Bellos 2012). Having been involved in several of Howe's shows, Bellos decided that would be her last.

On 11 October, the day after the recording, Grant complained to Michael Grade. He argued that he had been invited on the show 'on false pretences', stating that Howe had focused on his 'credentials as a black leader', not on the issue of 'return/repatriations'. He also objected to the use of the tape. In sum, he argued that 'the makers of this programme behaved in a thoroughly unprofessional manner, and that I was treated shabbily in an attempt to humiliate me'. The complaint was passed to Dhondy, who defended the integrity of the programme and offered no apology. Grant, clearly dissatisfied, wrote to John Willis, Channel 4's Director of Programmes, objecting to the

> ghettoisation of my complaint. I am a Member of Parliament, and when I write to Michael Grade, I expect him to reply to me, and not to refer the matter to the Commissioning Editor for Multi-cultural programming. This amounts to nothing less than institutionalised racism. Because I am black, then you seem to feel that the matter had to be sorted out by black people, and that I can be fobbed off by Mr Dhondy.
>
> (BGI BG ARM 7/2/16)

Grant's complaints did not delay the show's transmission. After the programme aired, Grant received a series of letters rejecting his position. On 17 October, the African Caribbean Leadership Council formally distanced itself from Grant's comments. On 19 October, the UNISON Black Member's Committee did the same, and SCORE UK, the Standing Committee on Racial Equality, professed itself 'extremely disturbed' by Grant's comments. The General Committees of the

Archway, Alexandra and Hornsey Vale Labour Parties disassociated themselves from Grant's comments. The Tottenham Labour Party was more supportive, but did acknowledge that 'incautious and confused language' was used in the debate and therefore that 'steps much be taken to minimise the damage that has been done' (BGI BG ARM 7/12/15).

Fortunately for Grant, the show did not, as he had feared, end his career. Grant continued to advocate a version of the policy that he outlined on *Devil's Advocate*. Indeed, speaking in the House of Commons on 19 December 1995, he argued that 'a £100,000 option should be given to those wishing to return to Africa and the Caribbean' (Grant 2006: 123). Howe recalls that the programme marked the end of their friendship, and that, from that time on, Grant invariably referred to him as 'that well known idiot Darcus Howe' (Howe 2011j).

The Hot Seat

Occupants of the Hot Seat included big names such as Arthur Scargil, Winnie Mandela, Nigel Benn, John Fashnu and Chris Eubank. More often than not, Howe's cross-examinations led to heated exchanges. On an early show dealing with allegations of racism and nepotism at Stratford School, Muhammad Haque, chair of the London Collective of Black Governors, made no bones about his view that 'this programme is a dirty tricks programme, and you are doing the dirty for the racists'. Latoya Jackson took to calling Howe 'The Devil' during her appearance on the show. On two occasions, the show led Howe to fear for his life. Following his clash with Rastafarian actor and writer Shango Baku over the divinity of Haile Selassie, Howe recalls: 'the head of the Rastafarians in Brixton sent two men to my house to take me to their headquarters for a trial. They left without me' (*NS*, 18 November 2002). More serious was his encounter with Chief Mangosuthu Buthelezi. Howe's meeting with the Zulu leader was the climax of the show's fourth season. Howe flew to Durban for the confrontation. Howe had evidence which corroborated ANC claims that sections of Inkatha had taken money from the South African security services during the years of Apartheid. The information came from Phillips' contacts in the ANC, contacts that he had developed while being the president of the National Union of Students. Buthelezi 'arrived in the studio with a massive retinue'. More intimidating was news from Phillips 'that some people in the audience were bearing arms'. The worst of it, from what Howe recalls, was that as the show began, 'the braces clipped on to my trousers popped' (*Independent*, 25 October 1998). In front of a packed hall, Howe reeled off details of the funds paid by intelligence officers to the Inkatha Freedom Party from the security budget of the Apartheid regime. Buthelezi treated the claims with contempt. The programme ended with Buthelezi issuing a Zulu war cry. Following the show, Howe took no chances. He left immediately for Cape Town, then to Soweto and then home. Two days after the show was aired, the Durban studio was attacked by armed supporters of Buthelezi (*NS*, 6 September 2001).

The audience played a crucial role in holding the powerful and the famous to account. This was certainly the case in a 1995 edition of the show featuring Chief Constable Richard Wells, then leader of the South Yorkshire Police. The show, which was shot in the context of the controversial anti-mugging initiative Operation Eagle Eye, focused on the extent to which the police took racial violence seriously. Wells acknowledged that the force had had to rethink its attitude to black people. However, in the contemporary world, he argued, the biggest problem was communication, as a few *cause célèbres*, created by small pockets of racist officers, had persuaded minorities that the police could not be trusted. Other than introducing the show, Howe took a back seat, allowing the audience to put their case to Wells. The final word went to Frank Crichlow, who, drawing on his own experience, pointed out that small numbers of racist officers could 'ruin people's lives, hundreds of West Indian and black people's lives, continuously. . . . What I would like to see is an Eagle Eye to stop the deaths in police custody, an Eagle Eye in order to flush out some of the racism in the police force – we cannot walk the streets!' (*DA*, 27 September 1995).

'X-PRESS', screened on 10 August 1994, saw Dotun Adebayo and Steven Pope in the Hot Seat. The show focused on the publication of *Cop Killer* (1994) and the controversial marketing tactics used to promote it. *Cop Killer* was the fifth novel published by X-PRESS, an independent publishing house set up by Adebayo and Pope. Howe argued that the book was badly written, glamorized violence and the campaign to promote it, which consisted of sending out flyers to national newspapers with what appeared to be a bullet, was irresponsible.

Describing the atmosphere in the green room prior to the show, Adebayo recalls: 'I'll give Darcus this, and Trevor Phillips who was working on the show, they really knew how to put the fear of God into interviewees, they really knew it!' (Adebayo 2011). Adebayo's brother, a researcher on the show, refused to divulge anything of Howe's plans. 'We got to the green room, they'd sent a taxi, my heart was beating! Steve was nervous too, but not as nervous as me. They prepared the taxi to arrive with only a few minutes to go before they needed us on set.' Adebayo and Pope were rushed through make-up and then straight on to the set. Adebayo was convinced that the speed with which they were hurried through LWT was intended to put them on edge.

> The first person I saw on set was the brother of PC Patrick Dunne, a PC who had been shot in Clapham – when I saw that, I will tell you, my heart almost jumped out of my mouth – I've been a journalist all my life, you know what that symbolises, I couldn't control my emotions at that point, I was totally hyped! I wasn't a fool, I'd seen *Devil's Advocate*, I knew what the form was. I was a journalist, I knew I was there to get duffed up! We were sitting on these chairs, like electric chairs, waiting for the leaver to be pulled!
>
> (Ibid.)

Adebayo's nerves were not helped by Howe who was there in the background, 'clearly in his element, dressed for the occasion, his very presence dominating the arena!'. By the time the filming started, Adebayo was keyed up for a fight. Howe ramped up the dramatic tension during the show by producing a replica revolver. The audience was split, Adebayo had invited the team who put out the magazine *Skank* along for moral support. Adebayo's strategy was to come across as 'street', to imply that Howe was out of touch with contemporary youth culture, and this certainly came across in their exchanges over music. Adebayo and Pope countered Howe's claims about the quality of the prose by arguing that it was not so much about good or bad prose as it was catering to a specific market, and on this criteria, sales figures showed that they were succeeding.

Looking back, Adebayo comments: 'the great thing about Darcus at that time, when he was clearly at the top of his game, I defy you to find any journalist or presenter at the time, who could do that job as well as Darcus? . . . Darcus is a legend. Darcus has always been a positive militant person to look up to for me. Ever since Linton Kwesi Johnson did that tune, I remember thinking "I'm supporting him". Darcus, even before I met him, was something of an icon' (Ibid.).

Naturally, *Devil's Advocate* examined cricket. The very first show concerned the game. For Howe, this was a deliberate attempt 'to avoid the pre-set tracks

of what it is deemed right and proper for a black public figure to follow'
(UC Box VIII/7). Season 4 opened with Imran Khan in the Hot Seat. Howe
tackled allegations regarding ball tampering. Khan responded that whatever
he had done, it was nothing more than any other cricketer. Howe's response
reflected his faith in the universality of the moral code he had imbibed in his
youth. He argued, very simply, that this defence would not have satisfied his
mother. The show led to new opportunities for Howe. Impressed by what he
saw, Stewart Steven invited Howe to write for the *Evening Standard*. As a result,
Howe became a columnist, finding himself in the unlikely company of Nigella
Lawson and Brian Sewell. His first column appeared on 9 September 1994. On
that occasion, the column gave an insight into events around the making of
Devil's Advocate. On another occasion, Howe used the column to interview
Clare Short, who had previously been a guest on the show. The interview took
place in 1995. Short was in the Shadow Cabinet and with the Major government
divided and unpopular, she was preparing for Government. 'Over the years I've
had plenty of interviews. What I remember of Darcus was that he started off
by asking me to recall a line of poetry. It was very distinctive and I still have
a little affectionate memory of that.' Short quoted Yeats, '"The best lack all
conviction, The worst are full of passionate intensity."' I liked him and I liked
his style.' The verse lead into a discussion of her father, who used to quote the
verse, and Short's own approach to politics (*Evening Standard*, 4 April 1995). Of
Howe's impact on British politics, she comments: 'He was rigorous and critical
and then he became a national treasure without compromising. That's pretty
admirable' (Short 2012).

The sixth season of *Devil's Advocate*, which aired in 1996, was the last. Phillips
recalls that LWT were willing to commission a seventh series, but they were
offering less money so Howe pulled out (Phillips 2011). Over its 4-year run, the
show attracted praise and censure. Bellos looks back on it simply as 'that stupid
ludicrous programme . . . not to disparage the positive things that he did do early
on, frankly *Devil's Advocate* and a few other commentary things that he has done
have made him look a fool' (Bellos 2012). For Phillips, the show was ground-
breaking. 'It showed the black community not as a monolith, but a community
like any other where people had disagreements and took different positions'
(Phillips 2011). In terms of the journalism, he comments: 'people celebrate the
Paxman interview where he asks Michael Howard the same question fourteen
times. Darcus was doing that every week!' (Ibid.).

Notes

1 Dhondy was enjoying considerable success as a writer. In the 1970s, he had published *East End at Your Feet*, a collection of short stories, and *The Siege of Babylon*, a novel inspired by the 1975 Spaghetti House Siege. In the early 1980s, he had started writing for television with *Good at Art*, *The Bride* and *Come to Mecca*, airing on the BBC in 1983 and the first series of the sitcom *No Problem!* showing on Channel 4 in the same year.
2 Bellos returned to this theme in 'Bravo Bernie' *The Guardian*, 12 October 1993.

18

Slave Nation

Devil's Advocate had made Howe's name. In its wake, the *Independent* dubbed him a 'black media star' (1 March 1998), and the *Mirror's* 'Black Whose Who' described him as an 'influential TV presenter and journalist' (16 February 1999). Nevertheless, the *Devil's Advocate* formula, like the *Bandung* format before it, imposed limits on what Howe could achieve. The documentaries of the naughties, made with Diverse TV, allowed Howe to be more ambitious in scope. *White Tribe* and *Slave Nation* reflected contemporary public debates over the meaning of Englishness, with Howe playing the role of a modern-day anthropologist creating an ethnography of England's white population. Latterly, the focus of his programmes shifted. Reflecting long-standing trends, Howe himself became the centre of attention, the style more confessional. In addition to his major documentaries, Howe's celebrity and reputation for controversy meant that he was a regular on television and radio for the whole decade.

White Tribe

White Tribe was Howe's first major documentary. It picked up from where his 1998 *England my England* had left off. Both shows took Howe on the road, focusing on chance meetings. The 1998 *England my England* was Howe's first big television piece after the conclusion of *Devil's Advocate*. Howe was paired with Peregrine Worsthorne. Writing in *The Spectator*, Worsthorne expressed his surprise that Channel 4 'should have chosen a crusty old reactionary like me to take part'. He 'learnt later that the choice was not theirs but that of my West Indian co-"star", Darcus Howe, who, believe it or not, had made my presence a condition of agreeing to undertake the job' (11 April 1998). The two had crossed swords on an episode of *Devil's Advocate* dealing with the Royal Family. Worsthorne had appeared following Dhondy's suggestion that Howe examine a right-wing patrician. Howe had suggested Worsthorne, who he viewed as a worthy opponent as well as a good writer.

Howe used the show to make the case that the attitudes of white people in Britain had changed since the 1960s, that British racism, in the population at large, was if not dead then certainly dying. Worsthorne was more pessimistic, claiming that the weight of history meant that it would take several generations before British racism was dead. The analysis that Howe presented during the documentary reflected a more general perception, rooted in his own intuitions and experience. In essence, he was

> aiming to demonstrate in my grand tour of the state of English hearts and minds of all hues and classes that my childhood intuition that England was my home, that England was MY England was an intuition that, despite many setbacks, was a sound one. But that it had to be sought for and fought with a great deal of cunning and a sense of what in the English tradition of politics, religion and culture could be drawn on, to achieve this lifetime's ambition.
>
> (UC DHP Box IX/2)

Whatever their differences, Worsthorne evidently enjoyed working with Howe, his 'new and treasured friend' who, in Worsthorne's view, emerged from the programme, 'very much the hero of the hour' (*The Spectator* 11 April 1998).

Whereas *England my England* had focused on racism, *White Tribe* considered Englishness. Producer Narinder Minhas wanted to make a programme which inverted the focus of traditional programmes about race. Rather than concentrating on black people as a beleaguered minority, it considered a crisis of identity among England's white population. For Howe, the crisis was related to contemporary events (Minhas 2012). The loss of Empire, the prospect of Scottish and Welsh independence – much discussed after the devolution bills of the late 1990s, and the flimsiness of Blair's 'New Britain' all brought the nature of 'Englishness' into question. He also related the question to his own experience, arguing that he had been broadly accepted as British, but never English (*White Tribe*, 27 January 2000).

Minhas was ambitious for the show:

> Our real intention was to re-define what multicultural television should be in the new century. There's no reason why multicultural programmes should focus only on people with dark skin and live in the ghettos. Rather, its real future lies in the opportunities it provides for fresh perspectives on subjects that are often the

preserve of "whites". When did you last see three hours of primetime television on a significant issue fronted by a black man who is not a chef, stand-up comic or a footballer?

(The Guardian, 10 January 2000)

Part of Minhas' aim was to break out of the studio and take Howe 'on the road'. He envisioned Howe acting like a 'black Louis Theroux', conceiving the shows as 'obstacle courses' in which the Howe's unscripted interactions would drive documentary (Minhas 2012). Minhas was keen to work with Howe because of Howe's political unpredictability. Counter-intuitively during *White Tribe*, the left-wing, urban, radical Howe rejected the hunting ban and was prepared to give the racist comic Bernard Manning an opportunity to defend his material. Some of the interactions were pre-prepared, others serendipitous. His meeting with Norman Tebbit was a chance encounter at a Conservative annual dinner held in the Imperial Palace in Skegness. Howe describes the encounter as a 'clean cut draw, one all'. Remarkably, Howe did not discuss the 'cricket test' with Tebbit.[1] 'I didn't want any useless confrontation, because he wasn't going to change his mind and neither would I' (Howe 2011h). As for Bernard Manning, Howe comments: 'I have an instinctive respect for old fools! He was apologetic and extremely polite. I was never biblical or deeply religious about racists. I would take on the police, but I wasn't an opportunist. I could have confronted Manning, but people would say, "Oh yeah he's right but he's a shit that Darcus Howe"' (Ibid.). Channel 4 threw its weight behind the series, buying billboard space to promote the documentaries.

Howe continued his investigation of Englishness in *The Cricket Test with Darcus Howe*, 3 5-minute pieces that aired in August 2000, and *Slave Nation* which was shown in 2001. *Slave Nation* focused on protest, work and sex. In essence, Howe argued that the English had, by and large, lost their willingness to protest, had adopted a conformist attitude in the workplace and lost the joy of sex. Again, Diverse took Howe on tour, to sex shops in Soho, to a marriage enrichment course in Devon and, to an Egg call centre, to Switzerland with an anarchist Samba band, and, following the publication of the MacPherson Report, to Eltham, the London suburb where Stephen Lawrence had been murdered in 1993. What struck Howe while making *White Tribe* and *Slave Nation* was the poverty he encountered and the attendant 'stench of decay in homes, and a bitterness. The loss of self assurance.' Minhas comments: 'Darcus was visibly shocked by the views of the residents who consider themselves an ethnic minority in a town where they make up 90% of the population' (*Guardian*, 10 January 2000).

Slave Nation, like *White Tribe* before it, was given a primetime slot. It was not as well received as *White Tribe*. Certainly, the *Independent* welcomed Howe back: 'quibbles aside, it remains a privilege to watch people of diverse backgrounds being scrutinised by a brooding, powerful and teasing presence' (4 August 2001). Similarly, the *Express* considered it 'always good to see Darcus Howe back on our screens, not least as he's one of the few left on television, along with Jonathan Meades, actively allowed to roam free to criticise this fair country' (8 August 2001). *The Times* was less convinced, accusing Howe of a 'rather self-satisfied man who believes that you can camouflage the banality or fatuity of what you are saying by saying it very; very; slowly' (9 August 2001). Perhaps the subtleties of the show were lost on Gary Bushel who opined, '[a]ll Howe's TV shows are pants.... For real slave nations try filming in Kenya' (*People*, 26 August 2001). Significantly, none of the reviews acknowledged Howe's work outside of television. As far as the press was concerned, Howe was just another talking head, his activism and his years as editor of *Race Today* were wholly overlooked.

Darcus Howe is not a comedian?

Howe appeared on Mark Lamarr's talk show *Lamarr's Attacks* as part of the publicity for *White Tribe*. It was one of several appearances on comedy shows in the late 1990s and early naughties. In 1996, Howe joined Vic Reeves and Bob Mortimer on the comedy quiz show *Shooting Stars*. As part of Mark Lamarr's team, Howe entertained the crowd with an impersonation of Trevor McDonald and, through the medium of dance, with a representation of a salmon ascending a waterfall (1 November 1996). Reeves and Mortimer evidently enjoyed Howe's appearance (Thompson 2010), as did Howe, who later described the show as 'just songs, songs of freedom and bilious stupidity' (*Shooting Stars – the inside Story*, 30 December 2008). *The Real McCoy*'s parodied *Devil's Advocate*. Leo Chester, now Leo Muhammad, appeared as 'Darkman Howe ... the Devil himself' (5 January 1996). Howe's appearance on *Brass Eye* in 1997 was another matter entirely. Following a mock introduction by Chris Morris, Howe's only contribution to the show was the short, but memorable question, 'What's a "coco-shunter"?' Howe's interview on *Lamarr's Attacks* was part of the show's focus on Britain and Europe. Boris Johnson, Lamarr's first guest, demonstrated his inclusive credentials by declaring himself 'very much in favour of cappuccino and spaghetti albondiga'. Howe, for his part, spoke up for rice and peas. On a more serious note, he expressed a deep affection for England: 'I have never known a place that did such awful things in slavery and colonialism, and at the end of it say "I don't want to be that anymore." I think the present spirit of this country is not associated with colonial pomposity and imperial cruelty' (10 September 2000).

The N-bomb

In 2002, Howe made a brief appearance on *Edwardian Country House*, a series which tried to reproduce the dynamics of early-twentieth-century life. The climax of the show's fifth episode was a fancy dress ball for 50 people celebrating the British Empire. Howe, subversively, attended dressed as Toussaint L'Ouverture. His 2004 documentary *Who you callin' a nigger?* was altogether more controversial. Again, Howe and Minhas wanted to break the mould of multicultural television by investigating racism between different, non-white, ethnic groups. The notion of 'black-on-black' violence had surfaced in the mainstream media in 1998, following shootings in Lambeth and Brent. Howe was alerted to growing inter-ethnic conflict by his son Amiri. The title also recalled the 2002 controversy over J. Lo's, apparently affectionate, reference to her husband P. Diddy as 'my nigga'.

Starting in the West Midlands, investigating conflict between black and Asian youth, Howe discussed militant Islam and anti-Semitism, as well as violence between first-generation immigrants from Africa and second- and third-generation immigrants from the West Indies. Through a series of interviews, Howe established that inter-ethnic tension was a genuine concern for modern Britain. This conclusion troubled many. On the eve of the broadcast, Howe appeared on Channel 4 News with the musician Nitin Sawhney and Shahid Malik, a member of the Labour Party's National Executive Committee, to debate his findings. For Sawhney, the film presented 'inappropriate and irresponsible images' which ignored 'so many positive, positive examples' of inter-ethnic harmony. Malik went further, commenting, 'I think Darcus' piece is potentially quite dangerous because I think it exaggerates what is quite a small problem . . .' (8 August 2004). Malik was as critical of Howe's motives as he was of his journalism. 'It's sad', he commented, 'that Darcus feels he has to do something controversial to get media attention. He's the king of exaggeration . . .' (Ibid.).

In a sense, the debate reflected the old tension in multicultural programming between those who wanted to use television to present solely positive images of multicultural Britain and those who chose to face reality. The press was far more positive. The *Times* nominated *Who you callin' a nigger?* as the best documentary of the week (9 August 2004). The *Financial Times* described it as 'a vintage piece of Channel 4 . . . thought provoking and sometimes chilling' (13 August 2004), while Charlotte Edward's column in *The Telegraph* argued that the show cemented Howe's reputation as 'one of the country's most respected commentators on race issues' (8 August 2004).

Howe was disappointed by Channel 4's ambivalence to the documentary. Apparently, there were qualms over the title and 'It was scheduled at the darkest hour, 11 p.m. The programme was not once trailed on the channel, which is rare for output that promises an impact.' Even so, he was pleased with the public response, 'it stirred upwards of a million viewers into watching it . . . thousands of words have been written about it and feature articles too. Eighteen pages on C4's website hummed with responses' (*Broadcast*, 25 August 2004).

Howe's status as a television heavyweight was underlined in the same year by his appearance on *Question Time*, the gold standard of television politics shows. Howe joined a predominantly Welsh panel, including Ann Clwyd, broadcasting from Aberystwyth. Howe's presence was easily explained. The British National Party had won a rare victory in a Council Election in Burnley. The panel were united in condemning the racism in general and the British National Party (BNP) in particular. Nonetheless, Howe struck a distinctive note. Last to be called by David Dimbleby, Howe concurred with the panel that the BNP were to be resisted, but added, 'the BNP have to be taken on, head on, but they have to be taken on with those who they attack in the leadership' (19 February 2004). Evidently, while the political consensus on the platform deplored racism, Howe was still alone in emphasizing self-organization and black autonomy. Having dealt with the threat of the BNP, the panel turned its attention to immigration. Broadly, and in keeping with the contradictions of the mainstream consensus, the panel argued that while racism was wrong, immigration should be restricted. After all, one panellist argued, people were fearful that more immigrants would place a strain on public services. Having dealt with the BNP and immigration, the panel moved to the vexed issue of NHS dental provision. Remarkably, here too Howe had much that was distinctive to contribute:

> I had to travel from Streatham to Lewisham to get a dentist. And then, two months ago, I came out my door, turned left, four houses down the road I saw a huge sign,

"Dentist". I go there and there's an Asian old man and he brought three young Asian women from India. I walk up the street a couple of weeks later, another dentist. Do you know who's there? A Polish man who's bringing some other Poles to do dental work in south London. So the Labour Party's not doing anything. In the free flow of migration somebody told the Pole we need some dentists in south London. That is how it happens, and when we are full of dentists, Ann Clwyd will come here and tell us the Labour Party brought them!

(Ibid.)

Shifting focus

Following 2005, there was a discernible change of approach to Howe's documentaries. Minhas argues that the rise of reality TV had a profound impact on programme making. Since 2000, *Big Brother* had become an established part of British television. By 2005, reality TV shows, including *Love Island* and *Pop Idol*, were legion. Where ordinary folk led, celebrities followed, with celebrity spin-offs of *Big Brother* and *Love Island* as well as *I'm a Celebrity . . . Get Me Out of Here!*. The success of such shows demonstrated a public taste for confessional television and for seeing celebrities mocked and exposed warts and all. Television's changing ethos was not lost on Minhas. Indeed, Minhas concluded that the style of documentaries had to change, that there was no longer an audience for programmes that explored big ideas and grand narratives in the way that *Bandung*, *White Tribe* and *Slave Nation* had done (Minhas 2011). Documentaries would need to adapt their format, content and style to the challenge of reality TV. Where the women's movement declared the personal as political, commissioning editors like Minhas were now keen to explore 'issues' primarily through the lens of the personal.

Consequently, *Son of Mine* took a new direction. Howe was no longer the impersonal scripted voice making objective pronouncements. Rather, he was simply another subjective voice, in front of a camera with access to all areas of his life. In addition to the stylistic changes, there was also a change of focus. *Son of Mine* was primarily an investigation of Howe's personal life. There had been personal asides in the previous documentaries. Howe's ex-wife appeared in the final section of *Slave Nation*, and his son's wedding prefaced *Who you callin' a nigger?*, but in *Son of Mine*, what had been at the margin moved to the centre.

Howe was happy with the subject matter of the programme. He was far less happy with finished programme. Howe argues that the show's Director James

Quinn had already decided on the arc of the documentary before filming began. The documentary focused on Howe's relationship with his son Amiri Howe. The story it tells has a clear structure in which the relationship goes through a series of conflicts ultimately leading to a climactic resolution. In Howe's view, 'the worst documentaries are made to a plot and a plan, and then the director creates falsely a moment of profundity' (Howe 2011h). This, for Howe, was the main problem with *Son of Mine*.

If anything, *Son of Mine* was eclipsed by the publicity surrounding it. As part of the promotion, Howe appeared on Radio 4's *Midweek* alongside the comedian Joan Rivers. The flash point occurred over River's studious avoidance of the word 'black'.

> Howe: The use of the term black offends you.
> Rivers: The use of the term black offends me? Where the hell are you coming from? You have got such a chip on your shoulder. How dare you say that to me?
> Howe: I think this is a language problem.
> Rivers: No I don't. I think this is a problem in your stupid head. You had a child, you left them, your wife said you weren't there. You married a woman, you deserted her, now your son comes back he's got problems. Where were you when he was growing up, until he was eight years old?
> Howe: May we continue?
> Rivers: How dare you. Please continue, but don't you dare call me that. Son of a bitch.
>
> (*Midweek*, 19 October 2005)

Speaking to *The Times*, Rivers explained 'I just went NUTS! . . . I stopped the whole show, and just SCREAMED at him' (20 October 2005). The quarrel was picked up by the press, the *Independent* offered Howe a piece of free advice, 'You don't mess with Joan Rivers' (20 October 2005). Howe claims that the spat was over as soon as it began, all publicity is good publicity and they both had shows to promote (Howe 2011h).

Son of Mine was something of a game changer for Howe. Significantly, little of the coverage of the row with Rivers or the documentary mentioned Howe's back story. For some in the media, Howe was a man without roots, nothing more than a television personality. Implicit in much of the coverage was the assumption that Howe spoke for the sake of speaking, but lacked weight as a serious commentator. Howe's role as organizer of the Black People's Day of Action, his involvement in the Mangrove Trial, his association with Walter Rodney, or with John La Rose or with C. L. R. James went unremarked. Paul Vallely, writing for the *Independent*, summed up the impression of Howe created in the film thus:

> There was Darcus Howe's life's work on a neat little plate: a doughty portion of advocacy, with a dollop of Marxist historical inevitability, a cupful of excuses, a liberal sprinkling of rights with a deliberate underseasoning of responsibilities, and all stirred together in a recipe unchanged since his heyday in the Sixties.
>
> (22 October 2005)

Certainly, the article went on to flesh out some of his achievements, but the main point of this history was that Howe belonged to a different age, his perspective was no longer relevant. For all of the hype, the documentary was not aired on Channel 4, but on the newly created digital Channel More4. Whatever else the piece achieved, Diverse's documentary had lost the primetime.

New Statesman

From the mid-1990s, Howe was a regular columnist for the *New Statesman*. His work for the magazine earned him the Columnist of the Year at the 1998 Race in the Media awards. Howe's essays, perhaps more than the later documentaries, give an indication of his continuing political preoccupations. During his 17-year stint as a regular columnist, he touched on many themes that he had once explored in the pages of *Race Today*. On a couple of occasions, using recognizably Jamesian language, he used the column to advocate a Caribbean federation. He wrote about cricket; recounted episodes from the struggles of the 1970s and 1980s continuing his work as chronicler of the grass-roots struggle; as well as keeping a keen eye on the police. In lighter moments, he offered the readership his recipe for the perfect Christmas, salt cod followed by goose 'seasoned with herbs sown and reaped in the foothills of the Northern Range in Trinidad' (7 January 2002), and recounted some of the absurdities of his run-ins with the police. Characteristically, Howe used the magazine to campaign. One of his most immediately successful campaigns was a series of articles which played a part in the dismissal of James McGrath, Boris Johnson's political strategist (26 June 2008).

During the naughties, Howe's celebrity status proved double-edged. It allowed him to make a series of important documentaries, which undoubtedly broke the mould of multicultural programming. It also ensured him an audience in the

New Statesman, from which he was able to continue to popularize James' ideas, hold officialdom to account and to continue to campaign. However, at the same time, his fame overshadowed his early activities as a campaigner and organizer. As a result, when Howe encountered controversy, he was increasingly viewed, in the press at least, as a talking head, a man who was famous for being famous, or as Paul Vallely put it 'Britain's leading professional black man' (*Independent*, 22 October 2005). *Son of Mine* proved to be a turning point. While some praised Howe's bravery, others condemned him for using his family to regain the media spotlight. Nonetheless, the short termism of the media is itself double-edged, holding, as it does, the possibility of rediscovery.

Note

1   See: Fraser (2005: 306).

19

Fight to the Finish

On Monday 27 September 2010, more than a thousand people gathered to pay their last respects to Frank Crichlow. The funeral, the culmination of a week of mourning, took place at St Mary's of the Angle on Morehouse Road. The congregation and many more, who could not fit into the packed church, processed through Notting Hill to the West London Crematorium. The size and diversity of the crowd was a testament to the breadth of respect that Crichlow commanded. The mourners included the biggest names from Britain's Black Power Movement including Howe, Althea Jones-Lecointe and her husband Eddie who had flown in from Trinidad for the occasion, as well as Rhodan Gordon. There were also more mainstream black activists and politicians such as Lee Jasper and Paul Boateng; the film maker Horace Ové and hundreds of ordinary people, not political in any obvious sense, whose lives Crichlow had touched.

Boateng gave the eulogy, recalling Crichlow's activism, his smile, and his 'grace under pressure, and boy was there pressure' (Boateng 2010). Howe did not speak in the Church. Characteristically, he saved his words for the streets. Aided by 20 or so 'Vikings', black men in their 50s and 60s wearing berets, Howe brought the procession to a halt. Looking on helpless and bemused, the attendant police officers tried forlornly to get everyone moving again. Standing on the exact spot where he had launched the Mangrove demonstration 40 years earlier, Howe said this of his friend:

> ... he's arguably one of the most courageous West Indians who has ever lived in this country. [cheers] He came from a decent family in Trinidad, and he was not supposed to stand up against the British police and accuse them of corruption. He did that successfully. . . . I love Frank, he knows I loved him, a lot of people competed for a relationship and lost. Frank was my friend. And Frank was a Caribbean man who did ordinary things, like opening a restaurant, in extraordinary ways. We could not ask for more. Let the wagons roll. [cheers] Lets take this Viking to Valhalla!

(Howe 2010b)

After the speeches, the crowd moved off. As a sign of respect, Howe, not as fit or as young as he once was, walked the whole of the 2-mile route.

Killing me softly

Howe was diagnosed with prostate cancer in April 2007 at King's College Hospital in South London. The first signs of a problem, raised levels of Prostate Specific Antigen (PSA), were picked up as part of Howe's ongoing treatment for type 2 diabetes. A urine test revealed that Howe's PSA levels were 30, and normal levels would be around 0.1. The acid test was a physical examination: 'he drew the curtain and with a gloved finger penetrated my rectum. The cancer was there' (*Guardian*, 17 November 2009). The news was horrifying.

> Beads of perspiration dripped from my head and face. My entire body shook uncontrollably. Cancer to me meant death; Mrs Howe wiped my troubled brow. I sat gazing into the middle distance, my emotions shifting from one extreme to the next. I thought of my children and my grandchildren, guilt-ridden that I had imposed so much worry upon them.
>
> (Ibid.)

The consultant took a family history. Howe's father had died of a 'urinary infection', at least that is what it said on the death certificate. Howe's grandfather died, according to family lore, from a 'stoppage of water'. In both cases, the causes were urological. The consultant concluded that in all likelihood, Howe's forbears died of prostate cancer (*What's Killing Darcus Howe?*).

There was worse news: there was a good chance that the cancer had spread to his bones. If this was the case, there could be treatment but no cure. Howe was tested. The 10-day wait for the results was interminable: 'I have never been so terrified in my life,' he recalls. Howe's political battles had been nerve-racking, but he had known what to look for, he understood the moves that he could make. Cancer was uncharted territory. The news when it came was good. The cancer had not escaped the prostate. There was every chance that Howe would be well again (Howe 2011h).

Two important pieces of information emerged immediately from the meeting at King's College Hospital. First, Howe's consultant had a piece of non-medical advice. He recommended Saint-Émilion, now Howe's wine of choice. The second, Howe's consultant alerted him to the prevalence of the disease among black men from the Caribbean, America and the west coast of Africa.

Apparently, black men from these groups are three times more likely to suffer from the disease than white men are. In the shock of the moment, the import of these figures was lost on Howe. But as he regained his composure, he began to campaign. The key to reducing the death rate among black men was to get them tested early. To raise awareness, Howe was interviewed by nhs.uk, spoke at a fundraising event in Liverpool, wrote about his experience in the *Voice*, the *New Statesman* and the *Guardian* and began spreading the word informally using the one-in-ten method. At first, this was a difficult process. Howe recalls having to transcend his 'Englishness', that part of him that did not want to talk in public about his illness (Ibid.).

The first part of the treatment was a laparoscopic prostatectomy (*Guardian*, 17 November 2009). Howe admits that the thought of it terrified him. The second part of the treatment, less dramatic but no less necessary, was a 6-month course of radiotherapy. The treatment was successful. Howe publicly acknowledged his recovery in the *New Statesman* in January 2008.

The centrepiece of Howe's campaign was a Channel 4 documentary. Howe approached Hamish Mykura, with the working title 'Killing me Softly'. The documentary was given the green light and Howe was teamed up with BAFTA-award-winning director Krishnendu Majumdar. The result was conflict. 'We should have made a documentary of you making that documentary', comments Hassan: 'you would never have known that it was possible to have such conflict' (Hassan 2011).

The documentary, retitled *What's killing Darcus Howe?*, was shown as part of the *True Stories* series on More4 on Tuesday 24 November 2009. In a sense, it comprised two competing documentaries. Howe's aim was to make a film that encouraged young black men to have early prostate examinations. To this end, he befriended Mickey Lewis, the son of his friend Leo Lewis, persuading him to take the test. Majumdar, for his part, tried to examine the obstacles to better prostate health that he believed existed within the black community. For Majumdar, these included, a reluctance among West Indian men to submit to rectal examination, a general distrust of physicians and unhealthy habits such as drinking. In short, the documentary was an attempt by Majumdar 'to show him [Howe] that black men are part of the problem with prostate cancer . . . that black men may be at fault.' Majumdar set out the difference between him and Howe in the following terms: 'Darcus Howe is adamant that the authorities are to blame for the deaths of black men from prostate cancer. He doesn't think that enough is being done to raise awareness and encourage testing. But I don't share his politics. I think the problem lies with black men and their attitudes to health.' A notable flashpoint where these two different agendas collided happened during SunWalk, a breast cancer awareness event in Bristol:

> Majumdar: I think there'll be thousands.
>
> Howe: D'you think so?
>
> Majumdar: Yeah, thousands I think. Yeah, they're very organised this lot.
>
> Howe: I don't know what you mean by "very organised".
>
> Majumdar: I mean you get people, I mean its visible, I mean . . .
>
> Howe: Do you think black people are "very organised"?
>
> Majumdar: Its nothing to do with black people.
>
> Howe: No, I'm asking you.
>
> Majumdar: Yes.
>
> Howe: Oh. Your prediction is that it's going to be tremendously successful, and you're coming to show me how successfully white women can do things.
>
> Majumdar: No it's not that.
>
> Howe: Oh course it's that. And the implication is that one is a superior moral being and the other one is a load of monkeys from Africa. . . . You are just putting something false as has always been done to African and West Indian people.
>
> (*What's Killing Darcus Howe?*)

Looking back at the documentary, it was this suggestion that stuck in Howe's mind. 'They were thinking black people don't know how to organise like white people.' From Howe's point of view, Majumdar's comments reflected a lack of understanding of the recent history of Britain, and a lack of understanding of the black community and a lack of awareness of Howe's own work as the leading proponent of black self-organization.

To some extent, Howe's criticism of Majumdar's position is reminiscent of William Ryan's 'Savage Discovery' (1965) and *Blaming the Victim* (1971). Ryan's work excoriated *The Negro Family: The Case For National Action*, or the Moynihan Report as it is better known. The report controversially blamed black poverty in America on the black family. 'At the heart of the deterioration of the fabric of Negro society,' Moynihan argued, 'is the deterioration of the Negro family.' This in turn he blamed on the 'the tangle of pathology' within the black community. Ryan, a white psychologist from Boston, hit back, arguing that the liberal Senator's report was in fact an attempt to seduce 'the reader into believing it is not racism and discrimination but the weakness and defects of the Negro himself that account for . . . inequality.' In this sense, he argued, Moynihan blamed the victim. Howe's statement that Majumdar was in effect 'demonising' black men, echoes Ryan's concerns.

The documentary concludes with Lewis going to his GP. Howe appealed to the memory of Lewis' father, he appealed to Lewis' self-image as a man who feared nothing, and finally, he enlisted Lewis' mother. In this sense, Howe demonstrated that the resources necessary to persuade black men to consult their GPs are readily available within the existing culture of the West Indian community.

'I don't call it rioting. I call it an insurrection of the masses of the people.'

The 'England riots' of August 2011 led to a novel experience for Howe. For the first time in his long career, Howe 'went viral' thanks, in large part, to a poorly handled BBC interview. Howe's contribution to the public debate over the disturbances was distinctive, at odds with the reaction of the national press and leading politicians. The unrest which engulfed England's urban centres from 6 to 10 August became a political football immediately. David Cameron, cutting short his holiday in Tuscany, talked tough:

> Let me first of all completely condemn the scenes that we have seen on our television screens and people have witnessed in their communities.
>
> These are sickening scenes – scenes of people looting, vandalising, thieving, robbing, scenes of people attacking police officers and even attacking fire crews as they're trying to put out fires. This is criminality, pure and simple, and it has to be confronted and defeated.
>
> (*Guardian*, 9 September 2011)

Deputy Prime Minister Nick Clegg concurred, characterizing the unrest as 'needless opportunistic theft and violence – nothing more, nothing less' (Ibid., 8 September 2011). Labour Leader Ed Miliband stood 'shoulder-to-shoulder' with the prime minister, united in 'condemning the violence and vandalism we have seen on our streets' (Labour.org 2011). The responses were predictable and said more about the limits of mainstream political culture than they did about the events themselves. One remarkable feature of the 'England riots' was that there was much more public interest in the words of people outside the political mainstream. 'Hackney Heroine' Pauline Pearce and Tariq Jahan, whose son was killed in the violence, were taken up by the media as the authentic voice of the people rather than that of the party leaders.

Howe distinguished himself in two ways. First, as the only public figure who refused to condemn the violence and perhaps the first to offer an analysis that was free from moral panic. Secondly, as the only existing public figure who managed to hold the attention of the public when discussing the unrest.

For Howe, the 'England riots' were no surprise. Speaking on ITN News on 6 May 2010, Howe argued: 'I won't be surprised, this summer coming here, if there isn't a social explosion that would make Brixton look like a holiday.' Howe was commenting on the issues raised by Clint Dyer and Robert Heath's film *Sus*. In so doing, he clearly linked police stop and search tactics to large-scale community resistance. He returned to this theme in *The Voice* on 4 August 2011. In reference to Operation Razorback, Howe argued that the Met, one of the 'most discredited institutions in the entire country', would 'raise the anti' in the run-up to the Notting Hill Carnival. He concluded by playfully recasting Amy Winehouse as the spirit of the people who would no longer put up with police interference:

> Look out for the Mangrove steel band and I'll be there dancing and prancing along
> the way in the band. And Amy Winehouse will be floating above the stars intoning
> her chant in the ear of authority: "No, No, No."

The article appeared on the same day that Mark Duggan was shot dead by police on Ferry Lane, Tottenham Hale. Two days later, Tottenham exploded in violence.

In the aftermath of the unrest, Howe spoke repeatedly about the causes of the insurrection. In essence, he argued that the unrest was the inevitable consequence of Operations Razorback and Trident. Operation Razorback was launched in the run-up to the Notting Hill Carnival. The Met's Chief Inspector Chris Allmey justified Razorback as a 'highly sophisticated and detailed operation aimed at ensuring those who set out with the sole intention of causing trouble at carnival will not succeed' (Met 2011). In practice, it meant a series of raids and 97 arrests in 2011. Operation Trident was an ongoing police initiative designed, in the words of Chief Superintendent Steve Dann, to tackle '"black-on-black" gun crime' (HOC 2008: 5). Notably, the officer who shot Duggan was accompanying officers working under the auspices of Operation Trident. The combined result of these initiatives, as far as Howe was concerned, was a 'rampant stop and search' campaign, targeting black young people, creating an atmosphere of harassment reminiscent of Brixton immediately prior to the insurrection of 1981.

Howe's first television discussion of the riots took place on 8 August on the BBC's *Newsnight*. Speaking to Gavin Esler, he argued that the seeds of the unrest had been clear for some time. The failure of the political class to anticipate the disturbances was rooted in the profound disconnection between Britain's politicians and young people black and white. Howe's approach to the England riots was notably different from that of Edwina Currie, who also appeared on the show. For Currie, it was important to draw two distinctions: the first was between the justifiable grievances of black people who suffered racism in the early 1980s, and the young people of 2011 who all had a 'reasonable chance' to have a good life regardless of their race. Secondly, between the justifiable grievances of black people in the early 1980s and their unjust response. Howe took a different approach. First, he argued that police racism was still part of the landscape. Specifically, elements within the police seemed 'drawn to humiliating a particular race in a particular place'. Secondly, Howe took no part in the chorus of condemnation.

The morning of 9 August unexpectedly brought Howe to national and international attention. On the face of it, it was just another BBC interview, barely 4 minutes of air time. But the fallout led to calls from CNN, the Huffington Post, appearances on US, French and South African Television and even a remix.

The interview started badly, with Fiona Armstrong introducing Howe as 'Marcus Dowe'. Again, the question of condemnation was raised. Howe saved his indignation for the police. Taking the interview back to Mark Duggan, he commented, 'there is a young man called Mark Duggan. He has parents, he has brothers, he had sisters, and a few yards away from where he lives a police officer blew his head off.' But it was the final exchange which really caused a stir.

> Armstrong: Mr Howe, if I can just ask you, you are not a stranger to riots yourself I understand, are you? You have taken part in them yourself.
> Howe: I am not a . . . I have never taken part in a single riot. I have been on demonstrations that ended up in a conflict. And have some respect for an old West Indian Negro and stop accusing me of being a rioter, because you won't tickle me to get abusive. You just sound idiotic. Have some respect.
>
> (BBC News, 9 August 2011)

In no time the video was posted on YouTube. By 11 the next morning, it was the second most popular clip on the whole site, having gained 656,439 hits. By 12 August, it had gained over 3 million hits and within a week more than 5 million. YouTube was not the only internet site that had been affected. By the afternoon of 9 August, a Facebook page campaigning for an apology had been created. Howe started trending on Twitter. Sensing the moment, Howe joined Twitter on 11 August. The following tweets from 11 August give a flavour of the reaction on twitter:

Sophia Nyananyo
Darcus Howe knows.

DREAM MCLEAN
Darcus Howe for prime minister

James Addison
Watched the Fiona Armstrong/Darcus Howe exchange – Armstrong is a tool. How can she bring any form of even journalism to the BBC? Fired.

Selina Spence
#darcushowe speaks the raw, unedited truth.

John Suppa
#darcushowe is the only man making sense in the midst of these riots, and they tried to shut him out . . . smh . . . #prayforlondon

Veronica Walsh
#darcushowe always delivers . . . #rtept

Barclay.TV
Darcus Howe serving up a good ole batch of West Indian Ether in the UK . . . http://t.co/QiprDhn Fiona Armstrong caught it . . .

Hasanah HM
Way to go, Darcus Howe!

Where the new media led, the old media followed. The interview and the subsequent apology were picked up by the British press and overseas titles such as the *Washington Post*, the *Toronto Standard*, the *Trinidad Express* and the *Trinidad Guardian*.

The day after the exchange was aired, the BBC apologized for 'poorly-phrased question' and 'for any offence that this interview has caused' (*Telegraph*, 10 September 2011). Speaking to the *Voice*, Howe welcomed the apology, adding, 'I would have sued if they didn't apologise. . . . I would have sued if I felt it was spite or malice but a lot them [BBC employees] know me and sent messages saying they were sorry. It was a miserable mistake' (12 September 2011). Armstrong phoned Howe a few days later to offer a personal apology (Howe 2011j).

Howe offered his most extended analysis of the causes of the riots on the Web-based American independent news program *Democracy Now!*. Here Howe argued that the insurrection was caused by the extensive use of stop and search powers. He noted the recent legal changes, a reference to the stop and search powers granted by the 2000 Terrorism Act and the abandonment in March 2011 of the requirement that all incidents of stop and search be recorded.

Secondly, Howe attributed the insurrection to the fact that young people were in the middle of the summer holidays. Thirdly, to the police murder of Mark Duggan – in the context of the general disarray of the Metropolitan police. During the disturbances, Howe claimed, the Met was effectively headless, Metropolitan Police Commissioner Sir Paul Robert Stephenson having resigned on 17 July 2011 due to his association with Neil Wallis, who had been arrested on suspicion of involvement in the News International phone-hacking scandal. Finally, Howe referenced celebrity culture with the attendant emphasis on fashion in the midst of the economic downturn as a reason why looting was so much more pronounced in 2011 than it had been in 1981.

The final and most unexpected result of Howe's intervention was 'Riot' a piece of music by the black American singer and violinist Marques Toliver. The piece, part of a collection entitled *Studying for My PhD Mixtape* released in December 2011, included an excerpt from the Armstrong interview. 'I guess it was partly because the interview section was very bold,' Toliver explains. The other aspect of the interview that appealed was that 'it just seemed as if there was a wall between him and the woman who was covering the story' (Toliver 2011). Howe's interview is one of many references to the politics of race included on the *Mixtape*. Others included a segment dealing with the eviction of 80 Travellers' families from Dale Farm in Essex and an interview with James Baldwin. With reference to the latter, Toliver explains: 'I just wanted to have different segments jumping throughout time showing how not much has changed despite all of the advances we have made as a people' (Ibid.).

For Howe, the riots and the response of British politicians were indicative of a more general political malaise. Speaking to the *Socialist Worker*, Howe described the political establishment thus:

> The parliamentary debate on the riots was unadulterated crap. I started watching it and I went to sleep. I've now been confirmed in what I've been saying for a long time: they do not know these black people at all. They ought to know them now, it's compulsory. And they know them less by the day.
>
> I don't think David Cameron knows any black person. When I say know, I don't mean casual friendship. Cameron is semi-literate about 90 percent of his own population.
>
> (16 September 2011)

Howe was equally critical of black politicians: 'there is a small black elite who are saying, "These ragamuffins have let me down." My response is quite simple: "Fuck you"' (Ibid.).

Diane Abbott's Twitter storm

In the sweep of a whole life, Diane Abbott's Twitter storm is a tiny episode. For perhaps 4 days it dominated the British media and then, the news cycle being the news cycle, it was forgotten. But for Howe, it was emblematic of the bankruptcy of modern British politics.

The storm broke in the context of public reaction to the conviction of Gary Dobson and David Norris for the murder of Stephen Lawrence. On the day after their sentencing, the following conversation occurred on Twitter:

Bim Adewunmi
Clarifying my "black community" tweet: I hate the generally lazy thinking behind the use of the term. Same for "black community leaders".
Diane Abbott MP
@bimadew I understand the cultural point you are making. But you are playing into a "divide and rule" agenda.
stephanie busari
@bimadew I agree! there is on homogenised black community. Black people in Britain are as varied as there are countries in the world!
Diane Abbott MP
@StephanieBusari @bimadew I am not talking cultural differences. I am talking political tactics. #dontwashdirtylineninpublic
Diane Abbott MP
@bimadew White people love playing "divide & rule" We should not play their game #tacticasoldascolonialism

It was Abbott's last tweet that caused the storm. Abbott quickly tweeted a clarification: 'Tweet taken out of context. Refers to nature of 19th century European colonialism. Bit much to get into 140 characters.' However, the clarification was too late and the '140 character defence' cut little ice.

The comment divided opinion on Twitter. Sensing a gaffe, politicians waded in, either to exploit Abbott's discomfort or to distance themselves from the comment. For Nick Clegg, the tweet was a 'stupid and crass generalisation'. There was partial support from the Labour Party which issued a statement saying, 'We disagree with Diane's Tweet. It is wrong to make sweeping generalisations about any race, creed or culture. The Labour Party has always campaigned against such behaviour and so has Diane Abbott.' Ed Miliband, in an attempt to draw a line under the controversy, apparently gave Abbott 'a severe dressing down' and demanded a public apology (*Independent*, 5 January 2012).

Howe appeared to discuss the affair on *Newsnight*. He defended Abbott by pointing to her long history of organizing in defence of the black working class and her public life spent fighting racism. Howe's point was that Abbott's comments should be read in the context of her whole career and in the context of the victory in the courts. Expressing his disbelief that she had capitulated to Miliband's demands, Howe was uncompromising in his criticism of the Labour front bench:

> I would have told Miliband "why don't you go to hell". . . . What concerns me is that Diane is in a Shadow Cabinet with people who are very inferior to her politically, and she is made Minister of Public Health, and they go out and speak about blacks, and she has to sit there waiting to listen to what the rest of them have to say which amounts to nothing.
>
> (Howe 2012)

A prophet without honour

For Howe, there are two threads that connect the events described in this chapter. The first is best understood by contrasting the political culture of Britain with that of the United States.

During the 'England riots', the authors were contacted by Josh Hurch of the *Huffington Post*. Hurch, interested in Howe's explanation of the insurrection, asked for a brief biography. At the end of the interview, Hurst expressed his shock at Armstrong's attitude during her interview with Howe. In America, he stated that public figures who had devoted their lives to the fight for racial justice were treated with respect as a matter of course. 'If this had happened here,' he opined, 'the interviewer would have been fired. It would have ended her career' (Hurch 2011). Hurch's point is indicative of a broader truth, that there is much greater scope for the media and the political establishment to treat black public figures dismissively in Britain than there is in America. The cases of Abbott and Howe, in very different ways, demonstrate this. The coverage of Abbott's tweet focused on her so-called gaffes, rather than on her record as a community campaigner, or her record in the Commons. Equally, Armstrong's tone with Howe was high-handed if not openly disrespectful. What is true of black public figures is equally true of black people more generally. Consider Johnson's support for James McGrath, the Mayoral advisor who thought it wholly appropriate to say that black Londoners who did not like the Mayor's policies should leave the capital. Equally, Majumdar's willingness to 'blame the victim' or in Howe's terms to 'demonise' black men is another indication that there is more scope for public criticism or public dismissiveness of black people in Britain as a group than there is in the United States.

To some extent, this dismissiveness is rooted in a different approach to each nation's history. The successes of the American Black Movement have forced the nation to acknowledge its racist past. Consequently, there is a media etiquette which ensures that national figures who emerged from the civil rights struggle are treated with respect. In Britain, there is a more equivocal view of the past. It is commonly assumed that racism was only ever a minor part of the British landscape, that it was restricted to crackpots on the fringes of national life; in short, that it was antithetical to the dominant tradition of enlightened liberalism that characterizes the British. By implication, black rights campaigners are guilty of overstating their case or misunderstanding British culture. Or worse still, black campaigners have wilfully exaggerated racism in Britain for their own ends. Of course, there are more subtle narratives of British history. Currie's perspective as outlined on *Newsnight*, is one example. On this account, racism is a thing of the past. Thus, while Howe should be congratulated on his work in past decades, his current point of view can be dismissed as archaic.

If the sort of disrespect shown towards Howe and Dianne Abbott is rare in the United States, similar attempts to portray veteran civil rights leaders who have not made their peace with the US establishment as fighting past battles are much more familiar. A figure such as Reverend Jeremiah Wright is presented as at best misguided and at worst a divisive race warrior, as someone who, in Barack Obama's words about his former pastor, is guilty of expressing views about the history of racism in the United States which 'widen the racial divide'. Yet as political analyst Tim Wise has argued, Wright and other veteran campaigners speak to the reality of a United States in which black people are still twice as likely as whites to be employed in low-wage jobs and twice as likely to be unemployed.

After Howe's public spat with Joan Rivers, journalist Paul Vallely penned a vituperative profile of Howe in *The Independent* which, among a litany of supposed sins, accused him of being irrational, prejudiced, confrontational, inconsistent, egotistic and of expressing a world view that was anachronistic. While wondering if Vallely would have written so dismissively and sanctimoniously about one of Britain's many right-wing white pundits, Howe's editor at the time, Peter Wilby, noted that it was the accusation that Howe held outdated and anachronistic views that seemed most curious. After all, Wilby observed, Howe had in his column in the *New Statesman* accurately predicted riots in the old Lancashire cotton towns, terrorist attacks by British-born Asians and growing tension between black and Asian youths that had recently erupted in hostilities in Birmingham. For Wilby, this highly personalized attack on Howe was illustrative of a broader trend in which anyone with politics to the Left of Tony Blair is dismissed as 'predictable, humourless, chippy and paranoid' in the mainstream press. To the extent that Howe or others of his ilk such as fellow *New Statesman* columnist John Pilger are tolerated and allowed in the papers at all 'they are treated as though they are rabid dogs' and their views labelled as 'controversial' or 'alternative' to denote to their readers that they should not be taken seriously and in order to marginalize them (*NS*, 31 October 2005).

A second aspect of modern British political culture that Howe has alluded to in his public statements is the mediocrity of the current British political class. Howe's loss of patience with the parliamentary debate over the England riots and the forthrightness with which he advised Abbott to tell Miliband to 'Go to hell' are based on Howe's feeling that party leaders have no understanding of the lives of ordinary people in general or black people specifically. As far as Howe is concerned, the extent of this division between rulers and ruled is a new feature of twenty-first-century politics. Modern British politicians no longer represent the people in any obvious sense. Rather their power is based on an alliance with the press, which Howe describes as 'one of the most vulgar institutions' (Howe 2012).

Still, Howe has not given up hope. The radical vision of a new kind of democracy that inspired him during the Black Power Revolution of 1970 inspires him today. For him, the political mediocrity and residual racism of British society are the product of a crisis in capitalism. But following James, Howe believes that there is a progressive moment in any situation, a new society growing in the womb of the old. Howe advocates a new culture of leisure; for leisure, as the ancients knew, is the mother of philosophy. In his most recent article, he explains: 'A shorter working day, a shorter working week, and a shorter working life. Don't think it's mad. We need time to access our thoughts. Capitalism has been good at force feeding us falsities: racial division, class inequality, alienation and disengagement, a world after capitalism means we must think long and hard again.' The result would be the kind of society that Howe glimpsed in Trinidad in 1970, that re-emerged briefly in Britain during the student sit-ins of 2010 and the Occupy Movement of 2011.

> I see streets lined with hundreds of citizens, immersed in critical discussion. A thousand Platos in every neighbourhood. We will return to the art of discourse, not the jargon fuelled rhetoric of the modern day politician, designed solely to keep us disengaged and baffled. No. A genuine political vernacular accessible to all. The building blocks of a new form of localized, popular democracy premised on equality of ideas.
>
> We think, therefore we are.

(Guardian, 30 August 2012)

Bibliography

Archival material

The National Archives (NA)

CRIM 1/4962/1 Central Criminal Court papers: Regina v. Peter Martin, GKT Dolo, Benedict Obi Egbuna
CRIM 1/4962/2 Central Criminal Court papers: Regina v. Peter Martin, GKT Dolo, Benedict Obi Egbuna
CRIM 1/5522/1 Central Criminal Court papers: Mangrove Nine
CRIM 1/5522/2 Central Criminal Court papers: Mangrove Nine
CRIM 1/5522/3 Central Criminal Court papers: Mangrove Nine
DPP 2/4827 Department of Public Prosecutions: 'Free Bobby' Demonstration 2 March 1970
DPP 2/4889 Department of Public Prosecutions: Oval Youth Club incident
DPP 2/4889 Department of Public Prosecutions: Oval Youth Club incident
DPP 2/5059 Department of Public Prosecutions: Mangrove Nine Contempt of Court
HO 325/143 Home Office Papers: Reports on Black Power and the Mangrove March
MEPO 2/11409 Metropolitan Police Papers: Evidence against Peter Martin, GKT Dolo, Benedict Obi Egbuna
MEPO 31/20 Metropolitan Police Papers: Evidence against the Mangrove Nine
MEPO 31/21 Metropolitan Police Papers: Evidence against the Mangrove Nine
PREM 19/484 Records of the Prime Minister's Office: Correspondence and Papers, 1979–1997
PRO/FCO 63/494 Cabinet Report: Black Power in Jamaica, 29 May 1970

The Institute of Race Relations Archives (IRR)

01/04/04/01/04/01/17 [Bootleg copy of the first edition of Black Power in Britain]
01/04/04/01/04/01/20 [Frank John's edition of CLR James' 'The Making of the Caribbean Peoples' and 'Black Power, Its Past, Today and the Way Ahead']
IRR 01/04/03/02/031 Black Eagle [Issue 2]
[uncatalogued] Black Defence Committee leaflet 1970

The George Padmore Institute Archives (GPI)

JLR 3/1/5 [The Black Panther Movement, 'Black culture for liberation' (flyer)]

JLR 3/1/5 [The Black Panther Movement, 'Repatriation/Retaliation' (flyer)]

JLR 3/1/5 [The Black Panther Movement, 'The People must know the Truth' (pamphlet)]

JLR 3/1/5 [The Black Panther Movement, 'The Police have done it again!!!' (flyer)]

JLR 3/1/5 [The Black Panther Movement, 'Black oppressed people all over the world are ONE' (flyer)]

JLR 3/1/5 [The Black Panther Movement, 'Untitled flyer dealing with the emergency in Trinidad and Tobago' (flyer)]

JLR 3/1/5 [The Black Panther Movement, 'Black Youth Forum' (flyer)]

JLR 3/1/5 [The Black Panther Movement, 'Untitled flyer dealing with the emergency in Trinidad and Tobago' (flyer)]

JLR 3/1/5 [The Black Panther Movement, 'Cultural and Political Evening' (flyer)]

Independent Radio News Audio Archive (IRNAA)

16 April 1981 Transcript of NMAC Press Conference

Kensington Central Library (KCL)

367 Man Mangrove Caribbean Focus Souvenir Brochure 1986
The University of Columbia Rare Book and Manuscript Library (UC DHP)

Box I Series I: CLR James, 1974–1996 (a)

1   Correspondence 1974, 1980–1986
2   Divorce, Regarding, 1981–1985
3   Correspondence James-Howe, 1976–1983, Undated
4   Condolences, 1989
5   Correspondence regarding James' death, 1989
6   James' Estate, 1989–1990, 2003
7   James' Funeral, 1989
8–9   James' Funeral–Photos, 1989 (2 Folders)
10   James' Finances, 1987, Undated
11   Interviews—Regarding James, 1981, Undated
12   Printed Material, 1986, Undated
13   Printed Material–Clippings, 1984–1990
14   Programs and Events, 1981–1989
15   Trinity Cross, 1987

Box VII

1   Statements, Index of, 1971
2–3   Statements of Witnesses, 1970 (2 Folders)
4   New Beginning Movement, 1971–1978
5   Police–General, 1973, 1980–1983
6   Police–Trinidad and Tobago–Complaint Against, 1979
         Race Today Collective
         Correspondence
7   1984–1990, Undated
8–9   A-T, 1976–1988
10   "Europe" –1980–1985, Undated
11   Permissions, 1989–1993
12   References, 1976–1978, 1986
13   Spencer, Marva, October 1989–January 1990
14   "West Indies", 1978–1988, Undated

Box VIII

1   Bradford Black Conference, 1978
2   Community Relations, 1972–1973, Undated
3   Dick, Patricia, 1988
         Reorganization of the Race Today Collective
4   General, 1988–1991
5   Dissolution, 1991
6   Drafts, Circa 1988–1991
7   Drafts and Notes, Circa 1988–1991
8   Rules, Circa 1978
9   Seminar–Black Aesthetic, Undated
10   United States Meeting–Transcript, Circa 1984
         West Indies
11   General, 1984, Undated
12   Oilfield Workers Trade Union, 1984–1988
13   Caribbean in Crisis–International Book Fair, 1985
14   Eulogy–for William Johnson, 1990
15–16   Speeches, 1978, 1988
17   Tribute to CLR James, 1989
18   "Black Sections in the Labour Party", 1985
         Bobby to Babylon
19–20   Drafts, circa 1980s
21   Galleys, circa 1980s

Box IX

Box X

19   Race Today, 1988 January/February
20   Teachers Action, circa 1970s

Darcus Howe papers

Howe's own copies of fliers have now been sent to the University of Columbia and form
    part of their archives.
[DH PC 1] Free Darcus Howe flyer.

The University of Warwick (UW)

MSS 149/2/2/15 The Realities of Black Power [Conference Programme]

London Metropolitan Archives (LMA)

PS MAR/A2/25 Marylebone Magistrates' Court Register 1968
PS MAR/A2/26 Marylebone Magistrates' Court Register 1968
PS MAR/A3/23 Marylebone Magistrates' Court Register 1968

Bishopsgate Institute

BG/ARM/7/2/11 Bernie Grant's press complaints correspondence regarding 'Devils
    Advocate'
BG/ARM/7/2/15 Bernie Grant's press complaints correspondence regarding 'Devils
    Advocate'.
BG/ARM/7/2/16 Bernie Grant's press complaints correspondence regarding 'Devils
    Advocate'.

Newspapers and periodicals

All England Law Reports – All ER
International Times – IT
Kensington Post – KP
New Statesman – NS
Race Today – RT
Race Today Review – RTR
South East London Mercury – SELM
Time Out – TO

Interviews

The interviews with Darcus Howe and Leila Hassan are available as MP3s at the George Padmore Institute in London and as an addition to the Darcus Howe Archive at the University of Columbia in New York.

Interviews with Darcus Howe

Unpublished introductory interview (Howe 2010) Howe, Darcus. Interviewed by Robin Bunce and Paul Field. The British Library, London, UK. 20 August 2010.

Unpublished interview concerning Howe's childhood (Howe 2011a) Howe, Darcus. Interviewed by Robin Bunce and Paul Field. Norbury, London, UK. 12 April 2011.

Unpublished interview concerning the origins of Black Power in Britain (Howe 2011b) Howe, Darcus. Interviewed by Robin Bunce and Paul Field. Norbury, London, UK. 23 March 2011.

Unpublished interview concerning Howe's influences (Howe 2011c) Howe, Darcus. Interviewed by Robin Bunce and Paul Field. Norbury, London, UK. 5 April 2011.

Unpublished interview concerning *Race Today* (Howe 2011d) Howe, Darcus. Interviewed by Robin Bunce and Paul Field. Norbury, London, UK. 6 October 2011.

Unpublished interview concerning Howe's relationship with the police (Howe 2011e) Howe, Darcus. Interviewed by Robin Bunce and Paul Field. Norbury, London, UK. 1 July 2011.

Unpublished interview concerning the Black People's Day of Action (Howe 2011f) Howe, Darcus. Interviewed by Robin Bunce and Paul Field. Norbury, London, UK. 15 July 2011.

Unpublished interview concerning the insurrection in Brixton (Howe 2011g) Howe, Darcus. Interviewed by Robin Bunce and Paul Field. Norbury, London, UK. 21 July 2011.

Unpublished interview concerning Channel 4 Documentaries 2000–2009 (Howe 2011h) Howe, Darcus. Interviewed by Robin Bunce. Norbury, London, UK. 05 August 2011.

Unpublished interview concerning the Notting Hill Carnival (Howe 2011i) Howe, Darcus. Interviewed by Robin Bunce and Paul Field. Norbury, London, UK. 21 October 2011.

Unpublished interview concerning Howe's work with Channel 4 1985–2000 (Howe 2011j) Howe, Darcus. Interviewed by Robin Bunce and Paul Field. Norbury, London, UK. 16 March 2011.

Unpublished interview concerning Trinidad's Black Power Revolution (Howe 2011k) Howe, Darcus. Interviewed by Robin Bunce. Norbury, London, UK. 22 March 2011.

Interviews with others

Unpublished interview (Abdullah 2011) Abdullah, David. Interviewed by Paul Field. Oilfields Workers' Trade Union, Circular Rd., San Fernando, Trinidad. 26 August 2011.

Unpublished telephone interview (Adebayo 2011) Adebayo, Dotun. Interviewed by Robin Bunce.

Unpublished e-mail correspondence (Ali 2011) Ali, Tariq. Correspondence with Robin Bunce and Paul Field. 29 December 2011.

Unpublished interview (Beese 2011) Beese, Barbara. Interviewed by Robin Bunce. The British Library, London, UK. 25 March 2011.

Unpublished telephone interview (Bellos 2012) Bellos, Linda. Interviewed by Robin Bunce. 31 December 2012.

Unpublished email correspondence (Bowring 2012) Bowring, Bill. Correspondence with Paul Field. 8 May 2012.

Unpublished e-mail correspondence (Coon 2011) Coon, Caroline. Correspondence with Robin Bunce. 11 April 2011.

Unpublished telephone interview (Cox 2011) Cox, Barry. Interviewed by Robin Bunce. 6 October 2011.

Unpublished interview (Dhondy 2010) Dhondy, Farrukh. Interviewed by Robin Bunce and Paul Field. The Royal Festival Hall, London, UK. 20 September 2010.

Unpublished interview (Dhondy 2011) Dhondy, Farrukh. Interviewed by Robin Bunce and Paul Field. British Film Institute, London, UK. 15 September 2011.

Unpublished telephone interview (Farrar 2011) Farrar, Max. Interviewed by Robin Bunce. 26 March 2011.

Unpublished interview (Forbes-Valdez 2011) Forbes-Valdez, Claudine. Interviewed by Paul Field. Eckel Village Anglican School, Trinidad. 28 August 2011.

Unpublished telephone interview (Goulbourne 2012) Goulbourne, Harry. Interviewed by Robin Bunce. 8 February 2012.

Unpublished interview (Hassan 2011) Hassan, Leila. Interviewed by Robin Bunce and Paul Field. Norbury, London, UK. 21 October 2011.

Unpublished e-mail correspondence (Hines 2010) Hines, Vincent. Correspondence with Robin Bunce. 28 March 2010.

Unpublished interview (Howells 2011) Howells, Ross. Interviewed by Paul Field. The House of Lords, London, UK. 9 June 2011.

Unpublished telephone interview (Hurch 2010) Hurch, Josh. Interviewed with Robin Bunce for the *Huffington Post*. 10 August 2011.

Unpublished email correspondence (Hyling 2010) Hyling, Alan. Correspondence with Paul Field. 29 May 2011.

Unpublished telephone interview (James 2011) James, Selma. Interviewed by Robin Bunce and Paul Field. 28 July 2011.

Unpublished telephone interview (James 2012) James, Selma. Interviewed by Robin Bunce and Paul Field. 19 April 2012.

Unpublished telephone interview (Johnson 2011) Johnson, Linton Kwesi. Interviewed by Robin Bunce. 14 November 2011.

Unpublished interview (Macdonald 2010) Macdonald, Ian. Interviewed by Paul Field. Ipswich. 1 March 2010.

Unpublished telephone interview (Mansfield 2011) Mansfield, Michael. Interviewed by Paul Field. 18 October 2011.

Unpublished interview (Minhas 2012) Minhas, Narinder. Interviewed by Robin Bunce and Paul Field. Cinnamon Soho, London, UK. 6 September 2012.

Unpublished interview (Murray 2011) Murray, Dereyck. Interviewed by Paul Field. Queens Royal College, Port of Spain, Trinidad. 26 August 2011.

Unpublished e-mail correspondence (Profitt 2011) Correspondence with Paul Field. 7 September 2011.

Unpublished telephone interview (Shah 2011a) Shah, Raffique. Interviewed by Robin Bunce. 18 February 2011.

Unpublished e-mail interview (Shah 2011b) Shah, Raffique. Interviewed by Robin Bunce. 15 March 2011.

Unpublished telephone interview (Short 2012) Short, Clare Interviewed by Robin Bunce. 08 February 2013.

Unpublished e-mail correspondence (Sivanandan 2011) Sivanandan, Ambalavaner. Correspondence with Paul Field. 27 June 2011.

Unpublished interview (Smith 2011) Smith, Carl. Interviewed by Paul Field. Queen's Park Savannah, Port of Spain, Trinidad. 29 August 2011.

Unpublished telephone interview (Toliver 2012) Toliver, Marques. Interviewed by Robin Bunce. 2 April 2012.

Unpublished telephone interview (Phillips 2012) Phillips, Trevor. Interviewed by Robin Bunce. 26 March 2012.

Unpublished interview (Waddell 2011) Waddell, David "Splav". Interviewed by Paul Field. Queen's Park Savannah, Port of Spain, Trinidad. 29 August 2011.

Unpublished interview (Woolford 2011) Woolford, Lenin. Interviewed by Paul Field. Queen's Park Savannah, Port of Spain, Trinidad. 26 August 2011.

Published works

Abraham, S., *Labour and the Multiracial Project in the Caribbean: Its History and its Promise*. London: Lexington Books, 2007.

Adams, T. R., [Untitled]. *Black Power Speaks*, 1, 1 (1968): 8–9.

Alexander, R. and Parker, E., *A History of Organized Labor in the English-Speaking West Indies*. New York: Praeger, 2004.

Alleyne, B., *Radicals Against Race: Black Activism and Cultural Politics*. Oxford: Berg, 2002.

Angelo, Anne-Marie, 'The Black Panthers in London, 1967–1972: A Diasporic Struggle Navigates the Black Atlantic'. *Radical History Review*, 103 (2009): 17–35.

Anim-Addo, J., *Longest Journey: A History of Black Lewisham*. London: Deptford Forum Publishing Limited, 1995.

Aspden, K., *The Hounding of David Oluwale*. London: Vintage Books, 2008.

Austin, C. J., *Up Against the Wall: Violence in the Making and Unmaking of the Back Panther Party*. Fayetteville: University of Arkansas Press, 2006.

Austin, D., 'All Roads Lead to Montreal: Black Power, the Caribbean and the Black Radical Tradition in Canada'. *Journal of African-American History*, 92, 4 (Fall 2007): 513–26.

—(ed.), *You Don't Play with Revolution: The Montreal Lectures of CLR James*. Oakland: AK Press, 2009.

Baldwin, B., 'In the Shadow of the Gun: The Black Panther party, the Ninth Amendment, and Discourses of Self-Defence', in J. Lazerow and Y. Williams (eds), *In Search of the Black Panther Party*. Durham and London: Duke University Press, 2006.

Bays, T., *Report of the Working Party on Community/Police Relations in Lambeth*. London: Public Relations Division of London Borough of Lambeth, 1981.

Bennett, H. L., 'The Challenge to the Post-Colonial State: A Case Study of the February Revolution in Trinidad', in Colin A. Palmer and Franklin W. Knight (eds), *The Modern Caribbean*. Chapel Hill: The University of North Carolina Press, 1989.

Berube, M. R. and Gittell, M., *Confrontation at Ocean Hill-Brownsville; the New York School Strikes of 1968*. New York: Praeger, 1969.

Bloom, C., *Violent London: 2000 Years of Riots, Rebels and Revolts*. London: Pan Books, 2004.

Brenton, S. and Cohen, R., *Shooting People: Adventures in Reality TV*. London: Verso, 2003.

Buhle, P. and Paget, H., *C.L.R. James Caribbean*. Durham: Duke University Press, 1992.

Bunce, R. E. R. and Field, Paul, 'Obi B. Egbuna, C.L.R. James and the birth of Black Power in Britain'. *Twentieth Century History*, 22, 3 (2010): 391–414.

Bunce, Robin and Gallagher, Laura, *Civil Rights in the USA, 1945 - 1968*. London: Edexcel, 2006.

Carmichael, Stockley, 'Black Power', in David Cooper (ed.), *The Dialectics of Liberation*. Harmondsworth: Penguin, 1968, pp. 150–74.

Carmichael, S. and Hamilton, C. V., *Black Power: The Politics of Liberation in America*. New York: Vintage Books, 1967.

Carr, G., *The Angry Brigade: A History of Britain's First Urban Guerilla Group*. Oakland: PM Press, 2010.

Carter, T., *Shattering Illusions: West Indians in British Politics*. London: Lawrence & Wishart, 1986.

Caute, D., *'68: The Year of the Barricades*. London: Paladin Books, 1988.

Cohen, A., *Masquerade Politics: Explorations in Structures of Urban Cultural Movements*. Oxford: Berg Publishers, 1993.

Colin, A., Ford, Tanisha, Springer, Kimberly, Ana Laura Lopez De La Torre (eds), *Do You Remember Olive Morris?* London: Gas Works and Remembering Olive collective, 2010.

Cooper, David, 'Introduction', in David Cooper (ed.), *The Dialectics of Liberation*. Harmondsworth: Penguin, 1968, pp. 1–14.

Cox, B., Shirley, J., Short, M., *The Fall of Scotland Yard*. Harmondsworth: Penguin Books, 1977.

Cudjoe, S. and Cain, W. (eds), *C.L.R. James: His Intellectual Legacies*. Boston: University of Massachusetts Press, 1994.

Daniel, W. W., *Racial Discrimination in England*. Harmondsworth: Penguin Books, 1968.

Darbeau, D., 'The Chains are Bursting' from *East Dry River Speaks,* Issue No. 3, in I. Oxaal (ed.), *Race and Revolutionary Consciousness: A Documentary Interpretation of the 1970 Black Power Revolt in Trinidad*. Cambridge, MA: Schenkman Publishing Company, 1969.

Deane, B., *Masculinity and the New Imperialism: Rewriting Manhood in British Popular Literature, 1870–1914*. Cambridge: Cambridge University Press, 2014.

Dhondy, F., *C.L.R. James: A Life*. New York: Pantheon Books, 2001.

Dickens, D., *Great Expectations*. Ware: Wordsworth Editions Limited, 2000.

Du Bois, W. E. B., *Black Reconstruction in America*. New York: Atheneum, 1977.

Duncome, S. and Maxwell, T. (eds), *White Riot: Punk Rock and the Politics of Race*. London: Verso, 2011.

Egbuna, Obi B., *Black Power in Britain*. London: UCPA, 1967.

—, 'Editorial: Hands off Rap Brown'. *Black Power Speaks*, 1, 2 (1968a): 1.

—, 'Black Power or Death!'. *Black Power Speaks*, 1, 1 (1968b): 4–7.

—, 'Preface', in Kwame Nkrumah (ed.), *Message to the Black People of Britain*. London: Black Panther Pamphlets, 1968c.

—, *Destroy this Temple: The Voice of Black Power in Britain*. London: MacGibbon and Kee, 1971.

—, *The ABC of Black Power Thought*. London: Negro Books, 1973.

Fanon, F., *The Wretched of the Earth*. Harmondsworth: Penguin Books, 1967.

—, *Black Skin, White Masks*. London: Pluto Press, 1992.

Forman, C., *Spitalfields: A Battle for Land*. London: Hilary Shipman Limited, 1989.

Frost, D. and Phillips, R. (eds), *Liverpool '81: Remembering The Riots*. Liverpool: Liverpool University Press, 2011.

Fryer, P., *Staying Power in Britain: The History of Black People in Britain*. London: Pluto Press, 1984.

Gilroy, P., *There Ain't No Black in the Union Jack: The Cultural Politics of Race and Nation*. London: Hutchinson, 1987.

Gittell, M., *Participants and Participation: A Study of School Policy in New York City*. New York: Praeger Publishing Company, 1968.

Gordon, J., *Why They Couldn't Wait: A Critique of Black-Jewish Conflict over Community Control in Ocean Hill – Brownsville (1967-1971)*. London: Routledge-Farmer, 2001.

Gordon, P., *White Law: Racism in the Police, Courts and Prisons*. London: Pluto Press, 1983.

Goulbourne, H., *Race Relations in Britain Since 1945*. Basingstoke: Palgrave Macmillan, 1998.

Granger, G., 'Corruption' from *East Dry River Speaks,* Issue No. 3, in I. Oxaal (ed.), *Race and Revolutionary Consciousness: A Documentary Interpretation of the 1970 Black Power Revolt in Trinidad*. Cambridge, MA: Schenkman Publishing Company, 1969.

Grant, E., *Dawn to Dusk: A Biography of Bernie Grant M.P.* London: ITUNI Books, 2006.

Green, J., *All Dressed Up: The Sixties and the Counterculture*. London: Jonathan Cape, 1998.

Guess, R., *History and Illusion in Politics*. Cambridge: Cambridge University Press, 2001.

Gutzmore, C. 'Carnival, the State and the Black Masses in the United Kingdom', in W. James and C. Harris (eds), *Inside Babylon: The Caribbean Diaspora in Britain*. London: Verso, 1993.

Harvey, F., *Rise and Fall of Party Politics in Trinidad and Tobago*. Toronto: New Beginning Movement, 1974.

Hiro, D., *Black British White British*. London: Grafton Books, 1991.

Hobsbawn, E., *Bandits*. London: Abacus, 2001.

Hobson, D., *Channel 4: The Early Years and Jeremy Isaacs Legacy*. London: I.B. Tauris, 2008.

Howe, D., *From Bobby to Babylon: Blacks and the British Police*. London: Race Today Publications, 1988.

Humphry, D. and Tindall, D., *False Messiah: The Story of Michael X*. London: Hart-Davis, MacGibbon, 1977.

James, C. L. R., *Nkruma and the Ghana Revolution*. London: Allison and Busby, 1962.

—, *Beyond a Boundary*. London: Stanley Paul/Hutchinson, 1963.

—, *Minty Alley*. London: New Beacon Books, 1971.

—, *Notes on Dialectics, Hegel, Marx, Lenin*. London: Allison and Busby, 1980.

—, 'Black Power', in Anna Grimshaw (ed.), *The CLR James Reader*. Oxford: Blackwell, 1992a, pp. 362–74.

—, 'The Case for West Indian Self-Government', in Anna Grimshaw (ed.), *The CLR James Reader*. Oxford: Blackwell, 1992b, pp. 49–62.

—, *The American Civilization*. Oxford: Blackwell Publishers, 1993.

—, *The Black Jacobins*. London: Penguin Books, 2001.

James, C. L. R., Lee, Grace, C., Chaulieu, Pierre., *Facing Reality*. Detroit: Correspondence Publishing Company, 1974.

John, G., *Taking a Stand: Gus John Speaks on Education, Race, Social Action and Civil Unrest 1980-2005*. Croydon: Gus John Books, 2006.

Kambon, K., *For Bread, Justice and Freedom: The Political Biography of George Weekes*. London: New Beacon Books, 1988.

Kiely, R., *The Politics of Labour and Development in Trinidad, Barbados, Jamaica, Trinidad and Tobago*. Kingston: The Press University of the West Indies, 1996.

La Rose, J., *The New Cross Massacre Story: Interviews with John La Rose*. London: Beacon Press, 1984.

Lovelace, E., *The Dragon Can't Dance*. Harlow: Longman Group Limited, 1979.

Lux, W., 'Black Power in the Caribbean'. *Journal of Black Studies*, 3, 2 (December 1972): 207–24.

MacDonald, S., *Trinidad and Tobago: Democracy and Development in Caribbean*. New York: Praeger Publishers, 1986.

Macey, D., *Franz Fanon: A Biography*. London: Verso, 2012.

Manzo, K., *Creating Boundaries: The Politics of Race and Nation*. London: Lynne Rienner Publishers, 1998.

Mark, R., *In the Office of Constable*. London: Collins, 1978.

Marx, K., *Letter from Marx to Arnold Rouge in Dresden*. Frankfurt: Deutsch-Französische Jahrbücher, 1844.

Millette, J., 'CLR James and The Politics of Trinidad and Tobago 1938-1970', in S. Cudjoe and W. Cain (eds), *C.L.R. James: His Intellectual Legacies*. Boston: University of Massachusetts Press, 1994.

Naipaul, V. S., *The Writer and the World*. New York: Alfred A. Knopf, 2002.

Narayan, R., *Barrister for the Defence: Trial by Jury and How To Survive it*. London: Justice Books, 1985.

Newton, Huey P., *The Huey P. Newton Reader*. (eds), David Hilliard and Donald Weise. New York: Seven Stories Press, 2011.

Olden, M., *Murder in Notting Hill*. Alresford: Zero Books, 2011.

Oxaal, I. (ed.), *Race and Revolutionary Consciousness: A Documentary Interpretation of the 1970 Black Power Revolt in Trinidad*. Cambridge, MA: Schenkman Publishing Company, 1969.

Palmer, C., *Eric Williams and the Making of the Modern Caribbean*. Chapel Hill: University of North Carolina Press, 2006.

Pantin, R., *Black Power Day: The February 1970 Revolution: A Reporter's Story*. Austin: University of Texas, 1990.

Peller, D., 'Race Consciousness'. *Duke Law Journal*, 4 (1990): 758–847.

Phillips, M. and Phillips, T., *Windrush: The Irresistible Rise of Multi-Racial Britain*. London: Harper Collins Publishers, 1998.

Podair, J., *The Strike that Changed New York*. New Haven: Yale University Press, 2002.

Policy Studies Institute, *Police and People in London, Volume 2, A Group of Young Black People*. London: PSI, 1983.

Regis, L., *The Political Calypso: True Opposition in Trinidad and Tobago*. Barbados: University of West Indies Press, 1999.

Rodney, W., *Groundings with My Brother*. London: Bogle-L'Ouverture Publications, 1990.

Ryan, S., *Race and Nationalism in Trinidad and Tobago: A Study of Decolonization in a Multiracial Society*. Toronto: University of Toronto Press, 1972.

Salway, J., *Reading The Riot Acts: Behind the Headlines and the Frontline*. London: Lambeth Archives, 2005.

Scarman, L., *The Scarman Report: The Brixton Disorders 10-12 April 1981*. Harmondsworth: Penguin Books, 1982.

Selvon, S., *A Brighter Sun*. Harlow: Longman, 1985.

—, *The Lonely Londoners*. London: Penguin Books, 2006.

Simpson, A., *I'll Never Forget What's His Name – A Popular Guide to the Scarman Report*. London: Commission for Racial Equality, 1982.

Singh, C., *Multinationals, the State and the Management of Economic Nationalism: The Case of Trinidad*. New York: Praeger Publishing Company, 1989.

Sivanandan, A., *A Different Hunger: Writings on Black Resistance*. London: Pluto Press, 1982.

Skinner, Q., *Visions of Politics, Vol. 1, Regarding Method*. Cambridge: Cambridge University Press, 2002.

Small, R., 'Introduction', in W. Rodney (eds), *Groundings with My Brother*. London: Bogle-L'Ouverture Publications, 1969.

Smith, A., 'Darcus Howe: A Political Biography', *Ethnic and Racial Studies*, 2014.

Smith, D. J. and Gray, J., *Police and People in London IV: The Police in Action*. London: Policy Studies Institute, 1983.

Smith, L., Cubbit, G., Wilson, R., Fouseki, K. (eds), *Representing Enslavement and Abolition in Museums: Ambiguous Engagement*. New York: Routledge, 2011.

Steele, J., *Turning the Tide: The History of Everyday Deptford*. London: Deptford Forum Publishing, 1993.

Stuempfle, S., *The Steelband Movement: The Forging of a National Art in Trinidad and Tobago*. Bridgeton, Kingston and Port of Spain: The Press, University of West Indies, 1996.

Sudbury, J., *Other Kinds of Dreams: Black Women's Organisation and the Politics of Transformation*. Hove: Psychology Press, 1998.

Thompson, B., *Sunshine on Putty: The Golden Age of British Comedy from Vic Reeves to The Office*. London: Harper Collins, 2010.

Thompson, K., *Under Siege: Racial Violence in Britain*. Harmondsworth: Penguin, 1988.

Tulloch, H., *Black Canadians: A Long Line of Fighters*. Toronto: NC Press, 1975.

Ture, K. and Thelwell, E. M., *Ready For Revolution: The Life and Times of Stokely Carmichael (Kwame Ture)*. New York: Scribner, 2002.

Turner, E., 'The Arts in Society', in S. Mackey (ed.), *Practical Theatre: A Post-16 Approach*. Cheltenham: Stanley Thornes Publishers (Ltd.), 1997.

Veenhoven, W. A. (ed.), *Case Studies on Human Rights and Fundamental Freedoms: A World Survey*. The Hague: The Foundation for the Study of Plural Societies, 1976.

Walmsley, A., *The Caribbean Artists Movement 1966-1972: A Literary and Cultural History*. London: New Beacon Books, 1992.

Wild, R., 'Black was the Colour of Our Fight.' *Black Power in Britain, 1955-1976*, Unpublished PHD Thesis, The University of Sheffield, 2008.

Williams, E., *The Negro in the Caribbean*. Connecticut: Greenwood Press Publishers, 1942.

—, *History of the People of Trinidad and Tobago*. New York: E World Inc., 1963.

Williams, J. L., *Michael X: A Life in Black and White*. London: Century, 2008.

Wise, T., *Color Blind: The Rise of Post Racial Politics and the Retreat from Racial Equity*. San Francisco: City Light Books, 2010.

Woodard, K., *A Nation Within a Nation Amiri Baraka (LeRio Jones) and Black Power Politics*. Chapel Hill: University of North Carolina, 1999.

Worcester, K., *C.L.R. James: A Political Biography*. New York: State University of New York Press, 1996.

Radio programmes

'Darcus Howe on CLR James', *Great Lives*, first broadcast 1 November 2002 on BBC Radio 4.

'Son of a Preacher Man', *Its My Story*, first broadcast 11 August 2008 on BBC Radio 4.

'Brixton Riots', *The Reunion*, first broadcast 25 March 2011.

Television programmes

World in Action, Interviewer Gordon Burns, 27 January 1978, Granada TV for ITV.

Skin, Director Jon Guilbert, 7 June 1981, London Weekend Television.

'What Chance for Scarman?', *London Programme*, Director Don Featherstone, Andrew Forrester and Tom Poole, 20 November 1981, London Weekend Television.

ITN News, 17 November 1983, Independent Television News for ITV.

Caribbean Nights, Producer Mary Dickinson, 14 June 1986–20 June 1986, BBC Television.

The Real McCoy, Producer Charlie Hanson, 5 January 1996, BBC Television.

'Europe', *Lamarr's Attacks*, Producers, Matt McCabe and Richard Wilson 10 September 2000, BBC Television.

'Home and Empire', Edwardian Country House, Producers, Donna Luke and Caroline Ross-Pirie, 21 May 2002, Wall To Wall for Channel 4.

Question Time, 19 February 2004, BBC Television.

Channel 4 News, 8 August 2004, Independent Television News for Channel 4.

'Darcus Howe interview with Fiona Armstrong', *BBC News*, 9 August 2011, BBC Television.

Bandung File (BF)

'President Nyerere In Conversation with Tariq Ali and Darcus Howe', *Bandung File*, Series Editors Darcus Howe and Tariq Ali, 17 October 1985. Bandung Productions for Channel 4.

'Viv', *Bandung File*, Series Editors Darcus Howe and Tariq Ali, 18 November 1985. Bandung Productions for Channel 4.

'Unfinished Revolution', *Bandung File*, Series Editors Darcus Howe and Tariq Ali, 9 May 1986. Bandung Productions for Channel 4.

'The Caribbean Today', *Bandung File*, Series Editors Darcus Howe and Tariq Ali, 23 May 1986. Bandung Productions for Channel 4.

'Michael Holding', *Bandung File*, Series Editors Darcus Howe and Tariq Ali, 30 May 1986. Bandung Productions for Channel 4.

'The Comediennes', *Bandung File*, Series Editors Darcus Howe and Tariq Ali, 6 June 1986. Bandung Productions for Channel 4.

'From Bandung to Harrari', *Bandung File*, Series Editors Darcus Howe and Tariq Ali, 12 September 1986. Bandung Productions for Channel 4.

'Raiding the Pirates', *Bandung File*, Series Editors Darcus Howe and Tariq Ali, 7 February 1987. Bandung Productions for Channel 4.

'The Gathering Storm', *Bandung File*, Series Editors Darcus Howe and Tariq Ali, 14 February 1987. Bandung Productions for Channel 4.

'C.L.R. James, the Grand Old Man', *Bandung File*, Series Editors Darcus Howe and Tariq Ali, 24 October 1987. Bandung Productions for Channel 4.

'Open art Exhibition', *Bandung File*, Series Editors Darcus Howe and Tariq Ali, 24 October 1987. Bandung Productions for Channel 4.

'Trevor Monerville – Unanswered Questions', *Bandung File*, Series Editors Darcus Howe and Tariq Ali, 21 November 1987. Bandung Productions for Channel 4.

'The Changing Face of Brixton', *Bandung File*, Series Editors Darcus Howe and Tariq Ali, 28 November 1987. Bandung Productions for Channel 4.

'Learie to Viv', *Bandung File*, Series Editors Darcus Howe and Tariq Ali, 12 December 1987. Bandung Productions for Channel 4.

'A Tribute to C.L.R. James, 1901–89' *Bandung File*, Series Editors Darcus Howe and Tariq Ali, 27 June 1989. Bandung Productions for Channel 4.

Devil's Advocate (DA)

'The Battle For Stratford School', *Devil's Advocate*, Producer Trevor Phillips, 15 April 1992. London Weekend Television for Channel 4.

'Bernie Grant', *Devil's Advocate*, Producer Trevor Phillips, 13 October 1993. London Weekend Television for Channel 4.

'Latoya Jackson faces The Devil's Advocate', *Devil's Advocate*, Producer Trevor Phillips, 9 November 1993. London Weekend Television for Channel 4.

'Is the Labour Party Sexist?', *Devil's Advocate*, Producer Trevor Phillips, 13 November 1993. London Weekend Television for Channel 4.

'Imran Khan', *Devil's Advocate*, Producer Trevor Phillips, 03 August 1994. London Weekend Television for Channel 4.

'X-Press', *Devil's Advocate*, Producer Trevor Phillips, 10 August 1994. London Weekend Television for Channel 4.

'Chief Buthelezi', *Devil's Advocate*, Producer Trevor Phillips, 21 September 1994. London Weekend Television for Channel 4.

'Sir Peregrine Worsthorne', *Devil's Advocate*, Producer Trevor Phillips, 31 August 1994. London Weekend Television for Channel 4.

'NIGEL BENN', *Devil's Advocate*, Producer Trevor Phillips, 13 September 1995. London Weekend Television for Channel 4.

'Chief Constable Richard Wells', *Devil's Advocate*, Producer Trevor Phillips, 27 September 1995. London Weekend Television for Channel 4.

'John Fashanu', *Devil's Advocate*, Producer Trevor Phillips, 15 March 1996. London Weekend Television for Channel 4.

Channel 4 Documentaries

England my England, Director Richard Lightbody, 11 April 1998, Panoptic Productions for Channel 4.

White Tribe, Director Paul Wilmshurst, 27 January 2000–10 February 2000, Diverse Productions for Channel 4.

The Cricket Test with Darcus Howe, Director Danny Cohen, 31 July 2000–02 August 2000, Diverse Productions for Channel 4.

'Sex', *Slave Nation*, Director Alex Harvey, 14 August 2001, Diverse Productions for Channel 4.

'Work', *Slave Nation*, Director Alex Harvey, 21 August 2001, Diverse Productions for Channel 4.

'Protest', *Slave Nation*, Director Alex Harvey, 27 August 2001, Diverse Productions for Channel 4.

Who you callin' a nigger?, Director Krishnendu Majumdar, 08 August 2004, Diverse Productions for Channel 4.

Son of Mine, Director James Quinn, 20 October 2005, Diverse Productions for Channel 4.

Is this my Country? Director Paul Yule, 25 April 2007, Diverse Productions for Channel 4.

What's Killing Darcus Howe?, Director Krishnendu Majumdar, 24 November 2009, Diverse Productions for Channel 4.

Film

Reggae, Director Horace Ové, (1971)

Pressure, Director Horace Ové, (1975)

The Mangrove Nine, Director Franco Rosso, (1973)

Websites

(Cameron 2010) https://www.gov.uk/government/speeches/speech-to-lord-mayors-banquet

(Cameron 2012) http://www.politicshome.com/uk/article/44536/pm_speech_to_the_council_of_europe_.html

(HOC 2008) http://www.publications.parliament.uk/pa/cm/cmhaff.htm

(Met 2011) http://content.met.police.uk/News/Carnival-troublemakers-targeted/1400002025517/1257246745756

(Perryman 2014) http://www.counterfire.org/articles/opinion/17171-springing-into-action

(Smith 2013) http://hatfulofhistory.wordpress.com/2013/12/28

Index